The International Canadian Studies Series
La Collection internationale d'études canadiennes

The *International Canadian Studies Series* offers a unique collection of high-quality works written primarily by non-Canadian academics. The Series includes conference proceedings, collections of scholarly essays, and other material (including poetry, novels, plays, and monographs). The Series publishes works written in either English or French.

La *Collection internationale d'études canadiennes* présente des ouvrages de premier ordre, rédigés surtout par des universitaires non canadiens. Elle comprend des actes de colloques, des séries d'articles et d'autres formes d'écriture comme des recueils de poésies, des romans, des pièces de théâtre et des monographies. La collection publie des ouvrages en français et en anglais.

Editorial Committee/Comité éditorial:

Guy Leclair
Chad Gaffield

International Canadian Studies Series

Collection internationale d'études canadiennes

IMAGES
OF CANADIANNESS

VISIONS ON CANADA'S
POLITICS, CULTURE, ECONOMICS

Edited by Leen d'Haenens

L. Balthazar, J.F. Conway, L. d'Haenens, J.S. Frideres,
H. Ganzevoort, M. Hart, R.M. Hébert, C.J. Jaenen,
D. Mitchell, J. Vrielinck, C. Remie, L. Roth

International Council
for Canadian Studies

University
of Ottawa Press

Institute
of Canadian Studies

Canadian Cataloguing in Publication Data

Main entry under title:
  Images of Canadianness: visions on Canada's
politics, culture, economics

(International Canadian studies series)
Co-published by the International Council for Canadian Studies.
Includes bibliographical references.
ISBN 0-7766-0489-9

  1. Canada.   I. d'Haenens, L. (Leen)   II. Balthazar, Louis   III. Series.

FC51.I48   1998   971   C98-901315-4
F1008.I53   1998

University of Ottawa Press gratefully acknowledges the support extended to its publishing programme by the Canada Council, the Department of Canadian Heritage, and the University of Ottawa.

 UNIVERSITY OF OTTAWA
UNIVERSITÉ D'OTTAWA

Cover Design: Robert Dolbec

ISBN 0-7766-0489-9

© University of Ottawa Press, 1998
  542 King Edward, Ottawa (Ont.), Canada K1N 6N5
  press@uottawa.ca   http://www.uopress.uottawa.ca

Printed and bound in Canada

CONTENTS

Introduction   1

Part One
The Political Debate   5

1   Reflections on Canada in the Year 1997-98   7
     John F. Conway

2   The Liberal Idea of the Canadian Nation-State   29
     Louis Balthazar

Part Two
Bilingual Canada: A Multicultural Mosaic   39

3   Identity, Cultural Production and the Vitality of Francophone
     Communities Outside Québec   41
     Raymond M. Hébert

4   The Belgian Presence in Canada   67
     Cornelius J. Jaenen

5   The Dutch in Canada   91
     Herman Ganzevoort

6   The Flemish and Dutch Migrant Press in Canada:
     A Historical Investigation   109
     Jennifer Vrielinck

Part Three
Canada from a Native Perspective   127

7   Nunavut: A Challenge for the Inuit   129
     Cornelius H.W. Remie

8   Television Broadcasting North of 60   147
     Lorna Roth

9   Indigenous Peoples of Canada and the United States of America:
     Entering the 21st Century   167
     James S. Frideres

Part Four
Canada in the International Arena   197

10   Of Friends, Interests, Crowbars, and Marriage Vows in
       Canada-United States Trade Relations   199
          Michael Hart

11   On Track for TAFTA? Developing Canada-EU Trade
       Relations in the 1990's   221
          Donald G. Mitchell

12   *Beyond Infrastructure.* Europe, the United States and Canada on the
       Information Highway: Where business and culture collide   237
          Leen d'Haenens

About the Authors   255

INTRODUCTION

Foreign news coverage on Canada has habitually been quite poor. Exceptions to this rule were articles and news items about – in chronological order – the 1970 constitutional crises and the resulting wave of terrorism by the *Front de Libération du Québec*, the Meech Lake fiasco (1990), the referendum on the Charlottetown accord. Other headlines in the foreign news were the Oka crisis (summer of 1992), the latest federal elections (November 1993), with the country-wide Liberal landslide, or the referendums in and about the separation of Québec. In background articles Canada is mentioned as an example of far-reaching political decentralization, as an officially bilingual country with a multicultural policy. Other recurrent themes are the debate on the right of self-government for the Inuit and the Indians and, more recently, Canada's firm stance against land mines.

This book offers backgrounds and explanations which may, among other things, elucidate the voting patterns of the Canadians and the Québécois. This book contains very different contributions and so could at first be perceived as somewhat disparate. It should quickly become clear to the reader, however, that its four-fold structure makes it possible to shed more light on a series of relevant – if relatively new – features of Canada, from a political, cultural, and economic angle. Each chapter contains articles from Canadian and European experts in their respective field. In each of these papers the intention has been to develop an original perspective on issues that are far from obvious.

In **Part One** (*The Political Debate*) the relationship between English-speaking Canada and Québec is discussed by two political scientists, one from Québec (Louis Balthazar) and one from Western Canada (John Conway). The central thesis of Conway's article is that the great federal experiment called Canada is profoundly at risk, most importantly because of what he calls "the English Canada/Québec conundrum" and an insufficient political resolve to concede, compromise, and innovate. Balthazar argues that most Québécois support federalism and comments on how – Canada being one of the most decentralized countries in the world – it can be that, under such conditions, Québec's potential partition from Canada continues to be such a topical subject in Québec politics. Some will reply that the Québécois are being manipulated by their nationalist elite. This may be true in part. However, other elites advocating the preservation of the Canadian Federation in its present form are just as adept at manipulation. Moreover, Québec's major newspapers do not support sovereigntists. Consequently, there must be other explanations for the current polarization between the French-speaking province of Québec and the other English-speaking components of Canada – explanations that do not question the legitimate and democratic nature of the Québec's political structures.

Part Two (*Bilingual Canada: A Multicultural Mosaic*) sheds new light on Canada's bilingual and multicultural nature. Raymond Hébert discusses the vitality of French-language communities outside Québec. After a brief overview of the components of identity among Canada's French-speaking minorities and a description of cultural production in the French language across the country, the author argues that the stronger the identity within a French-language minority, the greater the cultural production among members of that minority. In turn, perhaps, this increased cultural production leads to an even greater strengthening of that identity. Conversely, the weaker the identity to begin with, the more difficulty artists have in expressing it in their work, and the fewer works they produce. Only three French-language communities outside Québec can be said to have a strong identity and a concomitant relatively high level of cultural production: the Acadian community, centered in but not limited to New Brunswick; the Franco-Ontarian community; and the Franco-Manitoban community.

The following three articles by Cornelius Jaenen, Herman Ganzevoort, and Jennifer Vrielinck were written on account of a particular interest in the Belgian and Dutch immigration waves to Canada and their "cultural production" in the form of Dutch-language immigrant press. According to Jaenen, Belgians have always enjoyed a positive image in mainstream Canadian society inasmuch as they were seen as having upheld the work ethic, community values, and loyalty to the Crown. They are one immigrant group that has made an important contribution to the country's intellectual life, to education, religion, the arts, and literature. This is especially true in Québec, where university research, biotechnology, aeronautics, and computer science are all fields where they have played a most significant role. While immigrants of Belgian descent constitute a small community by any reckoning (about 90,000), the 1991 national census indicated that no less than 961,595 Canadians (one in thirty) said at least one of their ancestors was Dutch. Ganzevoort points out that the positive acceptance of the Dutch has meant that, unlike other ethnic communities, an antagonistic, protective ethnicity that is so often the response to non-acceptance by the host society, simply did not develop among the Dutch. As one of the results, the Dutch community seems to have little interest in maintaining a distinctive culture, separate from the social mainstream. The lack of religious homogeneity surely contributed to this absence of identity formation and group cohesiveness within the Dutch community in Canada.

Vrielinck takes a look at the ethnic press as one vehicle for retaining the Dutch language and culture. Over the years, Dutch-language immigrant newspapers, irrespective of why they were founded, have come to closely resemble one another. One of the most striking shared characteristics is the idealization of the fatherland, one where time would have stood still. The general picture of Flanders and the Netherlands in such papers is one that might have been true to life 50 to 100 years ago, and a highly idealized one it is: windmills, tulips, farms, pastures, and clogs are regular features. Another striking phenomenon is the use of the Dutch language. In the oldest newspapers this has never been of a high linguistic standard, but it is more or less kept up to par through input from Flanders and the Netherlands. English is added to broaden the readership, specifically to attract second-generation readers. This step inevitably leads to a slow but inevitable "Anglicization" of the newspaper. The only exception to this rule is *De Nieuwe Amsterdammer*. Nowadays the future of the Dutch-language immigrant press looks anything but rosy: in addition to substandard Dutch, the content of the reporting is sometimes of dubious quality. Both threats could be remedied by a greater direct contribution from Flanders and the Netherlands. However, the greatest problem – if that can be said to be a problem, since the other side of the coin is "perfect" integration – remains the fact that new generations of immigrant descent not only possess an inadequate command of the Dutch language, but that they have purely and simply lost interest in their roots.

In **Part Three** (*Canada from a Native Perspective*), Remie explores some of the major transitions taking place in Canada's Northwest Territories. In 1999 the Eastern part of the NWT will become a separate territory named *Nunavut*, which in the Inuit language means "Our Land." The Inuit of Nunavut will enjoy considerable political autonomy and will thus be given a chance to regain control over their lives. However, the demographic, economic, educational, and social realities of the day are so grim that achieving this will take considerable time. Roth looks into the role of the media as a tool for self-government for the First Peoples, and describes the different stages which First Peoples' television broadcasting has gone through in Canada's North – from outsiders' representations of the First Peoples and the impact of lobbies on the development of northern television to initiatives to "policy" the North and the establishment of *Television Northern Canada*. Frideres compares attempts made by both Native Americans and Canadian Indians to negotiate their position in society. In order to do this, Native Americans have used the courts in a reactive and defensive manner for well over a century, while it is only recently that Canadian Indians have asked the courts to expand and recognize their right to self-government. The author makes it very clear that the Indians in both Canada and the US are only going enter what he calls the "institutional spheres of the 21st century" if they start to play a far more significant, ongoing political and economic role.

In **Part Four** (*Canada in the International Arena*) Michael Hart illuminates the Canada-US relationship, which is sometimes problematic and hardly ever simple, and explains what a challenge it is for Canada – as a small, trade-dependent country – to live next door to a superpower, especially when it comes to managing its commercial relations with the US. FTA, NAFTA and WTO are proving to be effective negotiation tools for Canada with a view to harmonious future trade relations, while allowing Canada to keep its distinctiveness. Donald Mitchell assesses Canada's trade relations with the EU – Canada's largest trading partner after the US – and sees it more in terms of opportunities than of obstacles or inevitable disputes over commodities such as fish and fur. The author considers TAFTA (*Transatlantic Free Trade Agreement*) as a potential framework to launch a whole new wave of global trade liberalization, since the world's two most integrated trading blocs, NAFTA and the EU, are arguably best-suited to initiate such a change. Or is this day-dreaming? TAFTA is unlikely to happen in the next decade: the EU has already more than enough on its hands with the move to the single currency and Eastward enlargement, while North America is too absorbed by attempts to achieve closer economic integration with Asia and South America.

Finally, in the book's last article, Leen d'Haenens assesses the Canadian response to two specific challenges with regard to the Information Highway: infrastructure (hardware) development on the one hand, and cultural policy (software, content) on the other hand. Canada can build its own, export-based telecommunications infrastructure. The question of the future role of government in the expansion of global information networks is more problematic: striking the right balance between competition and regulation, copyright and intellectual property, Canadian content, privacy and the protection of information, and how can Canada, Europe, Japan, and the United States act reasonably in tune with one another? The article does not offer any ready solutions to all these questions, but attempts to provide some understanding of Canadian policy options in this respect.

This book came to being thanks to the financial support of the Association for Canadian Studies in the Netherlands and Flanders and the International Council for Canadian Studies. Finally I want to thank all the contributors for their time and expertise put in writing their articles. To them I express my deepest gratitude and appreciation.

Leen d'Haenens

Part One
The Political Debate

REFLECTIONS ON CANADA IN THE YEAR 1997-98

by John F. CONWAY

I   INTRODUCTION

Canada is profoundly at risk, most importantly because of the English Canada/Québec conundrum. But the risk does not just derive from that – this is not *the Québec problem*, this is *the Canada problem*. It became clear just how bad things had become when our federal transportation minister announced in 1994, despite his fresh election on the basis of the Liberal Red Book promise to save and renew Canada, that "the National Dream is dead"[1] as he warned Canadians that the Cdn$1.6 billion formerly spent on annual transportation subsidies – the St. Lawrence Seaway, passenger train service, the Crow Benefit[2], the ferries of Atlantic Canada, the Coast Guard – were on the chopping block, and have indeed since been severely cut. The effective end of our national policy of a **forced** and **subsidized** east-west transportation system, and the substitution of the free market and private enterprise as the foundation of our national transportation policy, drove another stake into the heart of Canada's federal system.

What is most deeply disturbing is that English Canadians have not yet awakened though we are on the edge of the abyss, have not yet realized the enormity of the risk facing Canada. Indeed, the mood abroad in English Canada is so cavalier that we may stumble thoughtlessly through a series of crises and urgent events, and suddenly wake up to find that this great federal experiment we call Canada has failed before its 135th anniversary in 2002. And it will have been a failure that could have been averted had we had sufficient political will to concede, compromise, and innovate.

In the interests of brevity and focus, the issues involved in our impasse will be examined separately, while recognizing all are inextricably bound together in one great morass of contradiction, contention and anxiety.

II   QUEBEC AND ENGLISH CANADA

There exists a large bloc of English Canadians – ranging from 30 to 40 per cent depending on which Gallup poll in which year you consult – who believe that the only road out of the English Canada/Québec impasse is to negotiate *special status* for Québec in our constitution.[3] Many have believed this for over thirty years, ever since the

---

[1] *Calgary Herald*, 13 June 1994.

[2] The "Crow Benefit" refers to the over half-billion Can$ annual transportation subsidy formerly paid directly to the railways to lower the cost of shipping Prairie grains to market. It was first put in place in 1897 in recognition of the costs borne by the Prairies in providing huge land grants and lucrative mineral rights concessions in order to ensure the construction of the Canadian Pacific Railway. It was first subjected to a series of annual cuts and then dismantled as a result of free trade agreements. Such proposals were strongly opposed by Prairie farmers.

[3] *Special status* for Quebec has been part of constitutional discussions between English Canada and

beginning of the Quiet Revolution. Indeed, since the emergence of the RIN in the 1966 Québec election[4] the Québécois have, with growing urgency, presented English Canada with a starkly clear option: special status or sovereignty. Ironically, the choices amount to the same thing in the final analysis – sovereignty will inevitably lead to some form of intimate association not dissimilar from the European Union (unless English Canada goes completely mad). What English Canada faces, then, is a choice between a very long and messy road to special status for Québec in some form of negotiated sovereignty association, on the one hand, and the shorter road to the same reality via negotiation leading to harmonious and voluntary constitutional change, on the other.

But despite the fact that at 30 or 40 per cent advocates of special status are a significant minority in English Canada, really on the threshold of majority status with the right leadership and commitment, the rest of English Canada, most importantly all the promi-

---

Québec from the outset. This concept insists that Québec, as the homeland of the Québécois nation, is not a province just like the others and requires unique and special powers to protect the language and culture of the Québécois while at the same time providing those political and economic levers seen as essential to protect the nation from economic exploitation and political oppression. The modern versions of special status were articulated in the early 1960s by two cabinet ministers in the government of Jean Lesage, René Lévesque, Minister of natural resources, and Paul Gérin-Lajoie, attorney-general. In its purest form, expressed by Lévesque and Gérin-Lajoie, it was a call for Québec to have the status of an *associate state* within Confederation, a concept that later inspired Lévesque's campaign for *sovereignty-association* during the 1970s. The actual content of *special status* has ebbed and flowed over time. Most recently, former Québec Premier Bourassa, the ambiguous and ambivalent federalist, described its minimum content in terms of the failed Meech Lake Accord: recognition of Québec as a *distinct society* in the written language of the constitution; the devolution of control over immigration to Québec; a withdrawal of the federal spending power from contentious policy areas in Québec (the right to opt out of federal programs and receive financial compensation); a veto over constitutional changes of vital concern to Quebec; the right to name three justices to the Supreme Court of Canada. English Canada's unwillingness to grant a significant form of special status, and the growing conviction among committed Québec nationalists and separatists that special status could no longer satisfy Québec's aspirations, has resulted in *special status* disappearing from official discourse as a viable constitutional solution to Canada's impasse. The historical fact is, of course, that ever since *The Québec Act* of 1774 Québec has enjoyed a special and protected constitutional status – and the unsuccessful 1992 Charlottetown Agreement sought slightly to augment that special status by granting Québec a guarantee of a minimum of 25 percent of House of Commons seats, veto power in the Senate on matters of language and culture, and the right of the Québec National Assembly to select Québec's senators while those of the other provinces would face popular direct election (thus ensuring that Québec senators were selected by the government of the day). It was a version of special status concocted by the English Premiers, and one not only not requested by the Québec government, but emphatically rejected by the Québec people in the 1992 Charlottetown referendum.

[4] The left-wing RIN, *le Rassemblement pour l'Indépendance Nationale*, contested the 1966 Québec election in two-thirds of the seats and astonished many by winning 7 per cent of the Québécois vote overall, including about 11 per cent in Montréal, doing particularly well among the young and better educated. A smaller, right-wing separatist party, le *Ralliement National* (RN), won another 4 per cent of the Québécois vote. Together, the RIN and RN won about 9 per cent of the total vote, much more than expected. The RIN vote was large enough in 13 of the seats to deprive the Liberal candidates of victory. As a result, the *Union Nationale* won a six seat victory over the Liberals. In 1968 all separatists and sovereigntists, left and right, united in *Le Parti Québécois* (PQ) led by René Lévesque. In 1976 the PQ under Lévesque won power and was re-elected in 1981. After Lévesque's retirement, the PQ was defeated in 1985. In 1994, led by Jacques Parizeau, the PQ won re-election.

nent political leaders, have exhibited a growing cranky unwillingness even to discuss the option. And in Québec, the strong nationalists and committed separatists insist that it is too late and only Québec sovereignty will now suffice to realize the dreams and securities the Québécois nation craves. Hence, the Québécois today have narrow and hard choices before them – accept federalism as it has evolved or choose sovereignty. One need not belabour the point that history tells us that presenting an aggrieved population such a zero sum choice can be very, very risky.

Political analysts and commentators appear profoundly puzzled as they try to understand and explain why Canadian politics and political debates, in a country repeatedly named by the United Nations as the best place to live in the world, have reached such a parlous state – dominated by the business lobby; an absence among established political and economic élites of a commitment to the project of the Canadian federation's survival; from 1993 to 1997, a separatist party as the Official Opposition in Ottawa;[5] the only other contender for the status of Official Opposition, winning that role in 1997, a Western-based protest party of the extreme right funded by oil and natural resource interests;[6] two once great federal parties – the NDP and the Tories – in tatters and disarray;[7] a separatist party in power in Québec, preparing carefully for a referendum after the next provincial election, having narrowly lost the 1995 referendum by less than one per cent; our health, education and social support infrastructures on the verge of collapse; the population deeply cynical and increasingly withdrawing from active political participation.[8]

---

[5] Lucien Bouchard, Secretary of State in the Mulroney government, left the party after the 1988 election when the prime minister re-opened the Meech Lake Accord in order to placate English Canada. He was soon followed by a handful of other Québec nationalist Members of Parliament and founded the Bloc Québécois in the House of Commons, a party dedicated to Québec separation. In the October 1993 federal election Bouchard and the Bloc won 54 of 75 seats in Québec with 49 percent of the popular vote. Leading the party with the largest group of MPs on the opposition benches, Bouchard became leader of the Official Opposition in Ottawa. In 1995, Bouchard replaced Jacques Parizeau as PQ leader and Premier of Quebec. In the 1997 election the Bloc, now led by Giles Duceppe, won 44 of Québec's 75 federal seats with 38 percent of the popular vote.

[6] In May 1987 Preston Manning, son of the former Social Credit Premier of Alberta, Ernest Manning, founded the Reform Party as a western protest party with the slogan *The West Wants In*. In the 1988 election, the party contested 72 of the 86 seats in the four western provinces, winning 7 per cent of the western vote and no seats. In October, 1993 the Reform Party won 52 seats, 51 of them in the four western provinces and 46 of those in the two most western provinces of Alberta and British Columbia. Manning, in fact, swept 20 of 26 seats in Alberta and 24 of 32 seats in British Columbia. In 1997 the Reform Party won 60 of the West's 88 seats and became the Official Opposition in the House of Commons. Reform won no seats in Central or Atlantic Canada.

[7] In the October 1993 election, Canada's social democratic party, the New Democratic Party, was reduced to 8 seats and the governing Tory Party, led by Mulroney's successor as prime minister, Kim Campbell, won only 2 seats. Canada's House of Commons elected a total of 295 Members of Parliament in 1993. The Liberal Party, under Jean Chrétien, won 178 seats and formed a majority government. In the 1997 election, now with a 301 member House of Commons, the Tories and NDP recovered only slightly, the Tories winning 20 seats with 19 percent of the vote, and the NDP 21 with 11 percent. The Liberal Party was reduced to 155 seats, a four seat majority government.

[8] Voter turnout prior to 1993 in Canadian federal elections was generally well over 70 percent. In 1993 that fell to 69.6 percent, and in 1997 to 66.7 percent. A 14 May 1997 Gallup Poll found that the Canadian federal government, the House of Commons, and political parties were three of the four

A large part of the answer can be found in the fact that for thirty years and more the development of Canada's two founding national identities has been blocked. In the case of the Québécois nation this chronic national frustration is clear, and is central to Québécois politics. The signposts are like a litany of failure:[9] the *War Measures Act*; the dirty tricks of the federal secret police; the economic fear campaigns; the "stab in the back" of '81; the collapse of the Meech Lake Accord in a welter of English Canadian hostility; the Charlottetown insult; the 1993 and 1997 election of Québécois sovereigntists as a majority of Members of Parliament from Québec in the House of Commons; a sovereigntist party firmly in power in Québec; a near victory for the sovereigntists in the 1995 referendum and another referendum inevitably expected in 1999 or 2000; the need for the Québécois to prove they are serious by electing the PQ in Québec and the BQ in Ottawa again and again; and so it goes, over and over and over the same ground again and again in what is becoming a dreary repetition and re-affirmation of an increasing polarization. Should we be surprised if Québécois nationalism is getting a bit frustrated, tired of having to repeatedly demonstrate how serious the Québec problem is and that it won't just go away as English Canadians keep hoping? In the meantime, the fullest and freest development of the Québécois nation has been largely stymied, put on hold, postponed.

Ironically, the national identity of English Canada has suffered more, has not only been more thoroughly blocked in its development, but has been badly distorted, perhaps even damaged beyond repair. The fact is that thirty years of thwarting Québécois nationalism and denying special status to Québec, which became a self-destructive obsession, has distorted the national identity of English Canadians and put on hold the development of a clear and positive sense of English Canadian nationhood. (Opposition to special status for Québec and the aspirations of the Québécois nation have come dangerously close to becoming for far too many English Canadians all that is left uniting Canada's nine Anglophone provinces). In a sense, English Canada had to give up, indeed deny, its own national project in order to justify the fight against the Québécois national project, usually by embracing extreme decentralization and the language of provincial rights and the equality of provinces. In doing so, English Canada by and large proved unable to transcend the historical dead-end of seeing Québec through the prism of the interests of the English Canadian minority in Québec.

In place of a positive English Canadian national identity, we substituted an effort to build a phony *national* identity that encompassed all in some hyphenated lowest common denominator. Thus bilingualism was inflicted upon us – something Québec never asked for and didn't want, and most in English Canada resented even while tolerating it for the sake of national unity. Well, now it's official – bilingualism has

---

lowest scoring Canadian institutions regarding public respect and confidence, far behind banks and large corporations.

[9] Details on the following events are documented in my 1997 book on Quebec and English Canada, *Debts to Pay*, as are details regarding the Meech Lake Accord and its collapse, the Charlottetown Agreement and its defeat in a national referendum in 1992, and the 1995 sovereignty referendum.

failed. Then there was the multiculturalism myth – that Canada was a mosaic of many cultures and national identities of which the Québécois were but one and English Canadians another. The effect of this was to deny the essential bi-national, bi-cultural reality of Canada, while effectively masking the continuing hegemony of English Canada. (The multiculturalism doctrine was also later used to trump the claims of the aboriginal nations and to deny what is now conceded by many to be Canada's tri-national essence – English Canadian, Québécois, and aboriginal.) Official multiculturalism ignored the sociological reality that immigrants have largely joined – and uniquely and often dramatically influenced – one or the other of the English Canadian or Québécois nations through a sort of functional integration (while resisting assimilation). Then there was the equality of provinces constitutional myth, a fabrication of Trudeau determined to use the nine English Canadian provinces to hammer Québec into submission. This myth has had dangerous consequences and has pushed us to the ridiculous point where individuals can seriously argue that, even in our democracy, one or two tiny provinces can veto the constitutional aspirations of 80 or 90 per cent of the Canadian people – surely an unsustainable and even suicidal position. This last myth fed into the increase in the centrifugal forces of provincialism as the status of premier was elevated from premier of a province to co-prime minister of Canada. This new-found power and influence of the premiers was used in a cynical game as English Canadian premiers argued that, given the equality of provinces, it followed that nothing could be given to Québec that was not given to all other provinces, and that the consent of the premiers and governments of the English Canadian provinces was required to grant accommodations to Québec. This was somewhat codified in the 1982 constitution whereby constitutional change requires the consent of 7 of 10 provincial governments – still a far cry from the equality of provinces notion, but close enough to be worrisome.

This premiers' game of using the Québec crisis to enhance the powers of all provinces was realized effectively in the Meech Lake Accord which granted many of Québec's minimum constitutional demands only by conceding the same package to all provinces. A similar effort was made by the premiers in the Charlottetown Agreement – provincial powers were even more enhanced at the expense of federal powers. One should not underestimate the impact of these efforts on the people. The message was clear – the only way to save the Canadian federal system was to destroy it, was to render the federal government – the political institutional essence of the Canadian nation – impotent and virtually powerless. The English Canadian people rebelled – some, a minority, for distasteful reasons: hostility to Québec and the Québécois; others, by far the majority, for solid reasons: a refusal to participate in the triumph of provincialism and the effective end of a Canada characterized by a reasonably strong federal government able to govern the entire nation.

As a result of the Charlottetown referendum there was some hope, if only for the briefest of moments. The Agreement's overwhelming defeat in both English Canada and Québec ensured that the process did not immediately lead to an even deeper English/French cleavage than we have always faced. In that defeat, both the Québécois and English Canadian nations affirmed, contrary to the federalist political élites, the importance of developing their national identities and demonstrated a keen awareness of the political tools needed for such a task. The Québécois once again told English Canada that either special status with real powers, or sovereignty, is necessary for the evolution of the Québécois nation. There was nothing new in that. What was novel was that English Canadians sent a clear message along similar lines. English Canadians want a strong federal government able to develop national policies both to overcome regional disparities and to resist the American pull which can only increase under the regime of the FTA.[10] English Canadians also affirmed that they want a federal government able to continue national programs with national standards in areas like Medicare, financing post-secondary education, pensions, and social security, and to develop in future new national programs in areas like day care, culture and an extension of national policies into post-secondary education and manpower training – the very areas Québécois nationalism sees as most sensitive.

The slight hope engendered by the defeat of the Charlottetown Agreement was severely tested by a succession of dramatic events further eroding the possibilities for the future survival of Canada intact – the Bloc's 1993 victory in 54 of Québec's 75 seats with 49 per cent of the vote; the PQ's victory in the September 1994 Québec election, in which the two sovereigntist parties won over 50 per cent of the popular vote; the near victory of Québec sovereigntists in the 1995 Québec referendum; the Bloc's retention of 44 of Québec's 75 seats in 1997 with 38 per cent of the vote; and the Reform Party's victory in 60 of the west's 88 seats with 44 per cent of the western vote, running largely on a crude anti-Québec platform and winning the status of Official Opposition in the House of Commons. As a result, Canada is even more deeply polarized than ever, and the hopes for a mutually acceptable accommodation between English Canada and Québec have never been dimmer.

Whatever the final outcome, there is no question that the political earthquake of 1992 to 1997 has cleared the table of a lot of baggage, making it clear that the future of the federation can only be served by constitutional changes that can accommodate the aspirations of both the Québécois and English Canadian nations. Given the contradictory nature of those aspirations, the only accommodation possible – short of a breakup of the federation – is meaningful special status for Québec, and a strong central government for the nine English Canadian provinces. If the last thirty years of constitutional and political carnage culminating in the 1992 to 1997 *sequelae* of disasters tell us anything without qualification or ambiguity, they should tell us this. The chickens scattered over the past thirty years have finally come home to roost. With the Reform Party pushing Québec to leave, and the Bloc pulling towards its audacious dream of a sovereign Québec, never before have the choices before Canadians been as crystal clear: special status or separation.

---

[10] The FTA, or Free Trade Agreement, was concluded between Canada and the U.S. in 1988 and was the central issue during the 1988 federal election. The Mulroney government was returned and proceeded to negotiate the North American Free Trade Agreement (NAFTA), passed in 1993 just before Mulroney's resignation as prime minister.

III   THE REFORM PARTY AND THE WEST

It is not without a certain tragic historical irony that the region which spawned the innovative political movements which pioneered both Canada's universal social programs, and the doctrine of an interventionist government, has now become the source of a right-wing movement seeking to destroy those same programs and to emasculate government as a tool of the popular will.

It was the Social Credit in Alberta under Aberhart which first insisted that all citizens had a right to a basic social and economic security, that there ought to be programs to ensure that the provinces of the disadvantaged regions be provided the means by the central government to secure a national minimum level of services at reasonably comparable rates of taxation (since codified into the 1982 constitution), that ability to pay be removed as a barrier to access to education and health services, that provincial and federal governments ought to be used aggressively to realize the people's will whether business interests agreed or not.[11] It was the CCF in Saskatchewan under Douglas which went further in building a comprehensive system of health and social security, innovated in the area of central economic planning, and envisioned a strong role for public and co-operative ownership in the economy.[12] These movements marched out of the West to win the hearts and minds of all Canadians and became such a political threat to the Liberals and Tories that a new national political consensus emerged, shared by all parties, incorporating the basic doctrines of the democratic welfare state and the interventionist government.

The Social Credit and CCF were also regional and agrarian protest movements demanding a better deal for farmers in a modernizing industrial capitalism and a better deal for the West in Confederation. The costs of industrialization through a tariff wall weighed heavily on farmers who were caught in a cost/price squeeze – their tariff protected industrial inputs for agricultural production continued to go up in price as Canadian industry demanded protection from external competition; meanwhile the things they produced for world markets, especially wheat and other grains, went through boom/bust cycles in response to global competition. Thus the movements demanded abolition of the tariff, or at least some tariff relief, as well as government interventions in marketing and transportation to assist farmers. Out of this agitation many gains were made, most importantly regulation of the grain trade, orderly marketing, and transportation subsidies. For the West as a region, relegated in Confederation to the near colonial status of producer of natural resources and captive market for Central Canadian industry, the movements advocated new national policies to encourage economic diversification in order to decrease the West's economic vulnerability due to the

---

[11] The Social Credit movement, led by William Aberhart, was elected in Alberta in 1935 and re-elected in 1940. After Aberhart's death in 1943, Ernest Manning assumed the leadership. After Manning's 1944 election victory, he took a sharp right turn and the popular, anti-capitalist features of the Social Credit movement were jettisoned.

[12] The CCF, or Co-operative Commonwealth Federation, led by T.C. Douglas, was elected on a radical social democratic platform in Saskatchewan in 1944 and it governed until defeat twenty years later.

uncertainties of world markets for its resources. Again, some gains were made – supports for agricultural diversification, some tariff relief, subsidies for the development of industry related to the West's natural products.

But the reforms first advocated and pioneered by Aberhart's Social Credit in Alberta and Douglas' CCF in Saskatchewan were not universally supported in the West. The business lobby, especially the private grain trade and natural resource and oil interests, fought each reform tenaciously and often fanatically. After Aberhart's death, his successor, Ernest Manning, took a sharp right turn, making Alberta ever since the political home of the extreme right in the West and the private political preserve of the oil companies. The political polarization in B.C. between the radical B.C. Socialist Party/CCF and the highly politicized business lobby resulted in a strong and vigorous right wing opposition in that province to all the reforms. There was, therefore, always a strong red-neck right in the West, financed by the business lobby, especially the resource and oil interests, and politics in the West was characterized by a deeper class and ideological cleavage than elsewhere in Canada. Thus, while the CCF in Saskatchewan pioneered Medicare, the strongest resistance to extending Medicare nationally was expressed by other more conservative Western provincial governments.

The strong showing of the Reform Party in the West in the 1993 and 1997 federal elections reflects the continuing and now growing strength of this red-neck right. But the Reform phenomenon has many layers of meaning. Certainly it is no surprise that Alberta went Reform – it is the West's right-wing bastion. But the significant successes of Reform in British Columbia, and the more modest successes in Saskatchewan, do not reflect the final political triumph of the right in the West. At least, not yet. Indeed, the forces that united behind Reform candidates are quite complex. First, of course, there is the solid right-wing base which Reform successfully hijacked from the Tories. But Reform in the West was not centrally seen as right-wing by many westerners who supported the party, certainly not in 1993 and not universally so in 1997. Other groups of westerners, not right-wing in any sense, voted Reform for other reasons. At one level, the vote for Reform in 1993 and 1997 was an echo of the strong opposition in the West to the Charlottetown Agreement – the Reform Party alone among all parties in English Canada opposed the Agreement. Second, Reform got its kick-start as an expression of Western alienation, stealing from the NDP the role of champion of the West in Confederation. Thus a large part of the western vote for Reform can be seen as an expression of both western bitterness about the old National Policy involving the West's subordinate political and economic place in Confederation, and a sense of boiling frustration about the failure of the other parties, including the NDP, to develop a new set of national policies to address the region's grievances.

Finally, there was the Québec canard. Ever since Riel, the anti-French, anti-Catholic, anti-Québec sentiment in the West has been carefully played like a violin by generation after generation of western politicians. During the height of the post-World War II political consensus, and most particularly the Pearson/Trudeau years of "national unity through bilingualism to fight Québec separatism", western politicians exercised some restraint, accepting federalist advice that provocations against the Québécois nation could only help the separatist cause in Québec. The collapse of the Meech Lake Accord, and the Charlottetown referendum campaign, made explicit anti-Québec politics more acceptable, the former constraints slipped away, and the gloves came off. The Reform Party, more or less alone, exploited this festering anti-Québec, anti-bilingualism mood quite successfully, and particularly brutally and irresponsibly in the 1997 election. Thus many Reform voters – voters who reject Reform's right-wing social and economic agenda – voted to express their crankiness about the perception of Québec's favoured *spoiled child* place in Confederation. Moreover, Québec seemed to be a major roadblock to the West's aspirations for a new national economic policy and a new industrial strategy. (And hadn't Québec voted for free trade in 1988, something largely opposed everywhere in the West except in Alberta?)

In the 1997 election, another reason for voting Reform, quite apart from its ideology and program, was prominent among western voters. Secure that Reform could not possibly win power, many westerners voted Reform in order to deny the Bloc the status of Official Opposition. The spectacle of a sovereigntist party, half-heartedly serving as the official opposition in the House of Commons, defending all of Canada from the predations of government policy, seemed bizarre and, for most in English Canada, totally unacceptable. With the Tories and the NDP in no position to embrace that role, many voters in the West decided to give it to the Reform Party (just as voters in Ontario, for obvious strategic reasons, decided to do what they could to ensure a Liberal majority government).

The rise of the Reform Party as the major federal party in the West, and the Bloc Québécois as the major federal party in Québec, more than anything, confirms the implacable impasse we have reached. Never have the two solitudes been so completely isolated from one another. One wants to destroy that which makes Canada a humane and decent society and offers us the right-wing bromides of extreme neo-conservatism: the social barbarism of the free market unconstrained by the popular will as expressed through democratic government. The other is in the House of Commons for no other reason than to lead Québec to sovereignty and has, therefore, no interest whatsoever in developing new national policies or a new constitutional accommodation. And they feed off each other in a frenzy that could destroy Canada. Every time a Reform MP speaks, another batch of votes is added to the separatist column in Québec as further proof is provided that there is no place for Québec in a new and more satisfying constitutional arrangement. Every time a Bloc MP speaks, Reform's contention that it is time to get tough with Québec is confirmed. There is no dialogue; just posturing in preparation for the final denouement, a denouement that Reform Party leader Manning has suggested on a number of occasions could involve a civil war.

IV   THE ESCALATION OF RHETORIC IN ENGLISH CANADA

Manning and the Reform Party are not the only ones guilty of engaging in what amounts to civil war talk. NDP premiers Harcourt and then Clark of British Columbia, and Romanow of Saskatchewan, no doubt trying to stave off the threat of the Reform Party, have also repeatedly uttered some destructive, anti-Québec bombast. Their comments have ridiculed the BQ and PQ leaders, questioned their motives, and engaged in threatening talk apparently to try to scare the people of Québec off the separatist option.[13] One of Romanow's suggestions – deeply ominous in its implications – conveyed the notion that even if Québec elects the PQ and votes for sovereignty in a referendum, there is simply no legal and constitutional way for Québec to leave Confederation. Romanow has repeated this theme endlessly from 1992 to the present, though restraining himself during crucial and sensitive votes in Québec. This kind of hostile, lawyer's gibberish can only escalate the war of words – and, history tells us, after uttering warlike words, politicians find it extremely difficult, as political confrontations spiral out of control, to prevent verbal conflict from becoming military conflict. Furthermore, this kind of talk confirms the widely held belief among many Québécois nationalists that English Canada is guilty of bad faith in dealings with Québec – after all, English Canada recognized the right of Québec to self-determination when the PQ was first elected and affirmed Québec's right to determine its constitutional future, up to and including sovereignty, with the participation of the prime minister and many English Canadian premiers in the 1980 and 1995 referendum campaigns in Québec. Back in 1970, when the *War Measures Act* was imposed, and the army occupied Québec, English Canada, through Ottawa, clearly drew a line in the sand indicating that illegal and violent methods to achieve sovereignty would not be tolerated. As a result, the Québec sovereignty movement united as never before and threw itself into the democratic struggle for sovereignty, achieving remarkable victories and near-victories in the last 30 years. Now that the sovereignty movement appears to be on the threshold of an unexpected success, it would be not only an act of bad faith, but also an extreme and deliberate provocation for English Canada and Ottawa to use the pretext of a Supreme Court ruling, or an arbitrarily inflated definition of the *majority* needed to win a sovereignty referendum (something considerably greater than 50 per cent plus one), to refuse to recognize and accept a democratic victory for sovereigntists in a future referendum in Québec.

Then there is the threatening talk from some quarters in English Canada that if Québec decides to leave, huge chunks of the province's territory will be carved out, a corridor will be forced through to link Ontario and Atlantic Canada, Québec will not be welcome

---

[13] Romanow accused the separatists of a "con job," and described Parizeau and Bouchard as "master illusionists" who believe in "yogic flying." Harcourt threatened the territorial integrity of a separating Québec, and warned that if Québec stays in Canada, "Québec and British Columbia... would be best of friends, ... but if they decided to separate... we'd be the worst of enemies." Harcourt also re-iterated strong opposition to special status. After Harcourt was replaced by Clark as NDP leader and Premier of British Columbia, Clark continued to challenge Québec's right to separate, to threaten a sovereign Québec's territory, and to reject any form of special status for Québec.

in NAFTA, economic and political relations will be hostile and full of conflict – and so the bellicose talk feeds upon itself.

Let's be honest. Much of this is nothing less than dangerous civil war talk and constitutes the worst possible way to ensure harmonious relations between English Canada and Québec whatever the final constitutional outcome. Why are prominent English Canadian federal politicians, premiers and even the prime minister doing this – electoral opportunism to pander to English Canadian red-neck hostility to Québec; economic, legal and military blackmail to scare the people of Québec? It won't work – indeed, it plays into the hands of the committed and uncompromising separatists in Québec.

At the very least, such threatening, bellicose talk sets the stage for bitter confrontations between English Canada and Québec, whether Bouchard and the PQ are re-elected or not, whether another referendum on sovereignty in 1999 or 2000 passes or not. Such talk also limits our options and ties our hands. What do we do in English Canada if Bouchard and the PQ are re-elected, as seems inevitable, and a referendum passes, as seems quite likely, particularly given the fact that the Bloc was again returned in 1997 as the major federal party representing Québec in the House of Commons? Refuse to negotiate? Force Québec to make a UDI[14] and then invade? What is the strategy? What is the plan? Remember, for the first time in the history of Québec, since the 1994 Québec election, the people of Québec have been democratically represented in both the House of Commons and the Québec National Assembly by separatist parties. In terms of international law, political morality, and any conceivable theory of democracy, we are now in a very different situation than in the past when the people of Québec elected a separatist party to speak for them in the National Assembly and a federalist party to speak for them in Ottawa – thus both separatist and federalist politicians from Québec could justly claim to speak for the people of Québec. Now a clear majority of those elected to speak for the people of Québec – both in Québec City and in Ottawa – are committed to sovereignty and if a referendum in 1999 or 2000 affirms that option, then a refusal by English Canada to negotiate in good faith would find little respect or recognition in the international community. Indeed, in such a situation many countries might well recognize a UDI by Québec.

In the interests of our future, of keeping our options open, of salvaging the federation, we can only hope that the Mannings, Clarks and Romanows, and all the other belligerent voices in English Canada, would shut up. They are not helping the situation.

V   THE TRIUMPH OF NEO-CONSERVATISM

All this is happening in the context of the triumph of neo-conservatism, a triumph which has disarmed us. The decade-long pursuit of the neo-conservative agenda initiated by Mulroney, and by most premiers, most notably Bennett and Vander Zalm of British Columbia and Devine of Saskatchewan, achieved what appears to be a final – and

---

[14] Unilateral Declaration of Independence.

hopefully only very temporary – success at the very moment many of us thought the agenda had been decisively defeated. The ambitious agenda amounted to nothing less than a major re-structuring of Canadian society and the economy, and a re-writing of the post-Depression, post-War political consensus of Canada as a society based on a mixed economy, generally committed to incremental increases in a universal social security net, a humane regulation of the worst features of unregulated, free enterprise capitalism, and slowly advancing standards of living for wage and salary earners. The neo-conservative agenda constituted an effort to overturn that consensus and to turn the clock back sixty years and more to the era of the unregulated free market, private greed and unrestrained individualism, and a modified social Darwinism as the basic creed governing interventions to assist the weak, the afflicted and the vulnerable.

The key items of the agenda are well-documented: (1) cutbacks in social spending, including the significant erosion of Canada's social security net; (2) an assault on the incomes and living standards of wage and salary earners, while increasing the total share of wealth generated flowing to capital and its privileged servants; (3) a weakening of federal power *vis-à-vis* the provinces; (4) a program of deregulation and privatization, and a move to free market forces as the engine of social and economic development; (5) a free trade deal with the US as a prelude to the establishment of a continental free market encompassing Canada, the US and Mexico; (6) a deliberate process of discrediting and disabling government as a popular democratic tool available to the people to shape the economy and society, largely by burdening governments with huge annual deficits and a crippling debt, and by shifting the increasing tax burden from the rich and the corporate sector to those in the middle income category, thus provoking a tax revolt.

Mulroney scored some considerable successes in implementing the agenda during his eight years and nine months in office, but not without finally paying a price. The prime minister who set records in the elections of 1984 and 1988 was driven from office in June 1993 as a result of month after month of the lowest approval ratings ever scored by an incumbent prime minister, leaving office as arguably the most reviled prime minister in Canadian history. His party suffered for his sins in the 1993 election when it was reduced from the status of majority government to two seats in the House of Commons. Neo-conservative governments in British Columbia and Saskatchewan suffered similar fates in October 1991, when the NDP in those provinces, after years in parliamentary opposition fighting the implementation of the neo-conservative agenda, swept to power. The earlier victory of Rae's NDP in Ontario in September 1990 on an explicit and aggressive anti-neo-conservative platform further indicated a popular revulsion at the agenda and its impacts. On the political front it appeared that the people had spoken – the neo-conservative agenda was over and governments opposed to the agenda had a mandate to proceed to re-build.

Then, in an unanticipated *volte face*, the three NDP premiers, and the national NDP leader abandoned social democracy and embraced neo-conservatism as the new national political consensus. The victory of the business lobby was complete and beyond anything even its most optimistic members could have hoped for. The message to the public was very clear. Mulroney, Devine, Vander Zalm and the other neo-conservatives were on the correct course after all. The public debt and deficit made it impossible to do anything but cut social, health and education spending. The money lenders were calling the tune and elected politicians had no choice but to dance to it, despite winning popular mandates to govern otherwise. Further, the business lobby was also correct. There was no solution to be found in tax reform, government intervention in the economy, or public ownership and state economic planning. This move to fiscal neo-conservatism by the three NDP premiers and the national NDP leader, as well as their earlier enthusiastic support for Tory efforts to constitutionalize a weakened federal government and stronger provinces via the Charlottetown Agreement, discredited both the NDP as a political party and social democracy as a political and economic doctrine. Canadian social democratic leaders lost their way and joined the neo-conservative crusade.

The turn to fiscal neo-conservatism by the NDP leadership had a significant impact on the popular consciousness. Now deprived of the parliamentary leadership of the NDP in resisting neo-conservative logic and doctrine, and observing the spectacle of the NDP, upon election to power, agreeing that the problems of debts and deficits needed to be addressed by cuts in social spending, and further that the business lobby had to be appeased in the interests of economic viability, popular resistance began to falter. Increasingly, polls revealed that the public, formerly quite unwilling to buy the neo-conservative rationale, began to do so. A shift of enormous significance took place in public opinion in the aftermath of the right-turn of the NDP leadership. After a decade of unsuccessful efforts, a shift in the public consciousness to share in a new neo-conservative political and economic consensus at the core of Canadian public life began to occur. It appeared that what Mulroney, Vander Zalm and Devine had failed to accomplish – indeed had sacrificed their political credibility and careers to achieve – began very quickly if incompletely to be accomplished by the NDP premiers and the national NDP leader. It was a watershed in Canadian political history, constituting what could be the death of social democracy in Canada. It was not surprising, therefore, that the Rae government in Ontario and the federal NDP were virtually annihilated at the polls in subsequent elections, while the NDP governments in British Columbia and Saskatchewan salvaged themselves by imposing only a moderate version of neo-conservatism even as they kept speaking the language of social democracy, at least during elections.

Therefore, at the time of a potentially great national crisis we are disarmed by the neo-conservative consensus. Social programs are under attack and our underclass faces new and unprecedented levels of social barbarism. Government as a tool for realizing the popular will is discredited, and politicians either fear to exercise their powers, or are ideologically committed to refraining from doing so. For the first time in our recorded polling history, a majority of Canadians oppose programs of economic supports for the poorer regions – a key cement binding the federation together. And as universality with minimum national standards in social, health and education programs continues to be eroded, the daily political ties that bind individual loyalties to the distinctiveness of the

Canadian experiment are weakened. As individuals – especially the middle class whose access to social programs is increasingly under attack even as their tax rates remain high – begin to see that they are in the rat race alone and unprotected, the law of the jungle will begin to prevail and commitment to Canada as a society and as a political experiment will wither and die. And who can be proud to be part of such a Canada?

VI   CAPITAL'S ABANDONMENT OF THE CANADIAN NATIONAL PROJECT

The Canadian business lobby, representing the giants of corporate Canada, deeply committed to neo-conservatism, free trade, and globalization, have virtually abandoned Canada as a national project. Indeed, the new globalization/neo-conservative cant insists the truly successful corporation must now compete on the world stage. For a corporation to even have a vision of *nation* or a *national stage* on which to act, is considered backward and old-fashioned. At its most basic economic level this simply confirms a central law of capital – grow and expand, or die – and should not therefore be surprising.

But at the political level the implications are profound. What corporate capitalism is telling the people of Canada is that, having used Canada in the initial stages of development, the success stories of corporate Canada now want to abandon nation building. Indeed, given the central and successful role of the business lobby in our neo-conservative politics of the last decade, Canadian business has done everything it could to dismantle what has been constructed since 1867. Let us recall that these corporate success stories have roots in the 19th and early 20th centuries and that they unashamedly shaped and then used Canadian national policies – the tariff, protection of Canada's banks and financial institutions, subsidies, grants of public lands and mineral rights, etc. – to build their successful enterprises. Now, having achieved success, they are ready to meet world competition and understandably wish to move onto the world stage. But these enterprises want to do so unencumbered by any commitment to Canada as a national project. The very country they exploited to achieve success, the business lobby now wishes to renounce, to put behind them. This the business lobby cannot be permitted to do – they owe the Canadian people a great deal and if they will not fulfill their political and economic obligations willingly, they must be forced to do so.

Ironically, a significant number of Québec-based corporations and financial institutions constitute an exception to this general trend. Significant elements of the business lobby in Québec have come out for sovereignty – an unprecedented development – indicating a conviction that they see their future as tied to a sovereign Québec unencumbered by a declining English Canada. The potential political significance of this should not be underestimated. The Québec business lobby, especially the large corporate and financial sector, spoke with one voice against sovereignty throughout the 1960's and 1970's, and played a key role in the economic fear campaign that helped defeat sovereignty during the 1980 referendum. The economic fear trump card is no longer effective. During the Charlottetown referendum, economic fear, frequently bordering on deliberately manufactured hysteria, was used in both English Canada and Québec to stampede

Canadians to vote Yes. It failed utterly. In the 1993 federal election, economic fear was used against the Bloc in Québec with little effect. In the 1994 Québec election, economic fear was again used unsuccessfully by federal forces in efforts to deny Parizeau and the PQ a victory. In the 1995 sovereignty referendum the economic fear card was again played and doubtless contributed in some small measure to the narrow defeat of the Yes, but not enough to suggest its use will again sway significant numbers of Québec voters (though it might help to firm up the core federalist vote, and it certainly seems to have its most dramatic impact in English Canada).

VII   THE END OF THE OLD NATIONAL POLICY

The old National Policy, the core economic strategy of Canada as a nation, is finished. But we have developed no new National Policy, no new core economic strategy, but free trade, free markets and globalization. It goes without saying that an economic strategy singularly characterized by free trade and free markets amounts to no economic strategy at all.

The reader will recall that the old National Policy really amounted to an industrialization/ modernization strategy in order to build the east/west economic foundation of the nation, rooted in tariff protection to keep the home market for local industries, protection for financial institutions, and the extraction of resources for world markets. This strategy depended heavily on exploiting the Canadian people as a captive market, and exploiting the natural environment in the rapid extraction of resources for export. Above all, the strategy required strong and interventionist federal and provincial governments.

The strategy had a clear regional dimension. The peripheral regions – the West, the North and Atlantic Canada – provided the captive markets and the resources. Southern Central Canada – a narrow, heavily populated region along the Great Lakes and the St. Lawrence – was the focus of industrialization. Québec played a mixed role – there, industrial development was more heavily based on the exploitation of cheap and plentiful labour, Québec's vast natural resources were opened up and the Québécois provided a lucrative captive market. Ontario shared these characteristics with Québec, but tended to enjoy the advantage of being the focus of more modern, technologically innovative industrial development. Ontario also enjoyed the advantage of being the dominant province of the nation, politically and economically; the location of head offices for transportation, financial institutions, and the great houses of wholesale and retail commerce; and the center of political power where national goals were defined. Confederation was really the project of the political and economic élite of Ontario, and that élite jealously guarded its domination and prerogatives in setting the national agenda.

That era is now over. The end had been coming for some time, politically and economi-cally. As the regionally based industries – natural resources, oil and natural gas, agriculture, the fishery, mining, hydro-electricity, etc. – in Atlantic Canada, Québec and the West grew in maturity and significance to the national economy, the peripheral regions became more assertive, demanding more say in setting national economic policy. And the regions, frequently restive in the past, became more successful in their political assertiveness and gained more national clout, particularly Québec after the Quiet Revolution and the West after the energy crisis of the early 1970's. The north/south economic pull, especially for Québec and the West, challenged east/west economic ties. Increasingly, trade with the US became more and more free – by the mid 1980's 80 per cent of trade between Canada and the US was free of tariff barriers, and protection was less and less important in Canada's economic life. The FTA of 1988 put a decisive and final end to the old National Policy. But, of course, the essence of the FTA was that no new national policy would be put in place as the remnants of the old were phased out – and the Canadian economy was expected eventually to go naked into continental and world markets.

But Canadians faced much more than just the end of the old nation-building policies of the past. Key cornerstones of the national material economic base were also disintegrating. In Atlantic Canada, the fishery, as we have known it, the cornucopia of the Grand Banks, is effectively over. On the Prairies, the wheat economy, as we have known it since the great wheat boom brought final success to Confederation's economic strategy in 1896, is effectively gone. The protections afforded Canada's broadly based traditional agricultural sectors – quotas, marketing boards, and tariffs – are about to disappear. In British Columbia the traditional forestry sector is in deep trouble, and faces a period of massive re-adjustment and re-tooling to reconcile popular demands to save what little is left of old-growth forests, the necessity to exploit the smaller trees of new growth forests, and the need to produce wealth and provide jobs for the many communities dependent on the forest industry. The accelerating flow of our western resources southward under the FTA has urgently raised the specter of what will be left for the West after we have drained the conventional oil and natural gas from the Western Basin, denuded our forests, and begun to pump our fresh water southward. Is the West to trade the role of hewer of wood and drawer of water for the Canadian national economy for the same role for the whole continent? And, if that occurs, just how long can we sustain a viable economy to support our people, services and infrastructures? In Ontario, the incredibly rapid de-industrialization since the FTA has called into question the province's traditional role of industrial heartland of the nation. Where are the new national policies on the fishery, the grain trade, agriculture in general, forestry, water, natural resource exploitation in general? Where is the new national industrial strategy? Where is the over-arching national economic strategy to tie the regions together in a viable and symbiotic way? There are none. We are on the verge of becoming an economic basket case and all we hear is free market and globalization cant.

The death of the old National Policy, and the absence of a new one, has had some unanticipated effects in Québec. Some Québec business leaders and nationalists have argued that the FTA has been much more beneficial for Québec than for the rest of Canada (remember, the FTA would not have passed had Québec not voted solidly for Mulroney in 1988). The resulting rapid decline in the out-dated, traditional tariff protected industries has cut one of the last ties that bound Québec to the east/west economy. This decline in Canadian oriented industry has opened up opportunities for growth among Québec-based and US-based enterprises, and Québec's economic future is increasingly seen in a continental and global context rather than in the context of the Canadian federation.

A study conducted for the *Caisse de dépôt* found that Québec exports to the US between 1988 and 1992 had surged in all economic sectors, and this growth had been significantly greater than that experienced by Canada as a whole. Another study found that between 1981 and 1995 Québec's exports to the rest of Canada grew by 67 per cent, while international exports grew by 208 per cent. From 1991 to 1995 Statistics Canada reported that interprovincial trade grew by under seven per cent, as a result of a dramatic shift to foreign markets, especially the American market. This shift to foreign markets was biggest in Alberta and Québec. In fact, Québec's 1995 interprovincial exports were lower than those of 1990, and Québec suffered a Cdn$1 billion trade deficit with the provinces in that year, while enjoying a Cdn$3.8 billion surplus in foreign trade. Meanwhile, Alberta's deficit in interprovincial trade grew from Cdn$2 billion in 1991 to Cdn$3 billion in 1995 at the same time as its foreign trade surplus grew to almost Cdn$11 billion. In fact, Ontario was the only province to report an interprovincial trade surplus in 1995 of almost Cdn$26 billion, and a foreign trade deficit of just over Cdn$5 billion. In terms of trade between Ontario and Québec, Ontario's trade surplus with Québec more than doubled to almost Cdn$6 billion in 1995. This changing economic reality was accompanied by a shift in public opinion. In January 1994, Gallup found that although 53 per cent of Québécois believed the Canadian economy would be worse off without Québec, opinion regarding the province was almost equally divided, with 35 per cent of Québécois believing their economy would be better off and 37 per cent believing it would be worse off. Meanwhile, 74 per cent of Canadians outside the province believed the Québec economy would be worse off, another example of the two solitudes. The depth of this economic disagreement was confirmed when a poll found that 60 per cent of non-francophones blame Montréal's high unemployment levels on the sovereignty debate, while only 28 per cent of Québécois share this view.

The political implications of this difference of views are worth careful scrutiny. Let us recall the role played by campaigns of economic fear to battle the PQ and sovereignty in the 1970's. The claims were ominous: Québec separation from the Canadian economy would bring economic hardship, a flight of investment, high unemployment – in short, economic catastrophe. Economic fear was key to Lévesque's failures in the elections of 1970 and 1973 – so much so that the PQ placed sovereignty on the backburner and promised good government first, followed by a referendum, in order to reassure the Québécois. In the referendum of 1980, the economic fear campaign was absolutely decisive in giving the federalist side its 60/40 victory. During the 1992 Charlottetown referendum, economic fear was used again by our political and economic élites, particularly intensely in Québec. It failed completely. And during the 1994 Québec election, Liberal leader Johnson made a desperate gamble that a combination of economic fear and a focus on the PQ's separatist commitment would work in his favour.

It didn't, but the danger was realized that by forcing the provincial campaign to center on the question of sovereignty and its economic consequences, Johnson handed a victorious Parizeau and the PQ a much stronger mandate to pursue the separatist option than otherwise would have been the case. Johnson's other risky gamble was to wrap himself and the provincial Liberals in the federalist flag – the first time an incumbent Premier of Québec had done so since the first days of the Quiet Revolution. Unfortunately for Johnson, having embraced the federalist option, he had no new vision to offer of the place Québec would occupy in a new set of national economic policies. It was not his fault, of course, because there were none, and there are none.

VIII   SIGNS OF HOPE

This is a dark picture, but there are signs of hope. The fact is, despite the unprecedentedly favourable context for sovereignty in 1995, the Yes forces failed to capture 50 per cent plus one. Further, the Bloc's loss of 10 seats (44, down from 54) and 11 per cent of the popular vote (38 per cent, down from 49) in the 1997 election suggests that there is at least a pause in the sovereignty movement's momentum, and the Bloc's decline might have been greater in the absence of Preston Manning and the Reform Party's anti-Québec crusade which became particularly shrill in the closing weeks of the campaign. Additionally, Bouchard's more modest version of the neo-conservative obsession with the deficit and debt has begun to tarnish his image and undermine his popularity in Québec. Given that another Québec provincial election must be held before the next sovereignty referendum, likely in 1999 or 2000 at the earliest, there is another window of opportunity to reach a settlement with Québec.

There is therefore time for English Canada to offer to open up a dialogue on special status for Québec within a re-constituted Confederation. It may well be our last chance to save the federation. But a good faith commitment from English Canada to grant Québec special status would have every chance of success. The fact is that most pro-sovereignty Québécois are reluctant separatists and would be quick to respond to a meaningful constitutional resolution of their grievances through the negotiation of special status. The biggest worry is whether the 30 to 40 per cent of English Canadians willing to consider special status for Québec can provide the leadership and vision to win sufficient support for such a solution among English Canadians. Given the hardness in English Canada to Québec after Meech and Charlottetown, and with the Reform Party and western premiers yapping and snarling at Ottawa's heels, it will not be a cake walk.

But it is not just the relentlessly looming Québec question that will hopefully force Canadians and their political and economic leaders to face reality and begin to develop effective policy responses. The collapse of the fishery in Atlantic Canada faces us with some rather stark choices and the momentum of the crisis will finally force us to deal with what could become the ruination of an entire region. The majority of experts and scientists insist that even the best case scenario for the recovery of the fishery will not be remotely sufficient for the traditional fishery to resume its former economic status as economic foundation for the region. Assuming this is a correct assessment, what do we do? Inevitably, as a nation, we will have to do something – if we don't do it willingly from compassion and sympathy, political and economic reality will finally force us to take some initiative.

Do we follow the harsh advice of *Globe and Mail* editor and leading neo-conservative ideologue Thorsell and allow the cruel logic of the free market – "the compulsion of the whip of hunger," as Max Weber once described it – to work its satanic magic by forcing massive depopulation?   As a solution, this is not only brutally reprehensible but ultimately irrational – in the long run the social, economic and political costs of such a Draconian policy would be incalculable. The displacement of tens of thousands of economic refugees from Atlantic Canada would create social havoc in other regions and lead to profound alienation and social despair among the involuntarily displaced population.

A more rational solution is a development strategy based on the considerable skills of Atlantic Canadians, and the existing resources of the region, premised on keeping the population in their already well-settled and successful communities. Obviously, part of the solution is a more regulated and careful approach to the traditional harvesting of fish in reconstituted in-shore and off-shore fisheries. We had reasonable if weak policies before, and even better advice from experts never acted upon. Even the weak policies, such as they were, were never fully or effectively enforced. But we will also have to take some public risks as a nation. Aquaculture is the obvious future of a modernized and sustainable fishery, but vast amounts will first have to be expended on research, development, and experimentation. Some individual entrepreneurs and corporations in Atlantic Canada are already doing so – but such individual efforts will not be sufficient to bring about the scale of re-development required in a timely fashion. Hence, a massive public investment in the fishery – at the very least in research and development – is necessary.

On the Prairies, as the wheat economy has declined, diversification into a variety of new cash crops for new markets has been occurring, often with a great deal of success. But this is occurring largely as a result of the entrepreneurial decisions of individual farmers – typically those large and debt-free enough to afford the risk. These successes can become models for a future new agricultural strategy for the Prairies. But again, individual entrepreneurial successes will not be sufficient to save the one in three Prairie farmers at risk, and the communities which depend upon them for economic survival. Again, we can take the advice of Thorsell and allow the free market to work out its logic – at the cost of the disappearance of between one in three and one in two farmers in the next decade or two, and the death of literally hundreds of rural communities. Again, the public leadership, initiative, and entrepreneurial supports of new state agricultural policies are urgently required. And there will inevitably be considerable political pressure from the increasingly desperate Prairie population on politicians to deliver.

In British Columbia the forestry crisis has reached the point where a jointly developed provincial and federal forestry policy is long overdue – and all sides in the debate, environmentalists and loggers, increasingly recognize that. Only the industry, and its political puppets, eager to enjoy the unrestrained right to exploit British Columbia's forests, continue to refuse to face reality. Similarly, in Ontario popular demands for a new national industrial strategy, once the enormity of what has happened sinks in, will be irresistible.

In other words, the politics of a vibrant democracy like Canada will force our leaders to take action, or finally result in their replacement by leaders who will. That fact provides an abiding sense of hope. But there are other reasons for hope as well. Canadians will not long remain opposed to using the federal state aggressively to further assist the poorer regions of this country. Many Canadians have been temporarily swept up in the well-orchestrated campaign of debt and deficit hysteria of the neo-conservatives and, in due course, rationality and humanity will return. Canada will not survive if we don't continue to address the issue of regional disparity – and even though our past programs never overcame such disparity, the absence of such programs would be catastrophic for the vulnerable regions. But even if Canadians' political willingness to provide further assistance to the poorer regions is slow in returning to former, pre-neo-conservative levels, there is always the Constitution.

The *Constitution Act, 1982* contained the following amendment to Canada's constitution, now in effect:

> 36.   (1) Without altering the legislative authority of Parliament or of the provincial legislatures, or the rights of any of them with respect to the exercise of their legislative authority, Parliament and the legislatures, are committed to
> (a) promoting equal opportunities for the well-being of Canadians;
> (b) furthering economic development to reduce disparity in opportunities; and
> (c) providing essential public services of reasonable quality to all Canadians.
> (2) Parliament and the government of Canada are committed to the principle of making equalization payments to ensure that provincial governments have sufficient revenues to provide reasonably comparable levels of public services at reasonably comparable levels of taxation.

No disadvantaged province, community, group or individual from a poorer region has yet used section 36(2) in a challenge in the Supreme Court to force Ottawa to act with more generosity. Former Newfoundland Premier Peckford once threatened to do so, but relented. Given what is happening in Atlantic Canada, the North, and the West, in conjunction with program cuts, it is only a matter of time before such a challenge is mounted. Regardless of the technical outcome, it would serve wonderfully to focus public attention on the deepening crisis of Canada.

There is also hope – and it is distasteful to have to say this, but things have become harsh and ugly – because, as every thinking Canadian knows, the unfettered free market cannot work in a humane and socially responsible fashion. Yes, we can concede to the neo-conservative economists, the free market works – the free market will "solve" the problems of Atlantic Canada through hunger and forced migration; it will "solve" the problem of Prairie agriculture by driving tens of thousands of farmers off the land; it will end the debate about oil and natural gas policy by pumping out all the oil and gas the market will take, leaving us the dregs; it will end the debate about forestry policy when the economically exploitable forests are gone; and so on. But the social, human and environmental costs will not be acceptable and the Canadian people will finally find those costs to be unacceptable.

As the cuts in social spending, and the massive withdrawal of government from society and the economy, continue, the consequences for the bottom one in four to one in three Canadians will be horrific and appalling. Canadians will find those consequences, and the resulting social unrest, abhorrent and repugnant. As young Canadians continue to face high unemployment, and as cuts in education spending close the post-secondary door on more and more of them, the consequences for a whole generation will quite simply be unacceptable, and Canadians will rebel and demand action. As the decline in real wages and salaries continues, and as employers use the current conservative climate to squeeze more and more out of their employees, the undulating strike wave already in motion will continue to sweep across the country and become increasingly politicized. As the dead-end Reform Party solutions (now increasingly pursued by Liberal and NDP governments), based as they are on simple-minded, blame-the-victim homilies, become clearer, Canadians will reject them and demand a shift in orientation. Regrettably there will be a lot of pain as Canadians re-learn the lessons their parents and grandparents learned up to and including the Great Depression and World War II.

Canadians will eventually come to a realization of how seriously Canada is at risk, at risk in so many ways. Indeed, many, perhaps most, Canadians have already come to that realization as revealed in their well-focused political behaviour of the last few years: in 1990 Canadians elected the Ontario NDP on a clear anti-neo-conservative program; in 1991 Canadians defeated neo-conservative governments and elected ostensibly social democratic governments in British Columbia and Saskatchewan; in 1992 Canadians defeated the Charlottetown Agreement; in June 1993 Canadian public opinion drove Mulroney from office; in October 1993 the governing Tory party was nearly wiped off the electoral map and Liberal leader Chrétien, who made a lot of anti-neo-conservative noise while in Opposition and during the campaign, was elected; in 1997 Canadians, especially in Atlantic Canada, punished Chrétien and the Liberals for reneging on their Red Book promises. The evidence, therefore, is clear that it is the political élites of all parties, not the people of Canada, who have failed to respond to the realities of the crisis.

As Canadians, especially English Canadians, come to realize the depth of the crisis, and as they watch the experiments with unrestrained neo-conservatism underway in Ontario and Alberta, they will finally reject the negative, anti-Québec, anti-feminist, anti-poor, anti-victim self-definition being offered to them by the Reform Party and other neo-conservatives. English Canada desperately needs to re-assert its sense of national identity and national purpose through a positive national project premised on the abrogation and re-negotiation of the FTA and NAFTA. Until those chains are broken and replaced by economic agreements that do not compromise Canada's sovereignty, independence and national integrity, English Canadians will only see the further erosion of the essence of who and what they are and want to become in future.

The other choice is clear: balkanization and fragmentation; a separate Québec; an isolated and impoverished Atlantic Canada; the eventual future absorption of provinces like British Columbia and Alberta into the American union, provinces where there is already a strong pro-US integration sentiment. In short, the other choice is the end of Canada, not with a bang but with a series of whimpers.

References

Conway, J. (1992). *Debts to Pay: English Canada and Québec from the Conquest to the Referendum.* Toronto: James Lorimer and Company.

Conway, F. (1994a). Reflections on Canada in the Year 1994, presented at a Canadian Studies Association/Canadian Historical Association/Canadian Political Science Association joint session at the Learned Societies' meetings at the University of Calgary.

Conway, F. (1994b). Reflections on Canada in the year 1994, *Journal of Canadian Studies* 29 (3): 146-58.

Conway, J. (1994c). *The West: The History of a Region in Confederation.* Toronto: James Lorimer and Company (second edition).

Conway, F. (1995a). Engelstalig Canada: krijgt Québec speciale status of niet? In L. d'Haenens (ed.), *Het land van de ahorn: visies op Canada: politiek, cultuur, economie.* Ghent: Academia Press.

Conway, F. (1995b). Reflections on Canada in the year 1994. In J. de Finney, G. Kealey, J. Lennox, & T. Palmer Seiler (eds.), *Canadian Studies at Home and Abroad.* (pp. 145-71). Montréal: Association for Canadian Studies.

Conway, F. (1996). The "folksy fascism" of the Reform Party, *The Literary Review of Canada*, June.

Conway, F. (1997a). *Debts to Pay: A Fresh Approach to the Québec Question.* Toronto: James Lorimer and Company.

Conway, F. (1997b). The political economy of Canadian federalism: a world without Canada? Approaching the next millennium. In M. Westmacott & H. Mellon (eds.), *Challenges to Canadian Federalism.* Toronto: Prentice-Hall.

Resnick, P. (1994). *Thinking English Canada.* Toronto: Stoddart Publishing.

THE LIBERAL IDEA OF THE CANADIAN NATION-STATE

By Louis BALTHAZAR

I   INTRODUCTION

It could be argued that the very foundation of modern Canada rests on a terrible ambiguity. For most English-speaking Canadian leaders in 1867, the British North America Act was creating a new nation. For French Canadians however, the new country was the result of a pact or a contract between provinces, especially between the French-speaking province of Québec, which received special guarantees of autonomy, and the other English-speaking components of Canada.

There does not seem to be any doubt that John A. Macdonald, for his part, would have much preferred that Canada be a legislative union in order to avoid the type of conflict that had tragically afflicted the United States federation and for the new government to be in a position to foster a strong east-west economic system. But, as a realistic politician, he accepted a compromise. Canada would be a federation because union would have otherwise been impossible. To avoid following the American model, however, provinces would be subordinated to the federal government, just like colonies in the British Empire. With the residual clause, the power of disallowance and the authority to appoint provincial lieutenant-governors, Macdonald was confident that, with time, the central authority would prevail so that a true national spirit would take shape. In 1868, he wrote a colleague:

> (...) I think the Dominion must win in the long run. The powers of the General Government are so much greater than those of the United States (...) My own opinion is that the General Government or Parliament should pay no more regard to the status or position of the Local Governments than they would to the prospects of the ruling party in the corporation of Québec or Montréal (Cook, 1969: 10).

This attitude corresponded well with the general liberal trend of the nineteenth century. Liberalism often espoused the cause of nationalism but the enlargement of nations was much more favoured than the creation of small entities through secession. Thus Macdonald, as Tory as he was, can be seen as a liberal nationalist and one of the first proponents of the idea of a strong, indivisible Canadian nation. Three factors, however, prevented this idea from being realized. First, Canada was still British North America, a quasi-sovereign state but in fact a colony of the United Kingdom. For many years, Canadian nationalism would be countered by strong imperial sentiments and devotion. Second, Canadian liberalism was fashioned by *laissez-faire* conceptions of the state. Ottawa would not act as a national government for the very reason that it hardly acted at all. Thirdly, this reluctance to intervene was reinforced by the political situation. The provinces – first among which Québec on account of its own traditional social structure that was so different, but also the Maritime provinces where regional allegiances and interests were well entrenched {- would not allow the federal government to assert itself too much. This political heterogeneity was recognized and given legal sanction by various judgments of the Privy Council's judicial committee in London which, as the final constitutional authority, was mostly ruling in favour of provincial autonomy. In spite of these factors, the liberal dream of the Canadian nation was kept alive and would come back in force in the 1930's. A new elite of intellectuals in the universities, in the civil service, in journalism and other circles would reanimate the national idea and give it strong credentials.

This paper is an attempt to assess the force of the liberal idea of a Canadian nation-state in the 1930's. Nationalism, socialism and new economic theories will be considered as ingredients of a modern conception of Canada leading to a serious revision of the British North America Act. In more ways than one, the intellectual effervescence of these years is the foundation of today's Canada. The fact that this is an English-Canadian phenomenon purporting to represent Canada as a whole gives a tragic twist to an otherwise enlightened movement.

II   THE NEW INTELLECTUAL ELITE

Given the relative prosperity of the 1920's and other factors, a growing number of Canadians had access to universities so that an impressive new generation of graduate degree holders was filling various posts in law, the civil service and schools of higher learning throughout Canada. Douglas Owram has done a magnificent job in identifying the personalities and their role in various movements like the League for Social Reconstruction, the Co-operative Commonwealth Federation (CCF), the Radio League, the Canadian Clubs, the Liberal party and, to some extent, the Conservative party when it was in power between 1930 and 1935 (Owram, 1986). People like Brooke Claxton, a lawyer, a professor at McGill University and later a prominent member of the Liberal government, Graham Spry, the founder of the Radio League and also active in politics, Adam Shortt, a history professor and a civil servant, Norman Rogers, a political science professor and a member of the King cabinet in 1936, Frank Underhill, a historian and the founder of the League for Social Reconstruction with Frank Scott and Eugene Forsey of McGill, Clifford Clark, an economist at Queen's University who would become deputy Finance minister, just to name a few, were all believers in a Canadian nation and a stronger, more active federal government.

Most of them belonged to institutions such as the Canadian Political Science Association or the Canadian Clubs, wrote articles in the Canadian Forum and, by 1935, the Canadian Journal of Economics and Political Science. Given the relatively small population of the country and in spite of its impossible geography, they formed a tight community of people who all knew each other and were amazingly mobile. They moved easily from academia or the practice of law to the civil service and vice versa. They also moved geographically, from the University of British Columbia to

Dalhousie for instance, although the core of their activity took place in the Toronto-Montréal-Ottawa triangle. Their ideas circulated well enough between Vancouver, Edmonton, Regina, Winnipeg, Toronto, Ottawa, Kingston, Montréal and Halifax.

However, in spite of the fact that many of these intellectuals lived in Montréal or came to the metropolis often enough, they had very little communication with French-speaking Canadians. A few men such as Édouard Montpetit, of the University of Montréal, and Father Georges-Henri Lévesque, of Laval, joined them occasionally but, by and large, it is fair to say, that the idea of a united Canadian nation was virtually nonexistent in French- speaking Québec. Even federal politicians such as Ernest Lapointe did not connect with the concept of political centralization.

The fact is that the Québec education system was falling far behind that of the other provinces and that Québec politics were very traditional and inspired by ideas that were foreign to modern liberalism. This allowed the English-speaking intelligentsia to ignore their Francophone compatriots. They just hoped that, in a not too distant future, some French-speaking intellectuals would join them and embrace their view of the Canadian nation. Still, conceiving a new framework for Canada – one which failed to take into account the aspirations of a high proportion of its population – did not seem to be a concern for them. It apparently never crossed their mind, from what it seems, that they were imposing an English-Canadian dream to Canada as a whole.

III   NATIONALISM

Oddly enough, it was a French Canadian who first promoted the idea of an independent Canada, free of any colonial obligation toward the British Empire. But Henri Bourassa's ideas, framed as they were in an orthodox Catholic philosophy, never had much appeal among English Canadians. When, in the 1920's, the new generation of intellectuals applauded the Dominion's gradually gained autonomy, which was legally sanctioned by the 1931 Statute of Westminster, they did not show any willingness to extend a hand to Henri Bourassa, a feeling that was amply reciprocated.

The pride of belonging to an independent Canada never went as far as using negative-sounding words as "separation" or "leaving" the Empire. Only the opponents of a complete Canadian sovereignty alluded to "separation," a case in point being R.B. Bennett who, while leader of the opposition, blamed the King government for establishing an embassy in Washington:

> I am wholly opposed (…) to the establishment of this embassy at Washington. It is but the doctrine of separation, it is but the evidence in many minds of the end of our connection with the empire. For that is what it means (...) because if we are a sovereign state we cannot belong to the British Empire (Mahant & Mount, 1989: 127).

One is tempted to make a comparison with today's situation. Many Canadians would like a Québec referendum question to include the word "separation." But, had Canadians been asked in the 1930's if they wished to "separate" from the British empire, would they have said yes as wholeheartedly as they agreed with Canada's newly acquired sovereignty?

Thus the new elites were very proud of their Canadian allegiance. They could, after 1931, conceive of their country as a nation. But they were not only concerned with their independence from Great Britain, they were also highly preoccupied with building a strong Canadian nation, free from American influences. This was particularly the case in the new popular phenomenon of radio broadcasting:

> Many Canadian stations were purchasing American programs; some stations affiliated with US networks. A survey conducted in major centers throughout Canada in the early 1930's found that 93 percent of Canadian high school students listened to American radio programs (Mahant & Mount, 1988: 152).

This was enough to arouse Canadian nationalism. Already, in 1930, the Canadian Radio League was founded by Graham Spry and Alan Plaunt in order to promote government intervention in broadcasting. The Bennett government was slow to react. But, after a Court judgment awarded control of broadcasting to the federal government in 1932, the Canadian Radio and Broadcasting Commission was instituted to establish Canadian content regulation. Eventually the Canadian Broadcasting Corporation (CBC) was created in 1936 on the British model with a mandate to draw all Canadians closer. But the inevitable duality of networks kept the French-speaking population quite apart from English-speaking Canadians.

The CBC was nonetheless a triumph for the nationalist cause. It was the voice of Canada and it was in the hands of the central government. For Canadian nationalists, it was a foregone conclusion that the problems were best dealt with at the federal level and that only a strong central government could bring about a united and independent Canadian nation. Historian Frank Underhill put it bluntly in the Canadian Forum:

> The real question at issue now is whether we are sufficiently nationally-minded to insist upon a national authority which shall be strong enough to supervise and direct our social and economic life or whether we mean to parcel up so much of the authority among nine provincial governments that our national government will remain impotent to meet national responsibilities (Owram, 1986: 224).

This opinion was shared by most liberal intellectuals of the time. Among them, Frank Scott, Brooke Claxton and Norman Rogers were the most outspoken. They firmly believed that Canada was a federation in which all national matters ought to be managed by the federal government and that provincial autonomy should be reduced to local questions. For them, the Fathers of Confederation were undoubtedly economic nationalists (Owram, 1986: 246). This is a typical feature of nationalists everywhere: promoting their cause as a return to the origins, fidelity to the source of the nation. As a consequence, nationalism often appears as conservative even in its radical demands:

> Those who sought to reform the constitution (...) were, far from defiling the sacred constitution, upholding its basic tenets. Proposed reforms could thus be posed not as dangerous innovations but as basically conservative attempts to return Canada to its founding principles (Owram, 1986: 247).

Nonetheless, in spite of the ardour of nationalist social scientists and civil servants in promoting a Canadian nation, they did not seem to be concerned with defining this nation. Of course, it was to include all Canadian citizens (i.e. British subjects until 1947). But was it to be bilingual? Bicultural? The latter word did not even exist, much less "multicultural." Liberal values could be considered universal but what if they were not shared by many Canadians, French Canadians in particular? These questions remained unanswered and "a single overriding sense of priority, purpose and authority" (Owram, 1986: 326) was still lacking at the end of the decade. This is often the paradox of nationalist movements, in that they fail to reach a substantial majority within the so-called nation. The nationalism of Canadian intellectuals remained elitist. But at the same time it was founded on a true sense of solidarity, compassion and a desire for social reforms.

IV   SOCIAL DEMOCRACY

The accession of Canada to full autonomy coincided with the most terrible social and economic crisis of the century. Canada, like all developed countries, was hit by the crisis throughout the decade and depression gave rise to various movements of frustration and in-depth questioning of the established order. This was made all the more intense by the fact that the nation's political leadership, in the Liberal opposition as well as in the Conservative government, seemed impotent and unable to bring about any valid plan for social reform. Liberal *laissez-faire* was such a strong habit that any meaningful government intervention in socio-economic matters seemed unthinkable for years.

It would be up to the intellectuals to shake things up and suggest new remedies. In 1932, Frank Underhill and Frank Scott, along with Eugene Forsey, Harry Cassidy, Graham Spry, and Irene Biss created the League for Social Reconstruction. The organization was designed to stimulate new thinking and foster new proposals for reform. In their criticism of traditional capitalism, League leaders were often led to recommending radical measures, coming close to harbouring Socialist ideals. By and large, however, they remained progressive liberals, on the model of New Deal Democrats in the United States, or social democrats, like Great Britain's Labour Party. They advocated strong government intervention, the creation of national public institutions, economic planning and several social services to be fulfilled by the government. But very few of them crossed the line to orthodox Marxism.

They invariably conceived reforms to be realized almost exclusively at the federal level. For them "the importance of collective action through national governments" was indisputable; this action should be "equally effective in every portion of the national domain" (Brady, 1933: 42) and called for a redistribution of legislative powers. The main problem to be dealt with was unemployment and "the failure of Canadian capitalism to provide men with work and their families with a decent living" (Cassidy, 1933: 55). The solution proposed was "a generous and humane system of relief, a scheme of unemployment insurance, and a program of employment stabilization, all of them on national lines under the leadership and the direction of the Dominion government" (Cassidy, 1933: 59).

In this context, a party was created, the Co-operative Commonwealth Federation (CCF), to operate at the federal level. Several members of the League for Social Reconstruction would form the brain trust of the CCF. In the Regina manifesto, at the founding of the party in 1933, many radical measures were put forward: (1) the creation of a national commission of planned economy; (2) the socialization of transportation and communications; (3) a new labour code. Since all of this would come under federal responsibility, constitutional amendments were deemed necessary.

Although the CCF was too radical for many intellectuals who remained closer to traditional party circles, there was constant contact between the CCF and other parties, through the intellectual community. Even within the Bennett government, the sense of crisis was felt acute enough that the Prime minister called in outside advisers, researchers and consultants (Owram, 1986: 178). In 1932, Clifford Clark, an economist teaching at Queen's University, became deputy minister of Finance and engaged in some economic planning, thus partially responding to the intellectual elite's wishes (Owram, 1986). Within the Liberal party, Vincent Massey, who was evicted from the embassy in Washington after Bennett took over the government, set himself to bring about political, economic and social regeneration to respond to the CCF call for change (Owram, 1986: 188). But no one was more representative of the links between the left-wing intellectuals and the Liberal party than Norman Rogers, a political science professor at Queen's University, who became minister of Labour within the King Cabinet in 1936. Rogers created the National Employment Commission that led eventually to the National Unemployment Insurance Act. Like all of his friends in the CCF, he was a staunch believer in centralization and the building of a strong "national" government. Social and economic recovery programs were also strongly supported by new economic theories.

V   NEW ECONOMICS

Doug Owram points out that the discipline of economics came of age in Canada in the 1930's (Owram, 1986: 192). John Maynard Keynes, who supported government intervention in the economy, did not publish his *General Theory of Employment, Interest and Money* before 1936. But he had become a renowned author as early as the 1920's and had many disciples in Canadian universities and, increasingly, in the civil service.

Even Conservative R.B. Bennett came to recognize the necessity of wealth redistribution before delivering his New Deal policies in 1935. He created a Royal Commission on Banking that recommended the creation of a central bank. The Bank of Canada was instituted in 1934, attracted the best minds in its councils (like Alex Skelton, John Deutsch and Louis Rasminsky) and would play an important role in regulating interest rates and currency value. During the 1930's, most Canadian economists were quite outspoken and not averse to recommending remedies to the flaws of the capitalist system. Adam Smith's paradigm of the invisible hand became considered as an illusion while a measure of control and regulation of private ownership was recommended. The Conservative government was persuaded to pass "a series of public works measures, first becoming involved directly and then providing a series of grants to the provinces" (Owram, 1986: 217). The new economic ideas, just like nationalism and the concern for social reforms, led to a quest for a greater role on the part of the federal government. Only the latter could adequately endeavour a redistribution of wealth, according to the intellectual elites and rising economists. Almost no consideration was given to the implementation of Keynes' theory on a provincial level. Québec economists, such as Édouard Montpetit, who opposed the creation of the central bank on the grounds of provincial autonomy, were quite isolated. The centralizing trend went as far as proposing that provincial budgets be placed under the control of the national bank in exchange for debt guarantees.

Consequently, "the very constitution of Canada appeared to be a structural problem, Reform of federal-provincial relations became, for many, the key to all other necessary changes" (Owram, 1986: 188).

VI   CONSTITUTIONAL REFORMS

It is no exaggeration to state that the Canadian liberal intellectuals of the 1930's literally despised the provincial governments. According to Frank Underhill, provincial administrations were "characterized by a tendency toward long periods of bad government alternating with relatively brief periods of competence. The exception was Québec which was privileged to have bad governments all the time" (Owram, 1986: 222).

It became therefore an obsession of the intellectuals that the constitution of Canada should be amended in favour of a definite pre-eminent role for the federal government so that it would fulfill its mission of being the national provider of services for the one Canadian nation-state. It is worth noting that, in the context of the worst economic crisis and the highest level of unemployment ever faced by Canada, the constitution was still seen as a priority. Frank Scott could state:

> No issue which faces the Canadian people is of greater importance than the problem of bringing the constitution up to date. Other matters loom more large upon the immediate horizon – unemployment, wheat marketing, the revival of trade must be seen to. But it is hoped that these difficulties are of a temporary nature, and in any case their solution involves us in constitutional questions which force us to examine with critical eye the present working of our governmental machinery. Even if they were solved tomorrow, however, the constitutional problem would still remain (Owram, 1986: 226).

Norman Rogers, both as a political science professor and as a minister in the King Cabinet, was also very outspoken about the need to reform the constitution and to falsify the theory, held dear in Québec particularly, according to which the Canadian constitution was a pact between provinces. For Rogers and a growing current of thought in the legal profession, the constitution was a simple law of the British Parliament instituting a new country. As a result, as W.P.M. Kennedy, a law professor at the University of Toronto, told a Parliamentary committee in 1935, there was no need whatsoever for the Canadian Parliament to consult the provinces to amend the constitution (Arès, 1967: 58). His colleague, Norman Mackenzie (1933: 247-8) had gone as far as suggesting "that the federal form of government is a clumsy device" but that the Fathers of Confederation "had achieved (...) a form of government which (...) would actually be a strong centralized government with almost unlimited power." All these arguments were brought forward in and out of a Dominion-Provincial Conference that was convened in 1935. One writer went as far as arguing "that the nation would benefit by the abolition of the provinces altogether" (Owram, 1986: 237) but provincial leaders were resisting and the Conference did not deliver any result. In such a context, one can understand the deep frustrations felt throughout the intellectual community when the judicial committee of the Privy Council in London ruled, in 1937, that most of the Bennett New Deal legislation was unconstitutional. This was enough to inflame Canadian nationalism. The Canadian Forum had an editorial entitled *Good-bye Dominion Status*: "(...) five old men in the Privy Council had threatened the meaningfulness of nationhood (...) we are nine peoples, not one" (Owram, 1986: 238).

The unbearable decision that "challenged the basic needs of modern Canadian nationalism" (Owram, 1986: 238) gave a definite urgency to a call that had been made for a serious independent commission that would bring about a complete overhaul of the BNA act. In August 1937, Prime Minister Mackenzie King appointed a Royal Commission on Dominion-Provincial Relations. The Commission was chaired by an old Liberal, Newton Rowell, who would eventually be replaced by a Québec notary,

Joseph Sirois, who was not connected to the English-speaking intellectual community that had called so vehemently for constitutional review.

As expected, the Report of the Rowell-Sirois Commission did recommend a thorough centralization of fiscal power and of the social programs. It was a great step in Canadian nation-building. Doug Owram (1986: 239) sums it up vividly as "the full-blown statement of a generation," the expression of the ideas of the best minds in English Canada. The report was released at a time when Canadian concerns were turned to other matters related to Canada's engagement in a world war. The federal government could not pay to the report the attention it deserved. Wartime necessities, however, converged with the report's recommendations. Provinces had to agree with Ottawa's taking over most of their fiscal power as centralization was in order at a time when national security was at stake. Also, one of the main proposal of the Commission, the creation of a national unemployment insurance system, was immediately implemented and the provinces were not in a position to resist a constitutional amendment transferring such responsibility to the federal government.

Was this a complete victory for the Canadian nationalists? Not quite. For in this whole process, Prime minister Mackenzie King remained, as a shrewd politician, very cautious and prudent. He somewhat resisted the centralist enthusiasm of most of his ministers and civil servants. He kept very close to Ernest Lapointe, his minister of Justice and Québec lieutenant, who constantly assured him of French-Canadian support. Lapointe would reflect another point of view on the Constitution, a message totally different from the voice of the English Canadian intellectual community. For good and deep-rooted reasons, Québec's French-speaking elites still saw Confederation as a pact and provincial autonomy as a sacred heritage to be preserved. Moreover, populist politicians, such as Ontario's Mitch Hepburn, added their voice to Duplessis's staunch resistance from Québec. King dealt very cleverly with these oppositions and he never quite reconciled himself with the idea of a strong nationalist and interventionist state. It was his successor, Louis St-Laurent, who would bring the centralist movement to its full-fledged expression in the 1950's.

VII CONCLUSION

In retrospect, the 1930's appear as the decade of a new start for Canada. The founding ideas of the modern Canadian nation-state were conceived, elaborated and expressed during these years. These ideas would come to fruition in the post-war era and Canadian nation-building would then progress constantly, except perhaps during the Diefenbaker and Pearson years. Canadian intellectual elites were not at ease with the old Conservative leader and his successor, Lester Pearson, who had to cope with the quiet revolution in Québec, showed some willingness to slow down centralization to pacify Québecers. Pierre Trudeau would revitalize Canadian nationalism and provide it with its great achievement and conclusion, the Constitution of 1982.

The great tragedy of this whole process, as stated above, was the total absence of French-speaking Québecers, at least during the seminal 1930's. This was later redressed in great part. During the post-war era, an intellectual elite that agreed with many of the tenets of modern Canadian federalism was formed in Québec. It had the disadvantage of falling behind but it brought fresh ideas and one could think, by the late 1950's, that the issue of Canadian unity would soon be settled once and for all.

Québec's quiet revolution unexpectedly dashed such hopes. Québec revitalized and modernized its autonomous posture. Not much was done, either to counter or to accommodate this trend. Especially with Trudeau in power, Canadian nationalism would go a long way to include French-speaking Canadians as individuals in the Canadian nation at large but would lamentably – albeit voluntarily – fail to meet the aspirations of Québec as a political entity. The tragedy of Canadian nationalism is that it never fully recognized that it collided with another strong nationalism in Québec. Even now, English Canada too often pretends to be speaking for all of Canada.

References

Arès, R. (1967). *Dossier sur le pacte fédératif de 1867 : la Confédération, pacte ou loi?* Montréal: Edition Bellarmin.

Brady, A. (1933). Public administration and social services. In *Canadian Problems as Seen by Twenty Outstanding Men of Canada*. Toronto: Oxford University Press.

Cassidy, H.M. (1933). An unemployment policy, some proposals. In *Canadian Problems as Seen by Twenty Outstanding Men of Canada*. Toronto: Oxford University Press.

Cook, R. (1969). *L'autonomie provinciale, les droits des minorités et la théorie du pacte, 1867-1921*, Etudes de la Commission royale d'enquête sur le bilinguisme et le biculturalisme. Ottawa: Imprimeur de la Reine.

MacKenzie, N. (1933). The federal problem and the British North America Act, *Canadian Problems as Seen by Twenty Outstanding Men of Canada*. Toronto: Oxford University Press.

Mahant, E.E. & Mount, G.S. (1989). *An Introduction to Canadian-American Relations*. Toronto: Nelson Canada (second edition).

Owram, D. (1986). *The Government Generation: Canadian Intellectuals and the State (1900-1945)*. Toronto: University of Toronto Press.

Part Two
Bilingual Canada: A Multicultural Mosaic

IDENTITY, CULTURAL PRODUCTION AND THE VITALITY OF FRANCOPHONE COMMUNITIES OUTSIDE QUÉBEC

by Raymond M. HÉBERT

Over the past thirty years, many indicators of the vitality of Canada's francophone communities outside Québec have been developed, though very few have been applied empirically.[1] The most obvious and widely used are demographic, including language transfer (or *assimilation*); the most complete recent compendium of data in this area can be found in Bernard (1990a, 1990b, 1990c). However, some authors have suggested that other factors contribute to the linguistic vitality of francophone communities: these include institutional completeness (Breton, 1964), legal and *symbolic* status (Breton, 1984), a combination of these factors (Giles, Bourhis & Taylor, 1977), socio-psychological factors (Landry, Allard & Théberge, 1991), and ideological and elite transformation (Hébert & Vaillancourt, 1971). Socio-economic status is also a factor, as can be inferred from Porter's (1965) work. We shall argue here that the quantity and quality of cultural production can also be used as an indicator of the vitality of francophone communities in Canada.

I THE DEMOGRAPHIC DECLINE OF FRANCOPHONE COMMUNITIES IN CANADA

Francophone communities virtually without exception have been in decline in both absolute and relative terms across Canada since the 1960's, under the impact of increased industrialization and urbanization in the post-war years. In recent decades, three additional factors reinforced the tendency towards assimilation of francophones to the anglophone majority: exogamy, declining fertility rates, and increased immigration.

Table 1 provides an overview of the distribution of francophones by mother tongue and language spoken at home in Canada and by province in 1991, as well as the rate of language transfer.[2] In addition to these sociological and demographic changes, francophone communities outside Québec have had to confront a more subtle yet perhaps more traumatic change since Québec's Quiet Revolution in the 1960's. Indeed, with Québec's revived and modernized nationalism (McRoberts, 1988), the destruction of the old French-Canadian identity which included francophones *from coast to coast* and the subsequent creation by many members of Québec's elites of a new myth of the inevitability of Québec's separation, many francophones outside Québec felt compelled to define a new identity for themselves. No longer members of a French-Canadian *nation* which stretched from Newfoundland to British Columbia,

---

[1] One notable exception is Wilfrid Denis's application of Breton's institutional completeness model in a recent study. See Denis (1993).

[2] Castonguay (1993) warns of pitfalls in the interpretation of Statistics Canada data in this field, due partly to changes in definitions and in the questions asked from census to census.

and cut off at least psychologically from their Québec cousins, they began to define localized, usually provincially-circumscribed, identities. Regarding the Franco-Ontarian identity, for instance, Marcel Martel (1993: 65) writes:

> Cette identité émerge partiellement en réaction à la nouvelle identité caractérisée par un rétrécissement de l'espace territorial de la nation canadienne-française – le Québec devenant le territoire du Canada français – et par une extension de ses frontières culturelles afin d'y inclure sa mosaïque culturelle.

Table 1:   *Population of French Mother Tongue and Home Language, Canada and Provinces (1991)*

	(1) Mother Tongue	(2) Home Language	(3) Difference	Rate of Language Transfer (%) (3/1)
Newfoundland	2,270	1,230	1,040	45.8
Prince Edward Island	5,590	2,935	2,655	47.5
Nova Scotia	36,630	21,585	15,045	41.1
New Brunswick	241,565	220,590	20,975	8.7
Québec	5,556,105	4,604,020	(+)47,915	(+).01
Ontario	485,395	300,085	185,310	38.2
Manitoba	49,130	23,545	25,585	52.1
Saskatchewan	20,885	6,350	14,535	69.6
Alberta	53,710	17,805	35,905	66.9
British Columbia	48,835	12,120	36,715	75.2
Canada	6,502,865	6,211,235	291,630	4.5
Canada excluding Québec	946,760	607,215	339,545	35.9

A Québec philosopher, Michel Morin (1992: 13), has taken up the same theme from the Québec perspective, pointing out the symbolic and other losses which this retrenchment has entailed for French-speaking Québecers themselves:

> En nous inventant ainsi au tournant des années 1960 une nouvelle identité, nous avons pratiqué dans notre conscience une rupture avec toute notre histoire et, partant, aussi bien avec ce qu'elle a d'humiliant que de glorieux. Pour effacer la figure du "porteur d'eau" ou du vaincu, nous avons du même coup effacé celle, pourtant dominante sous le régime français, du découvreur, de l'explorateur, qui était aussi celle du guerrier et du conquérant.

Be that as it may, this *rétrécissement* or abandonment of the whole of Canada as French Canadian territory on the part of important segments of Québec's élites and the parallel rise of the *Québécois* identity[3] limited to the territory of that province left Francophones outside Québec searching for their own. In Martel's (1993: 74) view, Québec nationalists since the 1960's "modifient radicalement la géographie de l'espace culturel canadien-français. Ils entraînent l'ensemble de la collectivité canadienne-française à se définir en valorisant la langue et l'appartenance au territoire provincial."

Still, it is an identity which francophone Québecers cannot completely eradicate from their own consciousness; as Paré (1994: 46) writes:

Canadienne-française, c'est le nom de l'autre dont on voudrait oublier le nom; c'est le jumeau trait-d'unionisé que la pensée québécoise moderne voudrait bien carrément mettre à l'écart, mais en vain.

Some authors are more scathing in their condemnation of Québec's attitude towards francophone minorities; Paré (1994: 47) for instance refers to the "rejet par le Québec de sa propre diaspora nord-américaine."[4]

---

[3] We shall avoid here attempting to define the actual content of this *Québécois* identity. Does it, for instance, include anglophones and *allophones* (persons speaking neither French nor English)? Most sovereignists today deny that the term has any specific ethnic connotation; however, an overwhelming majority of non-French Canadians in Québec reject the notion that sovereignists represent them, as even a cursory examination of provincial election results in Québec since 1976 illustrates. In the 1994 elections, almost 90% of non-French Canadians voted against the *Parti Québécois*. Mordecai Richler (1992: 77), the sovereignists' bugbear, said it all with his inimitable, scathing wit: "Jews who have been Québecers for generations understand only too well that when thousands of flagwaving nationalists march through the streets roaring *Le Québec aux Québécois!*, they do not have in mind anybody named Ginsburg. Or MacGregor, come to think of it." More recently, a member of the separatist *Bloc Québécois* in Ottawa, Philippe Paré, asked ethnic communities (other than Québécois francophones) to stay out of the referendum: "Just for once, couldn't you let the next referendum be decided by old-stock Québecers?", he asked a non-francophone ethnic representative in a public forum. Mr. Paré was reprimanded by his leader, Lucien Bouchard, for this remark; however, the incident clearly demonstrates the separatist movement's profound ambivalence on this issue. [For a report of the incident, see the Toronto *Globe and Mail*, Feb. 28, 1995: A10. In the *Globe*'s (March 1, 1995: A20) view, the incident highlights the fact that "The real reason for wanting to divide Québec from Canada (...) is to set up a new nation based on language and ethnicity – the language and ethnicity of the francophone majority."
[4] Paré (1992: 30-1) had developed this idea in an earlier work entitled *Les littératures de l'exiguïté*.

II   FRANCOPHONE IDENTITIES OUTSIDE QUÉBEC

Attempting to define francophone identities in Canada is a hazardous enterprise at best and one that must in part be speculative, given the vastness of the country and its great regional differences. In addition, there are obvious ideological differences among francophones themselves, be they Québecers or non-Québecers, regarding the *national* question: one can find many francophone Québecers who do not share the sovereignist dream[5] and who therefore may reasonably be assumed to have a different conception of their own identity, or who may perhaps still have a strong *French-Canadian* component in their identity. Inevitably, as well, the identity question in the present pre-referendum context in Canada becomes a political as well as socio-cultural issue. The 37 percent of Québecers who voted for the federal Liberal party in the 1993 federal elections surely have no doubt about their own identity as both Québecers and Canadians; though many in this group were anglophones, the majority were francophones, some of whom perhaps still consider themselves to be French-Canadians in the traditional sense of the word. As Claude Denis (1994: 48) has pointed out:

> Dans le contexte canadien actuel (...) le discours de l'identité est incapable de sérénité: c'est un discours de combat en même temps que de questionnement. On se demande, dans le cadre de conflits politiques (le débat constitutionnel par exemple) qui on est.

However fraught with these conceptual and ideological perils, we shall nevertheless attempt to define broadly the various francophone identities across Canada in light of recent scholarly research in this area. We shall then argue that the strength of these identities varies from region to region, and that this in turn leads to (or is caused by) variations in regional cultural production, which in turn increases or decreases the vitality of local francophone communities.

At the outset, it must be stated that the question of identity around the world is highly problematical in the late 20th century. In post-industrial societies, no longer is an identity given to us at birth by our ethnicity, our language, our religion, our history, our traditions: on the contrary, we are all active creators of our own identities, to a greater or lesser extent and more or less consciously. Julia Kristeva (quoted in Paratte, 1994: 227) poses this existential question and provides an answer:

---

[5] Opinion polls at the end of 1994 consistently indicated that popular support for sovereignty in Québec did not exceed 45 percent; this means (assuming that the overwhelming majority of non-francophones would vote against sovereignty) that the francophone population is split down the middle on this fundamental question. The results of the 1995 referendum confirmed this: the sovereignty option was defeated by a razor-thin margin, with over 60 percent of Québec francophones voting in favor of sovereignty.

> L'identité est-elle le résultat d'un déterminisme biologique et historique ou procède-t-elle d'un choix? Je suis de ceux qui croient que l'identité ce n'est pas l'origine: l'identité nous la choisissons. Ce n'est pas parce que je suis née en Bulgarie que je suis condamnée à choisir cette identité-là.

All francophones in Canada make a similar choice, more or less deliberately and more or less consciously, as do members of all ethnic groups in post-industrial societies. This means, then, that in such societies, there are more components to one's identity than the traditional ones listed above. It is possible to distinguish between at least two levels of identity, one global or universal, the other regional or local. At one level, we are all now, literally, *citizens of the world*. Because of the tremendous power, scope and ubiquitousness of the media, events in Croatia or Chechnya have the capacity to affect us immediately and profoundly. New and even more powerful technologies such as the Internet allow us to communicate and yes, *identify* with, people whom we have never met but who are every bit as real and significant to us, and often more so, than Grandma. For instance, recent research has documented the fact that Québec scientists publish over 95 percent of their work in English; even allowing for the fact that McGill University alone accounts for 40 percent of all scientific articles published in Québec, this figure indicates that most francophone scientists as well publish most of their articles in English. (R. Lacroix, M. Leclerc et al., and G. Paquin, quoted in Diallo, 1994: 68). Presumably these francophone scientists have found *communities* outside Québec with whom they share values that outweigh the value *language* which they otherwise priorize in their everyday lives.

This contemporary phenomenon of multiple *appartenances*, or *belongings*, has been well described by Québec sociologist Andrée Fortin (1994: 18), who posits the existence of two types of minorities, linguistic and cultural minorities on one hand, and structural or categorial minorities (groups based on common interests, sexual orientation, etc.) on the other. In this model, the traditional notion of *majority* dissolves; Fortin (1994: 19) refers to it as "l'insaisissable majorité." Of more direct relevance here is that "le rapport à autrui qu'entretiennent les minorités est éclaté dans le temps et dans l'espace." André Cloutier (1994: 34) has described the new environment in this way:

> Ce qui apparaît, ce n'est plus seulement un "lieu" harmonieux, facilement circonscriptible et capable de définir l'être de manière indubitable, mais plusieurs "lieux" plus ou moins radicalement distincts du "lieu" de la culture originelle et pouvant expliquer cette dernière.

In his analysis, Cloutier appears to argue that this situation only applies to minority francophones in Canada; we would argue that this situation is now generalized to all post-industrial societies, including Québec.[6]

---

[6] One recent tragic example of this was the deaths, mere months apart, of two Québec adolescents who imitated the suicide of Kurt Cobain, founder of the American rock group Nirvana: it seems obvious that, in their embryonic value systems, Cobain's death was of higher symbolic importance than any

Claude Denis (1994: 50) has a somewhat different perspective, which one might perhaps describe as post-modern; in his view, identity is a product of *discourse*:

> En ce qui concerne l'identité, plus rien n'est certain. Au niveau de la société, les réponses aux questions "Qui sommes-nous" et "Qui êtes-vous" ne paraissent plus évidentes. C'est alors que le discours de l'identité prend son envol. Les identités sont donc multiples, contingentes (par opposition à inhérentes à un individu ou groupe) et objets de luttes. Dans la constitution des solidarités sociales, l'identité prend ainsi le pas sur l'appartenance objective à un groupe. (...) L'identité a cette plasticité précisément parce qu'elle est un fait de discours.

If this is so, then the door is open wide to the political manipulation of identity by both nationalists and federalists in Canada, with the disturbing ethical and philosophical implications this has for a free society. A discussion of these issues is of course beyond the scope of this paper.

At another, perhaps more *primary* level, we live, eat, sleep, make love, play, and work in a highly specific context, surrounded by people Nature has given us (parents, children) and whom we have chosen (spouse, friends, coworkers). People in the first category necessarily share our ethnicity and usually our language and culture; people in the second category may or may not share these attributes. In more homogeneous societies, such as rural Québec, chances are most if not all people in both categories will share a common ethnicity, language and culture; in urban areas, in Québec and elsewhere, chances are there will be a much greater variety, especially among people in the second category. Among francophone minorities outside Québec, the situation is even more complex, since the very people Nature has given us (our parents, our children) may or may not share our language or our culture. To simplify, however, let us assume that at this *primary* level, our given or chosen identity includes one ethnicity, one language and one culture, though in reality the situation is much more complex.

Having made these distinctions, we can now attempt to describe the characteristics of the various francophone identities outside Québec. At the outset, and as a general proposition, it can be said that francophones outside Québec may or may not share the traditional view of themselves as *French-Canadians*; therefore, it is not correct to imply, as Martel and others do, that this identity is dead. The most one may say is that it has been rejected by many (but not all) francophones in Québec and by some (but probably not most) francophones outside Québec. Secondly, virtually all Canadian francophones grew up in the Catholic religion, and historically the Roman Catholic Church played a major if not dominant role in the establishment and maintenance of their communities, mainly before 1960. Most French-speaking Canadians, in Québec and elsewhere, remain at least nominally Catholic to this day. A third general

---

sovereignist dream. Indeed a sovereign Québec would be powerless, as is any contemporary State, to combat these cross-cultural influences.

statement that can be made about francophones outside Québec, with the exception of some Acadian communities in New Brunswick, is that they are much more exposed to English in their everyday lives than are most francophone communities in Québec. This means that most francophones living in all provinces except Québec are bilingual to at least some extent; most are fluently bilingual. This has led to the rise of what Roger Bernard has called a "bilingual identity" in some regions. According to Bernard (1994: 161), given the overpowering strength of English in the North American context, bilingualism affects an individual's personality at the deepest level and thus becomes the basis of one's personal identity; further:

> dans l'univers du bilinguisme, le français, langue maternelle, qui est normalement porteur de la culture française, est devenu effectivement une langue seconde et l'anglais, la langue première.

Elsewhere, Bernard (1990 (1): 113) has concluded that:

> très souvent, trop souvent, le bilinguisme, qui vient justifier et légitimer notre francité, conduit au transfert linguistique et à l'assimilation culturelle.

This theme is a recurrent one throughout Bernard's three-volume study, and it appears in other studies, mainly of Franco-Ontarians (see, for instance, Heller & Lévy, 1993). Its logical conclusion is that bilingualism, in the context in which francophone minorities find themselves in Canada, is inherently negative since it leads to the death of one's identity as a francophone. Bernard's analysis is of course simply an extension of Québec nationalists' view of the dangers which the English language represents as a *contaminant* of French culture in Québec and which found its ultimate legal expression in Bill 101 (the French language Charter) in 1977.

It also leads to outright condemnation of the policy of official bilingualism enshrined in *The Official Languages Act* adopted by the first Trudeau government in 1969 and revised by the Mulroney government in 1988, a policy which has allowed French-language communities across the country to survive and sometimes even thrive over the past thirty years. Typical is this statement by J.-L. Dion (1992: 388), a professor at the Université du Québec à Trois-Rivières:

> La stratégie fédérale élaborée par P.E. Trudeau et qui fait aujourd'hui ses ravages en douce fut de remplacer cette appartenance [to France or Québec] par une mythologie du bilinguisme *à la Canadian*.

Apart from distorting the nature of the official bilingualism policy itself, this statement ignores the fact that official bilingualism was the Trudeau government's response to the contemporary nationalist movement in Québec which insisted upon defining the new *Québécois* identity which itself excluded Francophones not residing in Québec, as we have seen above.[7] Several further comments regarding the nature of bilingualism

---

[7] It also ignores the fact that funding to francophone communities outside Québec through programs

among francophones outside Québec are in order. First, as mentioned above, virtually all francophones outside Québec are bilingual to at least some degree, and most are fluently so. Secondly, the linguistic situation varies widely from one francophone community to another across Canada (including Québec). Generally, the greater the concentration of francophones and the more the French language is used on a daily basis and in many spheres of life, the livelier and more vital the community *qua* francophone community. This is documented in an interesting study on linguistic insecurity and diglossia in New Brunswick by Boudreau & Dubois (1992: 19-20). The authors compared two regions within New Brunswick, the North-East region, where francophones (Acadians) constitute the majority, and the South-East, where they are in the minority. Respondents in the South-East:

> disent se sentir inférieurs aux autres locuteurs francophones, alors que les gens du Nord-Est disent se sentir au moins égaux aux autres locuteurs francophones en général et supérieurs aux autres locuteurs francophones de l'Acadie.

The authors (1992: 20) conclude:

> Cette enquête confirme le lien de causalité entre le degré de diglossie d'une région et le degré de l'insécurité linguistique qui naît chez les locuteurs de cette même région (...) L'insécurité linguistique peut agir sur les performances écrites et orales des locuteurs qui se sentent investis de l'intérieur par des préjugés négatifs. (...) De plus, l'insécurité linguistique pourrait jouer un rôle déterminant dans le phénomène du transfert linguistique.

This analysis points to a different path from Bernard's. Indeed, bilingualism *per se* is not the culprit here; rather it is a psychological sense of feeling inferior to the English--speaking majority and even to other francophones within the same province. The policy response, rather than limiting bilingualism by imposing limits on the language which is perceived to be a threat (the Québec nationalists' response), should, in light of the Boudreau & Dubois study, be to enrich the quality and quantity of French in the lives of those living in the regions that are disadvantaged in this area. Indeed this is by and large what the national organization (Fédération des jeunes Canadiens français, 1991, vol. IV) which commissioned the Bernard studies recommended.

Finally, bilingualism is indeed seen as a positive value by most if not all francophones living outside Québec, and for good reason: it allows them to be integrated into their environment. If this situation did not obtain, francophones would be obliged to live in virtual isolation, in a state of perpetual alienation in relation to their social, economic and political environment, a state which could not be sustained over a long period. In addition many francophones actually find pleasure in attending English-language

created under the *Official Languages Act* since 1969 has been in the order of many hundreds of millions of dollars, and that virtually all major francophone institutions outside Québec have received funding through programs created under this legislation since its inception. This has been a major factor in the survival and development of francophone communities outside Québec for the past 25 years.

cultural events, be they rock concerts or Gilbert and Sullivan operettas. It is entirely possible for a francophone in Moncton or Halifax or Winnipeg to attend a French-language play one evening and an English-language one the next; surely the result can only be the enrichment of one's personality. In this context, the challenge for minority francophone communities is to maximize the French-language cultural content in their daily lives; hence the crucial nature of cultural production in the vitality of francophone communities across Canada.

In summary, francophones outside Québec broadly share three characteristics: first, most francophones, with the exception of Acadians (whose identity antedates the French-Canadian one), still think of themselves at some level as *French Canadians*, and still include francophone Québecers within that identity. Secondly, most are still at least nominally Catholic. Finally, most if not all francophones are exposed every day to massive doses of English in the workplace, in shopping malls and in the media; as a consequence, most if not all are bilingual and most if not all see this as a positive value.

Let us now examine more specifically the regional identities of francophones outside Québec.

2.1   Francophones in the Atlantic Provinces

The great majority of francophones in New Brunswick, Nova Scotia and Prince Edward Island, and many in Newfoundland, are of Acadian stock and hold to this identity to the point where their representatives at the national association representing all francophones outside Québec fought for and obtained a change in the association's name which would recognize them explicitly.[8] Paratte (1994: 200) has defined the nature of the space and identity of Acadians in Nova Scotia in the following terms:

> Il y a donc bien un espace acadien réel, visible, audible, palpable, à commencer par un espace géographique aussi distinctif à certains égards que le bocage vendéen ou le marais poitevin: il n'est pas de région acadienne de la Nouvelle-Écosse qui ne soit avant tout rurale, et généralement proche de l'eau, rivières, baies et océan, ce qui appuie la réputation traditionnelle des Acadiens d'être des défricheurs d'eau.

Paratte's description applies generally to Acadians in all the Atlantic provinces. Indeed, when researchers at the *Université de Moncton* decided in the early 1990's to begin work on a *linguistic atlas* of Acadian dialects, they decided to focus upon maritime vocabulary of Acadian fishermen in New Brunswick, Nova Scotia and Prince Edward Island; the work will be entitled *Atlas linguistique des côtes francophones de l'Atlantique* (Babitch & Péronnet, 1992). However, Landry (1987: 258) points out that the first Acadians were mainly farmers and only became

---

[8] The association's former name was *La Fédération des Francophones hors-Québec* (FFHQ); since 1991, it is called *La Fédération des Communautés Francophones et Acadienne du Canada*.

fishermen after 1760, after the deportation, when they were forced onto land that was less suitable for agriculture. Acadians also have the longest history of any settled European group on the North American continent, a history dating back to the foundation of Port Royal in 1604. Though his analysis focuses on Nova Scotia, Paratte (1994: 199) points out that this is also a major characteristic of the Acadian identity:

> La dimension historique est fondamentale pour l'identité acadienne de cette province, où l'on parle beaucoup de projets de "village historique", de spectacles "son et lumière", de préservation de traditions: cette tendance, vraie à l'échelle de toute l'Acadie (...) est encore plus marquée dans une Acadie néo-écossaise.

There is some debate as to the geographical origins in France of the first wave of Acadian settlers in the middle of the 17th century, one common theory being that at least half of them would have come from the Poitou region, though historian P.D. Clarke (1994: 6) believes this population may have been more diverse than is commonly believed. On the other hand, Clarke (1994: 7) agrees that both the language and popular traditions imported from France were largely homogeneous:

> En Acadie (...) la linguistique et l'ethnographie tendent à soutenir l'hypothèse de l'homogénéité de l'apport linguistique et des traditions populaires. D'où la thèse d'une communauté de valeurs d'origine régionale transportée en Acadie, bref, celle de la survie de la culture rabelaisienne en terre d'Amérique.

There is general agreement as well that a certain number of French-language dialects are unique to Canada's Acadian populations. Researchers also agree that Acadian culture is based on a strong oral tradition (Paratte, 1994: 206). However, according to Clarke (1994: 36), this tradition, deeply rooted in popular culture, is rapidly disappearing, having given way to what he calls *modernism*, which necessarily involves critical analysis, historiography, and the written word, all of which has constituted an assault on this tradition, giving rise to a new culture and a new way of remembering:

> En l'espace de trois générations, la mémoire vivante en Acadie a disparu du champ d'énonciation public. (...) En effet, l'avènement de l'historiographie coïncide avec un sérieux effritement de la culture et de la mémoire populaires. (...) (L)a masse se rallia à une mémoire en accord avec la société moderne.

Despite its diminished influence in defining contemporary Acadian culture, however, the oral tradition remains a major core component of the Acadian identity. Finally, Acadians share powerful symbols that cross provincial boundaries and that reinforce their common identity as a *nation*: these include a distinctive flag, a *national* anthem, and a *national* feast day, August 15; all of these symbols date back to the late 19th century. These realities have led the Acadian sociologist Joseph Yvon Thériault (1995: 29-50) to describe the Acadian universe as being permanently divided between *l'acadianité*, the social and cultural sphere where the Acadian identity is forged, and the political sphere (*le politique*) which today is largely beyond the control of Acadians. This lack of control of *le politique* leads inevitably, in Thériault's (1995: 45) view, to the *ethnicisation* or the *folklorisation* of Acadia: "l'expulsion de l'identité hors du champ politique réduit cette dernière à l'ethnie." Thériault further distinguishes between ethnicity as a sociological *fact* and ethnicity as a *movement*, arguing that contemporary Acadia contains elements of a *movement*, "porteur d'un projet social ou politique."

Thériault's analysis thus rests on two sets of distinctions which might appear to some as spurious. First, the distinction between *le politique*, a mythical or mystical political space which would belong fully and exclusively to Acadians, and politics (*la politique*), a lower-level space where Acadians participate in elections and exercise their not inconsiderable power, particularly in New Brunswick, appears ingenuous; it certainly would be incomprehensible to the scores of Acadian politicians at all levels who currently wield real power in that province and who have scored major gains over the past thirty years in obtaining, for instance, a radically improved redistribution of state revenue in favor of the poorer Acadian regions and a virtually separate province-wide French-language school system. Secondly, Thériault's aim in distinguishing between ethnicity as a *fact* and ethnicity as a *movement* is a transparent attempt to raise Acadia to the status of a nation, despite very small numbers (a total of less than 300,000 in 1991, spread across four Canadian provinces; see table 1); this raises the issue of when an ethnic group is a *nation* and when it is not, an issue which is not resolved satisfactorily in Thériault's work. Indeed, if all ethnocultural groups, however small, are *nations*, then many of today's federations are truly *multinational*. Canada, for instance, would be home to over 100 *nations*, each of which, if one accepts Thériault's analysis, should be striving for ever-greater political autonomy. The implications for the modern state are mind-boggling.

Independently of Thérault's analysis, which is a reflection of much current thinking among Acadian intellectuals today, one can safely assert that the following elements constitute the core of the contemporary Acadian identity: a rural and maritime physical environment; a shared history and traditions dating back to the early 17th century; relatively narrow-based ethnic and linguistic origins; unique French-language dialects which remain alive to this day; a popular culture rooted largely in oral history; and distinctive *national* symbols.

2.2   Francophones in Ontario

The largest single group of people of French origin outside Québec is found in Ontario; however, this population is scattered over various regions of this huge province. Several of the large Franco-Ontarian communities are situated at or close to the Québec border; assimilation rates are lower there and it can reasonably be assumed that members of these populations share many elements of the *Québécois* identity, however defined.

Many others, on the other hand, are located in Southern and North-Western Ontario, where their existence has always been more precarious, in a social, economic and linguistic situation that has been described as being one of "marginalité absolue" (Paré, 1994: 60). Indeed, most if not all of these francophone populations have constituted a minority in the towns and villages where they live. A typical example is Sudbury, where one of the largest concentrations of Franco-Ontarians live: yet even here francophones constitute only 25 percent of a total population of about 100,000 (Paré, 1994: 48).

It emerges from Marcel Martel's (1993) attempt at defining elements of the Franco-Ontarian identity that this minority was historically closer to Québec and therefore shared many of Québec's traditional values, especially the Roman Catholic religion and an attachment to the soil heavily promoted by the Catholic clergy as an antidote to *modernism* and industrialization throughout the 19th century and the first half of the 20th. These three core values of religion, preservation of language in a hostile English environment and attachment to the soil attained almost mystical proportions, according to Martel (1993: 67):

> Le tout est empreint de mysticisme. Les Canadiens français deviennent les exécutants d'une mission providentielle: celle de conserver et de répandre un héritage catholique et français, riche en actes héroïques ponctuant le développement de ce continent. (...) Ces valeurs culturelles s'épanouissent au sein de la famille et d'un réseau institutionnel formé principalement par les paroisses, les écoles, les organismes de défense des droits des Canadiens français et la presse. Tous ont pour mission d'inculquer la fierté française, de solidifier la foi catholique et d'insuffler le goût pour la ruralité.

In the early 1960's, the rise of the Quiet Revolution in Québec and a new inward-looking nationalism there, along with the ongoing processes of secularization, industrialization, and urbanization, dealt mortal blows to all three pillars of the traditional Franco-Ontarian identity. The Franco-Ontarians' physical proximity to Québec and the family ties many of them had with Québecers meant that Franco-Ontarians, perhaps more than others, were deeply disturbed when many members of Québec's cultural and political elites abandoned the old French-Canadian dream of full duality, up to and even including the *sovereignty* of the French-Canadian nation across Canada, the mythic idea of "Canada, patrie des Canadiens français", si-de-by-side with English-speaking Canada (Martel, 1993: 68-70).

Martel (1993: 74) does not indicate what if anything has replaced the old Franco-Ontarian identity; indeed, though he believes a process of redefinition has begun, he does not indicate how far along it is or even where it might lead, though he believes a starting point is a territorial attachment to their own province and the need for a *new discourse* to justify their legal rights relative to other ethnic groups:

Au moment où les dirigeants nationalistes du Québec clarifient leur allégeance nationale au profit de l'État québécois au cours des années 1960, leur choix entraîne des répercussions dépassant les frontières québécoises. Ils modifient radicalement la géographie de l'espace culturel canadien-français. Ils entraînent l'ensemble de la collectivité canadienne-française à se définir en valorisant la langue et l'appartenance au territoire provincial. Ainsi les Francophones de l'Ontario doivent-ils inventer un nouveau discours justifiant la reconnaissance juridique de leurs droits, pour contrer l'idée qu'ils forment, après tout, un groupe ethnique comme n'importe quel autre.

This narrow conclusion, as compared to Martel's own analysis regarding "what is to be done", can be enriched somewhat if one adds to it elements of Paré's (1994) analysis, which concludes that, in the absence of a strong, unified identity, Franco-Ontarian writers and intellectuals share a particular burden in this area. We shall return to Paré's analysis below.

In summary, Franco-Ontarians, who are originally mainly emigrants from Québec, to this day share many characteristics with Québecers, including a shared language and a shared historical attachment to Roman Catholicism and to *the land*. As elsewhere, these values crumbled under the impact of urbanization, although to this day many Franco-Ontarians live in small towns and villages. The similarities in background of Franco-Ontarians to Québecers and their relative proximity to them made the rejection of the French Canadian identity by many Québecers in the 1960's more traumatic than elsewhere. However, starting in the early 1970's, attempts were made by artists, mainly in the Sudbury area, to define a new identity through their own cultural production.

2.3   Francophones in Western Canada

Most Francophones in Western Canada today can also trace their ancestry back to Québec; their forebears either immigrated directly from Québec or came to the West via the United States. However, settlement patterns and the local demographic context as it evolved through the 19th and early 20th century under the impact of massive immigration from Eastern Europe have meant that Francophones in the West today find themselves in quite different sociological circumstances from one province to another.

Two broad movements occurred in the 18th and 19th centuries which ensured that Francophones would play a major role in the colonization of the West. The first is aptly, and brilliantly, described in an essay by Nicolas van Schendel (1994) which at the same time describes the historical, Québec-rooted elements of this colonization along with its archetypal and symbolic components. Essentially, van Schendel (1994: 106) traces the beginning of this movement to the emergence of the *coureur des bois* in the 18th century, in almost dialectical opposition to the traditional figure of the *habitant*. The *coureurs des bois* were:

ces anciens Canadiens marginaux traversant, au cours du premier temps de la canadianité, les territoires autochtones à la périphérie du royaume néo-français pour y adopter la vie libre des bois et les manières de vivre pré-canadiennes. Bien entendu, cette figure se différencie de celle de l'habitant qui, à l'opposé, évoque l'image, dominante au cours de la même période, de ces anciens Canadiens enracinés, vivant sous la tutelle de leurs élites seigneuriale et cléricale et dont le "nous" minoritaire, à l'origine fortement imprégné d'amérindianité, sera par la suite maintenu à l'intérieur de frontières relativement étanches à toute influence étrangère.

The *coureurs des bois*, whose explorations were initially limited to regions contiguous to New France before the Conquest in 1760, eventually became the first *voyageurs*, whose territory literally extended to all of North America through the late 18th and early 19th centuries. The *voyageurs* were the first people of European ancestry to set foot in many regions of what is now Western Canada. Many took to spending the winter in their new *country*, taking Indian wives *à la façon du pays*[9]; this led to the emergence of a new nation, the Métis, whose rise ended tragically with the second Riel rebellion in Saskatchewan in 1885. The voyageurs disappeared in the middle of the 19th century with the end of the fur trade, leading, in van Schendel's (1994: 109) analysis, to the emergence of a new mythic figure, the *draveur*, a sort of *voyageur rapatrié*, a *voyageur* who has come home to his roots in Québec but who cannot be entirely reconciled to the idea of putting down roots and becoming a staid habitant.

The second broad movement is that of the establishment of Roman Catholic dioceses and parishes across the West throughout the 19th century. Missionaries had of course often accompanied the *voyageurs* in their travels on the Great Lakes and elsewhere in North America during the eighteenth century; however, in the early 19th century, with the emergence of the Métis nation and the growing numbers of expatriate Québecers, or *Canadiens* who decided to settle on the Prairies, the Church decided to encourage this pattern of settlement and indeed often took the lead by founding parishes in various regions of the West. Thus, after the foundation of the first archdiocese of St. Boniface in Manitoba in the early 19th century, the Church gradually headed West, setting up parishes across Saskatchewan and Alberta and subsequently new dioceses in Regina and Calgary in the early 20th century (Painchaud, 1987).

Components of the identity of Francophones in Western Canada are therefore both similar to, but markedly different from, those of Québecers. On one hand, Western Francophones almost universally have a historic attachment to the Roman Catholic faith and generally have rural roots, since the patterns of settlement encouraged by the clergy were similar to those in Ontario and Québec in the 19th century. On the other hand, the *voyageur* heritage has perhaps contributed to another trait which can more rarely be found among contemporary Québec francophones and that is, a genuine openness to other ethnic groups and cultures, a full acceptance of them regardless of

---

[9] Without an official, clerically-sanctioned marriage ceremony.

their contribution or otherwise to French language and culture.

At the outset, the *voyageurs* were initially obliged for their very survival to develop links with the Indian populations they encountered, and it can perhaps be argued that some of this openness to other languages and cultures is an element in the identity of modern-day francophones in the West. Indeed, many have carried this openness to the extreme of losing their own language and culture entirely (see table 1)! In any case this element may be found in the works of many Francophone artists and writers, from the early works of Gabrielle Roy to contemporary Manitoba poets and songwriters.[10]

West of Manitoba, the definition of francophone identity becomes more and more problematic. Though the *voyageur* history and rural pattern of settlement led by the Church is common to all Western regions, and though, of course, most Western francophones are descendants of settlers from Québec (with the exception of British Columbia), these elements do not seem to have coalesced into a firm identity which could withstand industrialization, urbanization, and immigration, with the result that francophones in Saskatchewan, Alberta and British Columbia are in the throes of attempting to define their contemporary identity beyond the traditional *French Canadian* one inherited from their ancestors. Very little documentation on this topic exists on Saskatchewan and British Columbia, which is in itself significant. However, a number of authors have commented on the francophone identity in Alberta, and their analyses converge. Dubé (1994: 87) speaks of "une communauté qui semble avoir en quelque sorte refusé une conscience d'elle-même en ne produisant que très peu de discours." Godbout (1994: 111) has a possible explanation for this lack of production:

> Il semble que la francophonie albertaine n'ait pas reçu un fondement historique et littéraire français qui soit adéquat pour maintenir sa langue et sa culture à un haut degré de vitalité.

After presenting the results of a content analysis of textbooks mainly written by Québec based Roman Catholic clerics used in the schooling of French Canadians in Alberta between 1906 and 1944, Godbout (1994: 125-6) concludes:

> L'élève franco-albertain n'avait donc pas de matériel historique et littéraire auquel il pouvait s'identifier localement, dans lequel il pouvait enraciner sa langue et sa culture chez lui. (...) [L]'absence chez les Franco-Albertains de préfiguration authentiquement française pertinente à leur milieu a mené à une configuration chez eux d'une histoire et d'une littérature ambivalentes, donc déstabilisantes, où la "fusion des horizons" linguistiques et culturels du français et de l'anglais ne se fait guère et une confusion de ces horizons en résulte.

---

[10]Regarding the many (and sympathetic) references to other ethnic groups in the work of Gabrielle Roy, see Bartosova (1994). Regarding contemporary writers, see Hébert (1994).

Whatever its causes, Roger Parent (1994: 244) acknowledges this cultural confusion, or the vacuum facing the Franco-Albertan artist, in the following terms:

> Quoi faire alors dans le cas d'une société éclatée, fragmentée où la culture est encore à dire, où l'artiste n'a pas cet écran de structures sociales sur lequel projeter l'image de son oeuvre? L'artiste doit alors créer dans un vide, ne sachant ni exactement quel est son public, ni quel est son horizon d'attentes, et parfois, ni même comment bien parler sa propre langue (...) Au théâtre, ce problème se trouve aggravé par le fait que les artistes d'origine franco-albertaine ne savent pas trop en quoi consiste leur identité.

This is broadly the context, in terms of identity, which confronts francophone artists throughout the Western provinces, especially those West of Manitoba.[11] What are the implications of this regional analysis of identity for cultural production per se? We shall argue here that there is a link between the quality and quantity of cultural production and the strength of the regional identity, however defined.

III   IDENTITY AND CULTURAL PRODUCTION

Broadly speaking, the strongest Francophone identities outside Québec, based upon the overview presented above, appear to be found in Acadia (especially in New Brunswick), Ontario and Manitoba. In all of these provinces, traditions and history were transmitted mainly orally through most of the 19th and 20th centuries; however, since the early 1970's, a strong written tradition has evolved, along with the emergence of strong role models among artists. Some of these include Antonine Maillet in New Brunswick, with her immensely popular works such as *La Sagouine* and *Pélagie-la-Charrette* (which won the prestigious "Prix Goncourt" in 1979, and thereby "consecrated" Maillet as a writer of international status); the artists' cooperative CANO[12] in North-Western Ontario, whose songs, poetry and theater virtually redefined the Franco-Ontarian identity in the 1970's; and Gabrielle Roy and Daniel Lavoie in Manitoba, whose combined work spans several decades.

Behind each of these internationally-renowned artists or groups in each of these provinces, literally dozens of others have followed. In Acadia, a history of Acadian literature was published in 1983[13] which traces the beginnings of this literature back to the 17th century. The contemporary period, however, is not documented extensively in this work, fortunately, according to Leblanc (1988: 187), since "il est impossible

---

[11] The analysis of themes, or "les thématiques," that may be found in the works of minority Francophone artists is beyond the scope of this paper. However, an essential, and ground-breaking, work on this topic is François Paré's *Théories de la fragilité* (1994).

[12] *Coopérative des artistes du Nouvel-Ontario*, a loose collective of actors, singers, musicians, poets and others. Major figures associated with this movement include André Paiement, Gaston Tremblay, Patrice Desbiens, Brigitte Haentjens, Rachel Paiement, and others. Later the group became a folk-rock group, under the direction of Marcel Aymar. See Paré (1994: 48-9).

[13] Marguerite Maillet (1983). *Histoire de la littérature acadienne: de rêve en rêve. Collection universitaire*. Moncton: Éditions d'Acadie. See Leblanc (1988).

d'être complet, et même toujours juste, parlant d'auteurs vivants." By all accounts, there are many of them, including major figures such as Herménégilde Chiasson, Claude Lebouthillier, Ronald Després, and Gérald Leblanc. Several publishing houses now exist in Acadia. Paratte (1994: 227) has counted nine in all, one of which has disappeared. The first, and largest, is *Les Éditions d'Acadie*, founded in 1972: it currently has a catalogue of close to 200 works (Bordeleau, 1992: 11). A critical anthology of Acadian literary works was published in 1979.[14] Acadia has also produced dozens of songwriters since the early 1970's, at least one of whom, Edith Butler, is internationally renowned. A recent compact disc anthology of representative works by Acadian songwriters, singers and groups contained 29 works by 21 different artists, on two discs.[15]

In Ontario, cultural production blossomed in the North-Western region starting in the early 1970's, as mentioned above. Two authors, Shannon Hengen and François Paré, recently documented this tremendous explosion of creative activity which lasted until the mid-1980's and the effects of which are still being felt today. Hengen's (1991: 60) focus is on the "Théâtre du Nouvel-Ontario"; where its development is traced from its beginnings in a church basement in the late 1960's to its "final stage, ongoing" of "having won province-wide acceptance and official approbation by the Ontario Arts Council." The troupe mounted 87 plays between 1972 and 1991, 44 of which were original creations or co-productions and many of which toured in Ontario and elsewhere. An interesting effort mentioned by Hengen was the 1990 mounting of a bilingual version of Shakespeare's Romeo and Juliet, with French translations of the Capulet family's speeches by Jean-Marc Dalpé, a popular contemporary Franco-Ontarian playwright. "With great success," according to Hengen (1991: 55):

> the British Renaissance classic renders poetically a political situation which has vexed Canadians since the British defeated the French in Montreal in 1760: the status of French language and culture in an anglophone milieu. For the young couple's determination to surmount inherited obstacles and forge a new alliance resembles efforts in contemporary Canadian culture toward a more integrally bicultural state.

We therefore apparently have here an authentic attempt at confronting the meaning of bilingualism in the Franco-Ontarian identity, bilingualism itself being, in the view of some, highly vexatious, as we have seen. Indeed, Hengen (1991: 59) quotes Arnopoulos[16] as having pointed out that "[t]he search for a new cultural identity was what the Théâtre du Nouvel-Ontario was all about." Although the "Théâtre du Nouvel-Ontario" has gone from success to success over the past 25 years, much creative activity has simultaneously been occurring in other fields in Sudbury and

---

[14] Marguerite Maillet, Gérard Leblanc & Bernard Émont (1979). *Anthologie de textes littéraires acadiens*. Moncton: Éditions d'Acadie. See Leblanc (1988).

[15] *Anthologie de musiques acadiennes* (1994). Musicor: Pointe-Claire (Québec).

[16] Sheila McLeod Arnopoulos (1982: 98). *Voices from French Ontario*. Kingston and Montreal: McGill-Queen's University Press.

surrounding area. Paré (1994: 47) echoes Arnopoulos in arguing that the North-Western Ontario movement, which he describes as "une forme (...) d'institution littéraire autonome", had as its primary objective "la formulation d'une littérature franco-ontarienne (...) spécifique et dont l'objectif ultime est la production de critères d'identité collective pour les Franco-Ontariens. Cette littérature et cette identité collective seraient essentiellement différentes de celles des Acadiens, des Franco-Manitobains et des autres peuples de la fragmentation canadienne."

Paré (1994: 49) vividly describes the breadth and scope of the movement, encompassing poets, playwrights, musicians, university professors, publishers, and even potters. However, he is more pessimistic than both Hengen and Arnopoulos in his conclusion. First, he points out that many of the main figures of the movement left Ontario for Québec in the late 1980's. Secondly, in his view the movement had within its own parameters as defined by its founders the seeds of its own disappearance: a strong emphasis on orality and spontaneity (which meant that many of the group's creations literally went up in smoke), a rejection of intellectual life in favour of a direct appeal to a less-educated public [Paré (1994: 57) points out that the group even cut itself off from the university, "l'un des plus importants agents de diffusion du littéraire dans toute société"], and an ideological (or perhaps psychological) insistence upon remaining marginal. Paré (1994: 60-1) concludes that literature cannot "transformer la souffrance accumulée de décennies de marginalisation en discours rédempteur", that "l'écriture, contrairement à ce que voulait CANO, n'engendre sans doute pas l'identité collective..."

Paré's conclusion in terms of the relationship between cultural production and identity cannot be sustained if one examines the experience of another small minority, the Franco-Manitoban one, where the artistic community has a history and ideological underpinnings since the late 1960's that are quite different from those of francophones in North-Western Ontario. First, contrary to the Sudbury region, French-speaking Manitoba did not see the rise of a *movement* of artists as such, only a gradual building up of an artistic community whose members have only loose links among themselves. Secondly, not being a *movement*, this community did not have a common ideology, nor even common origins (though most artists in Manitoba were born and raised in the province, many have come from elsewhere, mainly Québec, and have settled permanently in Manitoba). Third, from the beginning its production was written, recorded, and published, contrary to the Sudbury artists with their ideological emphasis upon orality. Finally, Franco-Manitoban artists have never disdained the university; indeed, some of their strongest support over the years has come from the local French-language university, *Collège Universitaire de Saint-Boniface* (Léveillé, 1994: 94) and, to a lesser extent, the two English-language universities in Winnipeg.

Francophone artists in Manitoba, it can persuasively be argued, have had a major role in defining and enhancing a strong Franco-Manitoban identity over the past 25 or 30 years. Building sometimes on geography (the Prairies and, to a lesser extent, the North), sometimes on history (Louis Riel, the Métis, the Voyageurs), sometimes on the bilingual reality (through the publication, for instance, of poems written in both English and French simultaneously – see Tessier, 1994), sometimes on the "openness to others" or the universality mentioned above, contemporary francophone writers, poets, playwrights and songwriters have produced hundreds of works which have both reflected and contributed to defining the Franco-Manitoban identity.[17] In terms of style, their production has ranged from the narrowly folkloric and provincial to the post-modern (Léveillé, 1994). Seen through the cultural products of its artists, the francophone identity in Manitoba appears to have the following elements (Hébert, 1994: 77):

> Affirmons d'abord, du moins à titre d'hypothèse, que la culture franco-manitobaine semble plus universaliste [que celle du Québec], en ce sens qu'on y trouve peut-être une plus grande acceptation de l'Autre. Lorsque l'artiste franco-manitobain veut déborder les cadres de sa collectivité, ce n'est pas vers le Québec qu'il se tourne mais bien vers l'univers; cela semble indiquer que le Franco-Manitobain aurait "fait sa paix" avec l'Autre, défini linguistiquement ou culturellement, et qu'il ne ressent aucun besoin particulier d'aller au Québec se réfugier chez ses cousins ou ses ancêtres. L'intégration de la langue anglaise dans la vie quotidienne, même sur le plan de l'activité créatrice, serait une autre manifestation de cette universalité.

After this brief overview of identity and cultural production in Acadia (and New Brunswick specifically) and French-speaking Ontario and Manitoba, it must be pointed out that cultural production, as one heads West and East, is much weaker both qualitatively and quantitatively. In Alberta, for instance, there are half as many francophone writers as there are in Manitoba (Parent, 1994: 241), although the size of the francophone community in that province is not much smaller than that of Manitoba, though the rate of language transfer there has been much greater (see table 1). In addition, two major works by Francophones published in recent times in Alberta were written in English,[18] an ominous sign in the sense that these authors apparently were not sufficiently confident in their writing abilities in French to publish in the language, a possibility raised by Dubé (1989: 103). This is quite a different phenomenon from that of writers in Manitoba, Ontario and elsewhere who integrate English in their work as a means of *apprivoiser* the language, taming it, making it less of a threat to the francophone identity by exorcising it in this way. In British Columbia, no significant works by francophone writers have been identified in the recent literature. In Newfoundland, francophone culture remains essentially an oral one (Thomas, 1994); this, coupled with the very small numbers of people who still speak French at home[19] has led to a situation where virtually no creative writing in French occurs in that province.

---

[17] For a broad description and analysis of this production, see Hébert (1994).

[18] Marie Moser (1987) *Counterpoint* and Jacqueline Dumas (1989) *Madeleine and the Anger.*

[19] A maximum of 3,000, according to Thomas (1994: 103); 1,250 according to the 1991 Canadian Census, see table 1.

IV   CONCLUSION

Our brief overview of the components of identity among francophone minorities across Canada and our even briefer description of cultural production in French across the country leads us to formulate the following propositions: the stronger the identity within a francophone minority, the greater the cultural production among members of that minority. In turn, perhaps, this increased cultural production leads to an even greater strengthening of that identity. Conversely, the weaker the identity to begin with, the more difficulty artists have in expressing it in their work and the fewer works they produce.

On this criterion, only three francophone communities outside Québec can be said to have a strong identity and a concomitant relatively high level of cultural production: these are the Acadian community, centered in but not limited to New Brunswick; the Franco-Ontarian community; and the Franco-Manitoban community. Based on recent literature, the French-speaking communities in Saskatchewan, Alberta and British Columbia can be said to have both weak identities and a low level of cultural production, as can the small francophone communities of Newfoundland and Prince Edward Island. On the surface, this indicator would appear to correlate broadly with other, more traditional indicators of the vitality of francophone communities outside Québec such as rates of language transfer and institutional completeness, although more research would be needed to establish a more direct and rigorous correlation among these various indicators. Our conclusion must therefore be viewed more as a working hypothesis to guide future research in this area.

One final point: it is not clear from the literature which comes first, a strong identity or a high level of cultural production. The experience of the three communities with the strongest identities differ considerably. Acadian identity survived for centuries with virtually no written cultural production; the contemporary Franco-Ontarian community's identity, at least in the North-West region, was produced virtually single-handedly by a dynamic group of artists in the 1970's and 1980's; while in Manitoba cultural production developed in an uncoordinated fashion starting in the 1960's, albeit with very strong role models such as Gabrielle Roy and Daniel Lavoie, and with a relatively strong identity related to the province's foundation by Louis Riel at the outset. Which comes first: a strong identity or copious, high-quality cultural production" Based on the experience of the various francophone communities in Canada outside Québec over the past thirty years, there appears to be no firm answer to this question; however, what is clear is that one is impossible without the other and that, without either, the future of small linguistic communities is grim.

References

Allias, M. (1989). The decline of French as a world language, *Manchester Guardian Weekly*, July 23: 15.

Association canadienne-française de l'Ontario (1991). *Un Canada à redéfinir: La francophonie ontarienne à l'heure des choix*. Vanier: Association canadienne-française de l'Ontario.

Babitch, R.M. & Péronnet, L. (1992). Atlas linguistique des côtes francophones de l'Atlantique, *Revue de l'Université de Moncton* 25 (1-2): 271-84.

Bartosova, M. (1994). Reflets du Manitoba dans l'oeuvre de Gabrielle Roy. In A. Fauchon (ed.), *La production culturelle en milieu minoritaire (Actes du treizième colloque du Centre d'études franco-canadiennes de l'Ouest)* (pp. 297-310). Saint-Boniface: Centre d'études franco-canadiennes de l'Ouest.

Bernard, R. (1990a). *Le déclin d'une culture: Recherche, analyse et bibliographie, Francophonie hors Québec 1980-1989*. Ottawa: Fédération des jeunes Canadiens français (Book I).

Bernard, R. (1990b). *Le choc des nombres: Dossier statistique sur la francophonie canadienne, 1951-1986*. Ottawa: Fédération des jeunes Canadiens français (Book II).

Bernard, R.(1990c). *Un avenir incertain: Comportements linguistiques et conscience culturelle des jeunes Canadiens français*. Ottawa: Fédération des jeunes Canadiens français (Book III).

Bernard, R. (1994). Du social à l'individuel: naissance d'une identité bilingue. In J. Létourneau (ed.), *La question identitaire au Canada francophone: récits, parcours, enjeux, hors-lieux* (pp. 155-63). Sainte-Foy: Les Presses de l'Université Laval.

Bordeleau, F. (1992). La voie régionale de l'édition, *Lettres québécoises* 65: 10-2.

Bourbeau, R. (1991). Évolution démolinguistique des francophones hors Québec, *L'Action Nationale* 81 (3): 330-42.

Boudreau, A. & Dubois, L. (1992). Insécurité linguistique et diglossie: étude comparative de deux régions de l'Acadie du Nouveau-Brunswick, *Revue de l'Université de Moncton* 25 (1-2): 3-21.

Boudreau, S. & Pelletier, P. (1993). De quelle culture êtes-vous?, *Éducation et francophonie* XXI(2): 39-47.

Breton, R. (1964). Institutional Completeness of ethnic communities and the personal relations of immigrants, *American Journal of Sociology* 70 (2): 193-205.

Breton, R. (1984). The production and allocation of symbolic resources: an analysis of the linguistic and ethnocultural fields in Canada, *Revue canadienne de sociologie et d'anthropologie/Canadian Review of Sociology and Anthropology* 21 (2): 123-44.

Cantin Merler, L. (1990). Le fait français: Pour la politisation des francophones, *Femmes d'action* 20 (1): 23-4.

Cardinal, L. (ed.) (1993). *Une langue qui pense: La recherche en milieu minoritaire francophone au Canada*. Ottawa: Presses de l'Université d'Ottawa.

Caron, G. (1990). Le fait français: Vivre hors Québec: Mode d'emploi S.V.P. ou la difficulté de s'intégrer aux communautés francophones isolées, *Femmes d'action* 20 (1): 19-20.

Castonguay, C. (1991). L'effondrement démographique des minorités francophones, *L'Action Nationale* 81 (8): 1076-9.

Castonguay, C. (1993). Mesure de l'assimilation linguistique au moyen des recensements, *Recherches sociographiques* 34 (1): 45-68.

CEFCO (1986). *Héritage et avenir des francophones de l'Ouest (Actes du cinquième colloque du Centre d'études franco-canadiennes de l'Ouest)*. Saint-Boniface: Centre d'études franco-canadiennes de l'Ouest.

CEFCO (1993). *Cahiers franco-canadiens de l'Ouest: Sociologie dans l'Ouest canadien: Théorie et pratique*. Saint-Boniface: Centre d'études franco-canadiennes de l'Ouest 5 (2).

Clarke, P.D. (1994). "Sur l'emprenier", ou récit et mémoire en Acadie. In J. Létourneau (ed.), *La question identitaire au Canada francophone: récits, parcours, enjeux, hors-lieux* (pp. 3-44). Sainte-Foy: Les Presses de l'Université Laval.

Cloutier, A. (1994). Les lieux de la minorité franco-canadienne, essai sur l'errance. In A. Fauchon (ed.), *La production culturelle en milieu minoritaire (Actes du treizième colloque du Centre d'études franco-canadiennes de l'Ouest)* (pp. 31-46). Saint-Boniface: Centre d'études franco-canadiennes de l'Ouest.

Dallaire, M.L. et Lachapelle, R. (1990). *Profils démolinguistiques des communautés minoritaires de langue officielle*. Ottawa: Direction générale de la promotion des langues officielles, Secrétariat d'État du Canada.

De Finney, J. (1998). Lecteurs acadiens d'Antonine Maillet: Réception littéraire et identité, *Revue de l'Université de Moncton* 21 (1): 25-41.

Demers, D. (1989). L'asphyxie des Franco-Ontariens, *L'Actualité* 14 (2): 63-5.

Denis, C. (1993). La complétude institutionnelle et la vitalité des communautés fransaskoises en 1992, *Cahiers franco-canadiens de l'Ouest* 5 (2): 253-84.

Denis, C. (1994). Théâtre et création nationale: l'aide étatique aux identités officielles. In A. Fauchon (ed.), *La production culturelle en milieu minoritaire (Actes du treizième colloque du Centre d'études franco-canadiennes de l'Ouest)* (pp. 47-63). Saint-Boniface: Centre d'études franco-canadiennes de l'Ouest.

Diallo, I. (1994). La recherche scientifique en milieu minoritaire: mythe et réalités. In A. Fauchon (ed.), *La production culturelle en milieu minoritaire (Actes du treizième colloque du Centre d'études franco-canadiennes de l'Ouest)*(pp. 65-74). Saint-Boniface: Centre d'études franco-canadiennes de l'Ouest.

Dion, J.-L. (1992). Les minorités françaises, sans métropole, *L'Action Nationale* 82 (3): 386-93.

Dubé, P. (1994). Je est un autre... et l'autre est moi. Essai sur l'identité franco-albertaine. In J. Létourneau (ed.), *La question identitaire au Canada francophone: récits, parcours, enjeux, hors-lieux* (pp. 79-99). Sainte-Foy: Les Presses de l'Université Laval.

Falardeau, P. (1990). Pour un espace francophone: Obsèques du réflexe minoritaire, *L'Action Nationale* 80 (10): 1451-9.

Fauchon, André (ed.) (1990). *Langue et communication (Actes du neuvième colloque du Centre d'études franco-canadiennes de l'Ouest).* Saint-Boniface: Centre d'études franco-canadiennes de l'Ouest.

Fauchon, André (ed.) (1994). *La production culturelle en milieu minoritaire (Actes du treizième colloque du Centre d'études franco-canadiennes de l'Ouest).* Saint-Boniface: Centre d'études franco-canadiennes de l'Ouest.

Fédération des jeunes Canadiens français (1991). *L'avenir devant nous: La jeunesse, le problème de l'assimilation et le développement des communautés canadiennes-françaises.* Rapport de la Commisssion nationale d'étude sur l'assimilation: Ottawa (Book IV).

Fortin, A. (1994). Territoires culturels et déterritorialisation de la culture. In A. Fauchon (ed.), *La production culturelle en milieu minoritaire (Actes du treizième colloque du Centre d'études franco-canadiennes de l'Ouest)* (pp. 7-28). Saint-Boniface: Centre d'études franco-canadiennes de l'Ouest.

Genuist, M. et al. (1986). *Héritage et avenir des francophones de l'Ouest (Actes du cinquième colloque du Centre d'études franco-canadiennes de l'Ouest).* Saint-Boniface: Centre d'études franco-canadiennes de l'Ouest.

Giles, H., Bourhis, R.Y. & Taylor, D.M. (1977). Toward a theory of language in ethnic group relations. In H. Giles (ed.), *Language, Ethnicity and Inter-group Relations* (pp. 307-48). London: Academic Press.

Godbout, L. (1994). L'enracinement historique et littéraire acquis dans le milieu scolaire et l'identité narrative? In A. Fauchon (ed.). *La production culturelle en milieu minoritaire (Actes du treizième colloque du Centre d'études franco-canadiennes de l'Ouest)* (pp. 111-31). Saint-Boniface: Centre d'études franco-canadiennes de l'Ouest.

Harvey, F. (ed.) (1992). *Médias francophones hors Québec et identité: Analyses, essais et témoignages.* Québec: Institut québécois de recherche sur la culture.

Hébert, R.-M. (1994). Essai sur l'identité franco-manitobaine. In J. Létourneau (ed.), *La question identitaire au Canada francophone: récits, parcours, enjeux, hors-lieux* (pp. 63-78). Sainte-Foy: Les Presses de l'Université Laval.

Hébert, R. & Vaillancourt, J.-G. (1971). French Canadians in Manitoba: Elites and Ideologies. In J. Elliot (ed.), *Minority Canadians* (pp. 175-90). Scarborough: Prentice-Hall (vol. 2).

Heller, M. & Lévy, L. (1993). Des femmes franco-ontariennes en situation de mariage mixte: vivre sur une frontière linguistique. In L. Cardinal (ed.), *Une langue qui pense: La recherche en milieu minoritaire francophone au Canada* (pp. 11-27). Ottawa: Presses de l'Université d'Ottawa.

Hengen, S. (1991). Théâtre du Nouvel-Ontario and francophone culture in Sudbury, Ontario, Canada, *American Review of Canadian Studies* 21 (1): 55-69.

Lafontant, J. (ed.) (1993). *L'État et les minorités.* Presses universitaires de Saint-Boniface: Les Éditions du Blé.

Lagacé, J. (1994). La francophonie au Canada: les femmes de Labrador City parlent..., *Femmes d'action* 23 (5): 38-9.

Landry, N. (1987). Les Acadiens et la pêche dans les Provinces maritimes. In R. Théberge & J. Lafontant (eds.), *Demain la francophonie en milieu minoritaire?* (pp. 257-66). Saint-Boniface: Centre de recherche du Collège universitaire de Saint-Boniface.

Landry, R., Allard, R. & Théberge, R. (1991). School and family French ambience and the bilingual development of francophone Western Canadians, *Canadian Modern Language Review/Revue canadienne des langues vivantes* 47 (5): 878-915.

Leblanc, R. (1988). Marguerite Maillet, histoire de la littérature acadienne de rêve en rêve, comptes rendus, *Revue de l'Université de Moncton* 21 (1): 182-93.

Leblanc, R. (1990). Comptes rendus: La réception des oeuvres d'Antonine Maillet, *Revue de l'Université de Moncton* 23 (1-2): 227-35.

Lemire, D. (1990). Mourir dans l'oeuf, *Femmes d'action* 20 (1): 25.

Létourneau, J. (ed.). (1994). *La question identitaire au Canada francophone: récits, parcours, enjeux, hors-lieux*. Sainte-Foy: Les Presses de l'Université Laval.

Léveillé, J.R. (1990). *Anthologie de la poésie franco-manitobaine*. Saint-Boniface: Les Éditions du Blé.

Léveillé, J.R. (1994). Le rôle du Collège Universitaire de Saint-Boniface dans la production culturelle en milieu minoritaire. In A. Fauchon (ed.), *La production culturelle en milieu minoritaire (Actes du treizième colloque du Centre d'études franco-canadiennes de l'Ouest)* (pp. 91-8). Saint-Boniface: Centre d'études franco-canadiennes de l'Ouest.

Lévy, L. (1990). Le fait français: "Sylvie, That's me": mariage mixte et transmission de la culture, *Femmes d'action* 20 (21): 21-2.

Louder R.D. & Waddell, E. (1983). *Du continent perdu à l'archipel retrouvé: Le Québec et l'Amérique française*. Québec: Les Presses de l'Université Laval.

Martel, A. (1991). *Les droits scolaires des minorités de langue officielle au Canada: De l'instruction à la gestion*. Ottawa: Commissariat aux langues officielles.

Martel, A. (1993). Compétitions idéologiques et les droits scolaires francophones en milieu minoritaire au Canada, *The Canadian Modern Language Review/La Revue canadienne des langues vivantes* 49 (4): 735-59.

Martel, M. (1993). De la certitude au doute: l'identité canadienne-française de l'Ontario de 1937 à 1967. In L. Cardinal (ed.), *Une langue qui pense: La recherche en milieu minoritaire francophone au Canada* (pp. 65-76). Ottawa: Presses de l'Université d'Ottawa.

McRoberts, K. (1988). *Québec: Social Change and Political Crisis*. Toronto: McClelland & Stewart (third edition).

Mocquais, P.-Y. (ed.) (1990). *L'Ouest canadien et l'Amérique française (Actes du huitième colloque du Centre d'études franco-canadiennes de l'Ouest)*. Saint-Boniface: Centre d'études franco-canadiennes de l'Ouest.

Morin, M. (1992). *Souveraineté de l'individu: Essai*. Montréal: Les Herbes rouges et Michel Morin.

Moulaison, G. (1988). La lecture idéologique de Pélagie-La-Charrette, *Revue de l'Université de Moncton* 21 (2): 33-5.

Painchaud, R. (1987). *Un rêve français dans le peuplement de la Prairie*. Saint-Boniface: Les Éditions des Plaines.

Paré, F. (1992). *Les littératures de l'exiguïté*. Hearst (Ontario): Les Éditions du Nordir.

Paré, F. (1994). *Théories de la fragilité*. Hearst (Ontario): Les Éditions du Nordir.

Paratte, H.-D. (1994). Écrire en Acadie de Nouvelle-Écosse: lieux littéraires et création en milieu minoritaire. In A. Fauchon (ed.), *La production culturelle en milieu minoritaire (Actes du treizième colloque du Centre d'études franco-canadiennes de l'Ouest)* (pp. 191-230). Saint-Boniface: Centre d'études franco-canadiennes de l'Ouest.

Parent, R. (1993). L'enseignement du français et la création culturelle de l'Ouest: Le point de non-retour, *Éducation et francophonie* 21 (2): 34-8.

Parent, R. (1994). Création culturelle et identité franco-albertaine. In A. Fauchon (ed.), *La production culturelle en milieu minoritaire (Actes du treizième colloque du Centre d'études franco-canadiennes de l'Ouest)* (pp. 241-54). Saint-Boniface: Centre d'études franco-canadiennes de l'Ouest.

Piché, M. (1990). Vision d'avenir: revitaliser les communautés francophones au Canada, *Femmes d'action* 20 (1): 27.

Porter, J. (1965). *The Vertical Mosaic: An Analysis of Social Class and Power in Canada*. Toronto: University of Toronto Press.

Richler, M. (1992). *Oh Canada! Oh Québec! Requiem for a Divided Country*. England: Penguin Books.

Samson, D. (1990). Affirmer notre valeur, notre identité: La notion d'identité bilingue et l'effritement d'une culture, *Femmes d'action* 20 (1): 26-7.

Schneiderman, D. (ed.) (1991). *Language and the State: The Law and Politics of Identity; Langue et état: Droit, politique et identité*. Cowansville: Les Éditions Yvon Blais Inc.

Tessier, J. (1994). De l'anglais comme élément esthétique à part entière chez trois poètes du Canada français: Charles Leblanc, Patrice Desbiens et Guy Arsenault. In A. Fauchon (ed.), *La production culturelle en milieu minoritaire (Actes du treizième colloque du Centre d'études franco-canadiennes de l'Ouest)* (pp. 255-73). Saint-Boniface: Centre d'études franco-canadiennes de l'Ouest.

Théberge, R. & Lafontant, J. (ed.) (1987). *Demain la francophonie en milieu minoritaire?* Saint-Boniface: Centre de recherche du Collège universitaire de Saint-Boniface.

Thériault, A. (1990). Les francophones hors Québec sont-ils les avant-postes du Québec?, *L'Action Nationale* 80 (2): 194-209.

Thériault, J.Y. (1995). *L'identité à l'épreuve de la modernité*. Moncton: Les Éditions d'Acadie.

Thomas, G. (1994). La production culturelle en milieu franco-terreneuvien. In A. Fauchon (ed.), *La production culturelle en milieu minoritaire (Actes du treizième colloque du Centre d'études franco-canadiennes de l'Ouest)* (pp. 99-108). Saint-Boniface: Centre d'études franco-canadiennes de l'Ouest.

Vaillancourt, J. (ed.) (1990). *Prairie Fire, a Magazine of Canadian Writing: A Special Issue on Franco-Manitoban Writing, Fiction & Poetry*. Winnipeg: Prairie Fire Press, vol. 11 (1).

Van Schendel, N. (1994). L'identité métisse ou l'histoire oubliée de la canadianité. In J. Létourneau (ed.), *La question identitaire au Canada francophone: récits, parcours, enjeux, hors-lieux* (pp. 101-21). Sainte-Foy: Les Presses de l'Université Laval.

THE BELGIAN PRESENCE IN CANADA

by Cornelius J. JAENEN

Flemings from Antwerp have been interested in the northern regions of North America since the Middle Ages when they participated in trade with the Viking colonies in Greenland and Vinland [Newfoundland]. They later became involved in the lucrative walrus hunts and the chartering and insuring of vessels bound for the Newfoundland cod fisheries in the 15th century. Cartographers associated with the University of Louvain, especially Gerard Mercator, played a key role in the transition to *modern* map-making. The maps of Gerard de Jode, Cornelius de Jode, and Abraham Ortelius were an important contribution to European knowledge of the region.

I   THE FRENCH COLONIAL PERIOD

In the period of French colonization (1604-1760) a few *Belgians* found their way to *la Nouvelle-France* and contributed to its economic and cultural development. A few Walloon Protestants from the colony on Staten Island (New York) associated with their pastor Pierre Minuit were involved with *Huguenots* in the fur and supplies trade with Québec. Among the soldiers, craftsmen and brides sent to the colony by Louis XIV's ministers there were found to be a few Walloon Calvinists and Flemish Lutherans. The craftsmen employed in Québec included master-builders, engineers, and one architect. In the 1750's a Flemish fortifications contractor along with some quarrymen, bricklayers and lime-burners were hired to strengthen the defenses of the fortress in *Louisbourg*.

The major contribution was to the nascent Catholic church in New France. Eight *Recollets* of the Franciscan order, three of whom suffered martyr's deaths, served as chaplains at military posts, as missionaries to the Amerindians, and as parish priests. Best known is Louis Hennepin of Hainaut, who accompanied the explorer Robert Cavelier de La Salle in search of the Mississippi, and who published *Ontdekking van Louisiana* (Amsterdam, 1688) and *Aenmerckelijcke historische Reijs-Beschrijvinge door verscheijde Landen veel groeter als die geheel Europa* (Utrecht, 1698), both of which went through numerous editions in several languages. Two Recollets from the Low Countries which would become Belgium (henceforth the "Belgian region") worked among the Gaspé fishing settlements and the Micmac Indians. Their early exploits were recorded by Chrestien Le Clercq, *Premier Etablissement de la Foy en Nouvelle France* (Paris, 1691).

The Jesuits were the principal missionaries to the Native peoples. Seven pioneer missionaries came from the Belgian region, among them Philip Pierson who worked among the Hurons and Sioux of the upper Great Lakes region, François de Crespeuil among the nomadic Montagnais, Jean-Baptiste Tournois among the Iroquois at Kanawaké reserve, and Pierre Potier with the Hurons of Detroit/Windsor. A final contribution in this colonial period was that of Pierre-Herman Dosquet, fourth bishop of Québec, who sought to raise the educational standards of clergy and laity and to eradicate the illicit brandy traffic.

II   BRITISH COLONIAL PERIOD

Following the cession of New France to the British Crown in 1763, few Belgians, apart from zealous missionaries, settled in British North America (1763-1867). There was some immigration to the coal mines of Nova Scotia and New Brunswick and to the towns of Québec which moved the Belgian government to open consulates in Montréal, Québec and Halifax. But many of the miners who came to Nova Scotia moved on to join compatriots in the Pennsylvania mining towns. Belgian authorities quickly became concerned about the welfare of emigrants. In 1842 conditions on board steamships leaving Belgian ports were strictly regulated and consuls were required to report regularly on the welfare of nationals working abroad. In 1856, for example, the consul in Montréal reported that factory workers were in great demand there and would find favourable working conditions, as would farmers and tradesmen throughout Québec. However, the trickle of Belgian emigration at this time was directed more to the United States, especially to Michigan, Indiana, and Wisconsin, than to the British colonies.

In 1859 the colony of the United Canadas appointed a Select Committee on Immigration which recommended that assisted passages and grants of free land offered to British nationals be extended to Belgians. In response to this new policy, a group of ninety-nine families arrived in Québec in 1862 under the direction of an independent agent named A. H. Verret. This laid the groundwork for subsequent immigration policy in the new Dominion of Canada created out of four British colonies in 1867, to which the new provinces of Manitoba, British Columbia and Prince Edward Island were soon added, as well as the extensive North-West Territories.

III   EARLY CANADIAN IMMIGRATION POLICY

The creation of the Dominion of Canada in 1867, with overlapping provincial and federal jurisdiction in the field of immigration, resulted in the provinces of Québec and Manitoba and the federal government in Ottawa seeking a share of the flow of immigrants from Antwerp to North America. Legislation was soon in place providing free land grants and homestead patents to industrious settlers in Western Canada. The first Immigration Act, 1869, created a class of *preferred countries*, including Belgium, which were regarded as *civilized* Christian constitutional monarchies resembling Great Britain, and therefore choice sources of immigrants.

Canadian authorities employed six means of attracting new settlers. Firstly, they appointed immigration officers – the first of whom was Edouard Simaeys, originally from Tielt in West Flanders – for Europe with offices in Antwerp. These immigration agents portrayed Québec and Manitoba with their Catholic majorities and bilingualism as particularly suitable places. Flemish farmers and Walloon miners and industrial workers were considered "desirable" according to the instructions issued Joseph Marmette, special immigration agent in 1883. The most successful agent was Désiré Tréau de Coeli, a trilingual Belgian from Hull, appointed permanent immigration agent in Antwerp in 1898. He gave weekly lectures, published a monthly bulletin in both French and Flemish for distribution to teachers, clergy, ticket agents, etc., and arranged for Canadian participation in the universal and local exhibitions.

The second approach was the enlistment of the railway and steamship companies through bonuses paid for every immigrant landed at a Canadian port of entry. Assisted passages were also offered on participating steamship lines such as the Allen Steamship Line, the White Star Line and the Belgian government-subsidized Red Star Line to immigrant families. The North Atlantic Trading Company, composed of European shipping agents, was organized secretly by W.T.R. Preston in London to divert immigrants destined for the United States to Canada. But there were abuses which were addressed in part on the Belgian side by the *Société de Protection des Emigrants*, organized in Antwerp in 1882, and the *Oeuvre de l'Archange Raphaël*, organized in St. André-lez-Bruges in 1888. The Oblates opened an emigration center in Antwerp under the direction of Father C. Delouche.

Thirdly, a publicity campaign was launched in the regions of Belgium most susceptible to provide the type of immigrants required. A *Commission du Travail*, established in 1886, had reported on appalling labour conditions and relations in the industrialized regions of Wallonia and had recommended emigration for the impoverished. Many Flemings were accustomed to sojourn in northern France or the industrial centers of Wallonia. Canadian efforts were directed to attracting this migrant labour force in the hope that a chain migration would ensue.

Fourthly, Canadian authorities subsidized the publication of pamphlets written by successful immigrants. This propaganda included J.V. Herreboudt's *Le Canada au point de vue de l'émigration* (1890), Gustaaf Vekeman's *Guide des émigrants au Canada* (1890), Louis Hacault's *Notes de Voyage au Canada* (1890) and Gustaaf Willems, *Les Belges au Manitoba, Lettres authentiques* (1894). Steamship companies published their own immigration literature. But all recruiting had to be carried out with circumspection because Belgium had placed severe restrictions on emigration when reports of gross misrepresentation and exploitation of emigrants came in from consular offices abroad.

A fifth approach was the official sponsorship by provincial governments of visits by articulate and successful immigrants to their villages and regions of origin to induce their countrymen to join them abroad. These *return men* enjoyed some success but they came under close scrutiny by the Ministry of Justice because their activities violated many of the protective measures the Belgian government had put in place to eradicate fraud and deception.

Finally, tours of prospective areas of settlement in Canada were arranged for Belgian officials and journalists. Louis Hacault as journalist with the *Courrier de Bruxelles* was so impressed by rural Manitoba that he settled there himself. The engineer Georges Kaiser toured western Canada with a French colonization company group in 1887 and ten years later published his observations in *Au Canada* (Bruxelles, 1897). In 1900 a group headed by Louis Barceel visited western Canada in the interests of Antwerp businessmen. The following year, the vice-consul in Ottawa, E. R. de Vos, was instructed to investigate prospects in agriculture, mining, business and investment and report back to Brussels on the accuracy of private assessments from individuals who had been given guided tours. Finally, in 1929 Louis Varlez and Lucien Brunin were commissioned to report on all centers of Belgian settlements in Canada. Their tour was at the expense of the several provincial governments and the Canadian Pacific Railway Company, all of which had an interest in promoting immigration.

IV   PERIODS OF IMMIGRATION

Emigration to Canada can be categorized as falling into four periods, coinciding with adverse conditions in Belgium and apparently favourable conditions in Canada. In the period before 1896 the majority of Belgians who came to North America arrived in New York and remained in the United States. There was some spillover into south-western Ontario from Detroit and environs. Québec made the greatest effort to attract Catholic industrial and agricultural workers and publicized opportunities for newcomers in such brochures as the abbé P. J. Verbist's *Les Belges au Canada* (1872). Appeals for experts in agriculture from the institutes at Vilvoorde and Gembloux resulted in the introduction of flax culture and the linen industry and in the commercial growing of sugar beets and sugar refining in the 1870's. The introduction of new technology and the arrival of experienced farmers enabled both Québec and Ontario to develop butter and cheese-making on a commercial scale. There were also several projects to set up bloc settlements but the only one which enjoyed a limited success was Gustaaf Vekeman's colony in the Sherbrooke area of Québec in the 1880's, where numerous Flemings took up mixed farming.

In this first period of immigration – coinciding with industrial unrest in Wallonia and population pressure in the Flemish region – Manitoba held out possibilities of building a new and more prosperous life on the 65 hectares of free land then offered as a "homestead". Few knew the difficulties of pioneering in a strange land, a rigorous climate and a challenging environment physically and socially. Soon a sizable community developed in St. Boniface and small farming hamlets like St. Alphonse, Bruxelles, and Mariapolis emerged in the southwestern part of the province. A visionary French priest, the abbé Jean Gaire, dreamed of a chain of francophone parishes stretching across western Canada and proceeded in his recruiting efforts to attract a number of Walloon settlers from the province of Luxembourg. Walloon glass workers began arriving in Ontario's nascent industry, while miners took jobs in the collieries of Nova Scotia and Vancouver Island.

The second period of immigration began in 1896 with the coming to power of the Liberals who pursued a vigorous policy of building up eastern Canadian industries and western Canadian agriculture through enhanced immigration. In 1903, direct steamship links between Belgium and Canada avoided the necessity of departing from Britain or arriving at American ports where agents tried to divert new arrivals to the American Midwest. Also, in 1906 new legislation moved away from an agricultural bias to a program to attract Belgians to mining, construction, forestry and industry. About thirteen thousand arrived during the next eight years – miners, navies, craftsmen and a wide spectrum of agriculturists including dairymen, market gardeners, fruit growers, beet and tobacco growers. In 1903 the Union Belge was organized in Montréal to coordinate the social, recreational and business activities of a growing community in Québec, and two years later the Belgian Club was organized in St. Boniface with similar objectives for the Manitoba community.

Another fourteen thousand followed in the decade after the First World War, many recruited by the railway companies, the sugar beet manufacturers, and the tobacco companies. Ontario's Belgian-born population doubled numerically in the 1920's as the Dominion Sugar Company recruited field and factory workers in the Flemish region and the growing of flue-cured tobacco caught on in the sandy soils of southwestern Ontario and attracted Belgian growers from the neighbouring United States and directly from Europe. Belgians figured prominently in market gardening and dairying in the Richelieu valley of Québec, the Red River valley in Manitoba and the Fraser valley in British Columbia.

The last and greatest period of immigration from 1945 to 1975 did not result in the emergence of new Belgian settlements as most new arrivals went either to urban centers or to settlements already established by their predecessors. Economic pressures after World War II influenced more Belgians than ever before to look abroad for a better life. The decline of the coal, iron and steel industries centered in Wallonia, as well as the loss of the Belgian Congo in the 1960's and the return of many professionals and technicians to a depressed economy, provided strong incentives for emigration. However, it is worth noting that it was the Flemish-speaking region, which was now becoming industrialized, that provided the majority of the emigrants. In Canada, immigration policy shifted in 1962 from *preferred groups* to individuals with desirable education, training and skills. Now immigrants came from the industrial, commercial and professional sectors more often than from the agricultural sector. Québec attracted about two-thirds of these immigrants, especially teachers and professors in disciplines outside traditional provincial programs, professionals, and skilled workers, particularly in the domains of biotechnology, aeronautics, and computer science.

In Canada, the Belgians constitute a small community by any measure. In 1991 only 31,475 said they were of Belgian origin with another 59,435 indicating Belgian as one of their origins. In other words, if respondents who mentioned "Belgian" as one of their multiple origins are included, the total reaches 90,910. Flemings outnumber

Walloons four to one and are found across the country, with a particularly important bloc in southwestern Ontario and in Manitoba. Walloons have gravitated to Québec and to small francophone communities across the western provinces.

This Belgian-origin population is spread unevenly across the country. In comparative terms Québec's share of Belgian-origin population declined in the 1980's, while Ontario's share increased and also benefited from inter-provincial migration. Some of these immigrants and migrants went to Ontario's tobacco belt, but the greater number went to the commercial and industrial Greater Toronto region. Elsewhere in Canada, communities followed the general trends of urbanization and occupational mobility. There is a large concentration of about 43 percent of the total in Ontario, and Québec and Manitoba each have about 17 percent of the total Belgian-origin population. This population is more rural than urban, except in Québec, where it is overwhelmingly concentrated in the Montréal region, and in British Columbia, where more than half live in urban communities. In Manitoba, one third are found in the greater Winnipeg region, while in Ontario they are concentrated in the southwestern counties – up to 1921 in Essex and Kent, but more recently also in Norfolk county and metropolitan Toronto.

V   TRADE AND INDUSTRY

In 1895 Ferdinand Van Bruyssel, a former consul general in Montréal, warned prospective immigrants that professionals should not contemplate pursuing their careers in Canada unless they had sufficient resources. The caution did not apply to industrialists and financiers. Even before there was direct steamship service between Antwerp and Canadian ports in 1903, glass products and structural iron and steel were in sufficient demand to sustain a network of Belgian importers and entrepreneurs in Canada. Gérard Macquet, for example, organized Québec's department of transport in 1887 which undertook the immediate construction of forty-eight metal bridges. The following year, under Van Bruyssel's direction, the *Comptoir Belgo-Canadien*, a conglomerate originally including fourteen major companies, was incorporated to negotiate railway construction and maintenance and public works in general. From 1902 to 1975 the Belgo-Canadian Paper Company, under the direction of Hubert Biermans, operated successfully at Shawinigan until it was absorbed into what became Consolidated Bathurst. In 1922 the Belgian Trade Syndicate had been organized in Brussels which provided information and personnel essential to such successful ventures as Alexis Nihon in ceramic, marble and granite products, the Miron holdings in cement and concrete, and the Simard family in shipbuilding. In 1932 the Liège-based Franki company began the construction of large buildings on piles from Montréal to Vancouver. A few years later, it was Louis Empain who opened what was then an unprecedented resort center, Domaine de l'Esterel, in the Laurentians north of Montréal featuring a luxury hotel, a commercial complex, a sports club, and a theater.

Activity spread to other regions. Union Minière Canada revived the northern mining community of Pickle Lake in Ontario, for example. At the turn of the century several financial organizations with interlocking directorates, backed by Antwerp banks and investment conglomerates, were incorporated to buy up large tracts of land on the western prairies and in the Okanagan valley of British Columbia, to promote Belgian settlement, and to participate in the urban booms of Winnipeg, Edmonton and Calgary.

In 1929 Leon Dupuis organized the Canadian-Belgian Chamber of Commerce in Vancouver, which played a role in western Canada similar to that played by the Comptoir Belgo-Canadien in central Canada. By using the Hudson's Bay railway route, the Dupuis enterprises had no real competitors in rails, structural steel, wire, cement and glass until the outbreak of World War II.

Belgians became active again in 1945, especially in mining and the petroleum industry. Through a number of organizational changes, including Sogémines and Solvay in mining and the metallurgical industries, Genestar emerged in 1965 as a major player. Canadian Petrofina, Canadian Hydrocarbons, Great Northern Gas Utilities are but a few of the Belgian-backed companies that contributed significantly to the economy and industrialization of a region previously limited to agriculture. By 1960 Belgium ranked just after the United States and the United Kingdom in investments in Canada.

VI   MINING

In the 1880's miners in Hainaut were actively recruited for their particular skills by the Dominion Coal Company which operated mines at the Glace Bay, Dominion, and Reserve Mines in Cape Breton. A consular report for 1896 indicates that many of these men were dissatisfied with wages and working conditions in Cape Breton and that they moved on to the smaller mining centers of the Inverness, Pictou, and Stellarton (Nova Scotia). The report goes on to say that when they had earned sufficient money to move on again, they left with their fellow workers from Italy and Slovakia for the mines of Pennsylvania. This pattern of migration continued as many left the United States to return to Canada, first to Vancouver Island, and eventually to Alberta.

Walloon miners, who had a reputation for being radical and anti-clerical, were well acquainted with their syndicalist tradition, and experienced in organizing unions and workingmen's political associations when they immigrated. In 1909 they were caught up in a bitter struggle between the Dominion Coal Company and the United Mines Workers of America, who were seeking certification. Those who favoured unionization lost their jobs and the right to company housing. The company found that replacements hired in Belgium to break the strike tended to make a common cause with their dismissed compatriots. There were many similar strikes at other Nova Scotia mines in the pre-war years. At Springhill mines, Jules Lavenne emerged as a militant leader and member of the Socialist Party of Canada.

In 1888 James Dunsmuir hired for his Vancouver Island collieries a number of Belgian miners, especially experts in explosives, who were anxious to flee the repression following bloody strikes and riots in Liège and Charleroi. Exaggerated accounts of ideal working conditions were transmitted to these miners by the Knights of Labour through Paul Watelet in Thuin who acted as their agent. Disgruntled miners soon began writing to Belgian newspapers describing the frequent work stoppages, extremely dangerous working conditions, and anti-union policy of the company. When miners joined an international union and went on strike for better wages and safer working conditions, Chinese replacement workers were brought in to break the strike. By 1912 the Belgian workers were at the forefront of the organization of the Syndicalist League of North America and when strike organizers were arrested, they organized a Miners Liberation League to work for the release of the detainees. But the intransigence of the mine owners and the provincial authorities convinced the majority of these men to move into other sectors of the wage economy.

At the turn of the century miners from Wallonia began arriving at the collieries in Alberta to work for West Canadian Collieries, founded in 1903 by a group of French and Belgian entrepreneurs, and for Canadian Coal Consolidated, a Paris-based firm. Léon Cabeaux, a well-known union leader who had organized a particularly violent strike in Hainaut in 1886, settled in Lethbridge and soon attracted disgruntled compatriots from the collieries in Pennsylvania. The miners soon became deeply involved in labour radicalism, since in Alberta the mine disasters were among the worst anywhere, and there were no provisions for the welfare of families of the miners maimed or killed on the workplace. Frank Soulet, Joseph Lothier, and Gustave Henry emerged as dedicated socialist union leaders. In the strikes and demonstrations at Drumheller in 1919 and again in 1925 a youth called Lambert Renners was shot and injured by the police. This incident went to the Supreme Court of Canada but Renners received no compensation. This embittered the Belgian miners who blamed both the Communist Party for inciting violence and the Catholic Church for supporting the "establishment."

As early as 1896, Belgians from overseas and migrants from North Dakota found employment in the lignite mines around Estevan and Bienfait in Saskatchewan where working conditions were no better than elsewhere. In 1931, in a period of rural distress when jobs were scarce, the miners went on strike for better working conditions. Police and firemen broke up a protest rally at the Estevan town hall, injuring scores of people and killing three workers. Louis Revay was among those vulnerable immigrants arrested, charged with unlawful assembly and ordered deported. Fortunately, by this time the Belgian government, had provided funds for the repatriation of such persons.

VII   AGRICULTURE

Belgian immigrants excelled in five domains of agriculture, besides the usual mixed farming: market gardening, dairying, sugar beet culture, tobacco growing, and fruit growing. In the 1870's a couple of Flemings experimented with flax growing and market gardening around St. Hyacinthe, Québec. Other farmers, who came to Québec in the late nineteenth century as part of the provincial government's effort to modernize agriculture, introduced the growing of sugar beets, hops, and chicory. The Québec government also sent delegations to visit the agricultural institutions in Gembloux and Gentbrugge, and the horticultural college in Vilvoorde, with a view to introducing intensive farming to local haphazard farming approaches. There was no end of possibilities, as Johann Beetz discovered when he introduced silver fox farming which became a very lucrative business.

In Ontario, market gardening was one of the first occupations undertaken by the newcomers to the Windsor and Lake St. Clair regions. After World War II there was renewed activity, especially around Leamington which became the canning and food processing center for Ontario. Gerhard Vanden Bussche, for example, developed overhead irrigation systems for growing tomatoes and strawberries, and developed new greenhouse watering systems at his Klondyke Gardens reclaimed from marshland.

In Manitoba, market gardening which was dominated by Belgians boomed throughout the interwar years around Winnipeg. But following the Second World War the younger and better educated moved into urban occupations. In British Columbia's Fraser valley, Belgians also took up market gardening but they never dominated the field as did their compatriots in Manitoba.

Flemish immigrants experimented successfully with growing apples, apricots, and sand cherries in the seemingly inhospitable climate of Manitoba. Retired consul Léon Dupuis on Salt Spring Island in British Columbia had a carefully tended vineyard and served his own wines decades before the Okanagan wineries came into existence. Indeed, the success of the Okanagan valley in fruit growing began in 1890 with the Okanagan Land and Development Company, in which eight Belgians held a large number of shares. Seven years later, the Belgo-Canadian Fruit Lands Company, with headquarters in Antwerp and directed locally by Raoul de Grelle and Fernand De Jardin, began its operations. In 1908 a number of its shareholders formed their own Belgian Orchard Syndicate, bought land from the parent company, planted seventeen thousand apple trees in ten-acre blocks, built their own packing-house, and by 1936 the syndicate reportedly sold annually 40,000 boxes of apples and considerable quantities of pears, peaches, plums, onions, and tomatoes. In 1909 the Belgo-Canadian Land Company invested in undeveloped lands east of Kelowna and built up productive orchards under irrigation. The following year, the Vernon Orchard Company, organized in Belgium but registered in British Columbia, developed orchards near Swan Lake. In 1912 the Land and Agricultural Company of Canada, whose head office was in Antwerp, invested money made from land sales in Saskatchewan in its subsidiary Black Mountain Water Company for the irrigation of a vast acreage of bench land. These developments aided in the recognition of the Okanagan valley as one of the prime fruit-producing areas in Canada, the growth of service centers at Kelowna, Penticton and Vernon, and directly involved immigrants and their descendants in agriculture in an area once considered semi-desert.

Dairy farming was another common Flemish occupation pursued in Canada. Flemings first became established around Montréal and Sherbrooke, were noted for their intensive production, and their important support of creameries and cheese factories. In southwestern Ontario, Flemings who first took up mixed farming soon changed over to either dairying or market gardening. In 1879 the Bossuyt brothers took up dairying in the environs of Winnipeg and St. Boniface, and soon names such as Nuyttens, Van Walleghem and Anseeuw became respected names in the Manitoba Dairy Association. The Bossuyt dairy and later the Anseeuw dairy in Fort Whyte became showplaces for foreign visitors and guests of the provincial department of agriculture. Beginning in the 1950's, urban sprawl took over much of the valuable land of these dairies which gave way to large, modern, centrally located production facilities in the urban center. Just as dairying was proving less attractive in Manitoba, Belgians took it up in the Richelieu valley south of Montréal. The prosperity of the Sabrevois area is attested to presently by the presence since 1962 of a large *Club Belgo-Canadien*.

In 1875 the Québec government began experimenting with the growing of sugar beets but it was the Ontario Agricultural College in Guelph that set up test plots and interested local businessmen in inviting entrepreneurs in Michigan, where the beet sugar industry was thriving with the help of experienced Belgian field workers, to start up a plant in Wallaceburg in 1902. In 1912 the Dominion Sugar Company began its own recruitment of seasonal workers in Flanders and by 1920 began providing subsidized fares, while the earlier group of workers provided housing for new immigrants on the small farms they had acquired. In this way Belgian communities were built up in the vicinities of Chatham, Windsor, and Sarnia. Then the depression of the 1930's affected the industry and dissatisfied workers began leaving for the more lucrative but no less arduous labour of tobacco culture. Others, especially the youth, sought employment in the developing glass, plastics, and auto accessories manufacturing.

Beet growing was introduced in Alberta in 1903 by the Knight Sugar Company that turned to Flemish migratory workers for the back-breaking work in the fields around Raymond, promising them passage money and housing. However, twenty-seven families that arrived in 1912 were bitterly disappointed because none of the promises were kept and at the outbreak of World War I the company closed down, leaving the immigrant workers stranded. In 1925 another American company opened a modern plant in Raymond and recruited workers in Flanders. The families that came were very dissatisfied with housing provisions – usually just abandoned houses or remodeled chicken coops and granaries – and the scheduling of their wages. A Beet Workers' Industrial Union was formed and it affiliated with the Farmers Unity League, organized by the Communist Party in 1930. The following year, the British Columbia Sugar Company acquired ownership of the Alberta refinery and organized a Growers Association to divide the growers and their hired workers and thus break down any common front against management. The Growers Association received the support of the Alberta government in its wage disputes with the workers on the grounds there was a Red plot to overthrow constituted authority. When the company opened a new plant in Picture Butte in 1936, it signed profit-sharing agreements with the growers to undermine workers demands for better wages and living conditions. In 1941 the growers were able to use displaced Japanese Canadians as cheap labour, so the remaining Belgians left.

In 1939 Baron Kronacher and a New York investor opened a sugar refinery in Fort Garry. Dairy farmers living near the plant, mostly Flemings, began growing sugar beets on a crop-sharing basis for the Manitoba Sugar Company. When a local Catholic priest exposed some of the evils of the system, he was quietly transferred by his bishop to a remote northern Ontario parish. By the 1950's prospective Belgian workers had good reason to heed the earlier warnings of their consular officials and emigration societies. The conditions demanded were not acceptable so recruitment of Belgian field workers came to an end.

It was primarily the cultivation of flue-cured tobacco as a commercial crop on the sandy soils around Tillsonburg and Delhi in the 1920's that drew Flemings away from market gardening and beet growing in southwestern Ontario. According to the 1921 census, 63.4 percent of the Belgians in Ontario had migrated to the tobacco belt of Kent, Essex, and Lambton counties. In the ensuing decade the tobacco buyers exploited small farmers through the system of barn-buying and the growers' plight was aggravated by the onset of the great depression and the decline in prices. Although the large, cohesive patriarchal family functioned well as a unit of production, many of the growers became hopelessly indebted.

In this crisis the Flemish growers took uncharacteristic action and became instrumental in the organization in November 1932 of the Southern Ontario Flue-Cured Tobacco Growers' Association. This group filed an unsuccessful complaint with the combines investigation office that the tobacco companies were fixing the purchase and price of the crop, so they organized their own marketing association with representatives from both growers and buyers, an arrangement which remained in effect until 1957 when it was decided to adopt the European system of selling by auction. George Demeyere emerged as the community leader charged with finding international markets for the marketing board with federal government support. The communities of Tillsonburg, Delhi, Simcoe, and Aylmer relied on tobacco wealth to build malls, massive banquet halls, modern sports complexes and to send their youth to university. Each year the tobacco harvest attracted about ten thousand transients to southwestern Ontario, creating enormous social problems. So in 1966 students were sent out from Belgium to bring in the harvest. This developed into a cultural experience as well when the students gave language lessons, staged plays and gave concerts to reawaken a sense of Flemish culture.

In the 1950's about twenty Flemish growers decided to leave Ontario to try to establish tobacco culture on the sandy soils around Joliette in Québec. Others, noting the success of their neighbours who had moved to Joliette, turned to other sandy regions in the Maritimes suitable for tobacco growing and introduced tobacco growing in Nova Scotia in 1958, in Prince Edward Island the following year, and finally in New Brunswick in 1963.

In the mid-1980's domestic tobacco consumption began to decline rapidly, therefore many Belgians in southwestern Ontario turned once again to growing vegetables and small fruits for local canneries. However, young people are more inclined to turn to the larger urban centers for employment.

VIII   URBAN ACTIVITY

While tracing urban activities, it is certain that from the beginning a number of immigrants settled in urban centers. In 1872, for example, Count Leopold d'Arschot arrived in Québec City with workers in tow to open a potato-base starch, vinegar and strong glue factory. The following year, Jules Van Nieuwenhuyze arrived with men experienced in flax growing and some weavers intent on opening an establishment in St. Hyacinthe for manufacturing linen.

Single men coming to western Canada made St. Boniface their first destination where many remained to work in the local brickyards, lumber yards, slaughter houses, meat-packing plants, and flour mills. Others moved on from St. Boniface to Belgian contacts in Deloraine and eventually Forget in Saskatchewan, where a consul was named to assist them. In Weyburn sufficient numbers found employment, especially in the brickyards, so that a section of the town became known as Belgium Town. As they moved westwards some found seasonal employment through their ethnic contacts in the factories of Chicago or Moline during the winter months. Among the more enterprising was one François Adam, an engineer with connections in high financial and political circles, who took up fur trading and successfully competed with the Hudson's Bay Company in person each year on the London market. Upon learning of the coming of the railway, he turned his ranch into the townsite for Camrose in Alberta, built twelve large business blocks and operated several businesses himself.

After World War II Belgians were caught up in the movement from rural to urban communities. This was particularly evident in the greater Winnipeg area, as insurance agencies, hardware stores, lumber yards, plumbing and building suppliers, electrical suppliers and repairers, bakeries and confectioneries bore recognizable Belgian names. The same urbanization occurred in Ontario as Belgians became car dealers, innkeepers, insurance agents, salespeople, and retailers. Some started their own businesses. One great success story began with Michael DeGroote's trucking company in Elliott Lake, which developed in time into the Laidlaw's enterprises which became the largest school bus operation and the third largest garbage disposal company in all of North America. Immigration to Québec after 1950 was directed almost entirely to the Montréal area where Belgians made their mark as teachers, college and university professors, researchers, doctors, bankers, brokers, musicians, and artists.

IX   RELIGION

In 1821 the *abbé* Charles Nerinckx recruited nine candidates at Malines for the North West missions, among them Pierre de Smet, a Jesuit from Termonde, and Auguste-Joseph Brabant, from the American College in Louvain. Father Brabant taught for a couple of years at St. Louis College in Victoria, then learned the Wakashan tongue of the Hesquiat who lived on the northern part of Vancouver Island. During his many years of labour among these people he became an authority on their history and customs. In 1899 he opened the first "industrial school" for Native children in British Columbia.

In 1846 the diocese of Vancouver Island was created and its first bishop brought out some Belgian and Dutch priests, including Charles-Jean Seghers of Ghent, who became diocesan administrator in 1871 and bishop of the diocese two years later. Seghers directed his attention to the evangelization of coastal native communities as far north as the Yukon and to laying the foundation of educational and charitable institutions for the colony. He was succeeded in Victoria by Jean-Baptiste Brondel, a native of Malines, who is remembered for having decreed that all missionary work, whether with Indians or Europeans, would be conducted in English. When Brondel was transferred to an American diocese, Seghers returned and almost immediately undertook another missionary journey to the Yukon. These bishops had laid the foundations of an enduring Catholic presence on the Pacific frontier which remained attached to the American church until 1903.

The Oblates of Mary Immaculate extended their missionary work to western Canada and the first Belgian of the order arrived at Lac La Biche in 1874. In 1883 Leonard Van Tighem began teaching the Blackfoot at a residential school south of Calgary as well as serving three pioneer communities, hearing confessions and preaching in English, French and German, and on a few occasions in Italian and Hungarian as well. He laid the foundations of the first school of agriculture in southern Alberta and through irrigation showed the ranchers how to grow quality fruits and vegetables. During the next century at least forty-six other Belgian Oblates devoted their lives to the Indian, Inuit, and isolated communities. They taught in the boarding schools they managed for native children, composed dictionaries and grammars of the various native languages, and evangelized over a vast territory.

In 1879 Belgian Redemptorists arrived at *Sainte Anne-de-Beaupré* to take over the healing center and shrine, which had been a place of pilgrimage since 1658, from their American correligionists. They soon extended their preaching missions to other ethnic communities in Western Canada in response to an invitation from Archbishop Langevin of St. Boniface. Father Guillaume Godts, who had visited parishes on the prairies that included Flemings, took charge of a parish and the monastery in Brandon and was directed to turn his attention to the Ukrainians. Father Achille Delaere arrived from Flanders to undertake this work, conscious that it was necessary to adopt the Eastern rite, with its Church Slavonic liturgical language rather than Latin, yet follow the Vatican directive to keep his vow of celibacy although Ukrainians preferred married priests. In 1901 Delaere and four companions were assigned to open a new monastery in Yorkton, adopted the Eastern rite and the Julian calendar. More Redemptorists came from Belgium as Ukrainian parishes multiplied, and a residential high school for girls and St. Joseph's College for boys were opened. Delaere began publishing in Ukrainian a modest church paper, *Holos Spasitelya* (Redeemer's Voice) in 1923. The Belgians began to retire from this pioneer work as Ukrainian Basilians arrived.

Flemish communities in southwestern Ontario benefited from the presence of the American diocese of Detroit created in 1833, where numerous Belgians lived, that had a succession of Belgian-born bishops and administrators: Rese, De Bruyn, Lefevre, Van Renterghem, all of whom paid attention to the needs of the Flemings, including those in neighbouring Ontario. The Fathers van Scheut, the popular appellation of the Immaculate Heart of Mary Mission Society, came regularly to minister, as did the Dutch Priests of the Sacred Heart in London. From 1878 to 1919, Franciscan friars at Chatham also took a special interest in parishes with a concentration of Flemings.

Then, in 1927 Capuchin monks opened a monastery in Blenheim and were given a special mission to serve Dutch and Flemish Catholics. They succeeded in bringing families back to active support of their parish and separate Catholic public schools. They extended their ministry to St. Boniface, where the Walloons worshipped with other francophones in the cathedral while Flemings were assigned a chapel where Fathers De Munter and Van den Bossche cared for them. In 1917 Canada's only Flemish ethnic parish – Sacred Heart – was created in the Belgium Town section of St. Boniface, and ten years later it was assigned to the Capuchins from Ontario. Full services – catechism, confessions, sermons, retreats, etc. – were offered in Flemish until 1935 when catechism was taught in English only and 1955 when all sermons were given in English. This erosion of the use of Flemish followed naturally on generational assimilation and the lack of sustained immigration. From 1931 to 1972 the Capuchins, with reinforcements from Belgium from time to time, maintained a small monastery at Toutes Aides, a remote community three hundred kilometers northwest of Winnipeg, from which they would serve not only Belgians but many ethnic groups and native peoples in at least five mission stations.

Among the other religious communities are: the Trappist monks who in 1862 founded a monastery at Oka, famous for its cheese; the Benedictines of Saint-Wandrille led by Dom Joseph Pothier, internationally known for his achievement in restoring Gregorian chant into contemporary worship, who in 1912 founded the monastery and retreat center of St. Benoit-du-Lac; the Premonstratensians from Tongerloo, who built an imposing monastery at Lacolle, south of Montréal; and the Brothers of Our Lady of Lourdes from Oostakker, who opened the Dom Bosco Home in Calgary for emotionally disturbed teenagers in 1959.

X   EDUCATION

Very soon after Confederation in 1867, the Department of Public Instruction in Québec City placed orders in Belgium for textbooks, teacher's guides and manuals on pedagogy. Laval University relied heavily on Louvain University as a model for its organization. In 1908 Auguste-Joseph de Bray of Louvain University organized the *Ecole des Hautes Etudes Commerciales* in Montréal, supervised its construction and hired its staff. It went on to enjoy great success under the direction of Henry Laureys, an economic geographer, who added a simulated trading establishment and a museum of commerce and industry to the institution. Alfred Fyen, a former officer in the Belgian army, founded a series of trade schools: in 1907 a school for training surveyors in Québec City; in 1908 the reorganization of the Ecole Polytechnique in Montréal; in 1912 the *Ecole des Arts Décoratifs et Industriels* and then the *Ecole d'Architecture*. To each institution he brought a sense of organization and discipline important to establishing high standards in new educational domains. Charles De Koninck played an important role in university affairs in his capacity of professor and dean of the faculty of philosophy at Laval from 1934 to 1965. He surprised many by advocating a non-confessional school system to replace the traditional Québec dual confessional system.

As school enrollment mushroomed, partly owing to the 1950's baby boom, Belgium became a source of teachers from kindergarten level through to university graduate schools. There is little doubt that their liberal ideas contributed not only to the Quiet Revolution in the province but also to the student movement in the universities and junior colleges (CEGEPs).

In the rest of Canada, Flemings generally supported Catholic public schools where such existed, while Walloons joined French Canadians in demanding instruction in French as well. Maurice Baudoux of La Louvière, for example, as a parish priest in Saskatchewan, became a staunch supporter of French rights and campaigned successfully for French radio broadcasting in western Canada, before becoming Archbishop of St. Boniface. Only two communities of religious women were active in Canada, the Sisters of Notre-Dame-de-Namur in Ontario and the Ursuline Sisters from Tildonk, Manitoba.

Belgians created only one educational institution serving solely their ethnic community – Scheppers College in Swan Lake, in rural Manitoba, operated by the Brothers of Our Lady of Mercy from Malines, as a boys' boarding school and agricultural college offering basic agricultural and manual training, along with academic subjects and religious instruction in Dutch. Twelve brothers came from Belgium and classes began in an imposing brick structure in the autumn of 1920. Each year there were between sixty and seventy-five boys in boarding, in addition to local day scholars. The great depression played havoc with their project and by 1932 the bold ethnic experiment had come to an end.

The work of Gustave Francq in labour relations in Québec can justly be regarded as educational. At the turn of the century he became active in labour politics, as a union executive for seventeen years, as a militant member of the Labour Party fighting for the eight-hour day and universal suffrage, as an organizer of working class clubs in Montréal, as owner and editor of the bilingual *Le Monde ouvrier/The Labour World*, a newspaper which appeared in 1916 with a mission to educate the public on labour, class, and gender issues. In addition to being president of the provincial Minimum Wage Commission, Francq was also active in organizing sports facilities, food co-operatives, lobbying for minimum wage legislation and women's rights until his death in 1952.

XI   CULTURAL LIFE & ASSOCIATIONS

In addition to holding important positions in colleges, universities, academies, learned societies, libraries, archives and museums, Belgians have made significant contributions in music, theater, and the fine arts. Behind the founding of the *Académie des Beaux-Arts* in Montréal in 1873 was none other than the colonizing priest P. J. Verbist. Guillaume Mechtler, apparently the first Canadian to have been paid for his compositions, was organist of Notre-Dame Church in Montréal from 1789 to 1832. Other famous organists followed in the early twentieth century – Benoît Verdickt at Lachine, Auguste Leyssens at Sorel, Joseph Vermandere at St. Joseph's Oratory in Montréal from 1919 to 1937. In 1865 the renowned violists Jules Hone and Frantz Jehin-Prume settled in Montréal. Jehin-Prume founded the *Association Artistique*, Québec's first professional chamber music company, among whose members were gifted compatriots Erasme Jehin-Prume and Jean-Baptiste Dubois. The latter gave courses for the general public that were paid for by the provincial government. Sohmer Park, inaugurated in 1889, featured Belgian musicians in its concerts and many of them remained in Québec to teach music. Joseph-Jean Goulet, for example, played an important role in the founding of the Montréal Symphony Orchestra, which began with a core of Belgian musicians in 1894. His brother, Jean Goulet, conducted the majority of choral productions in Montréal up to 1955 for the *Société Canadienne d'Opérettes* and the *Variétés Lyriques*, founded by another brother – Charles. In 1933, Henri Vermandere founded and directed for many years the choir school called *Chanteurs à la Croix de Bois*. At about the same time, pianist Severin Moisse and violinist Maurice Onderet took up their distinguished careers as soloists and teachers in Montréal.

The paintings of Henri-Leopold Masson, a native of Namur, which reflect his love of the Gatineau region near Ottawa, are known internationally and hang in galleries across Canada. Among the artists who have attained regional fame are Francis Coutellier, Guy Gosselin, Michel Meerts, Jan Mirck, Claire Miron, Raymonde and Léon Plonteux. In the field of sculpturing, Marcel Braitstein, Josef Drenters, Auguste Hammerechts and Pierre Hayvaert have been outstanding. Hayvaert is remembered especially for his work for the Québec pavilion at Expo 67.

In 1903 Alphonse Ghyssens, with the support of the Count de Bellefroid and Baron Kerwyn de Lettenhoven, organized the *Union Belge* in Montréal (reorganized in 1939 as the *Union Nationale Belge*) to bring together Walloons and Flemings. However, in 1964 the two linguistic groups each founded their own social association: the *Vlaamse Kring van Montreal* and the *Association Belge de Langue Française de Montréal*.

In Manitoba the Belgians organized few associations to preserve their language and cultural heritage. From the turn of the century the Walloons in St. Boniface participated in both the *Cercle Molière*, a nationally reputed drama group, and the *Société Lyrique de Gounod* while the Flemish community organized the La Vérendrye band the *Onder Ons* dramatic club. Both groups joined in 1905 in supporting Louis de Nobele in the organization of the *Club Belge* in St. Boniface. It began as a social and cultural association with a special mission to assist newcomers in making contacts, finding jobs and farmsteads. Although it was strictly non-partisan, it was here that people came to discuss political and social issues, community concerns and business affairs. Its benevolent and charitable activities were carried out through a Ladies Auxiliary, a Belgian Mutual Benefit Society, and a Belgian Credit Union Society in co-operation with the Flemish Sacred Heart parish. It also became the umbrella organization for the various sports and recreational activities associated with all the Belgians on the prairies. To this end it had a branch in Ste. Rose-du-Lac for twenty years. The club sponsored and publicized the activities of scores of archery clubs, Belgian bowling tournaments, bicycle racing, and pigeon racing. Provincial semi-finalists still go on to compete at the *national finals* in Detroit or some southwestern Ontario location. At its inception the club operated in both French and Flemish, but now official minutes and correspondence are in English.

In 1962 a unique association, *Vlamingen in de Wereld*, made its appearance in Ontario when Dr. Arthur Verthé and Marcel Vertommen came to the Belgian Club in Delhi to arrange for exchanges with the mother country. In 1965 a world congress of Flemish representatives from all over the globe was organized in Brussels. Canadian Flemings were represented by delegates from the Belgian Club in St. Boniface, the Belgian Club in Delhi, and a delegate from Tillsonburg. In one of the first exchanges university students from Flanders worked during the day harvesting tobacco and spent the evenings teaching Flemish language and literature, or putting on plays and concerts. This combination of field workers and cultural agents continued until the mid-1980's. Since then smaller groups of both Walloon and Flemish students have continued to come.

XII   BELGIAN AMERICAN INFLUENCES

The influence of Belgian communities in the United States on activities in Canada has already been mentioned. Detroit became in several ways the cultural center for North American Flemish communities. In 1911, for example, the *Nationaal Toneelverbond* began furnishing dramas and theatrical expertise to Flemish groups in both the United States and Canada. By 1922 there were at least four Flemish theatrical companies in

Detroit, of which *Kunst en Vermaak* made regular visits to southwestern Ontario. Three years later, a club known as *Den Vriendenkring* was launched to extend ethnic activities into the educational field. A small school was opened in Leamington to teach Flemish and a Dutch-language library was organized. In 1927 the Windsor Dramatic Society began to stage dramas for the Flemish tradesmen, auto workers and business people, the *Vlaanderen's Kerels* undertook to provide both entertainment and language instruction at Chatham, and *De Jonge Jeugd* promoted cultural activities in Wallaceburg. With some assistance from the Belgians in Detroit, a Flemish choir was organized in Windsor to complement the efforts of the drama society. Most of these groups fell victim to the depression in the 1930's, but the parishes attempted to continue some of the social and cultural activities.

The Flemish nationalist movement also entered Canada from the United States. In 1919 an organization called *Flandria-America* was organized in Michigan by war veterans to support the Flemish nationalist struggle in Belgium. From Michigan its activities soon spread into Ontario. Adolf Spillemaeckers often visited the communities of Wallaceburg, Leamington, Blenheim, and Delhi until 1925, when he was deported to Belgium by American immigration authorities. It was not long before he was back, this time legally, and from his base of operations in Detroit he spent many weekends in Ontario promoting Flemish drama, music, literature, and language study for *Flandria-America*.

In 1962 the work of all these early associations was taken over by *België in de Wereld*, an umbrella organization launched at Detroit by Rev. Arthur Verthé and Marcel Vertommen. It had the support of the Belgian embassy in Ottawa for its activities in Canada. Very soon it changed its name to *Vlamingen in de Wereld* to more accurately reflect its ethnic character and mission.

The Catholic Church in the United States also played an important role in Belgian communities in Canada. St. Anne's parish in Detroit was the spiritual home of many Flemings in Windsor, and as this parish grew it assumed an important role in the cultural and recreational field. The diocese of Detroit had been canonically constituted in 1883 and had a succession of Belgian-origin bishops; Rese, De Bruyn, Lefevre, Van Rentergem. It received many Redemptorist, Oratorian, and secular priests from Belgium, also two women's orders, the Sisters of Notre-Dame de Namur and the Sisters Servants of the Immaculate Heart of Mary. When Belgian Capuchins arrived in Blenheim in 1927, they took charge of most of the Flemish work in southwestern Ontario, with the exception of Windsor which continued to look to Detroit for its clergy.

In 1821, the abbé Charles Nerinckx, a native of Brabant and missionary in the United States, began to recruit clergy in Malines. It was there that he persuaded Pierre de Smet and eight other seminarians to join him. De Smet completed his priestly studies with the Jesuits in St. Louis and went west to Idaho and Montana, eventually extending his missionary activities into British Columbia and Washington. The

American College at the University of Louvain, founded in 1856 through the efforts of Bishop Peter Paul Lefevre of Detroit, became an important source of missionary clergy for both the United States and Canada. Father Auguste-Joseph Brabant, for example, was recruited there, served for several years as assistant pastor in Victoria, then opened a mission among the Hesquiat on the northern part of Vancouver Island, where he spent the next 33 years of his ministry. Prominent among the later recruits were Bishop Jean-Baptiste Brondel and Bishop Charles-Jean Seghers, whose diocese extended at one time from Oregon to the Alaskan border.

XIII SOCIAL RELATIONS

Both Flemish and Walloon immigrants brought with them strong traditions of the patriarchal family functioning as an economic unit. The role of the women was particularly crucial in the mining and agricultural contexts. In addition to their domestic chores, miners' wives often ran boarding houses for single men, offering such services as laundry and mending. The patriarchal family and the practice of pooled family resources were an asset in pioneering days in the prairie West. The same practice was current in southwestern Ontario, where tobacco farmers survived the depression years in good measure because of pooled family labour and pooled family financial resources.

During the first decade of immigration Walloons showed a greater tendency to come as family units, but the Flemings from the agricultural regions of the homeland tended to send one or two young men, occasionally the head of a family, to scout out the country, to earn some capital, and so pave the way for relatives, and eventually neighbours, to follow in the familiar pattern of chain migration. In this way, the community of Manor in Saskatchewan, for example, drew almost exclusively upon the Lommel area of Limburg province, which was an unusual region for emigration to Canada. For a brief period Manor was the seat of a Belgian consulate.

It is not surprising that Belgians have experienced relatively rapid integration into mainstream society. Outside Québec the Flemings have integrated into the dominant anglophone host society. Walloons in Western Canada often adopted French Canadian nationalist views regarding language rights and separate schools, but have generally supported the official national policies of bilingualism and multiculturalism. In Québec, the experience seems to have been different again, as both Flemings and Walloons became integrated into the now dominant francophone community.

In all regions this integration proceeded more on an individual basis rather than as a group experience. Belgian immigrants did not create their own ethnic sub-system, either on a regional or national scale. Roman Catholicism is one of the major distinguishing characteristics of the group, yet there is only one Flemish ethnic parish – Sacred Heart in St. Boniface – and no Walloon parish in all of Canada. This may be explained by the fact that unlike a number of other ethnic groups, Belgians never settled in ethnic blocs or reserves, although there was a concentration of settlements in southwestern Ontario and southern Manitoba. So-called "Belgian Towns" in St. Boniface, Glace Bay, or Estevan were not ghettos or self-sufficient ethnic enclaves but residential concentrations. The Belgian clubs in Montréal, St. Boniface, Delhi, and Sabrevois have increasingly served a heterogeneous community. Belgians, therefore, were never an isolated or segregated group in Canada.

This association with other ethnic communities may explain the departure from endogamy which characterized the first generation of immigrants. Local histories and church registers indicate that in the second generation marriages extended beyond ethnic boundaries into the wider Catholic community. In subsequent generations even the religious boundary is crossed as young people increasingly choose their mates from associates at school, the workplace, and recreational activities. The community's concentric worlds appear to expand with each succeeding generation.

This openness to other ethno-cultural groups has had other consequences. Flemings, as might be expected, have had a very low language retention rate. Outside of Québec they quickly adopted English because of its implications for economic advancement and social acceptance, just as in Québec in recent decades they have readily integrated into the francophone majority. The first generation of immigrants maintained active drama clubs, literary societies and social gatherings, but these soon gave way to mainstream cultural and social activities. A survey in Ontario's tobacco belt in the 1970's indicated that while children seldom spoke Flemish with their parents, and almost never with their peers, they retained a sufficient amount to communicate with their grand-parents.

There is no indication that Flemings and Walloons perpetuated their linguistic and ethnic battles in Canada. In the early years of settlement, Flemings in Ontario and Manitoba, like other ethnic minorities, asked for the services of priests speaking their tongue but the hierarchy was only infrequently able to meet their requests. Walloons were more fortunate as many of the Canadian clergy spoke French. In the 1920's, the Walloons shared with other francophones in western Canada and Ontario the abuse and verbal attacks of anti-French and anti-Catholic organizations such as the Ku Klux Klan, the Orange lodges and the reactionary wing of the Conservative party.

Politically, both Flemings and Walloons have consistently supported the same political party – either the Conservatives or the Liberals and rarely a third party – and have supported each other's candidate in municipal, provincial and federal elections.

The first generation of Walloon immigrants were more literate than their Flemish counterparts and as francophones they subscribed either to newspapers from Belgium or to French Canadian publications. The Flemings had their own North American newspapers coming out of the United States: the *Gazette van Moline*, which was published from 1907 to 1940, at which time it was incorporated into the *Gazette van Detroit* which continues to the present day.

Belgians have enjoyed a positive image in mainstream Canadian society inasmuch as they are seen as having upheld the work ethic, community values, and loyalty to the Crown. In numerous communities they reinforced Catholic values and traditions. They are one of the few immigrant groups who have actively promoted the development of francophone institutions in Canada, and one of the few immigrant groups to have actively participated in missionary work among other ethnic groups and the Native peoples. Belgian miners, dairymen, market gardeners, tobacco growers, and grain growers joined non-ethnic associations. Traditional recreational activities such as pole archery, pigeon racing, bicycle racing, and Belgian bowling were never restricted to their own community. Belgian investments in the nascent industries of this country greatly stimulated development and created jobs. In mining they actively supported unionization and the labour movement in general. In agriculture they have been pioneers in dairying, beet growing, tobacco culture, and market gardening. Everywhere they have made an important contribution to intellectual life, education, religion, arts and letters. This is especially true in Québec where university research, biotechnology, aeronautics, and computer science are domains in which their role has been most significant.

The acceptance of Belgians by both francophone and anglophone mainstream communities in Canada derives from their initial perception as *preferred immigrants*, their heroic image as valiant resistors of foreign invasion and occupation in 1914-18 and again in 1940-45, their rapid integration into the dominant society, their success generally as settlers, and their outstanding contributions in fields ranging from music and pedagogy to agriculture and engineering.

References

Asselin, J.P. (1981). *Les Rédemptoristes au Canada*. Montréal: Éditions Bellarmin.

Baudoux, M. (1953). Radio-Ouest Français, *Vie française*, VII: 435-41.

Beetz, H. & Beetz, J. (1977). *Johann Beetz*. Montréal: Éditions Leméac.

Brandt, Y. (1977). *Hutelet Heritage, 1688-1972*. Swan Lake.

Buitenhuis, P. (1987). *The Great War of Words*. Vancouver: University of British Columbia Press.

De Kegel, D. (1981). *Sport en etniciteit: volkssportenonderzoek bij de Vlaamse emigranten in Noord-Amerika*. Louvain: Catholic University of Louvain (unpublished MD thesis).

Demyttenaere, J. (1960). Scheme for young Belgian agriculturalists in Canada, *Migration News* 9 (3): 22-3.

Destrée, R. (1976). Louis Empain et l'industrie, *Art, vie, esprit* 41-2: 13-6.

Dewitte, P. (1981). Edouard Simaeys, een pennelikker uit Wakken, *De Roede van Tielt*, 12: 3-104.

Durieux, M. (1986). *Un héros malgré lui*. Saint-Boniface: Editions des Plaines.

Everaert, J. (1980). L'émigration en masse, *La Belgique. Sociétés et cultures depuis 150 ans*. Brussels (unpublished).

Gaire, J. (1898). *Dix années de missions au grand Nord-Ouest canadien*. Lille: Dom Bosco.

Gheur, B. (1985). *Retour à Calgary*. Paris.

Giscard, G. (1982). *On the Canadian Prairie*. Regina: Canadian Plains Research Center.

Greening, W. (1959). The Belgian role in Canadian economic development, *The Canadian Banker* 66 (2): 121-6.

Griffin, J. (1932). *The Contribution of the Belgians to the Catholic Church in America*. Washington: Catholic University of America.

Hacault, L. (1892). *Les colonies belges et françaises du Manitoba. Notes de voyage au Canada en 1890*. Brussels: Alfred Vromant.

Hennepin, L. (1688). *Ontdekking van Louisiana*. Amsterdam: Jan ten Hoorn.

Hennepin, L. (1698). *Aenmerckelijcke historische Reijs-Beschrijvinge door verscheijde Landen veel groeter als die geheel Europa*. Utrecht: Anthony Schouten.

Herreboudt, J. (1890). *Le Canada au point de vue de l'émigration*. Bruges.

Huot, C. (1974). Musiciens belges au Québec, *Cahiers canadiens de musique* 4: 69-71.

Jaenen, C. (1991). *The Belgians in Canada*. Ottawa. Canadian Historical Association, 20.

Jehin-Prume, F. (1889). *Une vie d'artiste*. Montréal (unpublished).

Journée, M. (1981). *De lokroep van een nieuwe frontier. Belgische emigratie in Canada, 1880-1940*. Louvain: Catholic University of Louvain (unpublished MD thesis).

Kaiser, G. (1897). *Au Canada*. Brussels: A. Lesigne.

Kurgan, G. (ed.) (1988). *La question sociale en Belgique et au Canada*. Brussels: Université libre de Bruxelles.

Kurgan, G. & Laureyssens, J. (1986). *Un siècle d'investissements belges au Canada*. Brussels: Editions de l'Université libre de Bruxelles.

Kurgan, G. & Spelkens, E. (1976). *Two Studies on Emigration through Antwerp to the New World*. Brussels: Center for American Studies.

Leau, L. (1912). *L'aisance qui vient. Vie du colon dans la prairie canadienne*. Paris: Bloud.

Le Clercq, C. (1691). *Premier établissement de la foy en Nouvelle France*. Paris: Amable Auroy.

Lemont, A. (1914). *La mission belge au Canada*. Montréal: Chambre de commerce du district de Montréal.

Lillard, C. (1977). *Mission to Nootka, 1874-1900*. Sidney: Gray's Publishing.

Magée, J. (1987). *The Belgians in Ontario: A History*. Toronto: Dundurn Press.

Motut, R. & Legros, M. (1980). *Ordinary Heroes*. Edmonton: University of Alberta Press.

Painchaud, R. (1987). *Un rêve français dans le peuplement de la prairie*. Saint-Boniface: Editions des Plaines.

Puissant, J. (1973). Quelques témoignages sur l'émigration hennuyère, 1884-1889, *Académie royale des sciences d'Outre-Mer. Bulletin des séances* 3: 443-63.

Rottiers, R. (1977). *Soixante-cinq années de luttes*. Regina: Association culturelle franco-canadienne de la Saskatchewan.

Stengers, J. (1978). *Emigration et immigration en Belgique au XIXe et au XXe siècles*. Brussels.

Stols, E. (1980). L'émigration des cerveaux, *La Belgique. Sociétés et cultures depuis 150 ans*. Brussels.

Trépanier, P. (1977). La colonie franco-belge de Namur, 1871-1881, *Asticou* 18: 14-32.

Van Bruyssel, F. (1934). *Jean Vadeboncoeur et Anne-Marie Lafrance, Canadiens-français*. Paris: Editions de la vie mondiale.

Van Der Heyden, J. (1920). *Life and Letters of Father Brabant, a Flemish Missionary Hero*. Louvain: J. Wouters-Ickx.

Vekeman, G. (1882). *Canada: het groote Noord-Westen*. Ottawa: Ministry of Agriculture.

Vekeman, G. (1883). *Lettres d'un émigrant, ou voyage au Canada. Suivi d'un appendice sur le Manitoba*. Brussels: Loge.

Vekeman-Masson, J. (1981). *La grosse île*. Québec: Editions la liberté.

Verbist, P. (1872). *Les Belges au Canada*. Turnhout: Etablissement Antoine Van Genechten.

Vermeirre, A. (1983). Un aspect de l'émigration au début du XXe siècle au Québec: H. Biermans, *Canadian Journal of Netherlandic Studies* IV: 14-9.

Vermeirre, A. (1987). *Les cinquante années de l'existence de l'Association Belgique-Canada*. Montréal.

Verthé, A. (1972). *Vlaanderen in de wereld*. Brussels: D.A.P. Reinaert.

Willems, G. (1894). *Les Belges au Manitoba. Lettres authentiques*. Ottawa (unpublished).

Wilson, K. & Wyndels, J. (1976). *The Belgians in Manitoba*. Winnipeg. Peguis Publishers.

THE DUTCH IN CANADA

by Herman GANZEVOORT

I   INTRODUCTION

Although Dutch immigrants have been settling in North America since the beginning of the 17th century, their presence in Canada in any significant numbers is largely a 20th century phenomenon. While Dutch commercial settlement by the Dutch West Indies Company had begun in the Hudson River valley as early as 1613, the people of the New Netherlands had few contacts with the French settlements developing to the north at the same time. The rather benign conquest of the New Netherlands by the British in 1664 permitted the Dutch to retain their religious and cultural identity well into the 18th century. As a result, the fall of New France to the British in 1763 did little to encourage Dutch Americans to pull up their comfortable roots and move to Britain's newest colony. However, during and after the American Revolution some Dutch American Loyalists did seek political asylum in the British North American colonies with the majority settling on the western frontier of Quebec. They were followed in the 1790's by other Dutch Americans seeking cheap farm land as the eastern American states reached their agricultural limits.

After 1815 American and European interest focused almost exclusively on the western frontier of the United States. Deteriorating economic conditions and religious conflict encouraged emigration from the Netherlands by the mid-1850's and brought about primary agricultural settlement in western Michigan, Wisconsin and Iowa. In the following decades Dutch settlements spread across the whole northern tier of the mid and western states. These settlements exerted a strong attraction on Dutch farmers and offered a relatively easy integration into American society. They attracted not only farmers but shopkeepers, skilled craftsmen, clerks and even professionals. The immigrants found a cultural and religious milieu that resembled that of small town Holland. Social displacement, language difficulties and loneliness, so much the common experience of most immigrants to America, were greatly mitigated (see Lucas, 1955).

However, by 1890, it was clear that the Dutch agricultural settlements had reached their physical limits. Like other American farmers, the Dutch were suffering from problems with land shortages, distribution, marketing, financing and transportation. Although new opportunities were opening up in the urban/industrial sectors, the city and factory held little appeal for many families who had been farmers for generations.

Seizing the opportunity to expand its own underpopulated and underdeveloped prairie region the Canadian government began to advertise the virtues of the "Last Best West". Dutch Americans and Dutch immigrants alike soon arrived to take up free homestead land or purchase millions of acres held by the Canadian Pacific Railway

Company and other companies. They, like so many others, responded to the promise of economic betterment and individual success based solely on the exploitation of the new frontier.[1]

The advent of World War I in 1914 and the economic recession that followed it significantly slowed the movement until well into the 1920's. At that time, Canadian government policy shifted to a general concern for agricultural development and employment across Canada as the prairie region had reached much of its settlement capacity. The massive unemployment and economic disruption caused by the Great Depression of 1929-39 saw the exclusion of all immigration with the exception of relatives of Canadian citizens and those with the financial wherewithal to immediately establish businesses or purchase farms.[2] The outbreak of World War II further reduced the number of Dutch immigrants to a mere trickle composed largely of economic and political refugees.

Starting in 1947 Dutch immigration resumed apace and in the two following decades immigrants made their way to all parts of Canada. The return of economic prosperity to the Netherlands in the early 1960's, thanks in large measure to the Marshall Plan, spelled an end to large scale emigration and with the exception of a few years in the mid-60's immigration has since not exceeded 2,000 Netherlanders a year.

II   SOCIAL CHARACTERISTICS OF DUTCH IMMIGRATION

The social characteristics of the Dutch immigrants were in great measure determined by what the Canadian government saw as the primary aims of immigration in the first sixty years of Dutch migration to Canada. In the 1890's Canadians viewed the West as the cornerstone of the country's future development. To accomplish the proper exploitation of the Prairies, the "empty" lands had to be peopled by European agricultural immigrants who could turn the raw frontier into productive farms (Timlin, 1960). The Dutch were highly favoured because they were of the right "racial" stock, had a reputation for hard work and cleanliness, and were familiar with democratic institutions. In other words, they were almost Anglo-Saxon and eminently assimilable.[3]

Due to this "agriculture first" policy, the great majority of Dutch immigrants who had settled in Canada by 1955 were either farmers, farm labourers or people with claimed agricultural experience. At the time of their emigration the majority were between the ages of 20 and 40 with an average of fifth or sixth grade education, often complemented by some technical or night school training. Prior to 1914 the movement

---

[1] R. Insinger to L. Pereira, 18 February 1892, Department of the Interior (Immigration Branch) Records, National Archives of Canada, Ottawa. Hereafter noted as DI/IBR,NAC.

[2] Ministry of External Affairs to the Central Emigration Foundation Holland, 20 August 1930 [Telephone transcript], Netherlands Emigration Service Collection, Glenbow-Alberta Institute. Hereafter noted as NESC, GAI.

[3] The Department of the Interior to H. Dixon, 11 May 1894, DI/IBR,NAC.

was predominantly family immigration as compared to that of the 1920's, which was overwhelmingly comprised of single individuals.

The post-1945 immigration was again primarily family immigration with agricultural workers predominating until 1950.[4] In 1950 the Canadian government, responding to the growing need for labour in the urban/industrial sector, abandoned the "agriculture only" category with the result that only 34 percent of the Dutch immigrants in that year were classified as farmers. From this point on skilled industrial workers, technicians, white collar workers, and professionals made up the bulk of the movement.

Unlike other European nations, the Netherlands has not experienced the kind of calamities that create mass emigration movements. The Dutch are generally reluctant emigrants, preferring their comfortable homeland to the unfamiliar. Failing internal migration or migration to other European countries, they regard overseas emigration as a last resort. While Dutch emigration to Canada cannot be seen as the flight of the destitute and oppressed, it can also not be regarded as the movement of a social or political elite. One could best characterize the movement as one composed of individuals and families of middling background, possessing the skills, desires and adventurous spirit to improve their life circumstances through emigration.[5]

Emigration from the Netherlands in the 1890's was, generally, a response to uncertain economic conditions. The corrosive effects of the 1873-1896 recession/depression affected most of the Atlantic economies to some degree and forced the Dutch government to initiate significant structural changes. Rationalization and reorganization introduced new methods, machinery, crops and standards in agriculture and new industries and processes stimulated development in the industrial sector. Unemployment and redundancy were the inevitable byproducts of such radical change.

Emigration to America seemed to present an alternative to unemployment and many looked to the government to take a lead in giving the movement direction. Some officials regarded emigration as unjustified risk-taking and opposed government involvement, although, most were content to let the emigration field regulate itself.[6] Others, primarily members of the Dutch economic elite, regarded emigration as a societal safety valve and an opportunity for the unemployed to achieve social and economic mobility. They also believed that immigrant recruiters, railway agents, land "sharks" and others who were spreading false propaganda had to be combated. To that end, a number of private emigration societies were organized, starting in the 1890's, to sponsor and organize the emigration of the unemployed (Hartland, 1959: 16-26-46). These were to be joined in the 1920's by Calvinist and Roman Catholic societies which sought to aid their coreligionists.

---

[4] A.S. Tuinman to the Netherlands Emigration Foundation, 6 November 1947, NESC, GAI.

[5] A.L Veenstra (1914). *Emigratie en de Nederlandsche Vereeniging Landverhuizing*. NESC, GAI: 1.

[6] B.H.M. Vlekke (1945). *The Evolution of the Dutch Nation* (1945: 322); W. Van Horne to the Department of the Interior, 26 June 1984, DI/IBR, NAC.

The outbreak of World War I, in 1914, curtailed emigration from the Netherlands for the next four years. Post-war problems and ongoing political and financial crises in North America offered little hope for a return to pre-war immigration conditions. The United States, fearing inundation by "racially inferior" immigrants and subversion by "Bolshevik" revolutionaries began to erect a framework of restrictive immigration legislation that favoured the British Isles and western Europe. Immigration quotas, based on the size of immigrant communities present in the United States, left the Dutch with a paltry 1,646 places annually. Canada, while open to Dutch farmers, was undergoing serious economic problems that discouraged immigration until after 1923. However, as the United States began to close its doors, Dutch emigrants were forced, many unwillingly, to consider Canada as an alternate destination.

The coming of the Depression in 1929 forced Canada to close its doors to all but the most well funded immigrants. The majority of those who remained interested in emigration decided it was more prudent to stay home rather than face the unknown in an alien land. The invasion of the Netherlands in 1940 by Germany ended all emigration until 1945. At that time Canada was faced with the difficult task of reestablishing the country on a civilian footing and was not prepared to immediately receive any significant number of immigrants.

While Canada was undergoing the process of post-war adjustment, the Dutch were evaluating their devastating war legacy. The facts engendered a deep pessimism shared by the general public and government alike. The statistics were ominous: over 200,000 hectares of land had been inundated by salt water, a condition that would retard crop production for years; 4 percent of all housing had been destroyed; factories and machinery had been looted by retreating German forces; spare parts were unobtainable; Germany – one of Holland's most important pre-war markets – lay in ruins, and tuberculosis was endemic in the human and cattle population.

Added to all of this misery was the inescapable fact that the high birth rate, which had driven the population to over 9,000,000, showed no sign of leveling off and job creation appeared to be a faint hope, especially in the agricultural sector, where approximately 33,000 young farmers were unable to find work. The struggle for independence in Indonesia and the loss of the Dutch overseas empire aggravated already existing problems. It is little wonder then that at least a third of the Dutch public seriously considered emigrating. With the United States virtually closed by the quota system and with Canada only a short distance away compared to other British Commonwealth countries, the Dutch government quickly cast aside its former "disinterest" and began to focus on Canada as the prime recipient of a planned emigration movement. A "Gentlemen's Agreement" was concluded with Canada in late 1946 and the following year saw the arrival of the first post-war Dutch farmers in Canada.[7]

---

[7] Interview by author with Ir. A.S. Tuinman, October, 1978, Calgary, Alberta.

Attempting to reduce the social and economic pressures by opening the "safety valve", the Dutch government actively sought to stimulate emigration by subsidizing travel costs, reorganizing the emigration system, and seeking to reach permanent numerical immigration agreements with host countries. Eventually a flexible arrangement was hammered out with the Canadian government that permitted the immigration of Dutch nationals according to the demands of the Canadian labour market.[8]

The Dutch recruited, selected and screened applicants according to Canadian criteria. The Canadians medically examined those who had passed the screening and the Dutch government transported the emigrants to Canada. On arrival the immigrants were once again medically inspected by the Canadians and then handed over to Dutch Canadian organizations for placement. The Canadian government demanded that every single immigrant or family head have a job before embarkation and the finding of such positions fell mainly on the fieldmen/representatives of various Dutch Canadian and Canadian churches and the Dutch agricultural attaché in Ottawa.[9] It was clear that Canada was interested in receiving Dutch immigrants but only if the problems were minimal, the costs low, and the benefits obvious.

In the two decades following 1945 hundreds of thousands of emigrants left the Netherlands in hopes of securing a better future. Spurred on by aggressive postwar Soviet expansionism some 152,000 went to Canada, 125,000 to Australia and 80,000 to the United States, South Africa, and New Zealand. The initial group of emigrants (1947-52) were predominantly neo-Calvinist farmers (orthodox dissenters from the Dutch Reformed Church). Roman Catholics, never a large part of the emigration from the Netherlands prior to 1947, began to make up a more significant part of the movement after 1952. The Canadian government's shift away from the exclusive recruitment of farmers in the early 1950's opened the door to a wider spectrum of Dutch citizens from urban as well as rural areas.

III   PERIODS OF IMMIGRATION

It is difficult to determine the actual number of Dutch or Dutch Americans who entered Canada for the purpose of settlement in the last one hundred years. Given that Dutch and Canadian figures are deeply suspect, the historian is left to give the best estimate possible. Taking into account all the extant figures, projections and reports, one arrives at some 200,000 immigrants. Determining the present size of the Dutch community in Canada also presents a problem in that census numbers are highly questionable due to the inconsistent manner in which ethnicity has been determined over time.

[8] Tuinman interview.
[9] Ann Felix to author, 6 March 1980; Tuinman interview, A.S. Tuinman to the Netherlands Emigration Foundation, 4 January 1949, NESC, GAI.

The results of the 1991 national census simply serve to underscore this problem. This census indicated that Dutch Canadians were to be found in all the provinces and territories with the largest concentrations in Ontario (179,760), British Columbia (66,526), and Alberta (54,750). The cities of Toronto (32,340), Vancouver (25,840), and Edmonton (16,230) had the greatest concentration of "Dutch people" in Canada. The census indicated that while only 133,265 people mentioned "Dutch" as their mother tongue and 358,180 gave "Dutch" as their only ethnic origin, some 603,415 claimed "Dutch" as one of their origins. In other words, 961,595 Canadians said one or more of their ancestors was Dutch. Designating oneself as Dutch for census purposes has become a matter of personal choice and not one based on birthplace or mother tongue. As Dutch Canadians become more assimilated, are distanced further in time from the first generation immigrants, and continue to intermarry with Canadians of other ethnic origins, the "Dutch" designation becomes more historic or nostalgic and possesses little real meaning in relation to an identifiable ethnic community.

It is unclear when the first Dutch immigrants arrived in the Canadian West but they were already there in the 1880's when Amsterdam bankers became involved with the Canadian Pacific Railway Company with a view to the acquisition of western lands for investment and cattle ranching. The completion of the railway in 1885 brought in Dutch entrepreneurs eager to scout out the possibilities on the new frontier and soon Dutch-funded mortgage and land companies were doing business on the Canadian prairies.

For some, the Prairies promised not just investment opportunities but also the possibility of relieving the Netherlands of its unemployed.[10] Their reports helped to bring about the arrival of a group of single Friesian farmers in Yorkton, Saskatchewan territory, in the spring of 1893. They were the vanguard of a larger group, supported by the Christian Emigration Society (organized and run by members of the Dutch economic elite), prepared to take up homestead lands. Supplementing their settlement with railway and farm jobs they began the difficult process of getting established. Few apparently succeeded and the majority retreated to Winnipeg and environs hoping to do better in the more populous districts of Manitoba (Lucas, 1955: 460).

Winnipeg soon became a focus of settlement for Dutch and Dutch American immigrants who were attracted to the more extensive opportunities of a relatively developed area. Some took up market gardening in the suburbs of Elmwood and East Kildonan while others looked for urban employment. Correspondence home to family, letters to the newspapers and the rapid growth of the city, brought others to try their luck. As the Dutch community grew, its clubs, churches and social organizations presented a significant attraction to those who shunned the bare-bones life of the homestead.[11]

---

[10] R. Insinger to the Department of the Interior, 18 February 1892, H. Dixon to the Department of the Interior, 15 July 1892, DI/IBR, NAC.

[11] J. Maurer (1915: 2). *Trip Report on Nova Scotia and Western Canada*. NESC, GAI.

City life did not, however, appeal to all. The majority kept their sights on economic independence on a homestead of 160 acres of free land. In the spring of 1904, a group settlement was established at Nobleford in southern Alberta by Dutch Americans from Iowa and Montana and settlers coming directly from the Netherlands. Thanks to extensive newspaper coverage in the United States and the Netherlands trumpeting the settlers' success and the opportunities for advancement, the community was soon joined by others wanting to share in the dream. Homesteads and aid were freely offered and by 1912 the community spawned its own daughter colonies as some of the earlier settlers sold out and moved north, some as far as the Peace River country (see Hoffman, 1983).

The well advertised success of the Nobleford settlement spurred immigrants to settle in other parts of the West. Manitoba saw Dutch farmers and hired hands at Portage La Prairie, Morden, Argyle, and Rosebank. In 1908 a group of Dutch Americans took up land near Moose Jaw, Saskatchewan, and were soon followed by settlers at Cramersburg in 1911. By 1914 single and married Dutch homesteaders had established themselves at places such as Leoville, Saskatoon and Morse. Free and cheap land remained a potent lure to those who regarded land as the basis of all wealth and security (see Ganzevoort, 1973).

The settlement in Nobleford also coincided with Dutch homesteading near Calgary and Edmonton. A colony settlement of Dutch Catholics at Strathmore in 1908 was paralleled by the development of a neo-Calvinist community, Neerlandia, northwest of Edmonton in 1912. Throughout the West, the Dutch became an integral part of the newly developing society. Whether single men or families, they were considered acceptable by their Canadian peers and they in turn felt much the same about their new homeland and countrymen.

Prior to 1914, the "Golden West" remained the focus of settlers and the Canadian government. Free homesteads and cheap railway land and an abundance of labouring jobs meant that the great majority of immigrants saw the prairies as the doorway to the future. While Dutch immigrants settled in every province and major city in Canada during the first two decades of the 20th century, their primary destination remained west of Winnipeg. Precise numbers are unclear, but it is estimated that some 20,000 Dutch and Dutch American immigrants entered Canada in the 1890-1914 period.

The outbreak of war in 1914 and Canada's involvement in it ended emigration from neutral Holland. Dutch military reservists returned home, while other immigrants joined the Canadian armed forces or sat out the war as neutral aliens. The hoped-for resumption of immigration after 1918 did not immediately materialize, however. Despite trends to urbanization and industrialization spurred on by the war, Canada had to deal with the legacies of high inflation, war expenditure, and the reintegration of wounded and demobilized soldiers. The economic recession which began in 1919 and caused social and political unrest spelled an end to high hopes for a vibrant postwar economy and the expected demand for thousands of foreign agricultural workers did not materialize (Hedges, 1930: 353). In the Netherlands the weak postwar economy and the collapse of the German mark augured ill for the future and drove the Dutch to search for opportunities overseas. Given American immigration restriction, Canada remained the only alternative. The reactivated Canadian propaganda campaign after 1923, primarily orchestrated by the railway companies, promised hope for those who wanted to leave their homeland. The majority of the arrivals in this period were overwhelmingly single or unaccompanied married men. The Canadian government preferred single men as they were more likely to take up work as farmhands or attempt homesteading. The very difficult nature of the work and the substandard accommodation – shacks, bunkhouses, converted sheds, chicken coops and attics – made an accompanying family a liability. Wages were also low and barely met the needs of a single man, thus making failure or vagabondage a real possibility.[12]

Mobility was the hallmark of male immigrants in the 1920's. Many never got the chance to own their own farms as most free or cheap land had been taken up by 1914. As hired hands they were at the mercy of the farmers with respect to length of employment and payment. They worked long hours and were often summarily dismissed without pay when winter arrived. Out of necessity, many crowded into the cities in the winter seeking food, shelter and employment. Some, however, preferred working for room, board, and tobacco on the farm or the rough life of the lumber camp to joining the aimless bands of men who drifted from place to place.

For many the dream of independence turned out to be a nightmare; an illusion destroyed by the reality that the homestead frontier was a thing of the past and that even successful Dutch settlements were now becoming crowded and forced to look at marginal land as an alternative for sons who wanted to farm. Many of the immigrants who failed to find a permanent place for themselves on the Prairies often ended up in Winnipeg and became permanent members of the oldest Dutch community in Canada, which numbered almost 5,000 people by 1929.[13]

As it became apparent that the West no longer held the promise of a rosy future, the immigrants turned to the East. However, neither the Maritimes nor Quebec met the basic criteria for success. The maritime provinces lacked good cheap land, markets, significant urban centers, and they had few agricultural jobs. Quebec also presented problems with its French language, Roman Catholicism (most immigrants were Protestant), lack of cheap land, and dearth of agricultural jobs. Those Dutch people who did choose Quebec settled primarily in Montreal to take advantage of the scarce employment opportunities in the construction trades and industry. As a result, Ontario became an attractive option for many.[14]

---

[12] K. Westra, *Life of an Immigrant*, unpublished manuscript in author's possession.

[13] *De Standaard*, 2 November 1929, NESC, GAI.

[14] Hartland, *De Geschiedenis*, P. Snoek to the Netherlands Emigration League, 11 November 1924, NESC, GAI: 155.

Ontario had a strong industrial sector based on a secure agricultural foundation. Urbanization and industrialization had drawn many farm workers to the cities and replacements were urgently needed. Immigrants found a steady call for their services from dairy, fruit, vegetable, tobacco, beet and mixed farmers. Winter was the most difficult period as farmers seldom had enough work to justify keeping a permanent farmhand. Some immigrants drifted into cities such as Toronto, Hamilton, and Windsor while others turned to the mines, mills and forest industries that dotted Northern Ontario.

Wherever employed, most immigrants in this period did not substantially improve their economic circumstances and some even saw them worsen. The post-war period had seemed to hold so much promise for the more than 15,000 Dutch immigrants who had arrived in Canada between 1918 and 1930 but it left all too many with unfulfilled expectations and deep fears about the future.

The coming of the Great Depression in 1929 not only dried up the job market and the flow of immigrants but it also encouraged, even forced, the repatriation of those who had not been able to find secure positions. Dutch consular officials reluctantly offered aid and assistance to the distressed and Canadian immigration officials carried out an active campaign deporting those who became "public charges" or found themselves in trouble with the law.[15] The number of such returnees was small as the great majority of Dutch immigrants accepted the idea that "survival" rather than "advancement" had become the watchword of the time.

One notable example of such "survival" was the successful settlement of 16 Dutch families on the Holland Marsh north of Toronto. The combined efforts of Dutch, Canadian and municipal governments managed to avoid the deportation of these families who had arrived in the 1920's and who had suffered severe financial hardship. Thanks largely to their pluck, courage, and sheer stubbornness, they were eventually able to make the venture succeed and achieve some security.[16]

Due to the fact that immigration was severely restricted, the number of Dutch immigrants who arrived during the 1930's barely reached 3,200 (Hartland, 1959: 162). Near the end of the decade, as conditions improved, new immigrants arrived to settle at Lacombe, Alberta and in Bulkley Valley, in Northern British Columbia. The outbreak of World War II in September 1939 and the invasion of the Netherlands in the following year virtually ended the immigration of Dutch nationals, with the exception of a small number of refugees among whom were members of the Dutch royal family.

---

[15] Included in the Netherlands Emigration Service Collection are Canadian government deportation lists and extensive files dealing with repatriated emigrants.

[16] Consul General J.A. Schuurman to the Ministry of Foreign Affairs, 9 December 1938, NESC, GAI. Schuurman observed that "The families on the Marsh don't want to leave, no matter how difficult things may be, perhaps only because they value their personal relations. They find it 'gezellig' [convivial]."

With the resumption of Dutch immigration to Canada in 1947 the new arrivals were initially directed to those areas that had seen successful Dutch settlement in the past. Dutch speaking "fieldmen" – mostly ministers and priests – placed immigrants in the most economically advantageous positions keeping in mind the necessity of maintaining social bonds.[17] The Dutch settlements in Alberta and British Columbia proved to be important sources of work and support and provided the means for the rapid dispersion and settlement of new immigrants. The Dutch community in Winnipeg functioned in much the same fashion. In Ontario the demand for immigrant labour exceeded the supply. Fruit, dairy, tobacco, and mixed farmers eagerly welcomed the families who made up the bulk of the movement.

Many immigrants, however, valued their independence, and given the chance, they soon bought out the aging farmers who had been their initial employers. Families, with grown sons and daughters who could substantially add to the family income, were initially the most successful in such ventures (for an excellent assessment of the role of Dutch agricultural immigrants in southwestern Ontario see Sas, 1957). Farm labourers, who had no long term interest in farming, regarded their tenure on the farm as a chance to learn the language and practices of their new homeland and looked forward to the day when they could leave for greener pastures.

As Canada became increasingly industrialized and urbanized in the 1950's, skilled and unskilled Dutch workers arrived to exploit all sectors of the new economy. The changing character of the immigrants inevitably brought about a change in the character of the Dutch community from predominantly rural/agricultural to urban/industrial. As agricultural opportunities and demand declined in the more heavily settled areas, some farm immigrants turned to the relatively underpopulated rural areas of Quebec, New Brunswick, and Prince Edward Island. While agricultural pursuits initially predominated in those areas, the immigrants' children and grand-children were inevitably drawn away from the farms as new opportunities opened up.

The same conditions that encouraged young men to emigrate in the 1890-1980 period also had an important effect on women. Prior to the 1930's occupational opportunities for women in the Netherlands were severely limited. Advancement and training, particularly for working class women was practically non-existent, especially if this led to job competition with men. Domestic service, whether in institutions or private homes, was one of the few positions open to the untrained single woman. However, it was poorly remunerated and seldom permitted the accumulation of sufficient funds to venture either into new directions or marriage.

Canada, however, had a great need for domestic servants in both rural and urban areas and salaries as high as Cdn$20 to Cdn$25 a month were comparable to those of an inexperienced farmhand. Demand was so great that by the 1920's eligible women were

---

[17] A.S. Tuinman to Netherlands Emigration Foundation, 2 November 1948, NESC, GAI. Competition among the various placement officers and organizations sometimes led to squabbling, sniping and charges of raiding.

advanced 50 percent of their passage money if they agreed to sign one-year contracts. Some young women saw domestic service in Canada as a way to advance themselves economically, a chance to see new places, or expand their social circle and perhaps even have a taste of adventure. Others wanted to emigrate to join their fiancés or families who had left the Netherlands. While the Canadian government sought to direct the immigration of domestic servants to the rural West, where the demand was greatest, the majority of the women preferred to work in the cities where the workload was significantly lighter and the opportunities to meet fellow countrymen, greater. While domestic servants most likely never made up more than 4 or 5 percent of the total emigration from the Netherlands to Canada, they remained an important part of the movement.[18]

More important to the long term success of Dutch settlement in Canada was the role of women immigrants in general. Settlers, in the West prior to 1914, recognized the absolute necessity of female participation in the homesteading venture. Bachelorhood was seen by most men as a temporary and unwelcome state. They regarded the civilizing process that turned wild grasslands into arable farmsteads as more than mere sod busting. The founding of a new society demanded the "gentle touch" of a woman's hand. Realistically, however, it was a woman's work-hardened hand that rocked the cradle, fed the chickens, did the washing up, knitted the socks and completed myriad other tasks so essential to survival. Women, more often than not, made the difference between success and failure on the prairies and Dutch women did not take second place to other women immigrants.

In the 1920's a married immigrant woman was usually regarded as part of the package when her husband was hired by a farmer. While he worked in the fields and the barn, she was expected to function as a servant in the farmer's household. In some cases the immigrant's wife or his daughters took up domestic service in the neighbouring town to supplement the often meager income. Independent immigrant farmers counted on their wives to sell butter or eggs to get their family through hard times. During the Depression a woman's income might be the only thing keeping the wolf of destitution from the door. During two world wars, with their husbands and fathers in the armed forces, wives and daughters often operated the farms on their own. Few tasks were beyond their abilities and these farms' productive capacity was often higher than in peacetime.

The postwar immigration presented new opportunities to single and married women alike. Although many Canadian farmers assumed that their contracts with immigrant families included the free labour of the female members they were often surprised when women demanded remuneration for hoeing beets, tying grapes, harvesting fruit, milking cows, and doing dozens of other farm tasks. As in previous decades, off-farm work was eagerly sought and those Canadians who looked to Dutch women for domestic service often had to compete with well paid employment in canning and basket factories or other agriculturally allied industries.

---

[18] G.L. Boer to the Central Emigration Foundation Holland, 5 February 1924, NESC, GAI.

As the Dutch settled in the cities in the 1950's, the whole area of industrial and service jobs opened up and women were as likely to be found working "on the line" as cleaning homes. Ready access to educational opportunities in the 1960's and 70's meant that the daughters of immigrants began to enter technical and professional fields alongside their Canadian sisters. There they have met the same challenges as other women in furthering their careers and establishing a recognition of the pivotal role they have played in the settlement and development of Canada.[19]

The desire to achieve economic independence led many immigrants to establishing their own businesses as quickly as possible. Most naturally gravitated to supplying the needs of their own communities first. Retail businesses selling familiar old country products often became outlets for the products of immigrant bakers and butchers and no Dutch community across Canada seemed complete without a "Dutch store". Immigrants combined their Dutch training and Canadian experience and offered a broad variety of services to their fellow immigrants, and within a short time, to the broader Canadian community.[20]

During the 1950's and 60's the Dutch seemed to dominate the gardening and landscaping sectors and were branching out into greenhouse production of flowers and vegetables. Inevitably, as the second and third generation achieved higher levels of education, they generally advanced beyond the entry level occupations of the first generation and moved into the professions, the civil service, and the corporate world.

As the Dutch immigrants have generally been held in high regard by Canadians, they have not suffered the social, economic or political discrimination that has been the experience of other immigrant groups. For the most part, the Dutch have lived up to the clean, hard-working, law-abiding stereotype that Canadians have cherished for over a hundred years and have presented no real threat to the societal status quo. While Dutch economic successes in such diverse places as western Ontario, southern Alberta or the Fraser Valley have occasionally led to mild outbreaks of envy, their commitment to integration or even assimilation has blunted any significant opposition to their inclusion. The economic success of the migration experience and the acceptance of the Canadian public has meant that the return rate to the Netherlands has been exceedingly low over the past one hundred years, perhaps less than one percent.

---

[19] The study of the role of women in the immigration movement and settlement has been sadly neglected and underestimated. Few would disagree that their contribution was essential.

[20] The material regarding the peddlers and other developing business enterprises is extracted from interviews and personal experience. The author accompanied his father on a horsemeat route and was personally acquainted with a number of grocery peddlers.

IV   THE INVISIBILITY OF THE DUTCH COMMUNITY IN CANADIAN SOCIETY

The positive acceptance of the Dutch has meant that, unlike many other ethnic communities, an antagonistic, protective, or even nostalgic ethnicity that is so often the response to non-acceptance by the host society, simply did not develop. As a result, the Dutch community seems to lack any significant or unique identity and the Dutch Canadians have little interest in maintaining a distinctive culture separate from the social mainstream. Integration and eventual assimilation have come to be seen as the natural, acceptable, and inevitable result of immigration.

One of the factors that mitigates against group cohesiveness and identity formation in the Dutch Canadian community is the lack of religious homogeneity. The religious identity of Dutch Canadians has been, in great part, determined by the attitudes and views that they held in the homeland. The great majority of immigrants to Canada prior to 1953 were of the Reformed tradition; a tradition that embraces not only the liberal and latitudinarian views of the Dutch Reformed Church, but also the most conservative of orthodox beliefs as represented by the dissenting neo-Calvinist churches. Relations between the different churches in the Netherlands was characterized by conflict and antagonism and that tradition has in part been transferred to Canada.

The Christian Reformed Church, originally a mission offshoot of the Christian Reformed Church of the United States, is the largest "ethnic" church with approximately 85,000 members. While it dominated the church life of the neo-Calvinist community in the prewar and immediate postwar period, its dominance was challenged in the 1950's as long standing Dutch conflicts over matters of common grace, church order, and other doctrinal issues reasserted themselves in Canada. Such disagreements led to the founding of the Canadian Reformed Church in 1950 and the Free Reformed Church in 1955. Also part of the neo-Calvinist community in Canada are the Protestant Reformed Church and the ultra conservative Netherlands Reformed Congregation.[21]

At present the great majority of Dutch Canadians belong to the Roman Catholic, United and Presbyterian churches of Canada.[22] These churches naturally have had little impact on, or interest in, maintaining or encouraging a uniquely Dutch religious expression. From the beginning the Roman Catholic church opposed "national" churches and did everything in its power to integrate and assimilate the Dutch immigrants into the larger faith community. The neo-Calvinist churches, despite their predominantly ethnic membership, have supported social integration and do not wish to be regarded as "Dutch" institutions. They emphasize that they are English language

---

[21] I am indebted to the Reverends J. Hielema and T. Hoffman for insight and information on the neo-Calvinists in Canada.

[22] Current statistical material regarding the Dutch community in Canada has been abstracted from the 1991 national census.

Canadian churches with a unique Calvinist message that seek to serve people of all social and cultural backgrounds. This diversity of religious expression has meant that even the Christian Reformed Church has had to speak from a minority position and its opinions have had little impact on the larger Dutch community.

However, neo-Calvinists have sought to give voice to their religious beliefs by developing alternative educational, social welfare and political structures. Starting in the 1950's Christian school societies were established across Canada and the result has been a network of parentally controlled Christian day schools, high schools and a number of Christian colleges. While social problems such as alcoholism, crime, and poverty have been minimal among neo-Calvinists, members have sought to provide social services based on a Christian perspective. The aging immigrant community has also been an increasing focus of concern, and housing and care facilities the result.

Modern urban and industrial employment has presented difficult choices for some members of the immigrant community. They have opposed membership in secular unions, Sunday work, and automatic union checkoff. The Christian Labour Association, founded in the 1950's, has challenged some of these issues in court and continues to play a meaningful role in industrial relations.

One of the most important vehicles for retaining cultural identity among immigrant groups in Canada has been the use of their native language. Among Germans, Ukrainians, Poles, and others, language has helped to solidify ethnic identity and mother language retention has always been a priority. This does not seem to be the case for the Dutch, as official studies have indicated that their desire for language retention was one of the lowest among all Canadian ethnic groups (O'Bryan et al., 1975: 128-30, 389). The reason for this seems to be directly related to a value judgment on the part of the immigrants as to the usefulness of their language in Canada.

Even before their departure immigrants were encouraged to take lessons in conversational English. Government officials, emigration societies, and even the churches urged the necessity of English fluency and stressed that integration was a desired goal, both economically and socially. First generation immigrant experience in Canada merely underlined the advice they had received at home. Successful settlement hinged on a sufficient command of the English language. The children of the immigrants, cut off from most institutions likely to contribute to language maintenance, with the exception of the family, acquired the language quickly as they entered Canadian schools and ultimately the workplace. By the mid 1950's Dutch Protestant churches began scheduling more and more English services to meet the needs of a changing community. The Roman Catholic Church, committed to the total assimilation of the immigrants in their Canadian parishes, encouraged the acquisition of English at every level.

It is not hard to understand why fluency in Dutch has declined in time. Outside the family the language is hardly ever used even among first generation immigrants. Even within the family, Dutch is only used infrequently. Fully fluent speakers may use it as their main language of communication among family members, but use drops by half among friends. Each succeeding generation seems to follow this pattern, indicating clearly that the use of Dutch diminishes the further one gets away from the first generation. In recent years some third generation Dutch Canadians have taken Dutch language courses at the university level but enrollment numbers are small and do not indicate a significant interest. Unless there is a massive infusion of Dutch immigrants in the near future, Dutch will soon be spoken only in the language classroom and the homes of recent immigrants.

An important factor that has helped other Canadian ethnic groups maintain their national character has been an ongoing and developing body of folk culture and traditions. Dance, music, literature and art unique to that group or its homeland inform and help shape the experience in Canada. Most Dutch immigrants brought little of such cultural heritage with them. While literacy was universal among them, much of what was read was either of a pious or practical nature. The neo-Calvinists, in particular, had no tradition of secular music or literature. As well, they opposed all forms of dance, art, theater, and film which they considered not consonant with their religious beliefs. Many Roman Catholics from the southern provinces of the Netherlands did come with a strong tradition of religious and secular festivals and more folkish cultural expressions. However, owing to the assimilative pressures exerted on them by the Catholic church and community in Canada, these traditions have not been retained. Given the educational level of the majority of the immigrants it is no wonder that they were not bearers of high culture. Their pragmatic views of the world and commitment to survival left little room for such fripperies.

The children and grand-children of the immigrants have, in the main, expressed little interest in Dutch culture or in giving expression to some unique vision of the Dutch experience in Canada. They were educated in Canadian schools, and their artistic interests have been expressed within the Canadian milieu. Painters, writers, musicians, photographers of immigrant background have sought, and found, a ready acceptance from other Canadians. Their vision is regarded as fully Canadian and not "ethnic" or distinct. While a few writers have focused on the nature of the group experience, they have not specifically directed their efforts towards the Dutch Canadian community but have rather sought acceptance in Canadian society at large.

Ethnic clubs and organizations have played a significant role in the maintenance of language and traditions for many immigrant groups in Canada but not in the Dutch community. The history of Dutch clubs from their genesis in Winnipeg in the early 20th century to the present day has been one of rise and fall, with few such clubs still in existence nowadays. A response to the need for community outside church circles, they were generally organized by a small coterie of first generation activists and most lived a short, underfunded and under-supported life. In recent years, with government subsidies, Dutch Canadian clubs across Canada have become involved in ethnic festivals where they dish up a potpourri of ethnic dance, songs, costumes and food that increasingly represents only a nostalgic or even romantic image of a community that is rapidly disappearing.

The reality is that these clubs only represent a small number of the members of the Dutch community. They have held little appeal for the neo-Calvinists and practically no appeal at all for the children and grand-children of immigrants. On a few occasions, primarily related to the role which Canada played in liberating the Netherlands in 1945, Dutch clubs and organizations have been able to unite for a common purpose, but this has not led to any national organizational development. As the number of first generation immigrants declines, organizations such as Dutch theater clubs, dance, choral groups and even the clubs themselves fold up and disappear. Their passing is hardly noted in the Dutch community.[23]

Another vehicle for retaining language and culture is the ethnic press. The Dutch community saw the development of a strong ethnic press in the 1950's, but this has declined steadily as death and assimilation eroded away the language and interest. At present there are two exclusively Dutch newspapers, the *Nederlandse Krant* (founded in 1954) and the *Hollandse Krant* (1969) and their circulation is dwindling. The only bilingual newspaper, *The Windmill Herald* (1958) offers a general overview of Dutch, Dutch Canadian, and Dutch American news, editorial comments, columns and advertisements for "Dutch" businesses. *The Windmill Herald* has an approximate circulation of 13,000 due in part to its use of English and its penetration of the Dutch American community. *The Christian Courier* (1945), with a circulation of 5,000, seeks to serve the Christian Reformed community and functions largely as a church organ and spokesman for neo-Calvinist opinion. A number of church magazines and newsletters continue to be published but their circulation is limited to their religious constituencies.[24]

As one of the larger ethnic groups in Canada, it could be expected that the Dutch would have a noticeable impact on the Canadian political process. Such has not been the case. While Dutch Canadian politicians can be found at all levels of government and in all political parties, none are regarded as, nor claim to be, representatives of their ethnic community. Given the lack of religious homogeneity, the broad dispersion of the Dutch across Canada, the absence of strong cultural institutions and a decided commitment to integration and assimilation, any Dutch Canadian politician would be a fool to depend on an ethnic constituency. Dutch Canadians also do not have an "ethnic" agenda and like most Canadians they favour the quiet middle way with a emphasis on small "c" conservatism.

---

[23] The material relating to the Dutch clubs and organizations has been gathered by interviews, formal and informal, in Calgary, Toronto, Vancouver and Winnipeg.

[24] Interviews with A. vander Heide, Burnaby B.C., May 1980, September 1996. Mr. vander Heide kindly supplied the information and statistics on Dutch Canadian newspapers and publications.

Dutch Canadians generally regard themselves as Canadians first and Dutch second. Loyalty to Canada has never been an issue and little has barred their way to full citizenship or opportunity. The result has been an abandonment of their ethnic identity. This has been an act of choice rather than chance. Even though certain elements of "Dutchness" have been preserved, particularly among the first generation, such cultural remnants have not been seen to be in conflict with the host culture. Pragmatism has been the rule in the keeping or discarding of things Dutch. For some the doctrines and expressions of neo-Calvinism held a high priority and most agreed that the Dutch traditions of family loyalty and solidarity were superior to the Canadian emphasis on individualism. As well, these aspects of their lives in the old country were seen as having relevance and ultimate benefit to the Canadian society. However, the preservers of such ideas constitute an increasingly irrelevant minority.

Some Dutch Canadians, and even outside observers, have expressed the hope that the more educated immigrants of the post-1950's would give voice and expression to the uniqueness of the Dutch experience in Canada. This has not been realized to any significant extent as most newly arrived immigrants have blended easily into the host society and, beyond social contacts, have had little effect on the larger Dutch community. As the culture of the Netherlands becomes increasingly North American in character, the difference between the immigrants and Canadians is reduced to a matter of language. Under such conditions emigration is hardly a world-shattering event and the limited resources of the ethnic community seem largely irrelevant to the new immigrants.

While some regard the loss of ethnic identity as a thing to be deplored, such is not the opinion of the vast majority of Dutch Canadians. They are not prepared to exert any significant effort to maintain what they regard as a disappearing community. Becoming the "invisible ethnic" is not a matter of great concern. Their view is that they or their relatives left the Netherlands to take advantage of the opportunities offered by a new country and that act was fulsomely rewarded. While there may be nostalgia for things Dutch, they would not trade their lives in Canada for life in the Netherlands. The commitment to the new homeland and the new language has drawn the immigrants step by step away from their native roots. Their children and grand-children, while perhaps curious about those roots, regard them as interesting but not necessarily essential to their identity. The great majority see their ethnic identity as largely irrelevant to their lives. They regard the extinguishing of that identity as part of a natural and desirable process that is producing a new and distinct society of which they and their children are an important part (for a general history of the Dutch experience in Canada, 1890-1980 see, Ganzevoort, 1988).

References

Ganzevoort, H. (ed.). (1973). *A Dutch Homesteader on the Prairies (Letters of Willem de Gelder)*. Toronto: University of Toronto Press.

Ganzevoort, H. (1988). *A Bittersweet Land*. Toronto: McClelland and Stewart.

Hartland, J.A.A. (1959). *De geschiedenis van de Nederlandse emigratie tot de Tweede Wereldoorlog (History of Dutch Emigration until World War II)*. The Hague: Ministerie van Sociale Zaken en Volksgezondheid.

Hedges, J.B. (1930). *Building the Canadian West*. New York: The Macmillan Company.

Hoffman, T. (1983). *The Strength of Their Years*. St. Catherines: Knight Publishing.

Lucas, H.A. (1955). *Netherlanders in America*. Ann Arbor: University of Michigan Press.

O'Bryan, K.E., Reitz, J.G. & Kuplowska, O. (1975). *Non-Official Languages: A Study in Canadian Multiculturalism*. Ottawa: The Secretary of State.

Sas, A. (1957). *Dutch Migration to and Settlement in Canada, 1945-1955*. Worcester, MA: Clark University (Ph.D. thesis).

Timlin, M.F. (1960). Canada's immigration policy, 1896-1920, *Canadian Journal of Economics and Political Science* 26: 517.

THE FLEMISH AND DUTCH MIGRANT PRESS IN CANADA
A HISTORICAL INVESTIGATION

by Jennifer VRIELINCK

I INTRODUCTION

The fact that Canada has long been a pole of attraction for an important inflow of migrants from places such as Flanders and the Netherlands is evidenced by the extensive social life and press activities which Flemish and Dutch Canadians have managed to develop over time. In this report, we will focus on the evolution of Flemish and Dutch migration to Canada. For a clearer view of the subject, a distinction has been made between Southern Ontario and the rest of Canada: first of all because of the exceptional situation regarding Flemish presence in Southern Ontario, and also because immigration flows between the United States and the other Canadian provinces have traditionally gone through Ontario. Precisely due to this central position, Ontario seems to be closely tied to press and social circles in the United States.

II FLEMISH AND DUTCH MIGRANTS IN CANADA
A BRIEF HISTORY

1927 was undoubtedly the peak year for Flemish and Dutch immigration to Canada, with no less than 2,369 Flemish and more than twice as many Dutch nationals crossing the Atlantic. After 1927 economic hardship forced Canada gradually to close off its borders; meanwhile, the rest of the world was facing massive unemployment. Between 1930 and 1937, barely a hundred of Flemish nationals gained permission to settle in Canada. This state of affairs lasted until the 1938 economic recovery (Verthé, 1974: 174). At the outbreak of World War II, 29,711 Belgians had emigrated to Canada; they were almost exclusively Flemish. Initially, most settled in the West.

2.1 Ontario

In 1910 Flemish immigrants began to settle in the Chatham and Wallaceburg areas. When it became apparent that the tobacco industry offered better prospects, many left the West for Ontario. The most important Flemish settlement was located at the heart of the tobacco-growing region, within the London-Kitchener-Dunnville triangle. Life centered around Delhi and Tillsonburg: Delhi became the hub of social life, while Tillsonburg dominated economic activity.

In the southernmost part of Ontario, on the Leamington-Chatham-Wallaceburg line, Flemish presence remained important despite losses to new tobacco-growing regions starting in 1928. The population there mainly consisted of bricklayers, farmers, and gardeners. Some continued to grow tobacco in addition to their main occupation. This settlement was without a doubt an important contact point between the so-called Flemish colony in Detroit and the Flemish population in the extended tobacco-growing region around Delhi and Tillsonburg. It also was Ontario's oldest Flemish settlement: around 1910, the majority of the settlers were sons of farmers who had not been successful in Detroit's heavy industry. Flemish migrants also went Eastward, away from the prairie provinces whose harsh climate hampered the profitability of work.

In the mid-1920's, another important settlement developed around Sarnia on Lake Huron. At first, the Flemish were solely active in agriculture. Partly because of its convenient location next to the lake, with Port Huron (US) on the opposite bank, Sarnia rapidly grew into a thriving industrial center. Most of the Flemish migrants were employed as technicians and manual laborers. There also was a small colony of tobacco farmers around Port Hope on Lake Ontario, 100 kilometers to the East of Toronto, the provincial capital. It is thus clear that the economic contribution of the Flemish population lay in the growing of tobacco. Fully half of the 4,500 farms in Ontario were under Flemish ownership. Toronto was home to about 1,000 Flemish natives who were active in a wide range of professions; university records of the time list students of Flemish origin. Several dozen Flemish natives had settled in the national capital, Ottawa, including university professors, journalists, etc. (Verthé, 1974: 175-6).

While we are mostly concerned with Flemish immigration here, it must be said that the number of Dutch immigrants was considerably larger. However, there was something special about the Flemish presence: nowhere else in the world do we encounter such typically Flemish settlements as in Ontario. With regard to profession and place of residence, the Dutch immigrants covered a wider area than the Flemish. In the 1950's, Dutch migrants were listed as the fifth ethnic group in Ontario with 216,000 individuals, as compared to 25,000 Flemish people (Verthé, 1974: 174-6).

Social life in Ontario developed in a haphazard way. Originally, the migrants were only in need of material security. In 1928, Flemish Capuchin monks came to Ontario with the intention of contributing to the development of Flemish social life (Verthé, 1974: 105). Due to hard times, no action was taken until ten years later. In 1939, a velodrome was built in Delhi, providing Flemish immigrants a place to practice their national sport (Verthé, 1974: 109). During the war years, cycling lost some of its appeal. Nevertheless, several associations were founded at that time. The theater group *Voor Huis en Haard* (Home and Hearth) was the first step; in 1946 the *(Delhi) Belgian Club* was founded (Verthé, 1974: 109). Lacking cafes of their own, the Flemish built a *Belgian Hall*. By the end of the sixties, the club boasted 3,000 members; the liquor license granted by the government – a highly exceptional occurrence in rigidly Protestant Ontario – most certainly accounted for the large membership.

The *Belgian Club* periodically published *club newsletters*, exclusively for its members (Verthé, 1974: 119). An actual magazine never appeared, partly due to close family and friendship ties with Detroit, where the *Gazette van Detroit* (a Dutch-language newspaper made by and for the Flemish migrants) was available. After all, the Flemish in Southern Ontario had more in common psychologically with the Flemish in Detroit than with those residing in Canada. During the early years, this common bond was strengthened even more by the existence of the Detroit velodromes, which Canada's Flemish immigrants took full advantage of in order to practice their national sport. The *Gazette van Detroit* also always included a Canadian page.

Toronto's *Belgian-Canadian Club* declined, especially because the migrants only used the capital city of Toronto as a halfway house on their way to a permanent settlement elsewhere. In fact, the role of a major city as a stepping stone is a very common element in migration. The *Belgian-Canadian Club* originally functioned as a reception center for newly-arrived Flemish immigrants. In Sarnia, the Flemish and Dutch migrant clubs merged into the *Canadian-Belgian-Dutch Club*; its membership was comprised of 500 families, 25 percent of which were Flemish and 75 percent were Dutch. The Wallaceburg *Canadian-Belgian-Dutch Club* was a daily meeting point for a pigeon racing union, a card game club and a rifle association. In Tillsonburg, a similar amalgamation of Flemish and Dutch social activities could be found in the *Canadian Benelux Unity Club*, a soccer club with fluctuating membership, its main activity being the organization of group trips to the Netherlands and Flanders. In Chatham, the *Kent Belgian-Dutch Club* acted as substitute for Flemish and Dutch cafes and pubs, offering dancing, bowling, archery and parties (Verthé, 1974: 176).

It is clear that Ontario, the Canadian province which borders the great lakes, is unlike any other province with respect to Flemish migration. Thanks to tobacco growing, among other factors, the Flemish contribution was particularly valuable on an economic and social level. However, their cultural contribution was quite small. In fact, especially in the early years, Flemish migrants viewed intellectual education and cultural pursuits as a luxury they could not afford. On the other hand, Dutch immigration was characterized by cultural contributions. The Dutch did not have much use for the *Gazette van Detroit*, presumably because its "simple Dutch" often lapsed into "pretty Flemish," and also because the news often related to Flemish families living in the United States.

In 1954, Laura Schippers founded *De Nederlandse Courant*. This was a bi-weekly magazine comprising various features which always filled up an entire page: *De Sport Courant* (sports), *The Dutch-Canadian Courant*, *De Reis Courant* (travel), *De Financiële Courant* (financial) and *De Community Calendar*. In October 1991, the *Dutch Canadian Association* created *The Link* in Ontario. Written both in English and in Dutch, this quarterly magazine mainly featured club news, unlike *De Nederlandse Courant*, which covered international news (from the Netherlands) and national news (from Ontario).

2.2   The other Canadian provinces

Even though the Flemish showed an interest for Canada early on, it was not until the end of the nineteenth century that the actual Flemish migration wave into Canada really began. This was mostly due to Canada's immigration policy. In addition to the propaganda promoting Canada as a land without restrictions, migrants were offered free lots of land. Due to their willingness to work, Flemish migrants were repeatedly defined as a preferred group. However, more often than not, Canada was seen as the legal entry gate into the United States, with Canadian citizenship as the entrance ticket. Most of the Flemish entering Canada were farmers and seasonal workers, often attracted by enticing slogans such as the "Golden West" and the "Granary of the World." Adventurers and gold diggers were also found in the group.

To appreciate the considerable Flemish presence in Western Canada, one only needs look at the towns in the Pembina hills region. The Flemish migrants played a part in founding Saint-Alphonse (1883), Bruxelles (1892), Mariapolis (1903), Somerset (1907) and Swan Lake (1919) (Verthé, 1974: 204). At the same time, Saint-Boniface[1] developed into the largest Belgian settlement in Canada. Through the efforts of the Capuchin monks, a Belgian Church came into existence and in 1905 *Le Club belge/The Belgian Club* was founded in order to promote social as well as business life. Moreover, Saint-Boniface was the gateway to the West. Many migrants had passed through Saint-Boniface to settle in Saskatchewan and Alberta, two provinces where thousands of Flemish lived, spread out over the endless plains, in the 1970's. Social life thrived until 1964, especially because of the *Belgian Club* in Edmonton. The members lived too far away from each other. Due to the great distances and the rough climate, social ties begin to fall apart. Furthermore, serving alcohol in public places without a license was forbidden in Canada. As Verthé (1974: 230) rightfully wondered: "(...) where on earth do Flemish throats wash down feelings of abandonment or homesickness with Coke or orange juice?"

Very few Flemish immigrants lived in the four maritime provinces of Eastern Canada. The situation was similar in the far North, apart from a number of missionaries, the only ones having made it this far in the beginning of the century. As for British Columbia, Canada's westernmost province, it boasted a larger number of Flemish immigrants. Most of these came from Belgium after the WWII or from the Congo after 1960. Generally speaking, the richest Flemish Canadians can be found here. The Flemish migrants who managed to amass a small fortune in other parts of Canada also tend to retire in the province, owing to the pleasant, mild climate of the Pacific Ocean (Verthé, 1974: 238). A *Belgian Club* was established there as well. In comparison with the other *Belgian Clubs*, this one enjoys much greater independence. This is largely due to the high local standards of living. No appeals for subsidies had to be made to the government or other authorities.

---

[1] Saint-Boniface is mostly a French-language community: those Flemish people who speak French like to settle there. Moreover, there is a religious reason: Saint-Boniface is a Catholic town, while the region around Winnipeg is considered to be Protestant.

In Montréal (Québec), the *Union belge* was founded in 1903; in 1966 the *Vlaamse Kring* (Flemish Circle) came into being. The latter has been sponsoring various events such as the *Ijzer* Pilgrimage Day and the Breughelian Feasts. Despite the thriving social and cultural life, there are no newspapers published by and for the Flemish. This is understandable, as all Belgian associations in Québec were led by French-speaking individuals. However, there are a number of publications intended for Dutch migrants, especially in British Columbia; they are distributed throughout Canada. According to Verthé (1974: 273), none of these publications are read by Flemish families: "(...) perhaps this can be partly explained by the smooth integration and easy adaptability of our emigrants (...)." The Flemish associations however, especially those in Québec, lacked self-confidence. With the exception of the *Vlaamse Kring*[2], Belgian associations pay little attention to Dutch or Flemish culture. Therefore, it is necessary to stress the great importance of an association such as *Vlamingen in de Wereld* (V.I.W.; *Flemish of the World*): this association has local clubs in a number of countries and is also active in Canada.

Those among the Dutch migrants known for their patriotic fervor were remarkably active in the publication of their own magazines. The most important newspapers were as follows: in 1954 *De Nederlandse Courant* and the *Hollandia News* were founded; in 1958 *Good News* appeared for the first time and in 1971 the last two titles were merged into *The Windmill Herald*, published by Vanderheide Publishing. This newspaper was issued twice a month in three editions: *Western Canada*, *Central Canada and the Maritimes*, and *US and the Overseas*. In British Columbia, *De Hollandse Krant* was founded in 1969: this monthly had a strong focus on the Dutch language and included a large section on Dutch literature. *The Link News* was created in October 1991 by the *Dutch Canadian Association – Ottawa Valley*. It is published every four months and is distributed free of charge. In the following section, we will explore in more detail several characteristics regarding content and format of these newspapers.

III   THE DUTCH LANGUAGE PRESS IN CANADA

3.1   De Nederlandse Courant

In 1954, when post-war Dutch migration reached its peak, *De Nederlandse Courant* was founded in Toronto; it was the first Dutch language newspaper in Ontario. Laura Schippers, a Dutch journalist, recognized the need of the newly arrived migrants for news from the Netherlands. The newspaper was launched from a small office in Scarborough. The first issue boasted four pages written by Laura, her husband and a few volunteers. Topics covered concerned the Netherlands and Dutch migrants. Publishing the newspaper monthly and later bi-weekly turned out to be a full-time job

---

[2] The *Vlaamse Kring* owes its name to the typical post-war phenomenon of Flemish cultural emancipation. Associations set up by Flemish migrants abroad are no longer called *Belgian*, but *Flemish*.

for Laura. The two thousand five hundred subscribers were not only from Ontario, but also from other parts of Canada. At that time, *De Nederlandse Courant* was the only Dutch language newspaper in Canada. In 1959, with the death of Laura Schippers, the task of chief editor was taken over by her husband until 1962. Afterwards, three businessmen bought the newspaper. One of these had a spouse who took charge of editing and layout. After a couple of difficult years, Thea Schryer became owner of the newspaper and took over the editing tasks. As a result of her enthusiasm and drive, the newspaper began to grow. Together with her children, she turned it into a family venture. Her leadership was a success and the newspaper became financially stable, even turning out a profit every now and then.

In the meantime, the Dutch-speaking migrant community was changing. Becoming more affluent. Logically, additional Dutch language newspapers appeared. *De Nederlandse Courant*[3] now totaled twenty pages with features such as *Nieuws van thuis* (News from Home), *Sport Community Nieuws*, *Interviews* and *Reistips* (travel tips). Employed staff provided editorial content, with news from the Netherlands selected from Dutch newspapers providing the balance. Thea Schryer held a readers' poll regarding the popularity of the newspaper (Deleu, 1994: 306). *De Nederlandse Courant* turned out to be the most popular newspaper thanks to the *Nieuws van thuis* feature. In 1979, a peak of four thousand subscribers was reached. In 1987 *De Nederlandse Courant* was awarded the *Lily Munroe Award for Excellence in Journalism* owing to its content, layout and contribution in maintaining and promoting multiculturalism in Canada. In the same year, the newspaper also received the *Canadian Ethnic Journalist Award* as a recognition of its level of professionalism.

In 1991 Thea Schryer sold the newspaper to businessmen Bas Opdenkelder and Theo Luykenaar. The total number of pages increased to approximately 24 pages. The newspaper was now published twenty-six times a year in tabloid format, featuring short articles in English as well as in Dutch. A large section was dedicated to travel news. The newspaper largely focused on Ontario and chose to run positive news coverage about the Netherlands. Thanks to efficient marketing, *De Nederlandse Courant* has continued to grow. In 1994 it had more than 4,000 subscribers and was also distributed in the *Dutch Stores* (shops where Dutch products were sold). The newspaper also tries to appeal to the younger generation. This means more and more articles written in English, even though a lot of attention continues to be given to Dutch language lessons and Dutch cultural events. The present publisher, Theo Luykenaar, sees the newspaper as a business, not a passion (Deleu, 1994: 307). Thanks to this strategy, the future of *De Nederlandse Courant* looks more promising than that of most other Dutch language newspapers in Canada.

---

[3] We base our summarized description of the content of *De Nederlandse Courant* on the following issues: June 4, 1994: 39(11); August 13, 1994: 39(11); January 11, 1995: 40(3).

3.2   The Link News

The Link News is very recent: it was founded in October 1991 by the *Dutch Canadian Association – Ottawa Valley*. The magazine is published four times a year and is distributed free of charge to members of the *Dutch Canadian Association – Ottawa Valley/Outaouais*, but complimentary copies are also available at the Dutch embassy in Ottawa and in about eight stores run by Dutch shop owners. The publication is financed through advertisements. Advertisers mainly include travel agencies, Dutch cafes, Dutch stores and moving companies. *The Link News*[4] contains articles in both Dutch and English, and totals approximately 23 quarto pages. Black and white photographs illustrate the editorial articles. Besides the leading article and the *Coming Events* section on the first page, the second page features an editorial: *The Editor Speaks*. The regular column *Nieuws uit Nederland* (*News from the Netherlands*) follows, supplemented with general announcements and letters to the editor. Also, one page is reserved for past events: in 1995 it featured a great number of photographs of celebrations in honor of victims of WWII. In addition, the newspaper includes missing person notices, human interest articles about Dutch Canadians, travel and gardening tips, as well as the *Business Notebook* with stock exchange news. In short, the articles are very general and rather varied. It is a typical club bulletin focusing on non-members. An indication of this are the various locations where *The Link News* is available for free.

3.3   The Christian Courier

The *Christian Courier* is a special case. It was intended from the start for a specific target group and with a well-defined purpose which is unlike that of any of the other newspapers discussed in this report. There are a number of reasons for mentioning it here. Besides typically religious matters, it also covers general news. The *Christian Courier*, previously the *Canadian Calvinist*, is now published entirely in English: Dutch has become obsolete. The evolution of this newspaper raises questions with regard to the future of those which are currently still published in Dutch.

On August 6, 1945 appeared the first issue of *The Canadian Calvinist*, founded by vicar Paul De Koekkoek (Witvoet, 1985a: 3). This issue was completely written in English. The majority of the readership had lived in Canada for 20 years or more and it would be several years before the start of the great immigration wave which was to follow the Second World War. In the first issues, vicar De Koekkoek pointed out the significant progress of Calvinism in Canada. Until January 15, 1946 *The Canadian Calvinist* was mimeographed. Starting on February 15, 1946, the monthly publication was printed in small format. During its second year of publication, the newspaper was expanded to eight pages, with a circulation of 550 to 1000 copies (Witvoet, 1985b: 5). In February 1948, the editorial team asked whether the magazine should continue to be published entirely in English, or if articles in the Dutch language could be included.

---

[4] This brief classification of features is based on *The Link News*, January 10, 1994.

The chief editor refused to take into account the large migration wave of Dutch people to Canada and referred to an existing Dutch publication written in Dutch, namely *De Wachter*, the Dutch language magazine of the Dutch Church. *The Canadian Calvinist* thus decided to remain an English language publication. Nevertheless, in the October/November 1948 issue, a section appears in Dutch for the first time (*Korte Berichten Holland-Canada* – Short News Holland-Canada).

Nineteen forty-nine saw the creation of a new monthly magazine with religious preoccupations called *Contact*. Its focus was mostly on Ontario, while *The Canadian Calvinist* was operating from *Huntingdon* (British Columbia) at that time. The first *Contact* issue appeared in August 1949 (Witvoet, 1985b: 7). The publication was run by the *Christian Reformed Immigration Societies in Eastern Canada*, and was written entirely in Dutch. John Vander Vliet was responsible for editing; John Vellinga took care of publishing. The magazine was printed in Chatham (Ontario). From March 1950, the first paid advertisements started to appear in *Contact*. Also in this issue, an article in English was found for the very first time.

In June 1950, the two publications began discussions towards a potential merger. Both parties understood that there was room for only one Dutch language Calvinist publication in Canada, but were divided regarding the manner in which cooperation should be achieved. *The Canadian Calvinist* wanted to remain an independent publication, while *Contact* preferred to be under the control of the migrant associations in order to prevent a take-over by another group. In the meantime, *The Canadian Calvinist* celebrated its fifth anniversary, having reached a circulation of 3,500 copies (Witvoet, 1985b: 6). When *Contact* celebrated its first year anniversary, it had a circulation of 2,000 (Witvoet, 1985b: 7). In 1950, 45 percent of *Contact*'s revenue came from advertising and the paper seemed to be generating sufficient funds to exist as an independent publication. From March 1951 *Contact* was printed in a larger format: *The Canadian Calvinist* had switched to this format one year before. Now *Contact* had a circulation of 2,900. *The Canadian Calvinist* could still count on 400 subscribers. In September 1951 the final issues of both magazines appeared; an agreement had been reached for the founding of one publication: the *Calvinist-Contact*. The new magazine was published twice a month and was printed in Chatham (Ontario). It featured articles both in Dutch and in English and was under the management of those migrant associations involved. It was especially the influence of *Contact* which seems to live on in the *Calvinist-Contact*. As a matter of fact, on the front page the word "Calvinist" was printed in smaller type than the word "Contact." Thus the first issue of the new *Calvinist-Contact* appeared on October 15, 1951, with John Vander Vliet as new chief editor: precisely the one person who previously never wanted to cooperate with *The Canadian Calvinist* – and who in fact quit after one year. He continued to write for the magazine, but was replaced as chief editor by John Gritter, a vicar from London (Ontario) (Witvoet, 1985b: 11). In 1954 the magazine moved to Hamilton, where publication and distribution were done by Bosch & Keuning Ltd. A new business manager replaced John Vellinga, who went off to found his own newspaper, the *Hollandia News*. These changes also heralded the end of John

Gritter as chief editor; his successor was professional journalist Adolf Otten. The *Christian Immigration Societies* retained ownership of the publication, which had 3200 subscribers. Otten introduced many changes in the publication, and in October 1954 the *Calvinist-Contact* became a weekly magazine published in tabloid format.

After five years at the *Calvinist-Contact*, Otten decided to leave: his views on life no longer matched the Calvinist outlook of the publication (Witvoet, 1985d: 15). Dick Farenhorst took over as chief editor and retained this position until 1976. Under Farenhorst's leadership, the magazine experienced a metamorphosis. Originally, the publication was written mainly in Dutch; in order to reach the younger generations, an English supplement of two to four pages was added in 1962: the *Christian Courier*. Five years later, this was replaced by *English Edition*, an eight-page supplement. English was used more and more as the working language, and in 1969 even the front page was in English. In 1973 only four pages were still written in the Dutch language. Farenhorst died on July 6, 1976 (Witvoet, 1985e: 17-21). During Farenhorst's illness Keith Knight gradually took over the latter's responsibilities, becoming chief editor and retaining the position until 1982. Articles in Dutch became fewer and fewer. In 1977, K. Knight Publishing Limited took over the *Calvinist-Contact* from the *Guardian Publishing Company Ltd*. Now Knight was chief editor as well as owner of the magazine. In 1981, Bert Witvoet became assistant chief editor, gradually taking on chief editorship. Knight remained publisher for some time, but then left to become chief editor for another Ontario newspaper. In 1983 the last two pages still written in Dutch were scrapped. *The Calvinist-Contact* was now a purely English-language publication. The last phase of this transformation occurred in 1992, when the title was changed to the *Christian Courier*. Now, the newspaper was published every Friday with a circulation of approximately 5,000. Bert Witvoet remained as chief editor and Stan De Jong was still director, a position he had assumed after Knight's departure. In 1995 the publication celebrated its fiftieth anniversary.

For the purpose of illustration, we will briefly look at the content of the new *Christian Courier*[5]. The articles contain general news from Canada and the Netherlands, as well as religious news. The publication includes an opinion page, an editorial by Bert Witvoet, reserves space for letters from readers. A number of pages feature ecclesiastic world news. Culture is also covered through a movie section. Advertisements may spread over as many as five full pages. These appear throughout the publication and are mainly from Dutch-Canadian advertisers (sometimes including text in Dutch): travel agencies, Dutch bakeries, banks, lawyers offices, senior citizens' homes, etc. The *Christian Courier* has undergone a transformation: because of this, it can be considered as a prototype of the other Dutch language immigrant publications. Even though a certain English influence was apparent from the beginning with the first issue of *The Canadian Calvinist*, we nevertheless see *Contact* evolve from a true Dutch language publication to a bilingual publication, which takes the final step in the eighties towards an integral English language publication. The editorial content of the *Christian Courier* is indeed unique because of the extensive coverage of religious

---

[5] Description based on a randomly chosen issue (March 17, 1995: 24-36).

matters. However, and contrary to other publications with the same religious focus, the *Christian Courier* includes a fairly extensive coverage of general news in Canada and the Netherlands as well as world news. Moreover, it has closely followed the evolution of the print media in general and has a sufficiently strong financial base to be able to issue up-to-date information on a weekly basis.

3.4   De Hollandse Krant

We mentioned earlier that *De Hollandse Krant* was founded in 1969 as an independent, monthly publication, with Dutch as its working language. The editorial column states that the magazine has no political or religious affiliation. The editorial board aims to provide information which is deemed interesting for Canadians and Americans of Dutch origin. The publication has an original layout, its most striking feature being its two front pages. The front page opens with the feature *Nieuws uit Nederland*[6] (News from the Netherlands). The publication does not contain color photographs; only the title of the magazine is printed in red. The editorial team is comprised of Gerard and Janny Bonekamp, who publish the magazine from Surrey (British Columbia). In addition, the publication employs staff in Ontario, Manitoba, Saskatchewan, Alberta and California. No major changes have been made to the content of the newspaper. Besides the regular feature *Nieuws uit Nederland*, with varied bits of news spread throughout the publication, there is an editorial from editor G. Bonekamp called *Onder Ons* (Between you and I) and letters from readers in the section *Wat anderen ervan denken* (What others think). In addition, the newspaper prints stories in English and in Dutch by well-known writers such as Annie M.G. Schmidt, as well as by readers themselves. It alternates between general news from the Netherlands and literature. *Windschrift* (Writing in the Wind), a literary feature by Maarten Timmer, shows that the editorial team as well as the loyal readership feel that preserving the Dutch language in their community is an important issue. The dissemination of knowledge – in this case the Dutch language – is the primary aim of the publication. This aim is even considered to be more important than providing current and topical news. Attention is also paid to leisure reading: besides literature, there is a small section on postage stamps, a chess column and a "poem of the month." The advertisements are spread throughout the publication; most of them are bilingual and are mostly from merchants of Dutch origin. The biggest advertisers are airlines, travel agencies selling trips to the Netherlands, the *Holland Shopping Center* (which sells articles from the Netherlands), car rental companies in the Netherlands, international moving companies, *Holland Video Productions* featuring videos of *Het Gouden Huwelijk* (Golden Wedding), *Nederland Oranje* (The Netherlands: House of Orange), *de Elfstedentocht* (the Eleven Cities Skating Race), yearly subscriptions to Dutch magazines. Also, there are one-off advertisements for dolls in traditional Dutch garb, miniature mills for the garden, Dutch pubs, etc.

---

[6] Description based on the following randomly chosen issues of *De Hollandse Krant*: June 1st, 1991: 263; January 1st, 1993: 290; September 1st, 1994: 302; February 1st, 1995: 307.

When looking at the different functions of the publication, we can conclude that in this case providing current and topical news is out of the question. Instead, providing the reader with leisure reading and general information are the primary objectives. In any case, *De Hollandse Krant* attains an extra dimension by publishing literary texts which, besides providing leisure reading, disseminate knowledge. It is surely a commendable initiative to help immigrants maintain their knowledge of the Dutch language by providing them with regular features and stories by great Dutch writers.

3.5   Hollandia News

In 1954, *Hollandia News* was founded by John Vellinga as a Dutch language publication for Dutch and Belgian immigrants in Canada and the United States. Vellinga began this publication after seeing – he was unemployed at the time – the *Canadian Calvinist* and *Contact* move to Hamilton (Witvoet, 1985c: 9). Four years later, the *Hollandia News* became *Good News*; the publication retained this name until 1971. In that year, both in addition to the publication's layout, its name was changed one last time as a result of the sale to *The Windmill Herald*[7]. From then on the publication would be a bi-weekly newspaper.

3.6   The Windmill Herald

For years, *The Windmill Herald* has catered to the younger generation through a supplement published in English. The three editions (Central Canada, US, Maritimes) do not show any notable differences in content. Vanderheide was chief editor as well as publisher of these editions, with staff in Bulkley Valley, Detroit, Grandville, and Winnipeg. The three editions focus on different regions and are part of a strategy to attract more advertisers. In addition, the division results in considerable cost savings: due to the high import taxes from Canada to the United States, it was much more profitable to publish local editions in both countries. The articles are published primarily in Dutch; the articles about the Netherlands are printed in the front part of the newspaper. In some of the issues, there also is some coverage of Belgian news. Newsworthiness standards are much higher. For example, the death of King Boudewijn and the crowning of King Albert II were mentioned, but the reader does not come across any short, general interest news from Belgium. The articles about the Netherlands usually cover the relationship between it and its former colonies: after all, some of the Dutch immigrants came to Canada from one of the colonies, not from the Netherlands. Furthermore, there are news about the Netherlands in relation to the land of migration and about the Netherlands as an EU member state. In addition, there is news about traffic accidents in the Netherlands as well as anywhere else in the world when Dutch people are involved. Here we are looking at what seems to be an informative function, but also at a social function due to the "homeland ties." This is a summary of previously published articles in selected newspapers: a source or journalist is never mentioned.

---

[7] This information is based on an article in *The Windmill Herald*, January 7, 1995: 4.

Van stad en platteland in Nederland (City and countryside in the Netherlands), a five page, regular feature, is typical of this type of publication: very short articles (an average of 17 lines) without a title and using the geographical location of the event as heading. Judging from their letters to the editor, readers seem to like this feature a lot. News from the reader's native district is usually read first. This letter from reader Tom T. Montrooy[8] speaks volumes:

To receive the Windmill is always a "Red-Letter-day" for me. It perks me up, puts a smile on my face, and I anxiously devour the latest details of what's going on in my *geboorteland* (homeland). For sure I skip a lot of minor news that doesn't concern me. What do I care if a cow fell into a canal somewhere in Friesland, or a barn burned down somewhere in Zeeland. But then I suppose it might be of interest to someone.

In short, the paper has a clear social and leisure function: the news aims to surprise its readers with tidbits of information from their former country of residence. Especially remarkable are the many advertisements interspersed between the short articles. An inventory of the most recurrent advertisers results in the following list (in order of importance): shops carrying Dutch items (herring, licorice, clogs, Delft porcelain, etc.) such as *The Wooden Shoe, Dutch Delight, The Dutch Market, Holland Shopping Center, The Netherlands Bazaar*; travel agencies selling trips to the Netherlands and car rental agencies there; insurance companies and funeral homes which usually refer to their Dutch background. The advertisements brim over with wooden shoes, tulips and windmills: an image of the Netherlands a century ago. Publisher Vanderheide also capitalizes on this nostalgic trend by regularly advertising commemorative tiles featuring old Dutch engravings and translated classic sayings from the Netherlands and Belgium, printed on his own press...

The Windmill Post, an English-language supplement featuring general information about the Netherlands, can be found in the center of *The Windmill Herald*. These articles are of a documentary and human interest nature. A few letters from English-speaking readers are even published. Only in the second half of the newspaper do foreign news articles begin to appear: again, these are summaries of material taken from other publications. Remarkably, news from Belgium is quite extensive in consideration of the Belgian-Canadian readership. The resignation of Leo Delcroix and the success of the far-right Vlaams Blok (Flemish Block) can thus be found in the issues we consulted[9]. Besides international news, articles about sport and leisure activities are also included. From these features one can again conclude that the readers are not all that young anymore: such features as *Handwerkje van de maand* (Handicraft of the month) and *Tuinhoekje* (Gardening Corner) are followed by primarily European and World Championship sport news. Additional pages include

---

[8] This passage is an excerpt from the letter of Tom T. Montrooy in *The Windmill Herald*, January 7, 1995: 14.

[9] We consulted the following issues of *The Windmill Herald*: Central Canada, September 7, 1993: 36 (741); US Edition, January 7, 1995: 37 (773); Central Canada/Maritime Edition, July 2, 1995, 37 (775).

The Little Windmill, a classified ad page, and *The Family Page* filled with announcements of births, engagements, weddings, birthdays, and jubilees.

In short, *The Windmill Herald* is not different from the other immigration press publications: the current news and information functions are completely absent. What is left is human interest and social-cultural information: homesickness for the homeland is the central theme.

IV   DISCUSSION

In conclusion, we can compare Canada with other Anglo-Saxon countries which are similarly considered to be popular immigration countries for the Flemish and Dutch. The United States has the longest history with regard to Dutch-speaking immigrants. Consequently, the oldest publications by and for Flemish and Dutch immigrants can be found there. These publications originated in a time when audio-visual media and communication methods were rather limited or even nonexistent. As a result, the level of newsworthiness of these newspapers was quite high in the beginning. They were after all the sole news channel for most of the newly arrived immigrants, especially regarding news from the "homeland." These publications lost this superior level of newsworthiness as soon as the audio-visual media began its irrepressible advance and the financially stronger native press in the United States became able to acquire technically superior equipment for the gathering and distribution of news.

In the course of time, the newspapers themselves have nevertheless undergone very little change. The layout has remained more or less the same and now looks outdated. As for news gathering, no positive change can be seen. The first newspaper received their news by mail or by telegraph. In the nineties, news gathering was still done by mail but no longer on the basis of direct sources. Volunteers select and compile news from the newspapers they read themselves. As most of the publications published by Dutch-speaking immigrants gather their news in this manner, we can generalize the loss of the current and topical news function. The more recent newspapers –we could call them the "post-AV (r)evolution" newspapers – were founded after the arrival of radio, television, and fast information transmission technology. These newspapers often seem no more than a mouthpiece for the social life of the Dutch community abroad. A prime example is *De Nieuwe Amsterdammer* (The New Amsterdammer), which publishes articles based on selected news from Belgian and Dutch newspapers and through a professional editorial team located in New York.

De Nieuwe Amsterdammer, founded in 1990 and the youngest newspaper geared toward Dutch-speaking immigrants in North America, is an independent publication based in New York. At a party held on the occasion of *Koninginnedag* (Queen's Day) at the *New Yorkse Nederlandse Club* (the New Yorker Dutch Club), Eleonore Speckens, the owner of the *Euronet* translation agency on West 39th Street, announced she wanted to publish her own newspaper. For this project she appealed to Benno Groeneveld, journalist at the Tros (Dutch public television broadcasting company), as well as the Dutch World Broadcasting Service and a number of professional magazines, as well as Yolanda Gerritsen, correspondent for Vara, Veronica, Avro, and VRT (Dutch and Flemish television broadcasting companies). Despite the enthusiasm of the journalists, the project was plagued by problems precisely because of their profession. The first official launch was canceled when President Bush announced the start of the Gulf War and the journalists had to rush off to cover the event. The second editorial meeting was also interrupted by President Bush, this time announcing the end of the Gulf War. Nevertheless, *De Nieuwe Amsterdammer* has been a success in more ways than one. According to Benno Groeneveld, this is because there are no other publications for Dutch people living in New York. There is a Dutch club, but it only accepts a certain class of members. The Dutch language broadcasts could be a binding factor within the community, but Groeneveld (Kagie, 1991: 30) disagrees: "...no one listens to them, would you believe I don't either, even though I work for them (...) in Australia, Canada and New Zealand, the Dutch immigrants all have their own newspapers."

In Canada there have been changes very similar to those in the United States. Here, a press made by and for immigrants also emerged early on. The objective of the publications was to pass on news from the homeland and to serve as a mouthpiece for immigrated Dutch and Flemish people. Nevertheless, Flemish people in Canada seem to be loyal readers of the *Gazette van Detroit*. The success of this Flemish newspaper in the United States has consequently never been equaled by another Flemish publication in Canada. On the other hand, the Dutch side boasts *The Windmill Herald*, *De Hollandse Krant* and *De Nederlandse Courant*. The latter is currently thriving thanks to the leadership of chief editor T. Luykenaar. It nevertheless faces a problem of aging readership. In order to remedy this phenomenon somewhat, the newspaper has gradually embraced the English language. This gradual change was also discussed in detail in reference to the *Christian Courier*, which is now published only in English and thus has renounced its origins completely.

During the early immigration days, we saw that both in the United States and in Canada the Dutch-speaking migrants had a real need for social clubs and, to a smaller extent, their own newspapers. Clubs such as these helped them tackle their legal and financial problems: the Flemish and Dutch migrants were after all hard workers who had yet to master the English language and who had hardly any formal education. The social dimension of these clubs originated precisely in this group bond: as soon as the immigrants had solved their financial problems and had more leisure time available, they turned to their clubs for all types of extracurricular activities. This led to the establishment of even more clubs, and therefore to a need for a new type of ·newspapers.

Let us now take a fifty-year leap back in time to the migration wave of Dutch-speakers to Australia and New Zealand: folk dance groups, theater companies and carnival organizations were founded right at the very beginning. We can therefore state that what was happening in the United States and Canada with regard to immigration at the turn of the century took place in Australia and New Zealand in the fifties. This also had a clear impact on social life and the publications of the Dutch-speaking immigrants in Australia and New Zealand: after all, the clubs and newspapers in the United States and Canada were founded during an era in which audio-visual media and communication methods were still very limited or even nonexistent.

In Australia as well as in New Zealand, the immigrants had various means available for obtaining news from the "homeland" or for communicating with it. There the clubs and publications had a different purpose: fostering a kind of micro-community within the adopted country. Besides, a clear distinction was made between Flemish and Dutch immigrants. This distinction also provides the answer to the question as to why the Flemish, in comparison with the Dutch in the United States and Canada, are more active with regard to their press and social life in Australia and New Zealand. Even though this kind of proposition is hard to prove, we suspect that the national character of the Dutch and the Flemish had something to do with it. Immigrated Flemish people tend to stick together during periods of difficulty and then to spread out without a trace, to anglicize their names, etc. In other words, the "we-feeling" rapidly disappears and makes room for complete integration in the new land. In any case, the immigrants who left at the end of the last century were forced to emigrate. The alternative was to become a victim of hunger and unemployment. Those Flemish people who emigrated later on – especially to Australia and New Zealand because of the migration quotas in the United States and Canada – choose another country of their own free will, thereby ensuring fast integration. On the other hand, the Dutch immigrants are more chauvinistic and consequently more conservative: they will not pass by any opportunity to celebrate the Queen's Birthday, the Prince's Birthday, Saint Nicholas, etc. with their fellow Dutchmen. Such activities are best organized within the framework of club life; in turn, these clubs can best present themselves by way of publications. Precisely because of the differences in national character, it is difficult to find a Dutch language publication which is geared towards both Flemish and Dutch immigrants. *De Nieuwe Amsterdammer* in the United States has been the most successful in this respect, at least as far as coverage is concerned. The title most likely appeals more to the imagination of the Dutch than to that of the Flemish.

Throughout the years, Dutch language newspapers have begun to look a lot like one another, regardless of their original purpose. One of the most noticeable, joint characteristics in the idealization of the mother country where time seems to have stood still. The general image of Flanders and the Netherlands in the newspapers is fifty to one-hundred years old, and heavily idealized: mills, tulips, farms, fields, and clogs are invariable part of the landscape. Another remarkable phenomenon is the use of the Dutch language. In the oldest newspapers, there seemed to be enough input from Flanders and the Netherlands to somewhat maintain certain linguistic standards. English was added in order to expand the readership – that is, to appeal to the second generation. This step inevitably led to a gradual but irreversible "Anglicization" of the newspaper, an occurrence which is discussed in depth in the section on the *Christian Courier*. On the other hands, for those publications which did not have much contact with the mother country but were published in Dutch, the transition to English happened gradually and – at least for the publisher – unnoticed. The Dutch as used in such newspapers no longer evolves along with the Dutch spoken in Flanders and the Netherlands: it sounds outdated, with the understanding that "anglicized" Dutch is awfully similar to antiquated Dutch.

Nevertheless, with the exception of *De Nieuwe Amsterdammer*, "Anglicization" has been irresistible. When speaking with or writing to us, most of the editors admitted that their newspaper had only a few more years to live, or at most the number of years the editors themselves will live. In short, the future of the Dutch migrant press is grim indeed. This threat to the newspapers is not only due to the lack of Dutch-speaking readers: this is a problem that could be solved by a transition to the English language. There is also the matter of content quality, which could be strongly improved, among other things through greater direct input from Flanders or the Netherlands. This could be encouraged by an awareness campaign in the Flemish and Dutch media sponsored by the Flemish and Dutch governments and aimed at the Dutch language press elsewhere in the world. However, the main problem remains the fact that in addition to having lost the use of the Dutch language, the current generations are no longer interested in their roots.

References

Anonymous (1994a). Dutch-Canadian-Association Ottawa Valley, *The Link News*, January 1: 1.

Anonymous (1994b). Vlamingen in de Wereld (Flemish in the World), *Vlamingen in de Wereld* 7: 20.

Anonymous (1995). The Windmill, *The Windmill Herald*, January 7: 4.

Deleu, J. (Red.) (1994). *The Low Countries, Arts and Society in Flanders and the Netherlands. A Yearbook 1994-1995*. Rekkem: Ons Erfdeel.

Kagie, R. (1991). Krant voor de Nederlander in New York, *NRC-Handelsblad*, July 19: 30.

Verthé, A. (1974). *Vlaanderen in de Wereld*. Brussels: Reynaert.

Witvoet, B. (1985a). The Canadian Calvinist years: 1945-1954, *Calvinist Contact*, September 13: 3.

Witvoet, B. (1985b). Two years of Contact: 1949-1951, *Calvinist Contact*, September 13: 5-7.

Witvoet, B. (1985c). The man John Vellinga, *Calvinist Contact*, September 13: 9.

Witvoet, B. (1985d). Calvinist-Contact in the fifties: 1951-1959, *Calvinist Contact*, September 13: 11-5.

Witvoet, B. (1985e). The Farenhorst years: 1959-1976, *Calvinist Contact*, September 13: 17-21.

Part Three
Canada from a Native Perspective

NUNAVUT: A CHALLENGE FOR THE INUIT

by Cornelius H.W. REMIE

I   INTRODUCTION

In this chapter some of the major transitions currently taking place in Canada's Northwest Territories will be explored. In 1999 the eastern part of the NWT will become a separate territory named *Nunavut*, which in the Inuit language (*inuktitut*) means "Our Land". The decision to create this territory was made in 1993 when representatives of the Inuit of the Central and Eastern Canadian Arctic and the federal government in Ottawa reached a final agreement on a landclaim after 17 years of negotiations.

This landclaim, also called *Nunavut*, was first filed in the early seventies, a period that witnessed increased White encroachment upon the Canadian Arctic. What preceded the claim in the early postwar years were: the militarization of the area through the establishment of large defense systems, the construction of permanent settlements, and the introduction of welfare colonialism. When major megaprojects that would affect their habitats and lifestyles were being considered, the Inuit people reacted against the radical transitions they were forced into. In their reaction, the Inuit focused on claims to native lands and demanded self-government. Initially the Canadian government only wanted to discuss Inuit title to what it considered to be Crown lands. Only when the process of constitutional renewal got on its way, did the claim to self-government become a serious point of discussion, the creation of a new territory being the outcome.

The 1999 establishment of the Nunavut Territory seems to fulfill a lot of Inuit dreams, but will it bring the future they hoped for, a future that will make them masters of their own destiny? Before I try to answer this question, I will first give a brief historical backgrounder on the development of Inuit-White relations. Then, I will focus on the post-war period which brought the Inuit sedentarization and welfare colonialism. Following a brief description of the landclaims and self-government movements, I will focus on the challenges that face the Inuit of *Nunavut* as the third millennium draws near.

II   HISTORICAL BACKGROUNDER[1]

The Inuit have inhabited the Canadian arctic for over 4,000 years. As the last wave of migrants to cross the Bering Strait, they soon spread over the arctic regions of North America and reached Greenland as early as 2,000 BC. Adapting themselves to life in the arctic coastal regions, they developed a nomadic lifestyle characterized by a winter adaptation to the sea-ice and a summer adaptation to the land. Survival depended

---

[1] This historical backgrounder is an abbreviated version of Remie (1993).

heavily upon a thorough knowledge of the arctic environment, sophisticated technology and elaborate patterns of collaboration, and mutual sharing. Hunting and fishing in small egalitarian family groups and bands, they lived a life that was adapted to the vagaries of nature.

Following initial contacts with Vikings who traveled the coastal areas of Labrador and Newfoundland a thousand years ago, the Inuit were – from 1576 onwards – increasingly exposed to explorers who were searching for a Northwest Passage to Cathay. Contacts with explorers were short-lived and had relatively little direct impact, but these contacts opened the door to a new breed of visitors to the arctic: the whalers and the fur traders.

Whaling in the Eastern Canadian Arctic started early in the 19th century. Whaling centers were located in Pond Inlet, Cumberland Sound, Hudson Strait, and in the north-western part of Hudson Bay. In the latter region, the heyday of whaling was the period between 1860 and 1870. In these areas whaling initiated the transition to dependency and caused a sharp decline in population as a result of the introduction of contagious diseases (Boas, 1888: 425-6). In the Western Canadian Arctic commercial whaling started comparatively late, in 1889 only, and boomed around 1894/95. It lasted for only fifteen years, but its effects on the local population were even more devastating than in the Eastern arctic.[2]

Hudson's Bay Company (HBC) fur traders penetrated the Canadian arctic early this century, when whalers were leaving for the southern hemisphere. Establishing its first trading post in 1911 in Chesterfield Inlet on the west coast of Hudson Bay, the HBC soon secured a monopoly in the trade and quickly established an impressive network of trading posts: during the heyday of fur trapping in arctic Canada – the 1925-1929 period – the HBC operated no less that 217 trading posts at 139 locations in the North-west Territories (Usher, 1971: 28). As the HBC exploited the trapping capabilities of its Inuit customers, the latter became increasingly dependent upon the HBC for the supply of basic commodities. Lured into the consumption of western goods, Inuit trappers soon found themselves caught in a web of obligations from which there was no escape.

The trapping of fur animals fundamentally upset the native hunting economy and led to total dependence. This became dramatically clear in 1929 when the fur trade collapsed, destroying what was left of the Inuit economy and turning the Inuit into virtual wards of the Hudson's Bay Company (Jenness, 1968: 25). Missionaries, who had come to the Canadian arctic in the wake of the fur traders[3], stepped in and gave a

---

[2] Diamond Jenness (1968:10) characterizes the impact of whaling in the Western arctic as follows: "In far northern Alaska, and in the Mackenzie River delta which adjoins it to the east, whaling crews left behind an Eskimo population reduced by European diseases and alcohol-promoted disorders to barely one-tenth of its earlier number, a population so demoralised that even today it has not recovered its pre-European virility".

[3] The Oblate Fathers established their first mission post in Chesterfield Inlet in 1912, a year after the

helping hand. They were assisted by the constables of the Royal Canadian Mounted Police who had come to the North in 1903.[4] However, the magnitude of the problems they faced was of such scope that their efforts were insufficient. When the Second World War broke out, the Inuit were a destitute people, impoverished and subject to all kinds of privations.

III   THE COLD WAR AND THE INTRODUCTION OF WELFARE COLONIALISM

The Great Depression and the years of World War II were difficult years for the Canadian arctic. Pre-occupied with solving economic problems in the South, the Canadian government in Ottawa almost forgot its North. It only woke up to its responsibilities after World War II. When US-Soviet relations deteriorated and developed into a cold war, Canada moved north. Within the context of NATO it agreed to the building of a Distant Early Warning line (DEW-line), a chain of radar stations to protect the North-American continent from a surprise attack from the north. The construction of the DEW-line sites started in Canada in 1952. By 1957 most stations were completed and had become operational.

During the construction phase of the DEW-line the Canadian government became aware of the problems of its northernmost citizens. The Inuit were found living under appalling conditions, impoverished and highly dependent on Hudson's Bay trading posts for their livelihood. Epidemics of polio and of tuberculosis had raged through the high Arctic in the late 1940s and early 1950s and had taken a heavy toll. The Canadian government reacted quickly and without hesitation. It developed a number of crash programs to improve living conditions in the North and to prepare the Inuit for their incorporation into the mainstream of Canadian life. A lot of time and energy and a seemingly inexhaustible amount of money were spent to achieve this goal. Ottawa's intentions may have been good, but its policy resulted in sheer paternalism and tutelage. What Ottawa eventually established in the Arctic, then, was a regime of "welfare colonialism."[5]

To raise standards of living, to "civilize" the Inuit, and to better administer social services, the Canadian government built permanent coastal settlements – twenty-eight in ten years – and the Inuit were forced to come live in these government-created villages (Billson, 1990; Coates & Powell, 1989: 10). The price the Inuit had to pay for

Hudson's Bay had opened a fur trading post there. As a rule, the founding of new mission posts followed the opening of HBC trading posts throughout the Canadian arctic.

[4] Although Canada claimed sovereignty over its present northern lands as early as 1874, it did nothing to enforce it. In 1903, however, when the Norwegian Sverdrup Expedition (1898-1902) which had claimed parts of the northern archipelago, and the presence of large numbers of American whalers in the Beaufort Sea and north-western Hudson Bay posed a threat to its sovereignty, the Canadian government established police posts at Herschel Island and Cape Fullerton. In the beginning, main tasks performed by the RCMP were keeping the peace among the drunken and fighting whalers and collecting customs from foreign whaling captains.

[5] For an analysis of welfare colonialism in the Canadian arctic, see Paine (1977).

reaping the benefits of western "civilization" was extremely high as a few examples will illustrate:

- The size of the new permanent settlements was such that too many hunters were concentrated in too limited an area. As a result, hunting spoils diminished which, in turn, led to increasing dependency on the welfare support provided by Ottawa's civil servants.
- To better administer the North, Canadian authorities initiated Project Surname which was to introduce family surnames in the arctic. The project was carried out in great haste and so many mistakes were made in issuing birth certificates that many Inuit got confused and felt they were losing their identity.[6]
- The new settlements were considerably larger in size than the largest traditional social units the Inuit had been familiar with, i.e. the winter camp. Traditional forms of leadership and social control were not attuned to these conditions. As a consequence, social life became disrupted considerably.
- Introduction of education alienated Inuit children from their parents. In the new schools they were taught subjects that did not relate at all to the everyday experience of northern life, let alone the traditional culture of the Inuit. The transmission of traditional survival knowledge was discontinued. As a consequence, the younger Inuit generation was no longer able to live off the land and it became dependent on wage-employment or its alternative, welfare.
- Life in the new permanent settlements required skills which the Inuit, lacking formal training and education, at first did not have. After they had acquired such skills, chances for employment still remained poor, because of the reluctance of White employers to hire Inuit labour. The resulting massive unemployment led to demoralization, apathy, and indifference to education.

Robbed of their personal identity, forced to leave familiar hunting grounds, put up in a strange house in a strange community of a size never before experienced, and constantly bossed around and reprimanded by White civil servants, the Inuit soon found themselves living a life that was regulated by southern "total institutions," a life heavily subsidized by welfare payments, pensions, family allowances and other social service payments (Billson, 1988: 304). The resulting alienation led to complete uprooting for the Inuit.

Characteristic of Ottawa's administration of the Canadian North was a total lack of political vision, at least until the beginning of the 1970s. A development policy was formulated only after large quantities of oil and natural gas were discovered on the Alaskan North Slope in 1968 and expectations had risen that large reserves of non-renewable resources also existed in the adjacent Mackenzie Valley delta and the Arctic archipelago. In March 1972 the Federal Cabinet presented the *Canada's North 1970-1980* plan, that set the priorities for Northern development: first people, then the environment, and after that economic development (Dosman, 1975: 98-9). In practice, these political priorities were implemented in reverse order.

---

[6] For a full description of Project Surname and its consequences, see Alia (1994).

Exploration activities boomed after the Yom Kippur war of 1973 and the ensuing Arab oil boycott. As the industrial lobby in Ottawa gained strength and momentum, the government caved in and started giving out licenses for mineral exploration and exploitation. Several megaprojects such as the Mackenzie Valley Pipeline Project, the High Arctic Pipeline Project (that would connect Cornwallis Island to either Québec or Manitoba), and the Arctic Pilot Project (the shipping of natural gas and oil from the High Arctic to southern Canada by way of mammoth submarines) a were being planned. In Québec, the *Quiet Revolution* had led to the James Bay Hydroelectric Development Scheme, which was to inundate large stretches of land of arctic and subarctic Nouveau Québec. Opposition against this technological megalomania was organized and it was then, in the early- and mid-1970s, that the federal government in Ottawa met with strong resistance on the part of the Inuit, who protested against the appropriation of their traditional lands, which they considered to be a further assault on their way of life or what was left of it.

IV   INUIT REACTIONS: THE CLAIM FOR LAND AND SELF-GOVERNMENT

Until the beginning of the 1970s the Canadian Inuit had reacted with resignation to the many changes that were forced upon them. Structurally weak leadership and no notion of being a people account for this. Only after young Inuit had gone through the Southern Canadian schooling system and had become familiar with white political institutions, did the sense of Inuit peoplehood awaken. When Southern pressures on the North increased, this grew stronger and took institutional form. Native organizations, such as the Committee for Original People's Entitlement (COPE-1969), the Inuit Tapirisat Canadami (ITC, established 1971), the Northern Québec Inuit Association (NQIA, established 1972), and the Labrador Inuit Association (LIA, established 1973) were founded. Their major aims were: the preservation of the Inuit language and culture, the promotion of a sense of dignity and pride in the Inuit heritage, and the achievement of full Inuit participation in Canadian society. Though ITC and other Inuit organizations presented themselves as non-profit, non-sectarian, non-political organizations, they were from the very start involved in political action, claiming large stretches of land from the government in Ottawa. Emphasis on land claims resulted from a number of land use conflicts[7] that occurred in the early 1970s, the period of the so-called "resource boom." Inuit organizations reacted by taking legal action to prevent resource exploitation or to postpone it until after they had been able to claim traditional lands and get these claims settled.

The first Canadian Inuit to settle a land claim were the Inuit of Northern Québec. Represented by NQIA, they were engaged in the lengthy negotiations that accompanied the James Bay hydroelectric project. Together with the Grand Council of the Crees, the leaders of the Northern Québec Inuit Association signed the James Bay

---

[7] Land use conflicts typical of the epoch involved mostly Inuit hunters and white seismic crews searching for natural gas and oil. For a good description of such conflicts, see Hackman & Freeman (1978).

Convention on November 11, 1975. Under this convention, the Inuit obtained financial compensation of Cdn$90 million, ownership of approximately 8,400 square kilometers of land and exclusive hunting, trapping and fishing rights in an area of approximately 86,000 square kilometers.[8]

The Inuit living in Canada's Northwest Territories, represented by Inuit Tapirisat Canadami, presented a comprehensive land claim to the Federal government in Ottawa on February 26, 1976. The claim aimed at the founding of a Nunavut Territory where the Inuit, through numbers and voting power, would be in charge for the foreseeable future. Also, the Inuit would have strong control over hunting, trapping and fishing, and they would hold surface title to at least 650,000 square kilometers of lands and waters, giving them a large land base and better control over what happened with regard to resource development. In short, what ITC wanted to achieve was self-government for the Inuit of the Northwest Territories. However, the Canadian government refused to discuss the political demands of ITC. Giving in to these demands would have far reaching constitutional consequences and the Canadian government was not ready yet to engage in such a discussion. But opposition against ITC's claim not only came from the Canadian government. Inuit in northern settlements, also opposed the claim and criticized ITC for "selling out" communities. As a result, Inuit Tapirisat had to withdraw the claim in the same year. In December 1977 it presented a new version of the Nunavut land claim,

Briefly after ITC had withdrawn its initial land claim, the Inuit of the western Canadian Arctic, represented by the Committee on Original People's Entitlement (COPE), presented their own claim, entitled *Inuvialuit Nunangat*, to Ottawa. This was done in May 1977 at a time when the option to build the Mackenzie Valley Pipeline was still open. Following the Berger Inquiry[9], a ten year moratorium on the construction of this pipeline was issued. In the fall of 1978 negotiations between COPE and the Federal government had proceeded so far that an agreement in principle could be signed. After that negotiations stopped for a while. They were resumed in 1982 and, in March 1984, COPE and Ottawa reached a final agreement. The final agreement provided the Inuit of the western Arctic with a financial compensation of Cdn$67.5 million in 1977 dollars, legal title to about 91,000 square kilometers of land and exclusive hunting, trapping and fishing rights in this area and in the Crown Lands of the Inuvialuit region. All this was granted in return for the surrender of Inuit interests in approximately 344,000 square kilometers of land and adjacent offshore islands and waters (Canada, 1984). Like the James Bay Convention, the Inuvialuit Final Agreement only settled a legal dispute over ownership of the land.

---

[8] Of this convention Cumming (1977: 33), legal advisor to the Inuit, wrote: "The James Bay settlement fails in dealing with the two essential requirements in a land claims settlement. On the one hand, it fails to do anything significant to effectively preserve the traditional identity. (...) On the other hand, the settlement does not provide a mechanism to bridge the people into the new identity of the emerging industrial society in Arctic Québec".

[9] For a full description of the Mackenzie Valley Pipeline Inquiry, see Berger (1977).

It said nothing about the political rights of the Inuit as an aboriginal people. These rights were dealt with in another forum: the process of constitutional reform.

The process of constitutional renewal got underway after 1982, when the Canadian constitution was repatriated. In various sections of the 1982 Constitution reference is made towards the existence of aboriginal rights.[10] These rights, however, were not identified and defined. This was the task of a series of Constitutional Conferences in which the Prime Minister of Canada and the First Ministers of the provinces, as well as representatives of the aboriginal peoples participated. Under the Trudeau government constitutional conferences were convened in 1983 and 1984. The approach to aboriginal rights taken during these conferences came to be known as a "Top-Down" approach. This approach opted for the entrenchment of a constitutionally guaranteed right to self-government, followed by negotiation at the federal and provincial level as to how the principle is to be interpreted in detail. Constitutional conferences held under the Mulroney government in 1985 and 1987 took a "Bottom-Up" approach to the problem of aboriginal rights. This approach favoured constitutional entrenchment of the aboriginal right to self-government after definition of this right at the local, provincial and federal levels. The former approach did not work because of the unwillingness of the western provinces to deal with the matter in a "top-down" way, while the latter was rejected by the aboriginal peoples.

In 1987, when the 4th FMC failed, the Meech Lake controversy further deteriorated the relationship between native Canadians and federal and provincial governments. The proposed Meech Lake Accord was an attempt to reconcile the political aspirations of Northerners and the political objectives of the Anglophone provinces with a view to bringing Québec into the constitution. The Meech Lake "betrayal", however, could not halt the process set in motion by the constitutional process, and new attempts were made to redefine the relationship between the Canadian Government and the aboriginal peoples. This was done during the Canada Round of Constitutional renewal which led to the Charlottetown Agreement of 28 August 1992. This unanimous agreement, a package deal, contained an important paragraph on self-government. It stipulated that self-government is an inherent right of Canada's Aboriginal peoples and this right would be entrenched in the Canadian Constitution. Furthermore, it stipulated that "governments and Aboriginal peoples would be constitutionally committed to negotiating agreements that would set out how the inherent right would be implemented (Canada, 1992: 6). The fate of the Charlottetown agreement is known. On October 26, 1992, it was rejected by a 54.2 percent majority of the voters.

During the process of constitutional renewal the Canadian government and the Tungavik Federation of Nunavut (which represented ITC at the negotiating table) continued their negotiations over the Nunavut land claim. In 1990 they reached an agreement-in-principle and a final agreement was signed and ratified by the Inuit in

---

[10] See section 15 (subsection 2), section 25 (subsection 1), section 35 and section 37 of the Canadian Constitution.

1992. Under this agreement the Inuit in the Nunavut settlement area would acquire the following rights and benefits:

- title to approximately 350,000 square kilometers (136,000 square miles) of land, of which 35,257 square kilometers (14,000 square miles) include mineral rights;
- equal Inuit representation in government on a new set of wildlife management, resource management and environmental boards;
- the right to harvest wildlife on lands and waters throughout the Nunavut settlement area;
- capital transfer payments of Cdn$1.148 billion, payable to the Inuit over 14 years;
- a Cdn$13 million Training Trust Fund;
- a share of federal government royalties for Nunavut Inuit from oil, gas and mineral development on Crown lands;
- where the Inuit own surface title to the land, the right to negotiate with industry for economic and social benefits from non-renewable resource development;
- the inclusion of a political accord that provided for the establishment of the new Territory of Nunavut and through this a form of self-government for the Nunavut Inuit.

However, by far the most important clause in the final agreement was the one in which the federal government of Canada committed itself to introducing legislation into Parliament pertaining to the creation of a Nunavut territory and a form of self-government for the Inuit of Nunavut.

Inuit leaders were afraid that the rejection of the Charlottetown Agreement would put the discussion about aboriginal self-government on the back burner, but the federal government lived up to its promises. On May 25, 1993, Prime Minister Brian Mulroney, Minister of Indian Affairs and Northern Development Tom Siddon, Northwest Territories Government Leader Nellie Cournoyea, and Tungavik Federation of Nunavut president James Eetoolook, formally signed the Nunavut final agreement (Canada, 1993: 1). To ratify the *Nunavut Final Agreement*, the Federal Government of Canada introduced two pieces of legislation into Parliament, the *Nunavut Land Claims Agreement Act* and the *Nunavut Act*. Both acts received Royal Assent on June 10, 1993. Both came into force on July 9, 1993.

V   IMPLEMENTING THE NUNAVUT FINAL AGREEMENT

Under article 37 of the Nunavut Final Agreement the *Nunavut Implementation Panel* was established. This panel, which includes one federal government representative, one representative of the government of the Northwest Territories, and two representatives of the Nunavut Tunggavik Incorporated[11], has to oversee and provide leadership of the implementation of the Nunavut Final Agreement, to monitor the

---

[11] Nunavut Tunggvik Incorporated (NTI) succeeded the Tungavik Federation of Nunavut as the corporation representing the interests of the Inuit people of Nunavut. It was incorporated on March 15, 1993.

implementation of the Implementation Plan and the development of the Implementation Training Plan, and to attempt to resolve any dispute that might arise between designated Inuit organizations and government regarding the implementation of the Nunavut Final Agreement (Implementation Panel, 1994: 11-2). Although a statutory body, the Implementation Panel has had a marginal role so far, as panel members from the very beginning have struggled with the nature and scope of the Panel's mandate (Implementation Panel, 1994: 12).

Far more important has been the role played by Nunavut Tunggavik Incorporated (NTI), which represents the Inuit of the Nunavut Settlement Area and which has as its main task "to jointly manage, with the Department of Indian Affairs and Northern Development, the various public boards (...) to be created within two years following the enactment of the Nunavut Land Claims Settlement" (Légaré, 1994: 17). These boards are: the Nunavut Wildlife Management Board, the Nunavut Planning Commission, the Nunavut Impact Review Board, the Nunavut Water Board, and the Surface Rights Tribunal. These boards are government institutions that regulate and manage renewable and non-renewable resources in the Nunavut Settlement Area. As instruments of government their decisions are legally binding. This has a direct bearing on the operations of the future Nunavut government. Légaré (1994: 17) has described this in following terms:

> (....) According to the Political Accord, Nunavut will be a public government and will hold the same jurisdiction as those already held by the Northwest Territories at the time of the signing ceremony (i.e. October 30, 1992). This means that the Nunavut Territory will have the same powers enjoyed by the provinces, except that it will not hold title to any land ownership, and might not therefore benefit financially from natural resource development. In fact, the land in the Nunavut Settlement Area ... will be owned either by Nunavut Tunggavik Incorporated (i.e. Inuit owned lands: 18 percent) or by the Federal government (i.e. Crown lands: 82 percent). Therefore, the Nunavut government might have no legislative authority over non-renewable resources (e.g. oil, mining) and might not get any share in royalties from development (e.g. Lupin, Nanisivik and Polaris mines). Also, since the public boards will be established well before any Nunavut government institutions (i.e. by 1995) this could give to these co-management boards added legitimacy in solely managing the Nunavut lands for years to come and in ignoring the priorities of the Nunavut public government in economic development.

These public co-management boards will not be the only ones with direct influence on the economic development policies of the future Nunavut government, Nunavut Tunggavik Incorporated, too, can affect such policies through the Nunavut Trust which manages the Cdn$1.17 billion capital transfer that comes with the Nunavut Final Agreement. The Nunavut Trust is responsible for protecting the money and investing it. The interest from the trust funds will be used to generate social and economic programs which are beneficiary to the Inuit (Légaré, 1993: 55). Examples of such programs are the recently established Nunavut Hunters Support Program which supplies financial assistance to hunting families, and the Small Business Assistance Program (NTI, 1995: 15). Under the aegis of Nunavut Tunggavik Incorporated, a host of other organizations and committees are involved in the planning of a Nunavut-wide economic development strategy. They do so to safeguard the interests of the beneficiaries of the Nunavut Land Claims Settlement, i.e. the Inuit, but at the same time this can lead to a power struggle with the future Nunavut public government, which not only represents the interests of the Inuit, but also of the non-Inuit residents of Nunavut. To avoid this, a close consultation process will be necessary between Nunavut Tunggavik Incorporated and the Nunavut Implementation Commission, which is preparing the establishment of the future Nunavut territory and government. What the level of preparation is to date, and what challenges the future Nunavut government will have to meet, will be discussed in the next paragraph.

VI   PREPARING FOR NUNAVUT: IDEAS AND CHALLENGES

The Nunavut Implementation Commission (NIC), an all-Inuit commission whose mandate is to prepare the establishment of the Nunavut territory and government, started its work in January 1994. Following a long process of public consultations NIC issued in March 1995 a report entitled *Footprints in New Snow*. This report addresses a great number of issues, the most important, being the structure of the future Nunavut government and the selection of a capital city for the future Nunavut territory.

According to NIC, the Nunavut Government should consist of a democratically elected Legislative Assembly with no fewer than 16 and no more than 24 members (NIC, 1995: 19) and the election of the first Nunavut Legislative Assembly should take place in May 1999 (NIC, 1995: 20). How the Legislative Assembly would function is left open in the report. In Nunavut there should be only two levels of government – territorial and communal – according to the NIC; no intermediate regional level is deemed necessary. The Nunavut government should also be highly decentralized. Use of new communications technologies could revolutionize the electronic delivery of government services to remote locations (NIC, 1995: 55). With respect to the Nunavut civil service, NIC emphasizes that Inuit participation in new government employment in Nunavut should reflect the demographic realities of the new territory (NIC, 1995: 45-6).[12] In order to achieve this, special attention should be given to the training of Inuit people for employment in the Nunavut government.

A considerable part of the report of the Nunavut Implementation Commission is devoted to the matter of selecting a capital city for the future territory, a matter that the NIC describes as "one of the most challenging ones" (NIC, 1995: 47), since much social prestige and considerable economic benefits are involved. In all, six communities expressed their interest in becoming a capital. Following considerable

---

[12] In Recommendations #6-8, NIC (1995: 47) states that "all planning proceed from an understanding that, at a minimum, Nunavut Government employment as of April, 1999, (should) be 50 percent Inuit by way of (1) overall composition, and (2) occupation of senior management positions".

analysis[13], the NIC believed that Cambridge Bay, Iqaluit, and Rankin Inlet best met the criteria used in the analysis. After much politicking and lobbying behind the scene, NIC presented its report *Choosing a Capital* at a press conference in Iqaluit on July 7, 1995, and announced that Iqaluit would be the best choice (Bell, 1995: 7).

In concluding my remarks on *Footsteps in New Snow*, a report which focuses on formal structures rather than on political substance, a few words should be said on what the Nunavut Implementation Commission perceives to be the major challenges for the future Nunavut government. In its report, NIC acknowledges that social and economic circumstances of Nunavut communities are not really healthy. NIC points at rather dim economic prospects and resulting social traumas, but expresses the hope that the Nunavut Agreement and the establishment of a Nunavut government will change the economic climate, and thus help remedy these social pathologies. NIC is optimistic about the effect of the Nunavut Agreement and the establishment of a Nunavut territory and government[14], but one can question whether such optimism is warranted. A quick glance at the major challenges the future Nunavut government will face may indeed put a big question mark behind NIC's optimism.

The first of these challenges is a demographic one. As in many Third World countries, population dynamics in Nunavut may seriously undermine whatever progress is made. The rate of increase of the Inuit population is more than twice that of Canada as a whole. In 1987 about 17,500 Inuit lived in the Nunavut Settlement Area.[15] NIC expects this figure to have risen to about 22,500 by April 1, 1999, an increase of almost 30 percent in twelve years (NIC, 1995: appendix A-6.2). A further characteristic of the Inuit population in Nunavut is the over-representation of the young in the population: in 1991, 39 percent of the Nunavut population was under 15 years of age (vs. 21 percent for the whole of Canada). The consequences of these demographic realities are considerable. As Irwin (1988: 37) has pointed out, there will be a high demand for work and a greater need for housing. Today, housing is already considered a very serious problem in Inuit communities as revealed by a study undertaken by the

---

[13] This analysis was made on the basis of following factors: existing infrastructure and amenities; potential for additional infrastructure, services and amenities; existing and potential transportation links within Nunavut and outside Nunavut; cost of living in the community; position/accessibility within the overall circumpolar region; attitude of the population of the community, taking into account its social, cultural and economic priorities; the extent of regional support; and climate (NIC 1995: 68).

[14] NIC (1995: 61-3) argues that the Nunavut Agreement creates investor confidence, makes Nunavut "open for business", and makes many economic ventures attractive to the Inuit. It will contribute positively to the development of the tourism sector, and supply the Inuit with new economic opportunities deriving from the opening up of new parks and conservation areas. NIC has high expectations with respect to the exploitation of non-renewable resources, referring in particular to the considerable mineral potentials of the Keewatin and Kitikmeot regions and the proven natural gas reserves in the Sverdrup Basin. NIC also points out that the Nunavut Agreement anticipates Inuit employment opportunities in the public sector, and the decentralization of the future Nunavut government can bring public sector jobs to the depressed communities.

[15] These figures have been calculated on the basis of figures provided by Robitaille & Choinière (1987: 28).

Inuit Women's Association in 1990 (Pauktutit, 1990, table 1.a)[16]. Given the present demographic trends, this situation will become worse (GNWT, 1989: 35). The trend towards smaller families and the increasing occurrence of incomplete nuclear families will also result in a higher dependency upon support from the state (Irwin, 1988: 37). Increased dependency on social assistance will in turn lead to "individualization of poverty and the undermining of the collective and traditional patterns of helping, sharing and co-operation centered on interconnected kinship systems" (Shewell & Spagnut, 1995: 41). Altogether, demographic trends in Nunavut are likely to put the developmental process under extremely high pressure. For the process to succeed, much will depend upon the economic prospects for Nunavut.

Economic prospects for Nunavut are gloomy as the report of the Special Committee on the Northern Economy of the Northwest Territories Legislative Assembly revealed in 1989. The report classified 46 out of 61 communities in the Northwest Territories as underdeveloped. The underdeveloped communities are as a rule small in size, have relatively poor links with the outside world, have a low labour force participation rate, have a high unemployment rate, have low educational levels and a very limited private sector (GNWT, 1989: 22-3). As the report points out, to maintain the current low level of employment 2,789 additional jobs have to be created by the year 2001 to keep up with the population increase. Bringing unemployment in the underdeveloped communities at the level prevalent in the developed communities would mean the creation of 5,757 new jobs by the year 2001; and if employment rate and labour force participation rate were to be equalized, 11,396 new jobs would have to be created by the year 2001 (GNWT, 1989: 25). With a limited potential to create new jobs, other than those which are government related, the report projects increasing levels of poverty.

Since 1989, when the Scone report was published, the situation has not changed very much. Unemployment figures are extremely high and in terms of jobs not much relief can be expected from the creation of the Nunavut bureaucracy. The Nunavut Agreement will generate no more than 40 new jobs to fill the ranks of the public management boards[17] and the creation of the Nunavut government will generate

---

[16] Table 1 (a), Community Concerns: Percentage Rating, lists following issues as *a problem* or *a serious problem:*

Alcohol abuse	89.7%
Drug abuse	92.5%
Solvent abuse	82.5%
Suicide	77.7%
Housing	92.5%
Unemployment	100.0%
Lack of recreation activities	82.0%
Poverty	78.9%
Family Violence	89.7%
Child sexual abuse	73.6%
Accidents	50.0%

[17] See Canada & TFN (1993), Schedule 4: Budget Estimates for Institutions of Public Government,

approximately 600 jobs in the public sector (NIC, 1995: 30). Considerable expansion of the private sector, as hoped for by NIC, need not be expected. Renewable resource development projects, highly subsidized by the Canadian Government, have largely failed as a result of international actions (such as the European Community's fur ban) and as a result of cultural factors (defective management due to the inability or unwillingness to give "orders," an attitude which is valued negatively in Inuit culture).[18] And large-scale development of non-renewable resource extraction is not to be expected in a Canadian economy that is subject to fundamental restructuring. In conclusion, Nunavut's economy will be characterized by high levels of unemployment, by poverty, and by high levels of government subsidization and welfare dependency.

An important factor that contributes to the high unemployment rate is the low level of schooling amongst the Inuit. The Scone Report notes that the school drop-out rate in the Northwest Territories is very high and the success rate in completing grade 10 is about 20 percent for the Inuit, a figure that results in a high level of functional illiteracy (GNWT, 1989: 36). Apart from a high drop-out rate, the level of schooling is as a rule below standard.[19] Deficient education among the Inuit population not only diminishes their chances for economic development, when the non-native population consistently benefits more from the educational process, poor levels of education among Inuit can also lead to what Irwin has called "structural racism" (Irwin, 1988: 44).

Poor levels of education, high levels of unemployment, poverty, high levels of government subsidization and welfare dependency will create severe tensions in Inuit society and the outcome may be a an even more deteriorated social climate than we have now. Socially, present day Inuit society shows all signs of uprootedness. A very high proportion (probably over 50 percent) of the adult native population is on welfare. It is destructive of individual and community integrity and self-respect, and leads to serious social pathologies (Franks, 1993: 8). The rate of alcohol abuse is frightening (Coates & Powell, 1989: 15-6), as is the rate of drug abuse.[20] The "hidden crime" of child neglect and spousal assault is on the increase (Rasing, 1994: 232-3), and the teenage suicide rate is of crisis proportions (Coates & Powell, 1989: 16). As to the latter, the Royal Commission on Aboriginal Peoples dedicated a special report to this

---

part 1: 1, part 2: 1, part 3: 1, part 4: 1, and part 5: 1.

[18] Non-involvement in someone else's behavior is one of the basic tenets of Inuit culture. It is based on the assumption that the adult Inuk is a person who has reached the state of *isuma* (reason) and therefore knows how to behave. Any comment on his or her behavior, let alone ordering someone to carry out a specific task, is valued negatively. For a good example of non-involvement, see Birket-Smith (1959: 52-3).

[19] Irwin (1988: 42) reports that tests carried out in the Keewatin district indicated that "Inuit entering adult education programs (...) tested, on average, 2.4 grades lower than their grade achieved in school". In turn, "poor levels of education produce high rates of failure in all training programs in the Arctic".

[20] According to Rasing (1994: 230), in Igloolik estimated drug use is 40 to 60 percent among individuals aged 12 to 40, while drug use is estimated at 70 to 80 percent of individuals in the 16 to 30 age group. These figures may well be representative of drug abuse in the entire Nunavut area.

phenomenon in which it stated that "suicide is clearly one of the most urgent problems" (Royal Commission, 1995: ix). How urgent a problem it is, is demonstrated by the figures: Inuit suicides are 3.9 times as high as the national average in Canada (Muir, 1991: 40) and the suicide rate is expected to increase in the coming 10 to 15 years (Royal Commission, 1995: 18).

VII   PROSPECTS FOR THE FUTURE

On the basis of the grim realities as outlined above, Irwin (1988: 41) states that "if current trends continue most of the Inuit living in the Arctic in the year 2025 will be second generation wards of the state whose society, economy and culture may have more in common with an urban slum than with the life of their grand parents." To overcome these problems he suggests that strong federal leadership is required (Irwin, 1988: 51). This may have been good advice at the time he wrote his report, but in the meantime the Nunavut land claim has been settled and the Inuit have now taken over the leadership in the developmental process in Central and Eastern Arctic. In this process there will be no place for any White tutelage, this time the Inuit want to solve their problems themselves. Under the present conditions of euphoria over the settlement of the Nunavut land claim, Inuit leaders may at times seem over-confident in what they may be able to accomplish. But self-confidence is exactly what is needed now, as it is the necessary basis for finding creative answers to the many challenges facing them. As the Inuit have always been very resourceful in overcoming adverse conditions, there is no reason to doubt that they will be able to do so this time. And though present conditions are indeed adverse, the general political setting is favourable: the Royal Commission on Aboriginal Peoples has recently issued its final report in which it proposes a 20-year agenda for change and renewal of the long troubled relationship between Aboriginal and non-Aboriginal peoples. The agenda focuses on action in four areas: healing of individuals, families, communities and nations; economic development; accelerating development of human resources; and institution building (Royal Commission, 1996: 133-6). The Royal Commission has shown that not implementing this agenda and maintaining the status quo will be a costly affair, not only in terms of human pain and misery, but also in terms of economic loss to Canada (1996: 139-40). No federal, provincial or territorial government in Canada can therefore afford to ignore the Royal Commission's agenda, and this is a completely new fact in the history of Aboriginal-White relations. For the Nunavut Inuit, this new reality may well be a key factor in overcoming the odds.

References

Alia, V. (1994). *Names, Numbers and Northern Policy. Inuit, Project Surname, and the Politics of Identity.* Halifax: Fernwood Publishing.

Bell, J. (1995). The commission's choice, editorial in the July 14 issue of *Nunatsiaq News:* 7.

Berger, Th. R. (1977). *Northern Frontier – Northern Homeland: The Report of the Mackenzie Valley Pipeline Inquiry.* Ottawa: Department of Supply and Services Canada.

Billson, J. (1988). Social change, social problems, and the search for identity: Canada's northern native people in transition, *The American Review of Canadian Studies* 18 (3): 295-316.

Billson, J. (1990). Opportunity or tragedy: the impact of Canadian resettlement on Inuit families, *The American Review of Canadian Studies* 20 (2): 187-218.

Birket-Smith, K. (1959). *The Eskimos.* London: Methuen.

Boas, F. (1888). The Central Eskimo. *Sixth Annual Report of the Bureau of American Ethnology to the Secretary of the Smithsonian Institution 1884-'85.* Washington: Government Printing Office.

Canada. Government of Canada (1984). *The Western Arctic Claim: A Guide to the Inuvialuit Final Agreement.* Ottawa: Department of Supply and Services.

Canada. Government of Canada (1992). *Our Future Together. An Agreement for Constitutional Renewal.* Ottawa: Minister of Supply and Services.

Canada. Government of Canada (1993). *Formal Signing of Tungavik Federation of Nunavut Final Agreement. Department of Indian and Northern Affairs,* Press Release of May 25.

Canada & TFN (Government of Canada & Tungavik Federation of Nunavut) (1993). *A Contract Relating to the Implementation of the Nunavut Final Agreement between the Inuit of the Nunavut Settlement Area as represented by the Tungavik Federation of Nunavut ("Inuit") and the Government of Canada, as represented by the Minister of Indian Affairs and Northern Development ("Government of Canada") and the Government of the Northwest Territories as represented by the Minister responsible for Intergovernmental and Aboriginal Affairs ("Territorial Government").* Ottawa: Department of Indian and Northern Affairs & Tungavik Federation of Nunavut.

Coates, K. & Powell, J. (1989). *The Modern North. People, Politics and the Rejection of Colonialism.* Toronto: James Lorimer & Company.

Cumming, P.A. (1977). *Canada: Native Land Rights and Northern Development.* Copenhagen: IWGIA Document 26.

Dosman, E.G. (1975). *The National Interest. The Politics of Northern Development 1968-75.* Toronto: McClelland and Steward Ltd.

Franks, C.E.S. (1993). *The Public Service of Nunavut.* Paper presented at the 11th Biennial Conference of the Association for Canadian Studies in the United States (ACSUS), New Orleans, November.

GNWT (Government of the Northwest Territories) (1989). *The Scone Report: Building Our Economic Future.* Yellowknife (NWT): Legislative Assembly.

Hackman, L. & Freeman, M.M.R. (1978). A land use conflict on Bathurst Island, Northwest Territories. In L. Müller-Wille, P.J. Pelto, L. Müller-Wille & R. Darnell (eds.), *Consequences of Economic Change in Circumpolar Regions* (pp. 235-49). Edmonton: Boreal Institute for Northern Studies.

Implementation Panel (1994). *Annual Report on the Implementation of the Nunavut Land Claims Agreement*. Ottawa: Department of Indian Affairs and Northern Development.

Irwin, C. (1988). *Lords of the Arctic: Wards of the State*. Ottawa: Health and Welfare Canada.

Jenness, D. (1968). *Eskimo Administration, V: Analysis and Reflections*. Montréal: Arctic Institute of North America Technical Paper 21.

Légaré, A. (1993). Le projet Nunavut: bilan des revendications des Inuit des Territoires-du-Nord-Ouest, *Etudes/Inuit/Studies* 17 (2): 29-62.

Légaré, A. (1994). *The Process Leading to a Land Claim Agreement and its Implementation. The Case of the Nunavut Land Claim Settlement*. Paper presented at CAG 94, May 20, Wilfrid Laurrier University, Waterloo (Ontario).

Muir, B.L. (1991). *Health Status of Canadian Indians and Inuit – 1991*. Ottawa: Minister of National Health and Welfare.

NIC (Nunavut Implementation Commission) (1995). *Footprints in New Snow: A Comprehensive Report from the Nunavut Implementation Commission, the Department of Indian Affairs and Northern Development, Government of the Northwest Territories and Nunavut Tungavik Incorporated Concerning the Establishment of the Nunavut Government*. Iqaluit: Nunavut Implementation Commission.

NTI (Nunavut Tunggavik Incorporated) (1995). A Message from Jose A. Kusugak, Special Report on Nunavut, Supplement to the June 9 issue of *Nunatsiaq News*: 15.

Paine, R. (ed.) (1977). *The White Arctic. Anthropological Essays on Tutelage and Ethnicity*. St. Johns: Institute for Social and Economic Research, Memorial University of Newfoundland.

Pauktuutit, Inuit Women's Association (1990). *A Community Perspective on Health Promotion and Substance Abuse. A Report on Community Needs in the Northwest Territories, Nunavik, Québec and Northern Labrador*. Ottawa: Pauktuutit.

Rasing, W. (1994). *"Too Many People". Order and Nonconformity in Iglulingmiut Social Process*. Nijmegen: University of Nijmegen.

Remie, C.H.W. (1993). Changing contexts, enduring relations: Inuit-white encounters in Northern Canada 1576-1992, *European Review of Native American Studies* 7 (2): 5-11.

Robitaille, N. & R. Choinière (1987). *Projections de la population inuit du Canada par Norbert Robitaille et Robert Choinière pour les Affaires indiennes et du Nord Canada*. Montréal: Université de . Montréal.

Royal Commission on Aboriginal Peoples (1995). *Choosing Life. Special Report on Suicide among Aboriginal People*. Ottawa: Minister of Supply and Services Canada.

Royal Commission on Aboriginal Peoples (1996). *People to People, Nation to Nation. Highlights from the Report of the Royal Commission on Aboriginal Peoples.* Ottawa: Minister of Supply and Services Canada.

Shewell, H. & A. Spagnut (1995). The First Nations of Canada: social welfare and the quest for self-government. In J. Dixon & R.P. Scheurell (eds.), *Social Welfare With Indigenous Peoples* (pp. 1-53). London: Routledge.

Usher, P. (1971). *Fur Trade Posts of the Northwest Territories 1870-1970.* Northern Science Research Group, Report 71-4. Ottawa: Department of Indian Affairs and Northern Development.

TELEVISION BROADCASTING NORTH OF 60[1]

by Lorna ROTH

The development of Canadian First Peoples' media policies, discourses, and practices is an important subject to examine toward the end of the twentieth century as aboriginal self-government comes closer to a negotiated consensus than ever before. First, there has been a restructuring of the Canadian broadcasting system to include aboriginal broadcasting as an integral element. Second, First Peoples' broadcasting lobbies have influenced the development of new mediating structures in Canada such as policy frameworks, a new broadcasting channel (Television Northern Canada), more open access arrangements with existing channels, and funding programs. Third, First Peoples' broadcasters have used television as an emancipatory tool. They see television as a vehicle for social and cultural action, for education, and for building national identity.

The use of media as a tool for self-empowerment in Canada is historically grounded within the approach of John Grierson, the first Commissioner of the National Film Board, and its now defunct Challenge for Change Program. It is within this tradition of using the media as a process tool rather than as an end product that First Peoples have set themselves the challenge of innovatively using broadcasting in an alterative fashion (Roncagliolo, 1991: 207), as a vehicle of transformation. Two kinds of transformations are the subject of First Peoples' television broadcasting history; first, the ways in which television has been used to reinforce indigenous languages and cultures and to build and promote stronger cultural and national identities; second, the negotiation of a national status for aboriginal broadcasting within Canadian legislation.

As television producers and broadcasting administrators have become leaders in Northern community and cultural life, their reshaping of the public media has enabled new forms of producer/community audience relationships to develop. These are different from those which generally exist within large metropolitan areas. Rooted as they have been in socio-cultural movements focused on broadcasting rights, First Peoples have turned to the networks of those organizing and receiving Northern and, more recently, Southern media to culturally, socially, and politically align their diverse communities with one another. Finally, given that Canada's Northern broadcasting infrastructure has been recognized, to date, as the most advanced aboriginal broadcasting system in the world, First Peoples' media initiatives, such as those described in this essay, can provide insights into the ways in which other Fourth

---

[1] This essay is an updated and corrected version of a chapter published in Holmes, H. & Taras, D. (eds.) (1996). *Seeing Ourselves: Media Power and Policy in Canada.* Second Edition. Toronto: Harcourt Brace and Company Canada, Ltd.: 173-91.

World[2] communities might chart the courses of their broadcasting development. First Peoples' demand for government financial and regulatory support for native-controlled broadcasting and for fairer portrayal and employment practices has resulted in a new, more inclusive public discourse. In the last two decades, increased access to indigenous (and ethnic) voices in public broadcasting systems has helped to reformat the international image of Canada as a state which supports its multicultural and multiracial discourses. The potential and actual roles that indigenous and other minority group communications have played in the process of Canadian self-definition have become highly valued, as Marc Raboy (1990a: 8) has observed:

> In Canada, a multiplicity of less-than-national, less empowered identity groups have struggled for recognition of their interests against the dominance of a one-dimensional Canada, and it is in fact their efforts that have maintained the Canadian difference against the overwhelming forces of continental integration in North America.

Through the opening up and management of (cross)cultural discursive spaces and mass-mediated public spheres in the North, First Peoples are combining the forces of post-modernity with their own particular cultures. This process has taken three decades and a dedicated commitment by First Peoples broadcasters and lobbyists. The result of their work has been the legal recognition and acceptance of aboriginal voices within the Canadian public and private broadcasting spheres, as integral participants in the developing fabric of a pluralistic community of communities – Canada.

I   THE CANADIAN NORTH

The North as a general category has been geographically defined by Louis-Edmond Hamelin, a well-known Québécois geographer, as being North of the 60th latitude line. Hamelin divides the North into three categories or zones. The first is called the "Middle North": the northern areas of the ten provinces, Labrador, and much of the Yukon where road access is possible (Hamelin, 1979: 332-3). Beyond the Middle North lies the "Far North", which takes in "mainly the Northwest Territories and corresponds in part to the Arctic climate", and the "Extreme North," which consists of the "Northern part of the Arctic archipelago".

Mythical notions of the North have made powerful inroads into the Canadian imagination. The symbolic North has been imagined and defined predominantly in

---

[2] Coined by Cree author George Manual, founding president of the World Council of Indigenous Peoples:

> The 4th [sic] World is the name given to indigenous peoples descended from a country's aboriginal population and who today are completely or partly deprived of their own territory and its riches. The peoples of the 4th World have only limited influence or none at all in the nation state [in which they are now encapsulated]. The peoples to whom we refer are the Indians of North and South America, the Inuit (Eskimos), the Sami people [of northern Scandinavia], the Australian aborigInes [sic], as well as the various indigenous populations of Africa, Asia, and Oceana [sic](Churchill, 1992: 10).

terms of Southern interests. Since cross-cultural contact, notions of the North have been fabricated by non-natives who have talked about it, analyzed it, made statements about it, settled it, ruled it, authorized certain views of it, managed it, and even produced it for Southern and "exotic" tourist consumption.

Ideas and fictions about the North have shifted focus throughout history as various Southern-based institutions set up outpost organizations to enact mandates originating outside of the North (Valaskakis, 1979). Among these controlling agents/agencies have been the early explorers (from Frobishers' 1576 voyage onwards), the missionaries (from 1578 onwards), the whalers (beginning in the early part of the 15th century), the traders (from the 1880's), the North West Mounted Police followed by the Royal Canadian Mounted Police (since 1903), the military (US and Canadian) (from the 1940's), and finally externally-controlled broadcasting and telecommunications institutions (since the 1950's). Southern voyagers' descriptions of the North and its peoples have influenced the ways in which the idea of the North has been defined by and to populations in the South. Indeed, Hamelin and others have suggested that present-day texts still reveal an echo of Voltaire's opinion of the Northerner as "the miserable Canadian settler, squatting 'in the snow between the bear and the beaver'" (Hamelin, 1979: 1). These mediated ideas, in turn, have found their way back to the North and have had effects on Northern peoples' identities.

Images of the North have oscillated between that of the frozen wilderness, a resource-rich hinterland, and a hotly-defended cultural heartland. Part of this identity involves romancing the "Mysterious" North (Berton, 1954); part involves denigrating it. The North is often treated as a beautiful "paradise which has temporarily lost its charm" (Hamelin, 1984: 167). On the other hand, it is also characterized as "inhospitable – such beauty as is only to be experienced with the comfort of the best survival equipment" (Shields, 1991: 173). It is hard to be indifferent to the North, its peoples, and its media representations.

II   FIRST PEOPLES' TELEVISION BROADCASTING HISTORY

A little less than two percent of the Canadian population, First Peoples have been historically located outside of the Canadian national project on many levels – territorially, socially, politically, economically, culturally. Having not had access to their own means of social definition and authority until the mid-seventies, First Peoples slipped easily into the position of being "subjects," not "citizens" of history and its mediated representations. Treated in an objectified manner, their absences and stereotypical portrayals in media in the first two-thirds of the twentieth century rendered First Peoples somewhat akin to landscape imagery. They were depicted as savages, or exotic representations of the ethnographic "Other".

First Peoples' energetic participation in the media as producers only systematically began after the Anik satellite commenced live broadcasting service in the North in 1973. They soon became aware of their apparent non-existence as living and historically-evolving cultural communities. In recognizing this absence, they began to demand a presence in all aspects of media production and distribution. It was, therefore, only after the intrusion of Southern media into the North that they began to contest their exclusion from traditional Canadian social and historical narratives. They called for compensatory histories and anthropologies, ones which would fill in the gaps, highlight their experiences and perspectives, and which would transform them from being displayed as passive objects to being active subjects of history (NQIA, 1974; ITC, 1976).

Looking backward from the mid-1990's, it is apparent that First Peoples have achieved remarkable changes in their media status. One might recall that 1901 was a time in which Thomas Edison filmed several Inuit people running amongst plaster icebergs in temperatures of up to 90° Fahrenheit for the amusement of visitors at the Buffalo exhibition (Raymont, 1981: *Magic in the Sky*[3]). Today, almost all of the 13 Northern regional Native Communications Societies produce 20 hours of radio and at least 4 hours of television weekly – from a native perspective. This, along with other Northern-theme programming, is distributed within the 13 Northern regions via Television Northern Canada, a Pan-Northern dedicated satellite service which commenced in 1992 and which broadcasts 100 hours of Northern-oriented programming per week to 94 Northern communities. In 1995, TVNC applied for permission from the CRTC (Canadian Radio Television & Telecommunications Commission) to be placed on the list of eligible channels to be picked up by cable operators in the South. In November of 1995, approval was granted, and recently several cable operators in the West have integrated TVNC in their signal packages. TVNC is also available on an off-air basis to those who own satellite dishes because its signal is not scrambled.

III   PHASES OF NORTHERN FIRST PEOPLES' TELEVISION BROADCASTING

Northern indigenous broadcasting has moved through several organizational phases. At first, aboriginal Peoples had very little opportunity to represent themselves. This was followed by a second stage characterized by protests and attempts to seize control by bypassing or ignoring federal regulatory procedures. Emergent from this was a growth period in which they gained access to a fairly broad range of media vehicles and federally-sponsored projects (i.e. radio, television, and community video) for their self-representation. More recently, First Peoples have gone beyond portraying themselves to their immediate communities. They now represent themselves to other native and non-native audience members. For instance, First Nations broadcasting initiatives are using new satellite distribution arrangements to redefine technology-access and cultural relations among themselves and between several of the Native Communications Societies, provincial broadcasters, and CBC's Newsworld audiences.

---

[3] Film cited by Peter Raymont, Director (1981). *Magic in the Sky*. NFB and Investigative Films Production.

3.1   Phase I – Early Northern Broadcasting: First Peoples' Representations by Outsiders

When CBC public radio was transplanted into the North in 1958, it presented itself as a fairly open medium to which First Peoples turned for cultural information about their own lives in the North. Partly because of lower costs, and because the technology is simpler, the languages and content of radio were tailored to the information needs of listeners. Emphasis was on local and national news, weather, road and flying conditions, flood and fire warnings and personal messages, such as health reports on relatives who were hospitalized down South (Government of Canada, 1965: 190). Native staff were recruited and trained in radio production techniques, and quickly reached managerial positions within the CBC Northern Service. The presence of a thriving radio service in the North set the context for the arrival of television. Accustomed to listening to relevant messages that conformed to their information needs, Northern residents expected a television service which would do likewise.

The early demand for television in the North did not come from the permanent native population, whose basic information needs required other kinds of communication facilities: telephone, trail radio, and community radio in their native language were high on their priority lists (NQIA, 1974; ITC, 1976). Rather, television broadcasting facilities in the North were developed in settlements that were of military, economic or administrative significance to the South and were introduced for two dominant reasons: to stabilize transient Southern work forces in Northern mining towns and to visibly/audibly demonstrate Canadian sovereignty in the North. Local native populations were not consulted by the CBC in its decision to expand service. Indeed, the federal authorities bypassed First Peoples entirely because they did not yet constitute a formidable lobby group.

In 1967, the CBC introduced the "Frontier Coverage Package" (FCP) to seventeen Northern remote communities.[4] The FCP was designed to be a temporary, pre-satellite television system, making use of reliable, inexpensive and easily-available videotape technology. It consisted of a "four-hour helical-scan videotape recorded in the South and bicycled on a one, two, three or four-week delay basis to various locations in the North for playback over local television transmitters" (CBC Northern Service, 1978a: 3). Programming for the Frontier Coverage Package consisted of a cross-selection of Southern programs, geared toward children's, teens' and adults' presumed interests. Although the CBC approved native-content programming in principle, no financial accommodation was made for the inclusion of native-language programming. Nor were relevant Northern subjects given particular importance in the schedule.

The establishment of a domestic satellite policy for Canada in the late sixties (1968-1969) and the launching of Anik A-1 in 1972 precipitated a new phase in First Peoples development in the North. In 1973, the satellite became operational, bringing telephone service, live television, and radio broadcasting to the same seventeen

---

[4] No plans for the addition of FM radio service developed until 1974.

communities hitherto receiving the Frontier Coverage Package. In 1974, the Accelerated Coverage Plan was approved, carrying live television to all Northern and remote communities with a population of 500 or more. In most cases, these communities were anxious to receive programming. In some (Igloolik in the Baffin region and in Northern Québec Inuit communities), there was reticence, framed by discussions of the right to cultural privacy. Josepi Padlayat, then Communications Officer for the Northern Québec Inuit Association, for instance, protested the disruption to community priorities that would be brought by foreign Southern broadcasting (1974). Padlayat had become aware of communications research, documenting the negative impact of Southern programming on Inuit culture and felt that unless there was to be a first-service in the Inuktitut language, television would act as a potent factor in eroding the culture and language of his people.

Concurrent with this protest, Southern communications researchers began to undertake longitudinal media impact studies. The gathering of data was followed by open criticism of the federal government's use of Northern television programming as an "alien culture socialization agent" (Coldevin, 1977a: 34). Native community input in the broadcast decision-making process and in the production of relevant cultural and linguistic television programming were strongly recommended as a method for mediating the potentially overwhelming impact of Southern programming (Valaskakis, 1976; Coldevin, 1977a, 1977b; Caron, 1977; O'Connell, 1975; NQIA, 1974; ITC, 1976). The establishment of production, training, and resource centers in the North and the formal encouragement of a two-way communication flow were considered necessary steps toward this accomplishment by all interested parties preoccupied with television's impact (Valaskakis, 1976; Coldevin, 1977a, 1977b).

In the process of evaluating their communication needs, First Peoples (mostly the Inuit) came to recognize that the academic data generated about media effects on individuals and cultural communities would not provide enough fuel for desired changes within the broadcasting system. A means of engaging federal government policy-makers and bureaucrats in a critical dialogue would have to be found and initiated by First Peoples' representatives. "Bridge discourses," which would mediate the relations between the unilingual aboriginal communities and the federal government, would have to be developed.[5] "Go-betweens" – First Peoples who could speak both their own and at least one of the official languages of Canada and/or non-native "interested parties" (activists, media researchers) who were acceptable to the native community leadership – would soon begin to play a valuable bridging role. They situated themselves "between" the two worlds, attempting to knit the disparate discourses of governmental regulatory policies and native cultural concerns together (Fraser, 1989: 11).

---

[5] The term "bridge discourse" comes from the work of Nancy Fraser (1989).

3.2   Phase II – The Impact of Lobbies on Northern Television Development

Two Inuit organizations played critical roles in researching and publicizing Inuit and Northern communication needs. The Inuit Tapirisat of Canada (Eskimo Brotherhood of Canada) and the Northern Québec Inuit Association worked persistently and systematically to alter federal government communications priorities in the North so that they would be more consistent with those of the Inuit themselves. Through legal and political channels, interventions at CBC/Bell Canada license application hearings at the CRTC, confrontations and negotiations with the CBC Northern Service, with the CBC's corporate management, and through publications, they promoted a new vision of Northern broadcasting. As early debates about the potential social impact of satellite communications entered the public domain, efforts to broaden and improve understanding of media applications in the North took shape in a series of projects, experiments, and field tests using conventional and satellite technology: HF two-way radio, FM radio broadcasting, portable VTR, and 16 mm. and Super 8 film. These experiments were generally designed to test the technical and social parameters of community-oriented media usage and control patterns. They represented a strategic way to provide media services to the North and became the acceptable method of mediating the divergent policy goals of the federal government (including those of the CBC) and those of the First Peoples (Roth, 1983a, 1983b).

More recent Northern media projects have generally fallen into three broad categories: (1) Field tests and experiments to test the viability of new technologies and to explore alternative forms of communications for the North [for example, the Anik-B experimental projects – Inukshuk, Naalakvik – and other media interactive media projects which took place in the seventies and early eighties]; (2) Projects designed to mitigate the potential negative effects or influences of Southern programming on native cultures (NFB film support projects of the early 1970's and a variety of community radio and television projects); and (3) Projects associated with the use of community media for organization and development purposes (community media projects) (Roth, 1983a, 1983b).

Media projects provided both the First Peoples and government sponsors with empirical data to substantiate their readiness to take on the personnel and technical management, technical and production operations, and financial accountability of full network operations. As Valaskakis and Roth observed some years ago, these projects were successful in training staff, in producing culturally-relevant, native-language programming, and in establishing the technical infrastructure to link several aboriginal communities laterally so that local residents could participate in inter-community discussions. Through federally-sponsored projects, Inuit have historically (re)constructed traditional folklore and heritage through programming which reclaims active use of native languages and promotes lived cultures ... The Northern native media project ... demonstrated their (First Peoples') competence as broadcasters to funding agencies as they met the basic communications needs in their communities (Roth & Valaskakis, 1989: 225-6). Evidence of project successes documented the point that First Peoples' broadcasting could be a legitimate undertaking and helped to chip away at government resistance toward Northern broadcasting subsidization through public funding.

3.3   Phase III – Policy-ing the North

During this period of experimentation up to the early eighties, the federal, provincial and territorial governments reacted to each new First Peoples' media challenge in an ad hoc manner. In 1980, a CRTC committee under the direction of the Vice-Chairman, Réal Thérrien, undertook an extensive Northern and remote community consultation to assess possible options and establish a set of principles to govern the "fair" expansion of television and pay-TV services in the North. The resulting report, "The 1980's – A Decade of Diversity: Broadcasting Satellites and Pay-TV," laid out a comprehensive and supportive framework for the Northern Broadcasting Policy that was to be adopted in 1983. In 1981, the Inuit Broadcasting Corporation was incorporated and licensed by the CRTC in recognition of their achievements and management potential as demonstrated in the interactive audio and video Inukshuk Anik-B satellite experiment (1978-1981). By 1982, the Applebaum-Hébert Cultural Policy Committee Report acknowledged that native peoples had gained a "special place in cultural policy" (Applebaum-Hébert, 1982: 11).

On March 10, 1983, after years of aboriginal lobbying and (in)formal consultations, the federal government announced a Northern Broadcasting Policy (NBP). This policy, the most important document in aboriginal communications development to date, elaborated five basic principles that established a significant measure of native participation in both media programming and the regulatory process:
1. Northern residents should be offered access to an increasing range of programming choices through the exploitation of technological opportunities.
2. Northern native people should have the opportunity to participate actively in the determination by the CRTC of the character, quantity, and priority of programming broadcast in predominantly native communities.
3. Northern native people should have fair access to northern broadcasting distribution systems to maintain and develop their cultures and languages.
4. Programming relevant to native concerns, including content originated by native people, should be produced for distribution on northern broadcasting services wherever native people form a significant proportion of the population in the service area.
5. Northern native representatives should be consulted regularly by government agencies engaged in establishing broadcasting policies which would affect their cultures (Federal Government News Release, 1983: 2).

The policy vehicle designed to operationalize the five principles was called the Northern Native Broadcast Access Program (NNBAP). Administered by the Department of the Secretary of State, Native Citizens Directorate (Canada), it was originally mandated to distribute Cdn$40.3 million over a four-year period to 13 regionally-based Native Communications Societies for long-term production goal of 20 hours of radio and 5 hours of television programming per week,[6] "expected" to be transmitted by either the CBC Northern Service or Cancom (a Northern satellite distribution service). NNBAP funding was provided to produce programming which enhanced native culture and the use of native languages.

Two key aspects of previous public discussions were missing from the framework of the NNBAP which rendered the policy problematic in its initial implementation phases. These included the lack of a funding allocation to provide employment training and the assumption that CBC Northern Service and Cancom would positively embrace their new distribution "expectations" without hesitation. With respect to training, it was assumed that Canada Manpower and Employment would assume the responsibility of providing money on an annual basis. This might have been a realistic expectation during the first four years, but as time wore on, as personnel changed, and as cutbacks were instituted, negotiations for this and other funding requirements became overwhelmingly difficult. The issue of adequate funding to meet the criteria of the Program's objectives remains increasingly problematic as federal budget allocations for Northern First Peoples' broadcasting continue to decrease annually.

As far as carriage of programming was concerned, the antiquated Broadcasting Act of 1968 did not obligate the CBC to comply with the CRTC expectation of donating its satellite transponder for distribution of aboriginal broadcasting. Nor did Cancom have any legal obligation to comply with the CRTC's policy statement. As a result, native broadcasters had to rely on moral suasion and "amiable negotiations" for program and scheduling arrangements.

The question of First Peoples' access to broadcasting distribution facilities was as much a moral as a political and financial one for the two networks involved. From the perspectives of CBC Northern Service and Cancom, carriage on its services involved unappealing infrastructure, schedule, and cost modifications. In view of this harsh reality, enshrinement of aboriginal broadcasting in legislation became an imperative for First Peoples. Without it, funding for training and distribution arrangement issues would remain unstable, erratic, and might eventually disappear.

As a result of these dissatisfactions and imperatives, the Northern Broadcasting Policy has been modified several times. In 1986, an otherwise positive program evaluation, undertaken by Lougheed and Associates, identified further problems with its fuzzy notions of "native culture" and "native languages," as well as its initial lack of realistic

---

[6] These figures were conceived in a study of minority languages in Europe. It was determined that in order to preserve a lesser-used language – one spoken by less than one million people (Alcock & O'Brien, 1980: 1.122), it would be necessary to broadcast in it for a minimum of 40 hours of radio and 20-25 hours of television per week, at peak viewing hours (Alcock & O'Brien, 1980: 3.120). The Alcock & O'Brien study was one to which the federal government referred in the design of the NBP and NNBAP. Obviously, the Canadian government could not afford the costs involved in such an undertaking and, therefore, reduced the number of hours for native-language broadcasting production support on the assumption that it was better to fund a portion of this amount than nothing at all.

planning around questions of training, distribution, and programming costs (Lougheed and Associates, 1986). In 1989, the CRTC undertook a study (Smith and Associates, 1989) to clarify the definition of native cultural programming. This was also in response to several private radio station management complaints (Yellowknife and Whitehorse) that the publicly-subsidized native radio station in each of the respective towns was intruding on their audience niches by playing Bruce Springsteen and Heavy Metal music, as well as by advertising in the English language. First Peoples argued that they had just as much a right to call Bruce Springsteen music "theirs" as did the private, non-native stations, and that because of budgetary constraints, it was necessary to sell advertising in English as well as the native languages. This, in addition to the other problems of NNBAP, impelled the CRTC to clarify what constituted native cultural programming and to resolve the difficulties of Northern television programming distribution.

Before the Smith inquiry was completed in 1990, the Secretary of State imposed a severe budgetary cutback on native communications funding. Federally-subsidized native newspapers (financed under another program called the Native Communications Program) were cut 100 percent; NNBAP television and radio services were chopped by 16 percent. These cuts were sharply criticized and in significant contrast to the federal government's attitude in the eighties when it had been fairly generous in its support of Northern aboriginal broadcasting. This was likely due to the impressive lobby efforts that Northern First Peoples had undertaken at the time.

There is some speculation that the cuts might also have had to do with the fact that in 1990, Elijah Harper, an aboriginal Member of the Manitoba Legislative Assembly, had refused to ratify and contributed to the defeat of the Meech Lake Constitutional Accord – the proposed new constitution for Canada. Furthermore, 1990 was the year in which a land conflict between the Mohawks of Kanehsatake and a neighbouring municipality, Oka, had begun to escalate into what would become a 78-day armed confrontation between the Mohawks, local and Québec provincial police, and the Canadian army. A native journalistic voice, documenting each of these mounting crises, would have added a very important perspective to the national debates surrounding these turning points in Canadian history. But because of financial cuts, First Peoples' journalists could not afford the costs of on-site coverage. Was this distancing and silencing process a conscious strategy on the part of federal bureaucrats or was it just an incidental part of an ad hoc decision-making process? I do not suggest a conspiratorial theory here. What I am suggesting, though, is that it is important to place the budget cuts within the overall political context.

It is interesting to note that the fiscal cutbacks of 1990 were just as much of a surprise to those administering the NNBAP and the NCP as they were to the native broadcasters themselves.[7] None of the evaluations undertaken to assess the quality of

---

[7] While in the Yukon in the summer of 1990, I interviewed a former federal bureaucrat who strongly

the Programs had ever suggested the possibility of terminating either of them. On the contrary, owing to their successes, independent evaluators had suggested fortifying them with increased budgets and a wider variety of services, if affordable.

Since the events of 1990, aboriginal peoples have commanded increased respect from federal circles. This respect, though evident in political relations, has not meant generous subsidization of media development. The effects of the cuts have been and continue to be fairly devastating. Native Communications Societies have had to lay off employees; the number of hours of production have been cut; programs have been canceled; production values have suffered in some cases. The disruption and damage caused to the relations of trust between the civil servants involved in the administration of native communications programs and the First Peoples have been immeasurable and can only be compared to the politicization effects that occurred around Chrétien's declaration of the White Paper on Indian Policy in 1969. The federally-instigated fracturing of its loyalty to what had become a commonly owned cultural and policy project reinforced an even stronger commitment on the part of First Peoples' broadcasters to figure out a way not only to diversify their funding sources, but also to expand their audiences in an effort to build both a political support group and an advertising base outside of their immediate regions.

While all of this was going on, the CRTC had been simultaneously collecting Comments on their Proposed Native Broadcasting Policy (Public Notice 1990-12), based on the results of the study undertaken by Smith & Associates, and were about to announce a new policy to the public. On September 20, 1990, toward the end of the Oka/(government) crisis, the CRTC released its Native Broadcasting Policy (Public Notice 1990-89) with a notable shift in title from what it had previously called the Northern Broadcasting Policy. Calling its new approach "flexible" and "minimalist," the Commission took into consideration the government budget cuts by relaxing its advertising restrictions on native stations as a way of augmenting their limited financial resources (CRTC Press Release, September 20, 1990). Borrowing from its Community Radio and its Broadcasting Policy Reflecting Canada's Linguistic and Cultural Diversity, the Commission clarified what it meant by an aboriginal broadcasting undertaking and native programming. It is one which is:

> owned and controlled by a non-profit organization whose board members are drawn from the aboriginal population of the region it serves. Its programming can be in any aboriginal language or in either or both of the two official languages, but should be specifically oriented to the aboriginal audience it is licensed to serve. It also has a distinct role in fostering the development of aboriginal cultures and, where possible, the preservation of ancestral languages. An aboriginal program is a program in any language directed specifically towards a distinct aboriginal audience, or a program about any aspect of the life, interests, or culture of Canada's native people (CRTC Press Release, 1990: 2).

believed that the decision to cut the budgets was made on the basis of bureaucratic and financial expediency rather than on concerted strategy.

In a community where there is more than just a native station, native broadcasters were given permission to advertise for up to an average of four minutes per hour each day with a maximum of six minutes in any given hour (CRTC Press Release, 1990). However, should the service be the sole broadcasting undertaking in a given community, all advertising restrictions were to be waived (CRTC Press Release, 1990: 1-2).

The Native Broadcasting Policy freed the notion of culture and language from its heritage containment framework and allowed for the potential development of programming based on other considerations. First Peoples were satisfied with the Native Broadcasting Policy in principle. But there were still several policy and program tasks left to achieve – the need to secure necessary program funding and the enshrinement of aboriginal communications rights within the Broadcasting Act. The former is still in danger of continuous erosion; the latter was accomplished in 1991, though representative aboriginal language rights are still not mentioned in the Act, to the disappointment of the First Peoples' lobbyists.

Legislation prior to 1991 specified that "all Canadians are entitled to broadcasting service in English and French as public funds become available" (Broadcasting Act, 7 March 1968, 16 & 17 Eliz. 2, c. 25; S.2(e)) and that the national broadcasting service should "be extended to all parts of Canada, as public funds become available." Native peoples had the right to receive programming in English and French, but not to broadcast.

Between 1968 and the passing of the present Broadcasting Act on June 4, 1991, the Northern broadcasting infrastructure has developed to include: thirteen regional Native Communications Societies in the North, CBC's Northern Service, CBC's Northern Québec Service, several private radio stations in Yellowknife, Whitehorse, and Iqaluit, 117 First Peoples' community radio stations across the country, and the TVNC dedicated Northern satellite transponder service. Aboriginal broadcasting is now addressed specifically in the Broadcasting Act, 1991, Section 3(1)(d)(iii), which states that -

> (d) the Canadian broadcasting system should:
> (iii) through its programming and the employment opportunities arising out of its operation, serve the needs and interests, and reflect the circumstances and aspirations of Canadian men, women and children, including equal rights, the linguistic duality and multicultural and multiracial nature of Canadian society and the special place of aboriginal peoples within that society...

The recent changes in broadcasting legislation mark a turning point in Canada's official recognition of collective over individual rights in broadcasting. The 1991 Broadcasting Act takes Canada's existing commitment to equality rights inscribed in the Charter of Rights and Freedoms (1982), the Multiculturalism Act, 1988, the Human Rights Act (1976-77) and the Employment Equity Act (1986) and applies it to the broadcasting field. These Equality Rights include: the right to be and express multicultural and multiracial differences, the prohibition of discrimination on the basis of race, national or ethnic origin, colour, religion, sex, age, or mental or physical disability, and the right to equitable job opportunities.

In the native broadcasting policy case, the federal government has demonstrated at least two parallel and contradictory policy tracks – that of positively responding to the aboriginal demands for broadcasting, on one hand, and that of pulling cultural funding away from aboriginal peoples on the other.

More specifically, early in the 1980's, the federal government had demonstrated its good will by financially supporting cultural broadcasting services within regions with significant aboriginal populations. On the other hand, by the 1990's, native broadcasting systems were operating smoothly and were no longer as much a priority on the federal agenda as they had once been. There were other federal concerns of greater import to those in government, such as the Meech Lake constitutional discussions, and the political/national questions about First Nations' expectations, costs, and roles within a new confederal system. Aboriginal peoples were also becoming more coherent about their demands for self-government; land claims treaties were in various stages of negotiations around the country. As communications became more sophisticated within native communities, First Peoples became more articulate about their demands on the federal, provincial, and territorial governments. They did not take the 1990 cuts sitting down and organized a national protest campaign as well as personal meetings with the Minister.

Ironically, it was the Minister himself who informed aboriginal broadcasters of what was needed – to build popular alliances in the non-native public and have them demonstrate to the government that they support native broadcasters and only then might the Minister listen to their and the native broadcasters' messages. The challenge that the Minister laid out at a meeting with First Peoples' broadcasters in March of 1990 was to be taken even more seriously than he expected. Indeed, activities with this goal in mind had already begun, under his eyes, in the late eighties, when one of the Native Communications Societies, Northern Native Broadcasting, Yukon had struck an arrangement with CBC's Newsworld for its half-hour program "Nedaa" to cross over the cultural and regional borderlines on a weekly basis, targeting an "imagined" Southern audience, interested in Northern First Nations issues and entertainment. Television Northern Canada was also in the works, preparing for their launch in 1992, with the eventual possibility of becoming a third national television service in the near future.

3.4   Phase IV – Emergent Trends in Northern First Peoples' Television Broadcasting

The essence of broadcast technology is its capacity to cross great distances. In Canada, in the past, state communications policies and regulations have restricted the number of broadcast licenses and their audience reach because of competition over scarce resources. Government broadcasting policies and programs have supported native projects and licensed undertakings which were intended for local community or regional broadcasting only. In no case within any of the existing Northern broadcasting policies has there been an exception to this restrictive principle until 1988. This was the year in which the federal government allocated Cdn$10 million to a national consortium to research and begin organization of a Pan-Arctic satellite channel distribution service. There is still no nationally-received aboriginal broadcasting service. Television Northern Canada, subsidized by federal funding, serves its 94 target communities in the North exclusively. A national cross-cultural audience reach was unforeseen in official policies or funding formulae for Northern Broadcasting Services. This has been because local and regional priorities have taken precedence in the context of Northern cultural development objectives for the obvious reason that, until local and regional strategies are in place, national considerations would not be paramount.

Recently, several factors have shifted the 13 regional Native Communications Societies' perceptions about the potential for national broadcasting. First, regional native audiences are fairly satisfied with their aboriginal services, as documented in the mandatory Native Communications Societies' surveys every few years. Second, a multiplicity of channels are becoming available through more sophisticated technology offered by signal compression. Finally, having become aware that "the institutions and processes of public communication are themselves a central part of the political structure and process" (Garnham, 1986: 37), professional native broadcasters have realized that their audience reach has never depended on technologies available to them and control of access to technology depended on government financing, government Ministers and private capital investors. With new satellite technologies and increased pressure on the communications industry for multiplication of its services, it is no longer possible for politicians and regulators to argue that there are too few frequencies available to allow for an expansion of native broadcasting. Thus, because of technological flexibility, it is now feasible to consider that an undertaking of any size, if financially viable, may broadcast its service to any local and regional or nation-wide audience. The potential is there for First Peoples to develop trans-regional networks that could influence a wide range of native and non-native audience members.

Television Northern Canada, the vehicle that could fulfill this objective, is the North's primary distribution system. Operationalized on January 21, 1992, it spans five time zones and covers an area of over 4.3 million square kilometers. Broadcasting a selection of television programs from seven Native Communications Societies, as well as CBC Northern Service, Government of the Northwest Territories (N.W.T.), Yukon College, and Kativik School Board of Northern Québec, TVNC is an exemplar of Pan-Arctic cross-cultural broadcasting. Broadcasters, as well as audiences, can see and evaluate their own and others' programs on a scheduled basis, thus having access to a variety of cultural productions originating from outside of their specific regions. The quality and range of program subjects carried by TVNC is impressive. Wrapped around with Broadcast News and weather reports supplied by Environment Canada, programs from each of the contributing Native Communications Societies and governmental entities cover cultural, political, social, and economic topics targeted at a diversity of age groups. National Film Board films are screened as are other acquired independent productions; documentary and children's programming are distributed and local soap opera-like segments are popular. In the "most appreciated" category is the Inuit Broadcasting Corporation's "Super Shamou" feature, which has become compelling viewing to youngsters and adults alike across the North. A blend of the South's Superman and the North's Magic Man, or Shaman, Super Shamou wears a cape, winks at the audience, and flies in the skies above Iqaluit on Baffin Island, overseeing the moral behaviour of the town's residents. Like Clark Kent, he intervenes when he sees someone about to get into or make trouble for him or herself. The Super Shamou segments are fascinating broadcasting strips, showing a way in which Inuit broadcasters have indigenized a social "comic" narrative of North American popular culture – to make it more relevant and appealing to Northern aboriginal viewers.

In general, TVNC's programs are fairly sophisticated from all of the contributing entities. Unfortunately, however, many remain accessible only to those who speak the program producers' language. To directly address the issues of narrowcasting, there are tentative plans to subtitle native programs so that language will not remain a barrier to comprehension of content for TVNC's network-wide audience and, eventually, for a Canadian national audience. Due to budgetary constraints, however, this option remains unaffordable at the moment, although steps in that direction are being carefully considered.

3.5   Cross-cultural Implications of TVNC

Television Northern Canada has already had the occasion to bring together an audience of native and non-native viewers that spans the Arctic. This fact, in itself, has enormous implications regarding the possibility of influencing the development of common public opinion trends. Moving South through carriage by provincial broadcasters, CBC Newsworld, and by cable operators will expand TVNC's potential to become an active participant in national dialogues. In the future, should money become available, international Fourth World connections may further extend possibilities for TVNC to become a key opinion-maker on a more global scale.

I believe that the extension of TVNC into the South is motivated by First Peoples' recognition that in order for them to maintain a stable presence within Canadian broadcasting and Canadian society, they must expand their influence by constructing new social, political, and cultural alignments. They are aware that using media as a tool for identity and nation-building might not be adequately empowering if there is not also a venue through which to address issues of broader (Canada-wide) common interest to a wider audience. In the words of George Henry, one of the founders of Northern Native Broadcasting, Yukon and former President of Television Northern Canada:

> We have to have the ability to give our messages a modern-day voice by our own people in order to promote and effect social change such as the misconceptions that Canadians have about the aboriginal people in terms of their languages, cultures, and customs. If you look at the last ten years, Indian people have been fighting to change the minds of the Canadian middle class or the middle ground. They're not really dealing with the politicians. They're not really dealing with the ethnic communities. They're trying to change the views of the middle ground in Canadian society. They've carved out their allies and that's where communications comes in. The more understanding and education you give people, the more tolerant a society you have (Personal interview with George Henry, August 7, 1990).

There are interesting and important, though yet unacknowledged, ramifications when minority broadcasters gain access to nation-wide audiences. Native Communications Societies' audience reach beyond the range of its own cultural and linguistic communities, planners argue, may provide multiple opportunities to disseminate otherwise inaccessible information, while at the same time persuading, lobbying, electronically constituting regional/Pan-Arctic or national publics, and building cross-cultural bridges and social alignments.

Despite federal financial cutbacks, aboriginal broadcasters have the symbolic support necessary for the extension of their Northern broadcasting services beyond their immediate regions, i.e. the 1991 Broadcasting Act, Southern Audience Interventions during Northern license hearings. Presence within mainstream broadcasting menus in the South, as promised in the 1991 Broadcasting Act, will, no doubt, provide First Peoples' broadcasters with the potential for influencing Southern-based public opinion about current and strategic aboriginal issues and decisions, but this will not be easily achieved, given the present financial climate.

Funding is clearly the key challenge. Ideas for fund-raising have included the development of a native broadcasting lottery, the creation of a fund based on a Southern cable service tax to subsidize Northern program production, the establishment of a Native Broadcasting Program Fund, such as that of Telefilm Canada (MacPherson & Campbell, 1993), and control over the establishment of the information highway services to the North. To date, none of these ideas have been approved or pilot-tested. Consequently, First Peoples' television producers north of 60, deprived of secure long-term funding, must plan their futures on Canadian airwaves without much economic confidence.

IV   THE SYMBOLIC DEMOCRATIZATION OF THE CANADIAN BROADCASTING SYSTEM

Gaining control over the production and distribution of their own cultural products through local and regional venues has involved First Peoples in negotiations with various levels of civil servants, cabinet ministers, and outsiders with common interests. As a consequence, indigenous peoples have introduced a level of cultural diversity and complexity to the bureaucratic process, unforeseen by most within the state apparatus. This has had the positive impact of assuring that governmental discourses on cultural and racial pluralism have actually been taken seriously and are reflected in the making and implementation of important decisions regarding native broadcasting.

The enshrinement of aboriginal broadcasting in the 1991 Broadcasting Act does not end this narrative. The Northern case goes beyond redress of imbalances and oppression to something like national self-determination. First Peoples are seeking a new place within the confederation of Canada. They are seeking a new social contract, a reconfiguration of power relations in Canadian society – a recognition that they, too, are founding nations.

Insofar as this manifests itself in communications spheres, it tells us that what First Peoples are essentially seeking is a national status, as opposed to a cultural status. In broadcasting, it has not been enough to enshrine communication rights in legislation, while leaving aboriginal broadcasters on the financial and political peripheries of Canadian society. First Peoples want to be integral to the national media scene. They want a Canada-wide (inclusive of the North and South) national aboriginal service, complementary to the French Radio Canada and the English CBC – a central and financially-stable presence on a nation-wide basis (MacPherson & Campbell, 1993).

What might a national First People's channel mean in actual terms? For instance, would some view such a development as the institutionalization of "media reservations"[8], or would it be viewed as a positive development on par with CBC French and English broadcasting of Radio Canada throughout the entire country? A great deal more thinking and research is needed on what it might mean for Fourth World frontier nations to achieve such a status in Canada and in other countries which "encompass" their peoples.

Seeking a national media status in broadcasting parallels First Peoples' political movements in self-government, territorial and environmental rights, among others. It goes beyond a repairing mode of thinking, i.e. repairing the damages of colonialism, and represents a national self-affirmation. It calls for the recognition of First Peoples as *national*, not just cultural *citizens*.

---

[8] This term was suggested by Thierry Le Brun.

References

Alcock, A. & O'Brien, T. (1980). *Policies to Support Radio and Television Broadcasting in the Lesser Used Languages of the European Community* (Consultative Draft). Northern Ireland: University of Ulster.

Applebaum, L. & Hébert, J. (1982). *Federal Cultural Policy Review Committee. Summary of Briefs and Hearings.* Ottawa: Minister of Supply and Services (Department of Communications).

Berton, P. (1954). The Mysterious North, *MacLean's Magazine*, 15 November: 11-19.

Berton, P. (1975). *Hollywood's Canada: The Americanization of Our National Image.* Toronto: McLelland and Stewart.

Caron, A. (1977). *The Impact of Television on Inuit Children's Cultural Images.* Paper presented at the International Communications Association Conference. Berlin.

Canadian Broadcasting Corporation (1978a). *Background and Historical Mileposts in the Operations of CBC Northern Service.* Ottawa: CBC Northern Service.

Canadian Broadcasting Corporation (1978b). *The CBC – A Perspective: Submission to the CRTC in Support of Applications for Renewal of Network Licenses.* Ottawa: CBC.

Churchill, W. (1992). I am indigenist: notes on the ideology of the fourth world. *Z Papers* 1 (3): 8-22.

Coldevin, G.O. (1977a). Anik I and isolation: television in the lives of Canadian eskimos, *Journal of Communication* 27 (4): 145-53.

Coldevin, G.O. (1977b). *Developmental Effects of Television via Satellite on Canadian Inuit Heads of Households.* Research Paper. Montréal: Concordia University, June.

Canadian Radio Television & Telecommunications Commission (CRTC) (1979). *Decision 79-320. Renewal of the CBC's Television and Radio Network Licenses*, April 30.

CRTC (1980). *The 1980's – A Decade of Diversity: Broadcasting Satellites and Pay-TV. Report of the Committee on Extension of Service to Northern and Remote Communities.* Ottawa: Canadian Government Publishing House.

CRTC (1985). *A Broadcasting Policy Reflecting Canada's Linguistic and Cultural Diversity. Public Notice 1985-139*, July 4.

CRTC (1989). *Review of Northern Native Broadcasting: Call for Comments. Public Notice 1989-53*, May 26.

CRTC (1990a). *Native Broadcasting Policy. Public Notice 1990-1989*, September 20.

CRTC (1990b). *Review of Native Broadcasting – A Proposed Policy.* Public Notice 1990-12, February 2.

CRTC (1991). *Decision CRTC 91-826. Television Northern Canada Incorporated.* Ottawa: CRTC, October 28.

Feaver, C. (1976). *The Politics of the Introduction of Television in the Canadian North: A Study of the Conflict Between National Policies and Needs of Native People in the North.* Ottawa: Carleton University (Unpublished MA Thesis).

Fraser, N. (1989). *Unruly Practices: Power, Discourse and Gender in Contemporary Social Theory.* Minneapolis: University of Minnesota Press.

Fraser, N. (1990). Rethinking the public sphere. *Social Text* 25/26 (8), 3 & 9 (1): 56-80.

Garnham, N. (1986). The media and the public sphere. In P. Golding, G. Murdock & P. Schlesinger (eds.), *Communicating Politics: Mass Communications and the Political Process.* Leicester: Leicester University Press.

Government of Canada (1965). *Report of the Committee on Broadcasting – Fowler Committee.* Ottawa: Queen's Printer.

Government of Canada (1968). *Broadcasting Act.*

Government of Canada (1982). *Federal Cultural Policy Review Committee. Summary of Briefs and Hearings.* Ottawa: Minister of Supply and Services.

Government of Canada (1983a). *Discussion Paper: Northern Broadcasting.* Ottawa: Minister of Communications, Minister of Indian and Northern Affairs, Secretary of State, February 18.

Government of Canada (1983b). *The Northern Broadcasting Policy – a News Release.* March 10.

Government of Canada (1991). *Broadcasting Act.* June 4.

Hamelin, L.-E. (1979). *Canadian Nordicity: It's Your North, Too.* Montréal: Harvest House.

Hamelin, L.-E. (1984). Managing Canada's North: challenges and opportunities: rapporteur's summary and comments, *Canadian Public Administration/Administration Publique du Canada* 27 (2): 165-81.

Inuit Tapirisat of Canada (1976). *Inuit Today,* Vol. 4 (9); Vol. 5 (7). Ottawa: ITC.

Inuit Tapirisat of Canada (1981). *ITC Project. List of Events in Northern Broadcasting.*

Lougheed and Associates (1986). *Report on the Native Communications Program and the Northern Native Broadcast Access Program.* Ottawa: Secretary of State.

MacPherson, L.W. & Campbell, W. (1993). *The Creation of a Canadian Aboriginal Film and Video Production Fund and a Canadian Film and Delivery System as an Economic Development Strategy* (Unpublished Proposal).

Northern Québec Inuit Association (1974). *The Northerners.* Québec: NQIA.

O'Connell, S. (1974). *Television Impact on Eskimo People of Canada.* Montréal: Concordia University Department of Educational Technology (Unpublished MA Thesis).

O'Connell, S. (1977). Television and the Canadian eskimo: the human perspective, *Journal of Communication* 27 (4): 140-4.

Peers, F.W. (1979). *The Public Eye: Television and the Politics of Canadian Broadcasting 1952-1968*. Toronto: University of Toronto Press.

Raboy, M. (1990a). From cultural diversity to social equality: the democratic trials of Canadian broadcasting, *Studies of Broadcasting* (Japan Broadcasting Corporation) 26: 7-41.

Raboy, M. (1990b). *Missed Opportunities: The Story of Canada's Broadcasting Policy*. Montréal: McGill-Queen's University Press.

Roncagliolo, R. (1991). Notes on "the alternative." In N. Thede & A. Ambrosi (eds.), *Video: The Changing World* (pp. 206-8). Montréal: Black Rose Books.

Roth, L (1983a). *Inuit Media Projects and Northern Communications Policy. Monograph on Northern Native Communications*. Montréal, Concordia University.

Roth, L. (1983b). *The Role of Communication Projects and Inuit Participation in the Formation of a Communication Policy for the North*. Montréal: McGill University (Unpublished MA Thesis).

Roth, L. (1994). *Northern Voices and Mediating Structures: The Emergence and Development of First Peoples' Television Broadcasting in the Canadian North*. Montréal: Concordia University (Doctoral Dissertation).

Roth, L. & Valaskakis, G. (1989). Aboriginal broadcasting in Canada: a case study in democratization. In M. Raboy & P.A. Bruck (eds.), *Communication For and Against Democracy*. Montréal: Black Rose Books Ltd.

Shields, R. (1991). *Places on the Margin: Alternative Geographies of Modernity*. New York/London: Routledge.

Smith, G. and Associates (1988). *Review of Native Broadcasting*. A Study Commissioned by the CRTC. Ottawa: CRTC.

Television Northern Canada (1987). *TVNC: A Proposal for a Shared Distribution Service in Northern Canada*. June.

Television Northern Canada (1992). *The Dawn of a New Era* (Publicity Pamphlet).

Television Northern Canada (1993). *Response to CRTC Public Notice 1992-13*. March 1.

Valaskakis, G. (1979). *A Communicational Analysis of Interaction Patterns: Southern Baffin Eastern Arctic*. Montréal: McGill University (Doctoral Dissertation).

Weir, E.A. (1965). *The Struggle for National Broadcasting in Canada*. Toronto: McClelland and Stewart Limited.

INDIGENOUS PEOPLES OF CANADA AND THE UNITED STATES OF AMERICA: ENTERING THE 21ST CENTURY

by James S. FRIDERES

I   INTRODUCTION

All around the world, indigenous groups, e.g., Maori of New Zealand, Saami of Sweden, Ainu of Japan, Indians of North America, are building solidarity over such issues as sovereignty and self-determination. Their efforts have thus far culminated in the writing of the Declaration of Indigenous Peoples Rights, which is now before the United Nations. Even though much of the land base of indigenous peoples has been lost and much of their political and social structure has been eroded, they have survived. In fact, many would say that they are experiencing a cultural renaissance.

While indigenous groups recognize that historical events have dulled their claims, they wish to survive as an ethno-cultural group, maintain their dignity and participate in the larger social and economic structures of their society. In practical terms this means they wish to control the use of land, water and natural resources which affect them. Of equal concern are economic and social policies which impact upon their lives.

Major confrontations between Indians and non-Indians have taken place over the past three decades as indigenous groups participate in ongoing social and political activities.[1] Issues such as self-government, sovereignty, and Native rights are central to Indians as they push for political and legal change in the United States and Canada. Before addressing the current structure of Indian policy in both countries, and how Indians have positioned themselves as they enter the 21st century, we need to provide a demographic profile of Indians and a brief history of Indian policy for each country. This introduction will provide the reader with sufficient background to fully understand current Indian policy and the political and legal decisions which are taking place as we head into the 21st century. It will also provide the reader with an appreciation of the issues confronting Indians.

---

[1] There is considerable diversity in the usage of terms to identify the original inhabitants of North America. Canadians tend to use generic terms such as *First Nations*, *Aboriginals* or *Natives*. More specific, legal terms are *Indians* and *Metis*. On the other hand, Americans do not use these terms and prefer to use *Amerindian* or *Native American* as their "marker" for original inhabitants of the continent.

II   DEMOGRAPHIC PROFILE

2.1   Canada

At the time of sustained contact with Europeans (1500), it is estimated that over 200,000 Indians occupied the land. After four hundred years of colonization, disease, and poverty, this number was reduced to less than half. However, since the beginning of the 20th century, a reduction in mortality and an increase in health care have led to a resurgence of the Indian population. Today the Indian population has increased to over 500,000 and if broader definitions are employed, the number increases to over one million (see table 1).

Today, Indians make up four percent of the total population. Their residential patterns reveal they are dispersed throughout Canada, making up less than one percent of the total population in the province of Prince Edward Island as compared with over sixty percent in the Northwest Territories. Forty three percent of Aboriginals live in the prairie region of Canada while only four percent in the Atlantic provinces. Slightly more than one fifth of the Indian population resides in Ontario while ten percent are in Québec. The remainder live in the northern regions of Canada. These patterns are a result of both the historical decimation of the Indian population in the East[2] and the forced migration of Indians from East to West as colonization took place.

The original inhabitants represent different legal and social categories.[3] For example, the category *Indians* is a legal term and individuals entitled to call themselves Indians must meet historical and legal conditions, e.g., must be a descendent of an Indian, must have government recognition through birth records, and must not be a descendent of someone who renounced their Indianness or cannot legally prove their Indian status.[4] Indians are further subdivided into those who may legally live on reservations (land set aside by the government and held in trust) and those who cannot. Another subdivision of Aboriginals are those who are legally defined as Metis (the biological product of Indians and European immigrants).[5] These individuals are legally recognized in the Canadian constitution and by provincial authorities in the provinces of Alberta and British Columbia. Yet, in other parts of Canada, Metis have no legal or political standing (Morse & Giokas, 1995). The third subdivision represents northern residents. Inuit (originally referred to as Eskimos) reside in northern regions of Canada and have achieved both legal and political recognition. The recent creation of Nunavut

---

[2] Beothuk-Indians in Newfoundland were exterminated by settlers and ceased to exist by the 20th century.

[3] In the present paper we will use the term *Indians* or *Native Americans* unless otherwise warranted. In the current legal literature, Canadian officials refer to Aboriginal as a way of encapsulating diverse groups such as Metis, Inuit, and Indian; all of which are legal entities.

[4] For example, for years section 12,1,b of the *Indian Act* stated that an Indian woman who married a non-Indian man would loose her Indian status as would her children. This clause was recently revoked but only for a select number of living individuals.

[5] Other, often derogatory names have been given to these individuals, such as *half-breeds.*

(a land area encompassing most of the eastern Arctic) gives Inuit political control over this area (Moss, 1995).

Table 1:   *Comparison of Aboriginal Population and Expenditures in Canada and the United States*

	Canada (1991)	United States (1990)
Status Indians	553,000	1,959,234
on reserve	326,000	1,306,234
off reserve	227,000	653,000
Non-Status Indians	405,000	---
Metis	192,000	---
Inuit (Eskimo/Alaska)	41,000	85,698
Percentage of total population	3.7%	1.2%
Number of Aboriginal bands/tribes	605	516
Land in Trust	1.11 M hec.	22.68 M hec.
Number of Reserves	2,364	287
Federal Funding	Cdn$5.4 billion	Cdn$6.6 billion
Per Capita Expenditure	Cdn$13,109	Cdn$6,621
Economic Dev. Expenditure	Cdn$347 million	Cdn$59.8 million
Education Expenditure	Cdn$928 million	Cdn$629 million
Health Expenditure	Cdn$836 million	not available

The Inuit will also be provided substantial sums of money to carry out their own development plans. The last group identified are those referred to as *non-status* Indians. These are individuals who may have all the phenotypical traits of Indians and/or live like Indians but are not legally registered as Indians.

Over five hundred years of colonization and tutelage have left Indians disorganized, alienated, powerless and with feelings of self-hatred. Socio-economically, Indians are the lowest of any ethnic group in Canada. Involvement in the labour force is minimal with unemployment rates running as high as 85 percent on reserves. The occupational structure for Indians also reveals important differences from the general Canadian population. Most Indians work in the primary industries while few are involved in managerial, professional, technical or even clerical jobs. Government transfer payments, e.g., social welfare, unemployment insurance, disability insurance, represent the largest single source of income for Indians. For those in the labour market, few make the median Canadian salary. In summary, job wise, Indians are un- and under-employed. While Indian education is changing, the current working age population has minimal education (less than grade nine). Today, perhaps because of the change in educational policy, the younger cohort is staying in school longer and continuing into postsecondary education.[6] Nevertheless, today we find that fewer than twenty percent of Indian students finish high school (compared to 75 percent of non-Indians) and an even smaller number complete some university.

Most aboriginal languages are extinct or near extinction. Data show that the ratio of home language use to mother tongue for all aboriginal language groups is well below 100. For example, only 71 percent use Ojibway, one of the major languages, as a home language (Silverman & Nielsen, 1992). The involvement of Indians in the criminal system is well known and Ducharme (1986) points out that nearly seventy percent of Indians have been incarcerated in a correctional center at some time before they reach 25 years of age.

After World War II, many Indians began to move to the cities. As a result, nearly forty percent live in urban areas. For those who remain on the reserves or in rural areas, living conditions are not unlike those in undeveloped countries. Half the Indian housing fail to meet basic standards of physical condition, with one third over-crowded and less than half the homes having sewer or water connections. Infantmortality rates are sixty percent higher than the Canadian average and Indians live, on average about 20 years less than the average Canadian. The major cause of death is "accident, poisoning and violence" with the rate per 100,000 population well over 150 and three times the Canadian rate. The Indian population in Canada is young, with nearly 40 percent under the age of 15.

The above figures accentuate the need for solving problems facing Indians today. These data also reveal that a larger number of Indians will enter the labour market over the next decade – into a labour market that cannot deal with the number now trying to enter the market. Nevertheless, over the past two decades, Indians have experienced some improvements in their quality of life. Living conditions and other measures of "well being" show there have been some improvements, e.g., life expectancy has increased, median income has increased, infant mortality has decreased. However, at the same time, we find that the difference between Indians and the general Canadian population on many of these measures is larger today than a decade ago (Fleras & Elliott, 1992).

2.2   United States of America

Researchers argue that at the time of first contact with Europeans, the Indian population in the North American continent was between two and fifteen million (Stuart, 1987; Stiffarm & Lane, 1992). After three centuries of contact, the population dropped to less than one eighth of that (Snipp, 1989) although the impact of disease, wars and settlement varied. As the 20th century emerged, the Indian population in the

---

[6] Prior to the 1960's, most Indians were sent to religious residential schools. Then, in 1960, Indians were sent to provincially funded public schools. More recently, Indian communities have established their own schools.

United States had declined to about a quarter of a million. Today Indians make up less than one percent of the total American population. Moreover, they are thinly dispersed throughout the states and even in areas of heavy concentration, the Mountain and Pacific regions, they make up less than three percent of the total population. In Alaska they only make up fifteen percent of the total state population. Nevertheless they are the fastest growing ethnic group in the United States, increasing 73 percent over the past five decades. It is a young group, with only eight percent over the age of 60 (compared to 17 percent of the total United States population) and nearly 40 percent under the age of twenty (compared to nearly 30 percent of the total United States population). The median age for Natives in 1990 was 26 while for all Americans it was 33.

In *United States vs. Rogers*, in 1846 the United States Supreme Court ruled that a Native American must have some biological heritage linking him or her to the original inhabitants of North America AND they would have to have some social acceptance within an Indian community. By the late 1800's, individual tribes were allowed to devise their own criteria for determining who was an Indian. Nevertheless, Congress has the final authority to determine who is Native American and they have consistently used the *blood quantum* theory.[7] Until the mid sixties, any person with 1/32 Indian blood could be placed on the Indian roll and considered Indian. However, as the numbers continued to grow, Congress enacted the 1/4 blood rule to be considered a legal Indian and eligible for various social and economic programs.[8] Intermarriage for Indians is common and this has added new concerns over defining who is an Indian. Today, over one third of Indian husbands have non-Indian wives.

Prior to World War II, most American Indians remained on the reservations. However, by the end of the war, nearly one hundred thousand had moved to urban areas. The federal governments' relocation program (1953-72), accelerated this process and took an additional one hundred thousand Indians off the reservations and into cities. In addition, twice that number moved to urban areas during this time period solely because they thought they could obtain a better life in the city, e.g., enter the labour market. By 1980, eleven metropolitan areas across the United States had Indian populations well over ten thousand (Los Angeles had the largest, with over sixty thousand). Five additional cities had Indian populations between five and ten thousand. However, we find that a majority of Indians still live in rural areas.

While over one hundred Indian languages still exist and are used in varying degrees, a similar number have become extinct or nearly extinct. The continuance of Indian languages occurs where large numbers of speakers are concentrated in rural areas, e.g., Navajo. Employment on reservations is low and unemployment rates are between 25

---

[7] In 1934 it was decided by Congress that anyone defined as an Indian would have to be a descendent from a legally recognized tribe and living on a reservation or have at least one parent with Native American bloodline.

[8] This policy was successfully challenged in 1985 when the courts ruled that the constitutionality of the use of the sole *blood quantum* theory was illegal.

and 36 percent. Their participation in the labour market determines their income and Indians have median incomes which are about two thirds of that of whites (McLemore, 1991).

Educational attainments of Indians are much lower than those of non-Indians. In 1991 only about one half of all Indians over the age of twenty four had completed high school compared to over two thirds of non-Indians (McLemore, 1991). Indians are achieving some control over the content and style of education and the proportion of Indian children in Bureau of Indian Affairs schools has decreased over time. By 1990, less than ten percent of Indian children were enrolled in Indian Affairs schools; the remainder attended nearby public schools. Today, more than 127,000 Indians are enrolled in colleges across the nation and about nine percent attend one of the twenty three Indian controlled community colleges (Feagin & Feagin, 1996). While most Indian colleges are small, poorly financed, and not fully accredited, this represents a major change over the past two decades. The percentage of Indians completing university has risen recently to nearly ten percent but when compared with non-Indians, it represents less than half the rate.

As would be expected from the above figures, quality of life for Indians is well below that achieved by other Americans. Health statistics show that Indians are still more likely to die early in life and that they live 15 to 20 years less than a non-Indian. And while infant mortality rates have been reduced substantially (82 down to 11 deaths per 1,000 births), Indians still have a higher rate than the country's average and suffer a disproportionate number of deaths from causes that reflect their poor quality of life.

III   NORTH AMERICAN HISTORY AS IT RELATES TO INDIANS

In the period of early contact until mid 18th century, Indians dealt mainly with European traders who wished to exploit the natural resources of the new world. At the same time, Catholic missionaries set upon a goal of converting Indians who they felt were capable of becoming Catholics AND who wanted to be converted. From the Indians' perspective, they tended to view the Europeans and missionaries as a nuisance, not a cultural or military threat. By the mid 1750's, the British, declaring war on the French, needed to stabilize their relationship with the indigenous population. As such, they created an Indian Department to establish formal relations with the Indians, protect Indians from traders and control the actions of colonists. After the Treaty of Paris (1753) was signed, France relinquished all its North American Territories to the British which opened the borders of Canada and promoted the settlement of lands by colonists. Many Indians objected to this act, e.g., Pontiac and his followers objected to the claim of sovereignty by Britain and captured several British forts, but their technological inferiority (especially in the area of arms and munitions) led to their eventual defeat.

Nevertheless, to demonstrate their concern over the treatment of Indians, Britain agreed to establish the *Royal Proclamation of 1763*[9]. This treaty of peace and alliance between Great Britain, France, Spain and Portugal, ended the *Seven Years War*[10]. The Proclamation is important for Indian people in that it has two provisions which are directed specifically at them. First, it states that abuses in colonists' purchasing land from Indians will cease. It explicitly states that colonists are forbidden to purchase land from Indians where the Crown had permitted Indian settlement. If Indians wanted to sell their land, they could only do so to the Crown. The second provision states that land outside the boundaries of Québec (1763), Ruperts Land, as well as lands located west of the source of the rivers that flow into the sea from the west and northwest, will be set aside for Indians. It clearly specifies that land within the area described above cannot be purchased by colonists without prior authorization by government authorities (Dupuis & McNeil, 1995).

British rule was disputed by the thirteen colonies and with the conclusion of the American Revolution (1776), the United States of America was created. By 1791, Upper and Lower Canada were established although they remained under British jurisdiction. Indian policy was controlled by the military until 1830, when it was replaced by a civilian agency. Overall, early Indian policies were bifurcated. At the global level, diplomacy, deliberations and treaty making were the cornerstones of the policy. However, at the local level, treaty breaking, intolerance and fraud were the basis for dealing with Indians (Thompson, 1996).

3.1   The United States of America

The Indian policy of the United States of America emerges out of the British policy prior to the American Revolution. Thus the *Royal Proclamation* (1763) forms the basis of American Indian policy. It is only the lack of clarity in the *Proclamation* that allowed the two countries to develop different Indian policies over the past two centuries. However, like Canada, which created a centralized Indian Affairs agency, the United States adopted such a bureaucratic structure. Today the Bureau of Indian Affairs centrally administers all Native American issues. As Brock (1993) points out, the United States legislation on Indians and Indian issues is complex, comprising over 5,000 federal statutes, 2,000 federal court opinions and nearly 400 ratified treaties and agreements.

Prior to the creation of the United States of America, the British government generally ignored Indian rights or Indian claims. Moreover, the small number of Europeans entering and developing the new country did not concern Indians, since the fur trade was at its pinnacle during the 1760's and all parties were benefiting from the trade.[11]

---

[9] The *Royal Proclamation* is not a statute but an edict by the British Government.

[10] While parts of the Proclamation were revoked in the *Québec Act* of 1774, the *Act* went on to say that nothing in the *Act* was to extend, nullify vary or alter any right, title or possession, however derived and all rights, titles and possessions were to remain in force as if the *Act* had not been passed.

[11] Much of the conflict occurring was that of inter-tribal warfare where Indian tribes were attempting

As colonization continued, the British unilaterally invoked the *Right of Discovery* doctrine, claiming control over all land and people. This doctrine was supported in 1823 with the Supreme court decision (*Johnson vs. McIntosh*) which ruled that Indians did not hold title to their land and thus could not sell it directly to non-Indians.

As the fur trade declined in importance the United States began to see the benefits of Indians as allies.[12] The tentative and vulnerable status of an emerging nation forced the Americans to sign treaties with Indians and recognize tribal authority (Brock, 1993). However, treaty signing didn't begin until after the American revolution and most took place between 1789 and 1871. Throughout the 19th century, immigrants began to settle and agriculturalize the land previously held by Indians. As the 19th century ended, no more treaties were signed and Congress began to remove Indians from their lands. By the early 20th century, much of the Indian land had disappeared, many Indians had died from wars and disease, and Indians were subjected to detribalization and assimilation policies (Cornell, 1988).

The result of such a policy was the basis for major Indian wars. As a result of these wars and diseases, Indians were forced to settle on lands set aside by the federal government for Indians, i.e., reservations. Nevertheless it was during this period that the American courts recognized the status of tribes as "domestic dependent nations."[13] In the *Cherokee Nation vs. Georgia*, 1831 ruling, the courts advanced the domestic dependent nations thesis. This ruling stated that tribes were distinct political entities which had inherent self-governing rights and were derived from the Indians' original occupancy of the land. It was a case where a weaker state placed itself under the protection of a stronger one, all the while remaining a state. One year later the *Worcester vs. Georgia* decision further strengthened this ruling. It declared that the state of Georgia did not have the legislative authority to supersede Cherokee law. Moreover, it determined that Indian internal powers of self-government were not restricted by treaties or federal/state acts. As Brock (1993) points out, the only limit was tribes attempting to engage in international treaties or contracts subject to Congressional authority. A more recent ruling in the *Native American Church vs. Navajo Tribal Council*, 1959, found that Indian tribes are not states, they have a higher status than that of a state.

Genocide and assimilation were the thrusts of all federal policy directives employed in the late 19th and early 20th century. Several strategies were employed to achieve these goals. First, the communal basis of Indian land tenure was removed and fee simple was given to many individual Indians. The *Allotment Act* (1887) gave individual Indians the right to own land and dispose of it. It struck at the heart of the Indian

---

to control the fur trade.

[12] Indian Affairs was placed under the direction of the War Department in 1789.

[13] It is important to remember that the legal doctrine of tribal sovereignty and the legal definition of the relationship between the federal government and tribal governments are applicable ONLY to Indians living within recognized communities, e.g., living on reservations. For example, urban Indians are excluded from this characterization as are Aleuts and Eskimos living in Alaska.

communal way of life and destroyed the indigenous social organization. Records show that between 1887 and 1934, 2.75 million hectares (60 percent of the Indian land base) was sold to white settlers. In addition, the Bureau of Indian Affairs began a major effort to interfere with the "day to day" operations on the reservations, engaging in direct management which struck at the very basis of Indian culture. New systems of government were introduced, the concept of individual rights was made an integral component of the new reservation and capitalism was unabashedly promoted in the reservations. It was also at this time (1871) that Congress declared that Indian tribes were no longer to be defined as "independent" nations. They also decreed that any powers Indians had were not inherent but delegated by Congress and thus could be removed at will by Congress. To facilitate this new policy and implement the provisions, the reservation system was created (1871-87).

This assimilation policy was carried on into the early 20th century. Then in 1934 a new direction in American Indian policy emerged under the leadership of the new Commissioner of Indian Affairs, John Collier. His new policy was to treat a band or tribe as a unit of community organization and build upon it. In many ways, Collier was an early advocate of self-government. Over the next decade, the Bureau of Indian Affairs developed nearly one hundred tribal governments, all within existing reservations. However, a new Indian policy was developed after World War II, now referred to as the *termination policy*. In 1953 the termination policy was implemented (lasting until the early 1960's) and thousands of Indians were removed from their rural communities. The termination of over one hundred reservations took place and the land ceased to be defined as a reservation; it now could be purchased by non-Indians.

3.2   Canada

As Britain entered the 19th century, it began to develop a new set of policies regarding Indians. It was clear by this time that Indians were no longer important military allies and the development of Canada refocused on issues of immigrant settlement and exploitation of the natural resources, e.g., furs, timber, minerals. As such, policies were implemented which gave the government the right to establish treaties, transfer the obligation of Indian integration to religious organizations and vest all Indian lands in the federal Crown.

By 1867 (Canada Confederation), all the basic features of Canadian Indian Policy were in place (Armitage, 1995). In 1876 the first comprehensive *Indian Act* was established; representing an amalgamation of many prior, disparate *Acts* relating to Indians and Indian lands. This new *Act* established a definition of "Indian"[14] as well as policy with regard to how the Crown would treat Indians (from the boardroom to the bedroom) and the rights and obligations of Indians, e.g., election of chiefs and

---

[14] Until recently, the term "Indian" was clearly defined under the Indian Act. It noted that *Indian* meant: any person of Indian blood reputed to belong to a particular band, any child or any such person and, any woman who is or was lawfully married to any such person. Since the 1970's there have been many changes to this definition although its central thrust remains intact.

councils, taxation rights, sale of Indian land, control of intoxicants, provisions for becoming a citizen of Canada and voting in federal/provincial elections. However, it is important to note that at NO time did the federal government act or define Indians as having nation status or having any inherent rights. During the next fifty years, yearly amendments were made to the *Indian Act*. The central thrust of the *Indian Act* was to control and assimilate Indians and all actions taken by the Crown were directed toward that goal. The administration of the *Indian Act* (since it was placed under civilian auspices in 1830) was through a superintendent, who had wide discretionary powers with regard to how to govern and deal with Indian people (created under the *British North America Act, 1867*). Today the Minister of Indian Affairs is responsible for Indians and their land through a large, complex bureaucratic structure consisting of over 20 departments, 5,200 employees and a yearly budget of over Cdn$6 billion (Frideres, 1995).

During the second half of the 19th century and well into the 20th century, the government of Canada dealt with Indians and their lands by entering into treaties with them. These legal agreements specified the rights and obligations of both parties although it is unlikely that the Indians fully understood the specific terms or consequences of the terms within the treaty. These treaties were undertaken because the British needed to settle large tracts of land quickly and unimpeded. On the other hand, Indians were forced to sign these treaties due to the devastating impact of diseases such as smallpox and tuberculosis, the decimation of the buffalo and (in the United States), the massacre of Indians opposing westward expansion. By the late 1920's, most of Canada had been "treatied out".[15]

At the end of World War Two, a joint committee of both the Senate and the House of Commons recommended new guidelines for future Indian Policy which resulted in a new *Indian Act* being passed (1951). This new *Act* included a political voice for Indian women, more self-government for Indians, easing of enfranchisement regulations, cooperation with provinces in delivering services to Indians and educational policies for Indian children. These sweeping changes to the *Indian Act* reversed the emphasis on assimilation and moved the policy toward integration into the social, political and economic mainstream of Canada.

In 1969 the government, wishing to facilitate the integration of Indians into Canadian society, introduced a *White Paper* which suggested that Indians no longer be a legal entity, reservations be dissolved and the *Indian Act* be done away with. If Indians and Indian lands no longer existed, there would be no reason to continue the large bureaucracy and provinces would take over services for Indians.

---

[15] In earlier times, Treaties of Peace and Friendship had been established with Eastern Indians. The *Royal Proclamation of 1763* was a form of treaty. However, it would not be until the mid 1800s that the major "numbered" treaties were taken with Indians. These treaties ceded most of the land west of Ontario to the Crown.

Indians objected to the *White Paper* and a coalition of Aboriginal, religious, and non-government organizations along with the provinces, lobbied the federal government to withdraw the proposed policy. In 1973 a formal withdrawal took place.

It was during this time that Indians began to refocus their efforts on self-government and sovereignty. Their cause was given a substantial boost when the Supreme Court ruled in 1973 that Indian rights existed independent of the Crown. While the court did not identify what these rights were, it was the first time that Indian rights were declared as existing. Subsequent actions by the federal and provincial governments have recognized broader Aboriginal rights. The *Canadian Constitution Act* (1982) recognizes "the existing Aboriginal and treaty rights of the Aboriginal peoples of Canada," and the *Charter of Rights and Freedoms* (1982) was qualified so as "not to abrogate or derogate from any aboriginal, treaty or other right or freedom that pertained to the aboriginal peoples of Canada..." One year later the *House of Commons Special Committee on Indian Self-Government* produced a report calling for an expansion of self-government so that Natives could be recognized as a distinct order of government in Canada.

IV   RECENT EVENTS AND NEW DIRECTIONS

We begin this section by identifying some recent events defined as *milestones* which would reconfigure Indian-White relations as well as begin the long process of integrating Indians into the larger society. We wish to identify four issues currently being negotiated by Indians in their push to achieve greater self-determination and obtain a better quality of life for themselves and their children.

4.1   Canada

After the demise of the *White Paper*, there was a concerted drive toward devolution of Indian affairs from the federal government to Indians. During the late 1970's and early 1980's, many provisions for Indian administration of various programs, e.g., education, community, were handed to Indian communities. Indian control over some programs has had moderate success but since funding remains solely in control of the federal government, control over the administration of programs seems to be a weak form of Indian control. There is no question that the federal government has moved to a less centralized and more flexible funding arrangement and allowed local Indian communities to take on greater administrative duties. However, after nearly twenty years of negotiations, it would seem that Indian self-government is nothing more than a community by community negotiation over powers and jurisdiction that approximate municipal governments (Fleras & Elliott, 1996).

In the push for Indian self-government, the federal government developed a policy of community-based self-government. The community-based self-government policy was announced in 1986 in an attempt to push through Indian development while side-stepping the *Indian Act*. A decade after its introduction, the *Indian Act* has been viewed as a vehicle for providing Indians a measure of self-determination while at the same time, a major impediment for Indians achieving self-government. In this strategy, the federal government offers Indian communities the chance to "throw off the yoke of colonialism" and take on self-determination and develop self-government. When it was first introduced, many Indian communities viewed the policy as a "make work" project while others saw it as a community development project. Others saw it as a way in which the government could off-load its responsibilities to Indians without providing Indian communities with commensurate power or resources. Today, fewer than fifty bands have reached the point of submitting a formal proposal to the Department of Indian Affairs and Northern Development. Most Indian leaders view it like other government policies directed toward Indians: restrictive in nature and specifying conditions that make it impossible for Indian communities to become less dependent on government institutions (Ponting, 1991). As Boldt (1994) points out, these policies are not developing the concept of Indian nationhood but rather new forms of constraint and dependency.[16]

4.1.1 Economic Development

Recent economic initiatives involving Indians and private enterprise are regional or local in scope. Perhaps the greatest impetus for involvement of Indians in the labour market was the passage of the *Employment Equity Act* (1986). This *Act* forced federally-regulated companies, e.g., banks, transportation companies, crown corporations, and corporations which obtained government contracts with a value of over Cdn$200,000 to review their employment policies and procedures with regard to four targeted groups: visible minorities, women, disabled people and Aboriginals. As a result of this *Act*, almost two thirds of all "equity" programs involving Indians were introduced over the past five years.

Sloan & Hill (1995) argue that an increased emphasis on corporate-Indian relations is also a response to changes in the business environment. Specifically, the changes in demographic and political realities have forced corporate Canada to rethink its policies with regard to Indians. For example, in the Northwest Territories, nearly 60 percent of the population is Aboriginal (Metis, Inuit, Indian). Government sources suggest that the Aboriginal population will grow by 50 percent in the next twenty-five years, and these figures suggest a changing customer base and a new profile for the workforce. Other considerations such as Aboriginal people controlling 20 percent of the land mass of Canada poses potential problems for developing or transporting natural resources, e.g., pipelines, utilities. Government policies have also contributed to this shift in thinking about Aboriginal peoples, e.g., employment equity legislation, human rights legislation, surface lease agreements, land claims settlements, and self-government are all new programs implemented by the federal government over the recent past. In some cases, corporate Canada has found linkages with Aboriginal peoples provides benefits to their operation. Companies dealing with Aboriginal

---

[16] For a listing and detailed explanation of various criticisms of this policy, see Ponting (1991).

people have opened new markets, and developed stable, long-term work forces, especially in the North. This fundamental shift in thinking has not taken place in corporate America. While Indians have a vision of economic development which is trimodal (entailing a revitalized traditional economy, a modern industrial base and government grants), this type of economic development simply will not stand the test of time nor allow Indian communities to become economically independent. Moreover, many Indians believe that once political autonomy has been achieved (self-government), Indian communities will become economically independent. Many Indians argue that with the passage of Bill C-115 (*Indian Act Amendment on Taxation*, 1988) which established the power of band councils to levy taxes on property on reserves, economic development is not far behind.[17] However, reality suggests that this is not the case and in fact, the causality of the argument is the reverse. Economic independence produces political independence.

Taxation has also been an economic issue Indians have dealt with for many years. Indians were exempt from taxation before Confederation and this is codified in the *Indian Act*. However, this exemption is limited to property situated on the reserve and income generated on the reserve. In 1983 the Supreme Court ruled (*R. vs. Nowegijick*) that an employer's physical location was the key to determine whether Indian income was taxable. They ruled that if an Indians' property was to be tax exempt, the employer had to be on the reserve. Nearly a decade later, it was decided that the physical location of the employer was not sufficient for determining whether or not Indian income was tax exempt. In *R. vs. Williams* (1993), the Supreme Court ruled that three factors had to be evaluated to determine the tax status: (1) the purpose of the exemption, (2) the character of the property, and (3) the incidence of taxation on that property.

While this test is more flexible than the earlier one, it is also less clear and predictable and does not afford total tax exemption for Indian income. This means, in practical terms, that even if the Head office of an Indian company is on a reserve, its property may still be taxable by the Crown. In addition, it is important to note that Indians still pay taxes. For example, Indians are liable for custom and excise taxes, they pay hospitalization taxes imposed by provincial governments and they must pay most federal and provincial taxes when making purchases off the reserve. In summary, after several Supreme Court cases, it seems there is little judicial support for the claim by Indians that there is an Indian right to tax exemption.

When Indians have tried to develop businesses which involve the sale of consumptive goods, e.g., gas, tobacco, the provincial governments have placed limits on the amount allowed to be purchased by the band tax free. After estimating how much of the goods would be sold to Indians, any additional amounts purchased by the band would have provincial taxes applied. Other retail sales on the reserve require that the band pay the applicable provincial taxes first and then the band applies for a refund of the original

---

[17] The Indian Taxation Advisory Board was established a year later to assist band councils in setting up appropriate tax by-laws.

tax paid. Attempts to become economically independent by solely on-reserve development will fail with some exceptions, e.g., oil and gas rich reserves. If an Indian community is to become economically viable, there must be sustainability to the economic developments and linkages to external markets. Indians need to consider an expanded economic model that will bring both employment and business opportunities and only through full participation in the mainstream Canadian economy can economic independence occur.

4.1.2 Land Issues

Peace and Friendship treaties were entered into with Indians in the Maritimes during the 1700's. By the mid 1800's, land treaties were imposed upon Indians in southern Ontario. From that time on until 1930, the Canadian government "treatied" with Indians from Ontario to Alberta and some of the Northwest Territories.

However, Map 1 reveals that most of Yukon, British Columbia, northern Québec, and the Northwest Territories were never treatied out. These land claims have been at the core of the major legal battles that have taken place over the past two decades and continue to take up time and money of Indians. There are currently 70 land claims waiting to be settled. In addition, many "specific" claims have yet to be settled. These are claims about lands taken away from Indians without proper compensation or in contravention with other conditions of the treaty. Since the Office of Native Claims no longer exists, Indians are now forced to negotiate a political settlement or take their case to court. Considerable time, effort and money have been expended by Indian communities in their attempt to receive compensation or reclaim lands illegally taken from them.

Map 1:   *Recent Canadian Land Claims Settled*

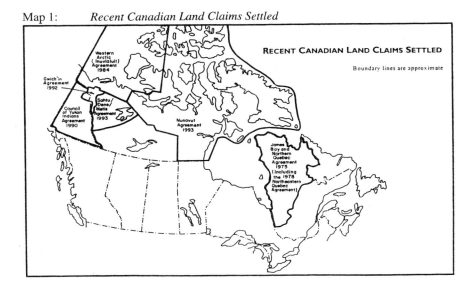

4.1.3 Self-Government

While Indians have been fighting for self-determination, sovereignty and self-government since the day Europeans landed on Canadian soil, their efforts were not successful until the landmark decision of the Supreme Court – *Calder vs. Attorney-General of British Columbia* (1973). This decision affirmed Aboriginal rights and paved the way for current demands for self-government by Indians. In 1982, Aboriginal rights were entrenched in the Constitution and gave, for the first time, formal affirmation and recognition of the existence of Aboriginal and treaty rights. Indian groups united in their fight with the federal and provincial governments over self-determination and sovereignty. While little progress was made during a series of First Ministers' Conferences on Aboriginal Matters (meetings held by the premiers of all provinces and Territories as well as the Prime Minister and other federal officials such as the Minister of Indian Affairs, 1982-87), the negotiations were significant on two fronts. First, they mobilized Indian groups and created a focused "enemy." This also provided a political and media platform for articulate Indian leaders, allowing Canadians to see Indians in a very different context than the usual stereotype. Second, the issue of self-government became a public topic and Canadians were exposed to the concept, its various meanings and possible strategies for implementation. Canadians were forced to assess the logic of the argument and how they might implement such a strategy. Finally, Canadians were exposed to the costs and benefits of such a strategy and the implications of what it would mean to a united Canada.

By 1987, there was a profound change in the mentality of politicians, courts and Canadians with regard to Indian self-government. Today discussions taking place focus on the form it will take, not whether or not it is going to happen. In short, as Brock (1993) points out, the right to self-government went from being a disputed item in the early 1970's to an accepted direction of government policy and negotiated constitutional clauses in 1992.

The creation of the *Canadian Charter of Rights and Freedoms* has allowed individuals and groups to approach the courts to challenge government policy. Under the new *Charter*, an alternative "backup" exists for groups when the political forces or will of the Crown has failed them. Each time constitutional stalls have occurred, Indians have approached the courts to affirm their rights. In the end, political negotiations between Indians and the government are taking place within a legal arena. Recent court decisions have been far more liberal in their interpretation of Indian rights than the political process. Even though court decisions such as Guerin, Simon, Sioui and Sparrow have confirmed Aboriginal rights, these decisions and others have also limited the prospect for Aboriginal self-government.[18]

---

[18] Court decisions are more zero-sum decisions which polarize the adversaries and limit the alternatives. Political decisions on the other hand allow for compromise and negotiation.

In their quest for self-government, Indians are negotiating with the federal government at two levels. At the more concrete level, they are requesting the transfer and delivery of services, ranging from education, health care to more exotic services such as gambling, from the federal government to their own communities. While many of these requests form the basis for self-determination, there is a sense of pragmatism involved in much of the substance within these negotiations; Indian people believe that they can prosper only if they are able to develop the policies (both economical and social), administer and deliver the services. As Brock (1993) points out, at the second level, the rhetoric is more aggressive and idealistic. The nature of discussion between the federal government and Indians at this level is more abstract and attempts to create an ethos in which the more specific negotiations take place. Indians feel they were successful in doing this throughout the debate regarding the repatriation of the *Canadian Constitution* (to ensure that Indians were beneficiaries of the *Constitution*) and they continue to feel it is an appropriate strategy. As such, Indians are continuing their demand for special status in the structure of Canada and they use the language of nationalism to place the issue in context.[19]

While negotiations over self-government are taking place under several guises, progress continues to move slowly. Aboriginals have expressed their frustration with the premises, scope and pace of the negotiations (Hogg & Turpel, 1995). The *Royal Commission on Aboriginal Peoples* (1990) was created to address the issue of self-government and make recommendations which were to be taken up by the government and implemented. Six years later and at a cost of over Cdn$60 million, the Commission has now tabled its Final Report. The Final Report recommends that Cdn$35 billion be spent on Aboriginals over the next twenty years, in addition to the over Cdn$6 billion it spends each year. The specific recommendations range from the Queen and Parliament issuing a royal proclamation acknowledging mistakes, the creation of an Aboriginal parliament, creation of an independent tribunal to decide on land claims, to training ten thousand Aboriginal professionals in the area of health and social services. The Commission feels that if the more than 440 recommendations were implemented, the social and economic gap between Aboriginals and non-Aboriginals would be reduced by 50 percent in twenty years.

While the recognition of the inherent nature of the right of self-government has been formally noted by the federal government, it does not answer the question as to what are the contents of these rights or how these rights will link and integrate with the political structure of Canadian society. Thus far the courts have been called upon to make these decisions and they have advanced the case of Aboriginal rights in a rather multidirected and disjointed manner. A review of the Supreme Court decisions over the past decade would not allow the reader to make any clear predictions about future decisions regarding Aboriginal rights.[20]

---

[19] There have been occasions when subgroups of the Indian communities, e.g., women, have taken issue with the leadership and accused them of being out of touch with the realities of their constituencies.

[20] Hogg & Turpel (1995) argue that the issues of Aboriginal rights and self-government are not

The concept of Aboriginal self-government is not easily reconciled with the existing political structure of Canadian society. As Hogg & Turpel (1995) point out, there are many principles in the present Canadian Constitution which are inconsistent with the recognition of Aboriginal self-government, the most important being the principle of exhaustiveness. This principle has divided all jurisdictions between the federal and provincial governments and leaves no room for Aboriginal government except for what might be delegated by the other two levels of government. In short, this means that Aboriginal self-government is much like municipal governments. Nevertheless some unique agreements for self-government have taken place, e.g., Sechelt Indians, First Nations of the Yukon. For example, the Sechelt Indians have negotiated a self-government *Agreement*. The *Agreement* notes that federal and provincial laws of general application apply to the Sechelt Indians and their lands. However, in the case of provincial laws, the laws of the Sechelt Band take precedence. Thus, if there is an inconsistency between provincial and Sechelt law, Indian law is paramount. However, when an inconsistency exists between federal and Sechelt law, federal law is paramount. Hogg & Turpel (1995) point out that the *Sechelt Act* is silent on the definition of inconsistency so that the narrow "express contradiction" test would probably apply.

Thus far in Canada today, the Crown has recognized the right of self-government[21] but has not established any framework by which to implement such a policy. While it is to be commended that Canadians have accepted the principle of self-government, it does little to help Indians achieve self-determination. On the other hand, the development of a formal framework for Aboriginals and its equal application across the more than 2,000 bands and 600 reserves would be nearly impossible. Moreover, this kind of approach does not take into account the different situations, cultures and aspirations of Indian peoples living throughout Canada. Hogg & Turpel (1995) suggest that a "contextual statement" (like that proposed in the failed *Charlottetown Accord*) be part of the Aboriginal self-government policy. This idea is that such a statement would frame self-government jurisdiction in light of the purposes and objectives that were desired by the specific Aboriginal group seeking self-government.

The contextual statement is based on the premise that Aboriginal government would be a third level of government, with its own jurisdiction. This model would ensure that the culture of Indian society (including languages, institutions, traditions) would be safeguarded and developed while helping Indian people maintain a link with their environment. Thus, Aboriginal government would have exclusive jurisdiction over issues identified above and allow them to control their own development. In the end, they would be able to achieve self-determination on a number of social, economic, and political dimensions. If this model were adopted by the other two levels of

---

suitable for resolution by the courts and would better serve all Canadians if they were dealt with through the political process.

[21] If self-government is inherent, then it would not be contingent upon federal or provincial recognition. On the other hand, if it is contingent upon governments recognition, then the right is not based upon the historical use and occupation of Aboriginal peoples over the land in Canada.

government, it would represent a major departure from the status quo and the powers given to Aboriginal peoples under the *Indian Act*.

The courts have given some indication that a limited right of self-government is possible. The *Sparrow* decision and the courts declaration that decisions about Aboriginals calls for a liberal and generous interpretation about Aboriginal rights (*Nowegijick*) supports this possibility. However, at the same time, the courts have noted that sovereignty and underlying title to the land remain with the Crown. Over all, the courts have not dealt with the substantive issue as to whether or not the right of self-government has been extinguished or still remains.

Both Indians and government agree that self-government expresses the desire of Indian peoples to control their destiny (Isaac, 1995). Indians feel that they need to determine their social and economic activities and be accountable to Indian leaders, not government or agents of the Crown. At the same time, the definition of self-government has been at the heart of the disagreement between Indians and the government. Governments feel the concept is too broad in meaning while Indians feel it is too narrow and restrictive (Canada, 1989). Moreover, the form of self-government is viewed differently by each group. Some Aboriginals want total sovereignty while others want to achieve some control over their lives but wish to stay within the federal structure of Canada.

The federal government and provincial officials are slowly trying to convince Indians that they have moved from a colonial wardship and assimilationist position to one which is supportive of Indian self-government. However, as Boldt (1994) points out, this is a partial myth. While there has been some movement in allowing Indians to take control of their affairs, it is also true that the same government structure remains (Indian Affairs) as it did in 1876 when the first *Indian Act* was implemented. Moreover, the self-government policy has been designed by Indian Affairs personnel, regulated by government and implemented by politicians. He argues that Indian special status will disappear, Indian self-government will become municipal government and institutional assimilation will take over. The wish to do away with Indian status can be seen in the 1969 *White Paper* and later the 1985 *Nielsen Report*. There is concern that another attempt is underway to do away with the legal status of Indians but this time under the guise of Indian self-government.

At present, 178 Indian bands have submitted formal proposals to the federal government to seek some form of self-government. Nearly half of these have progressed to the "agreement in principle" stage. While ostensibly this new policy is to serve Indians and help them toward self-determination, the truth may be closer to the fact that the policy is self-serving and does not provide Indians with the proper tools or resources to become economically or politically independent. As Boldt (1994) points out, this shuffle means that the Indians are being asked to deal with local issues on the reserves but remain under control of the federal agency through a complex set of rules, conditions and standards with regard to action Indians can take.

Hogg & Turpel (1995) argue that self-government will not take place through constitutional reform. They argue that it can only take place through a political accord with the existing two levels of government. A major advantage of such a strategy would be to reduce the cost and make the process expeditious. Rather than negotiate separate accords on all the various issues of self-government, a single negotiation could be signed. This process has successfully been used by the federal, Territorial and First Nations in the Yukon as they struggle to finalize an Agreement. Notwithstanding the above "successes," the Government of Canada still denies treaty status to any self-government agreement and this poses a major impediment to this type of solution.[22] However, some attempts using this model have been successful and in 1995, the Chiefs of Manitoba and the Minister of Indian Affairs concluded an Agreement which would dismantle the federal agency within the province and turn over funds and decision making responsibility to provincial Indian organizations.

There seems to be a concern by government that if Aboriginal self-government is obtained, the collective rights of Indians will come into conflict with individual rights of both Indians and non-Indians. Gibbins & Ponting (1986) argue that individual rights under the Canadian *Charter of Rights and Freedoms* is the very crux of Canadian citizenship. Thus, it is felt that individuals will stand to lose under "group" governments in which individuals have no rights. This has already been demonstrated when some Canadian bands have sought to thwart Bill C-31 which granted equal protection under the law to both Indian men and women (Ponting, 1993).

4.2   United States

When the Democrats came to power in the 1960's, they endorsed the notion of economic development among Native Americans. As Thompson (1996) argues, this was a time of cultural renewal for Native Americans; new policies of self-determination and plans for "partnership self-help" were promoted by senior government officials. Later the *Indian Education Act* was passed which allowed Native Americans to gain control over their schools and the funds given to them by the federal government. Soon to follow were the *American Indian Religious Freedom Act*, the *Tribally Controlled Community College Assistance Act*, the *Indian Child Welfare Act* (all in 1978) and finally the *Archaeological Resources Protection Act* of 1979.

Executive policy and legislative enactments since the 1960's suggest that the United States government is attempting to change its traditional trustee role. However, the reader should be cautioned that at the present time, the Bureau of Indian Affairs continues to exercise considerable influence over Indian affairs in most institutional contexts, e.g., education, housing, roads. The United States government, like the Canadian federal government, holds legal title to tribal lands and other major tribal assets. As such the federal government has considerable fiduciary duty to Indians and

---

[22] The question is whether or not a self-government agreement that has been denied the status of a treaty may still be constitutionally protected under section 35 of the *Constitution Act* (1982) as an expression of Aboriginal rights.

can be held liable if mismanagement is proven.[23] This trustee doctrine also supports a broader, non-judicially enforceable obligation accepted by the legislature and the executive in dealing with Indians. As a result, Anaya et al. (1995) point out, the Bureau of Indian Affairs increasingly sees its trustee responsibility as developing Indian self-government and not continuing its paternalistic style of governing.

In 1970 a new policy promoting Native American self-determination was initiated when the President declared the assimilation policy a failure and called for legislative measures to ensure Indian self-determination. In 1974 the *Indian Financing Act* was established with a budget of Cdn$50 million which would provide loans and grants for economic development on the reservations. This new policy was further set in motion by the *Indian Self-Determination and Education Assistance Act* (1975). The central thrust of this *Act* is to allow Native Americans to gain control of the planning and administration of all federal programs related to them.[24] It promotes an orderly transfer of programs and services from government to Indians. Other federal agencies, e.g., Secretary of Interior, Secretary of Health and Human services, now negotiate "self-determination contractors" with the tribes so they can plan, conduct and administer federal programs for the development of Indian resources.

With the 1980 election, a new conservative government was elected. This new conservative government (lasting until 1992), invoked a "termination by accountants" policy in which fiscal allocations to Indians were cut substantially. There were some notable exceptions to this "anti-Indian" government such as the *Indian Tribal Government Tax Status Act* (1982), which allowed tribes to enjoy tax exemptions as many states do. Nevertheless, this conservative government reaffirmed the goal of reducing Indian dependency on the federal government and pledged to support further Indian self-determination. The goal was to deal with Indians on a government-to-government basis.

In 1988 the *Indian Self-Determination Act* was amended to allow tribes to enter into a self-government "pact" with the federal government. Under this new agreement, Indian tribes extended their powers of self-determination to other areas of control, which until then, had been carried out by the Bureau of Indian Affairs and the Indian Health Service. As a result of this amendment, block grants are provided to Indian tribes and they set the priority of their needs, how programs will be established and carried out to meet those needs.

Some programs have actually incorporated Native American cultural perspectives into legislation's, e.g., *Indian Child Welfare Act* of 1978. The *Act* maximizes tribal jurisdiction over child placement and limits state intervention in such decisions. The *Indian Health Care Improvement Act* was implemented to improve Indian Health and

---

[23] Only recently did the Canadian courts impress upon the Crown that they held a fiduciary duty to Indians.

[24] This Act was recommended by the American Indian Policy Review Commission which had a number of Indians as members.

encourages maximum participation of Indians in the planning and delivery of those services. Other acts such as the *Indian Religious Freedom Act* and the *Native American Graves Protection and Repatriation Act* firmly spell out the "special relationship" between government and Indian tribes.

In 1994, President Clinton met with the leaders of all 547 federally recognized tribes in the United States. At that time, two executive orders were given. First, he publicly noted that tribal authorities were to be given the same deference and respect as that given to state governments. This means that federal officials will have to deal with tribal officials directly and not shuffle them off to the Department of Interior and the Bureau of Indian Affairs. Second, he modified the *Endangered Species Act* which allows Indians to collect and use Eagle feathers for use in various ceremonies. Following this meeting, Indian leaders met with the Attorney General and Secretary of the Interior to discuss ways to strengthen tribes' sovereign status.

4.2.1 Land

In 1946 an Indian Claims Court was created to help Indians achieve a just settlement for land claims disputes dating back to the turn of the century. During its tenure it heard 614 cases. Of these, 204 were dismissed as having no merit while the remainder were decided in favour of Native Americans. In 1978 it was disbanded and the 68 cases still remaining as well as all new cases are now heard by the Court of Claims. In all cases heard by the Indian Claims Court or the Court of Claims, land has never given back to the Indians. Successful claims netted nearly Cdn$1 billion but little of this was returned to the claimants. All expenses incurred in the trials had to be first subtracted and paid to the federal government before payment was made to the Indian claimant.

Under current constitutional arrangements, if Indians do not accept the decision of the court, they have to go back to Congress to obtain permission to sue the United States Government. As one could expect, many cases have yet to be ruled on by Congress. For example, the Sioux in the Black Hills area of the state of South Dakota claim that the Fort Laramie Treaty of 1868 was broken. The case has finally gone through the courts for which the United States Supreme Court set a figure of Cdn$122 million as compensation. However the Sioux do not want financial compensation but a return of the land. The Supreme Court refused to make a judgment requiring the return of the land, once again forcing the Indians to return to Congress, since only it has the power to deal with land (see *United States vs. Sioux Nations of Indians*, 1980).

As the seventies unfolded, land claims became an even more important issue. During the past two decades major land settlements such as the Alaska claims and the Blue Lake land claims of the Indians of Taos Pueblo, New Mexico have been settled. However, other land claims seeking reinstatement of tribal status and compensation for lost land and damages have yet to be fully dealt with.

4.2.2 Political

Unlike their Canadian counterparts, Native Americans have developed a powerful, politically active organizational structure.[25] The modern day "Red Power" movement started in 1961 at a Chicago conference which involved influential tribal leaders and a few radical, young, well educated Indians. Out of this conference was born the National Indian Youth Council. In 1964 this organization responded to the Supreme Court of the state of Washington's nullification of eleven federal treaties that had guaranteed the fishing rights of Indians living in the state. The Youth Council organized a protest lasting two years and culminating in the US Department of Justice appearing before the Washington State's Supreme Court on behalf of the Indians. Flush with such success, other "obstructive" confrontations by Indian organizations took place such as the occupation of Alcatraz Island (1969). In 1970 the American Indian Movement was established and quickly developed into a national organization. Members of this organization assumed militant strategies and began with a protest march (The Trail of Broken Treaties), the occupation of the Bureau of Indian Affairs Offices and the occupation of Wounded Knee (1973). It has continued to be a major political force for Native Americans. One year later, the International Treaty Council was created and provided a vehicle for taking their issues to the United Nations. In Canada, the National Indian Brotherhood was a powerful lobbying force during the 1970's but died out by the 1980's. In its place the Assembly of First Nations was created which is made up of chiefs from all of the bands in Canada. Since then, the emergence of splinter groups from within, such as legal and non-legal Indians, have reduced the effectiveness of this Canadian organization.

The goal of these organizations has been to regain their land base and have their collective rights as nations acknowledged. This linkage has happened in two ways: (1) the organizations have provided a platform for discussing common issues to all Indians, no matter where they lived, and (2) the suppression of the radical Indian movement by the government in the 1960's and 1970's produced a backlash which brought about greater solidarity among Indian groups. While they have accomplished many objectives, their impact has been dulled by several factors. First of all, they have not been able to develop strong linkages throughout the United States. Nor have they been able to create stable linkages with "mainstream" organizations, e.g., church groups, political parties. At best only a thin veneer has linked various Indian groups together. Second, structural and demographic differences between Indians such as socio-economic status, region, and politics have brought about disorganization and intragroup conflict to the overall movement. Nevertheless, Indians feel that their organizations have changed the federal governments policies toward Indians and produced some changes desired by Indians.

---

[25] When AIM (The American Indian Movement), a radical Indian organization attempted to establish itself in Canada, it was summarily rejected by nearly all Canadian Indian leaders. To the extent AIM existed in Canada, it was supported solely by young, radical Indians.

Indian mobilization has been divided between "tribal based mobilization" and "ethnic based mobilization." This bifurcation of mobilization has in part been brought about by the actions taken by government. Federal policy has vacillated between recognizing tribes as the foci of government programs and legislation and taking an alternative approach that "Indianness" was the relevant ethnic distinction for policy purposes. As a result, an analysis of Indian organizations reveals a three-layered structure: the tribal level, pan-tribal level and the ethnic level.

4.2.3 Sovereignty

Unlike those in Canada, tribal governments in the United States have long been recognized as having inherent powers. Moreover, the strategies for providing self-government differ between the two countries as we head into the 21st century. In the United states, it was decided over 150 years ago that Indians have the right to self-government and are to be viewed as domestic nations. Native Americans have not tried to use constitutional reform as a basis for achieving self-government since they already have this right embedded into the political structure.[26] Instead, Native Americans have used the courts to support their claims to self-government. Nevertheless, the political and legal structure of the United States has prevented Indians from achieving greater levels of self-determination.

The debate over self-government is not a political issue in the United States. As noted earlier, sovereignty is a given. However, this does not mean that there have not been debates over the issue. While the government of the United States has tried to restrict the rights of Indians, the courts have remained an integral part of Indian resistance to this infringement. Tribes resort to the courts on a regular basis to deal with state governments trying to exercise their "states rights" over Indian rights, including land claims (Ewan, 1996). In the end, the issues facing Indians are primarily in the legal and not the political sphere, so characteristic of the Canadian scene.

Time and time again, the American courts have set limits on the federal and state government's ability to encroach on tribal powers. Nevertheless, there has been some erosion of Indians rights over time, forcing tribes to take a defensive and reactive stance to legal issues. One noticeable change to this stance has been the establishment of the Native American Rights Fund in 1970 which is a nonprofit national legal defense firm, representing various tribes in lawsuits and negotiations for treaty rights. Nevertheless, courts have not always ruled in favour of Native Americans. For example, in 1996, the Supreme Court ruled (*Seminole Tribe vs. Florida*) that under the 11th amendment, a state may not be sued by an Indian tribe in federal court, even if the state is violating a federal law designed to protect Indians and the Indians are trying to protect themselves from a violation of a federal right (Ewen, 1996).

---

[26] It would seem extremely difficult to introduce constitutional reform in the US since change in the American Constitution requires an amendment to be passed by two thirds majorities in both houses of Congress as well as by three quarters of the states. In over two hundred years, there have only been 26 constitutional amendments passed. Moreover, Americans tend to see their Constitution as immutable.

As one can see from the above, no clear and coherent legal perspective can be seen developing over time as one reviews the decisions of American courts. The contradictory rulings seem to be based on a variety of "doctrines," and in the end, each decision can be explained by the politics of the day. Nevertheless, American courts have been fair and sympathetic to Indian concerns while the actions of Congress have not.

4.2.4 Economic

Recently, the federal government has attempted to develop industries on reservations. However, most of these industrial complexes have not been successful nor produced economic returns to Native Americans. Cottage industries on the reservations have also been encouraged and these have been marginally successful for a small number of individuals. There are substantial natural resources on reservations and there has been some attempt to develop these resources, e.g., reservations encompass about one third of all low-sulfur coal, six percent of the US total gas and oil reserves and nearly half of all known uranium reserves. However, it is difficult for small, independent businesses to enter into a transnational economy. To deal with potential economic developments on the reservations, forty tribes created the Council of Energy Resources Tribes in 1971. Today membership has increased to nearly sixty. This organization provides technical and financial assistance to other member groups and shares its expertise with Indian communities seeking to develop their economies. Another group, the League of First Nations (formed in 1995) is a group of independent Indian business owners (from Iroquois communities).

Presently, the threat to Indian economies (via taxation) on the reservations has tribes searching for new ways to forge ahead in the economic front. At stake is the long-held Indian assertion of sovereignty based on aboriginality in their own lands (Martin, 1996). The Supreme Court has once again opened this issue by ruling in a 1980 case (*Washington vs. the Confederated Tribes of Colville Indian Reservation*) and again in 1989 (*Cotton Petroleum Corporation vs. New Mexico*) that the existence of a tribal tax does not necessarily invalidate a state tax even when the result is dual taxation. Thus, if businesses were to locate on a reservation, they could be forced to pay both a tribal and state tax. Under such circumstances few industries or business would choose to settle on Indian land. In some cases, Indian tribes and state governments have signed agreements or compacts which provide for tax sharing, preventing dual taxation; such has been the case with the Fort Peck and Assiniboine Sioux tribes in Montana.[27]

Recent complications in economic development are a result of a Supreme Court ruling (*Department of Taxation and Finance of the State of New York vs. Milhelm Attea & Bros Inc.*) in 1994. Under this ruling, the state of New York is permitted to collect taxes on goods sold to non-Indians from Indian retailers. Making economic decisions

---

[27] Rather than fight the state and face exorbitant litigation costs, many Indian tribes are negotiating with the state to stop dual taxation on reservations.

even more unclear, the state of Oklahoma sued the Chickasaw Nation (*Chickasaw Nation vs. Oklahoma Tax Commission*) in an attempt to tax the sale of gas on Indian lands. The Supreme Court ruled in favour of the Chickasaw Nation (1995) saying that the state's attempt to impose a fuel tax interfered with the tribes right to self-government.[28] Outside the courts, the House of Representatives is considering a bill (1996) which will prohibit the Bureau of Indian Affairs from transferring any land into trust for any tribe unless the Secretary of Interior has been informed that a binding agreement has been established between the Tribe and the state regarding the collection and payment of state and local sales and excise taxes by non-Indians on Indian land.[29] While this bill has yet to pass the Senate, the chair of the subcommittee has been an outspoken opponent of Indian sovereignty.

The use of land and rights over water have become major economic issues for some reservations. For example, when the United States government first set up laws regarding water, it invoked the "prior appropriation" law which stated that the land closest to the origin of the water had first rights and then the next closest land, and so on. When reservations were established in the late 1800's, little thought was given to the force of this law. After many years of fighting, the courts created the Winters Doctrine of reserved water rights. Stated simply, all users of rivers had to go to court and the courts would then decide how much of the water they could use since all individuals (claims up and down stream) now had water rights. However, the determination of the amount of water rights for Native Americans was set at what one lawyer has referred to as "unconscionable" levels. As a result, many reservations are unable to sustain certain types of development due to lack of water.

A more recent economic activity (gambling) is now being developed by Native Americans and is a major economic enterprise. In 1994, Native American groups in more than twenty states operated over 200 gambling operations. No other commercial activity on Indian lands has matched the success of gambling operations that have been put in place over the past two decades and Thompson (1996) estimates that profits collectively exceed Cdn$5 billion each year. In comparison, Canada has only recently legalized casino gambling and fewer than six Indian casinos are currently in operation. In both countries, non-Indian companies such as management companies or equipment industries have aligned themselves with Indians in an attempt to cash in on the benefits of legalized gambling.

---

[28] Oklahoma is now considering enacting legislation that would impose the tax at the point of sale but allow Indians who pay the tax to apply for a refund.

[29] The argument is that revenues for the state are lost by allowing tax-free sales to non-Indians. In addition, non-Indian businesses claim these are unfair business practices. The state of New York, for example, claims that it loses Cdn$100 million each year.

V   CONCLUSION

In attempting to renegotiate their position in society, Native Americans have used the courts in a reactive and defensive manner while Canadian Indians have used the courts to expand and recognize their right to self-government. While Native Americans have used the courts for well over a century, it is only recently that Canadian Indians have approached the courts.[30] Historically, Canadian courts used narrow and positivistic approaches to resolve Indian claims. For example, the claim of self-government by Native peoples is based upon five normative claims (Macklem, 1995): prior occupancy, prior sovereignty, treaty agreements, self-determination and the preservation of minority cultures. However, when issues are taken to court, the cases are generally limited to one argument and do not consider the issues underlying other claims. This is one of the reasons why many Indians feel that courts are not the best place to resolve claims. Today Indians have moved to the political forum to solve legal and social issues facing their communities. For example, the political negotiations of the 1970's and 1980's led to the constitutional entrenchment of Aboriginal and treaty rights as well as major land claim settlements.

Today's Native peoples are suspicious of any actions taken by government or business which involve them. They have been taught costly lessons from the past and there is a view by Natives that government and business have a hidden agenda each time they approach them to support or partner. Similarly, they are wary of self-government as supported by the government. There is a feeling by some that it is a disguised way in which assimilation will be hastened and control will be in a more benign form.

After reviewing the actions taken by government with regard to Indians, we find that financial considerations are of crucial importance. Over the past two decades, the governments have been cutting the budget for Indians, downsizing, delegating services to Indian communities and decentralizing national structures. Many have argued that what government calls devolution is simply another way of channeling the government's responsibility to Indian communities. The issue remains as to whether or not Indians can deal with the new obligations without sufficient time to prepare, funds to support, and the will to integrate outside ideas into the Indian way of life.

Within the economic sphere, relationships with Aboriginal people are increasingly important to corporate Canada. In Canada, many companies have been implementing active corporate Aboriginal relations programs designed to build constructive partnerships with communities and expand employment and business opportunities for Aboriginal people.[31] On the other hand, this does not seem to be true for the United States.

---

[30] This seemingly reluctance to use the courts by Canadian Indians is partially due to the legal restrictions imposed by the Crown in limiting the Indians' ability to resort to the courts.

[31] This action may in part, be due to the creation of the *Employment Equity Act*, 1986 which forces private and public businesses to implement equity programs for women, disabled, visible minorities and Aboriginals.

Any commitment to Aboriginal people to integrate them into the economics of the corporate world must be multi-dimensional and long term. For any policy to achieve success, several aspects of the policy must be addressed simultaneously. First, the participation of Aboriginal peoples must be backed by the leadership of the corporation, including the Board of Directors. Anything less than top-down, corporate leadership to significant strategic commitments will result in failure. Second, policies must be implemented and integrated into the ongoing business corporate culture. Third, companies must promote education and training, beginning with programs to encourage young people to stay in school. This means that programs that both directly and indirectly influence school attendance must be supported. In addition, corporations must provide educational opportunities and support for Aboriginal students once they decide to continue their education. Fourth, corporations must provide access to pre-employment training in specific skills or business areas. Fifth, companies must enhance employment opportunities through a number of measures. For example, they might implement comprehensive work programs which increase the recruitment, retention and advancement of Aboriginal people. Targeted measures is another technique that can be effective in increasing the representation of Aboriginal peoples in workforces. A sixth strategy is to enhance Aboriginal business participation by providing business opportunities or developing business capabilities.

While examples of the above could be provided in both the United States and Canada, the actual number of successful, sustainable corporate-Aboriginal economic activities over the past two decades remains small. Companies are in the business of making money and if a market can be tapped without sharing it, private enterprise will do so. Only if Aboriginals are able to stop, slow down or otherwise frustrate the efforts of money-making ventures will corporations review alternatives such as establishing a joint venture with Aboriginal communities. Given the diverse interests and the immense power of major transnational corporations, negotiating with Aboriginals is not always necessary. The use of Indian political power (particularly in the United States) and the courts has become a major technique for Aboriginals to deal with corporate initiatives.

Today the American Congress has instituted a new pattern of assuming its federal trust responsibility that is similar to termination, as seen in some state-administered block grants for tribal programs or the outright elimination of tribal line items from budgets (Martin, 1996a). For example, the cuts to the 1996 Interior Appropriations budget averaged eleven percent compared to the 32 percent cuts for tribal fisheries, law enforcement, courts and child welfare.

These new "backlash" bills of the 1990's are similar to those enacted in the 1970's and 1980's. For example, in 1978-79, there were 13 anti-Indian bills introduced to Congress. A similar number were presented in 1985. These bills focus on eliminating indigenous water rights, tribal sovereignty, treaties and jurisdiction (Martin, 1996a: 29).

Nevertheless, Indians need to rebuild their vision, developing their traditional philosophies and using them as guiding lights to the future. Many Indians feel that because Indians are still distinct in society and despite the fact that many people have predicted their demise many times, they will continue to remain Indian. However, as Boldt (1994) points out, they may remain distinctive, but not necessarily Indian. Their distinctiveness is partially a function of being marginalized, holding specific legal status, experiencing racism, living on reserves and other social attributes. However, these are not cultural attributes which make them distinct. At present, Indians are experiencing a massive deculturalization process in which traditional social systems, normative patterns and other cultural practices are disappearing. Moreover, a culture of dependency has emerged. There is an urgent need for cultural revitalization to take place if Indians are to survive the next generation as Indians and not as member of a "culture of poverty." Members of the community (cultural maximizers) need to develop and socialize other members of the community with regard to Indian culture (from language to philosophy) (Boldt, 1994).

If democracy was the ultimate concern in dealing with Indians, treaty and other claims would have been settled long ago. Co-optation would be replaced by legitimate representation and government insistence on unilaterally proclaimed laws, e.g., Indian citizenship, would no longer be an issue. Nor would anti-Indian lobbyists use rhetoric to deny Aboriginal people their just entitlements as set out in the treaties.[32] Governments have a profound direct, day-to-day control over Native people and their lives. They are able to set budgets, determining how much money will be spent on such activities as education and social services. They also have what has been called "plenary power," meaning that they can do almost anything they want in terms of Indian-Federal relations. Such power can be used to grant self-government or terminate the federal relationship (Trahant, 1996: 30).

Both Americans and Canadians seem to want to recognize the distinctiveness of Indians and have not rejected outright the concept of self-government or self-determination. However, at the same time, both countries have hedged their support to such a reconceptualization, particularly if it means there will be changes to power structures and a redistribution of resources. In the end, while there may be some changes, the central policy structures and the definition of these policies still remains within the control of the federal government. If Indians are to enter the institutional spheres of 21st century America, they must begin to play a significant, ongoing political and economic role.

---

[32] In the United States, government actions are seen as turning tribes into felons because if the tribes did not accept the reduction of sovereignty, they would be committing crimes against the state. The states are arguing that they have supreme power, regardless of the existence of federal treaties.

References

Anaya, S., Falk, R. & Pharand, D. (1995). *Canada's Fiduciary Obligation to Aboriginal Peoples in the Context of Accession to Sovereignty by Québec.* Ottawa: Royal Commission on Aboriginal Peoples (Volume 1: International Dimensions).

Armitage, A. (1995). *Comparing the Policy of Aboriginal Assimilation: Australia, Canada and New Zealand.* Vancouver: University of British Columbia Press.

Boldt, M. (1994). *Surviving as Indians.* Toronto: University of Toronto Press.

Brock, K. (1993). The issue of self-government: Canadian and American Aboriginal policy compared. In D. Thomas (ed.), *Canada and the United States: Differences that Count* (pp. 252-70). Peterborough: Broadview Press.

Canada, Government of (1989). *Indian Self-Government Community Negotiations: Guidelines.* Ottawa: DIAND, Minister of Indian Affairs and Northern Development.

Cornell, S. (1988). *The Return of the Native: American Indian Political Resurgence.* New York/Oxford: University Press.

Ducharme, M. (1986). The segregation of native people in Canada: voluntary or compulsory, *Currents*, Summer: 2-3.

Dupuis, R. & McNeil, K. (1995). *Canada's Fiduciary Obligation to Aboriginal Peoples in the Context of Accession to Sovereignty by Québec.* Ottawa: Royal Commission on Aboriginal Peoples (Volume 2: Domestic Dimensions).

Ewen, A. (1996). A supreme question of power: High Court paves legal road to States' supremacy, *Native Americas* 13 (2): 26-9.

Feagin, J. & Feagin, C. (1996). *Racial and Ethnic Relations.* Upper Saddle River, New Jersey: Prentice Hall.

Fleras, A. & Elliott, J. (1992). *The Nations Within.* Oxford, Toronto/Oxford: University Press.

Fleras, A. & Elliott, J. (1996). *Unequal Relations.* Scarborough: Prentice Hall Canada Inc.

Frideres, J. (1995). *Native People in Canada: Contemporary Conflicts.* Toronto: Prentice Hall (fourth edition).

Hogg, P. & Turpel, M. E. (1995). Implementing aboriginal self-government: constitutional and jurisdictional issues, *The Canadian Bar Review* 74(2): 188-224.

Gibbins, R. & Ponting, J. (1986). An assessment of the probable impact of Aboriginal self-government in Canada. In A. Cairns & C. Williams (eds.), *The Politics of Gender, Ethnicity and Language in Canada* (pp. 171-245). Toronto: University of Toronto Press.

Isaac, T. (1995). *Aboriginal Law: Cases, Materials, and Commentary.* Saskatoon, Saskatchewan: Purich Publishing.

Macklem, P. (1995). *Normative Dimensions of the Right of Aboriginal Self-Government. Aboriginal Self-Government.* Selected papers commissioned by the Royal Commission on Aboriginal Peoples. Ottawa: Minister of Supply and Services, Canada: 1-54.

Martin, K. (1996a). Indians not taxed: will sovereignty survive? *Native Americas* 13 (2): 14-25.

Martin, K. (1996b). Under his authority, *Native Americas* 13 (3): 22-9.

McLemore, S. (1991). *Racial and Ethnic Relations in America.* Boston: Allyn and Bacon.

Morse, B. & Giokas, J. (1995). *Do the Metis Fall Within Section 91(24) of the Constitution Act, 1867? Aboriginal Self-Government.* Selected papers commissioned by the Royal Commission on Aboriginal Peoples, Ottawa: Minister of Supply and Services, Canada: pp. 140-277.

Moss, W. (1995). *Inuit Perspectives on Treaty Rights and Governance. Aboriginal Self-Government.* Selected papers commissioned by the Royal Commission on Aboriginal Peoples, Ottawa: Minister of Supply and Services, Canada: pp. 55-139.

Ponting, R. (1991). An Indian policy for Canada in the twenty-first century. In C. Remie & J. Lacroix (eds.), *Canada on the Threshold of the 21st Century* (pp. 431-46). Amsterdam: John Benjamins Publishing Company.

Ponting, R. (1993). Aboriginal dilemmas of the Federal State in Canada. In H. Ottens & F. Toppen (eds.), *Canadian Dilemmas: Environment and Constitution* (pp. 89-101). Canadian Studies Seminar, Hilversum, The Netherlands.

Silverman, R. & Nielsen, M. (1992). *Aboriginal Peoples and Canadian Criminal Justice.* Toronto: Butterworths.

Sloan, P. & Hill, R. (1995). *Corporate Aboriginal Relations.* Toronto: Hill Sloan Associates Inc.

Snipp, M. (1989). *American Indians: The First of This Land.* New York: Russell Sage Foundation.

Stiffarm, L. & Lane, P. (1992). Demography of Native North America: a question of American Indian survival. In M.A. Jaimes (ed.), *The State of Native America: Genocide, Colonization, and Resistance.* Boston: South End Press.

Stuart, P. (1987). *Nations Within A Nation: Historical Statistics of American Indians.* New York: Greenwood Press.

Thompson, W. (1996). *Native American Issues.* Santa Barbara: ABC-CLIO Publishers.

Trahant, M. (1996). Seeking representation, *Native Americas* 13 (3): 30-1.

Part Four
Canada in the International Arena

OF FRIENDS, INTERESTS, CROWBARS, AND MARRIAGE VOWS IN CANADA-UNITED STATES TRADE RELATIONS

by Michael HART

Canada's crowbar, our instrument to lever performance, our guarantee that neighbourly obligations must be fulfilled, our very locus standi as a nation derive not from the US Congress, but exclusively from international law and treaties. Even the most active lobbyists should never forget this fact.[1]
Allan Gotlieb, Canadian Ambassador to the United States (1981-88)

Getting things right with the US may be a prescription open to debate in Canada but it should never be a matter of neglect... Like a good marriage, we depend on each other in good times as well as bad. Geography has made us neighbours; trade has made us partners; and trade agreements have made it possible for us to live well with each other.[2]
Derek Burney, Canadian Ambassador to the United States (1989-93)

I   BACKGROUND

In 1994, in a study of the Canada-US free-trade negotiations, my co-authors and I concluded that "despite the problems posed by an often indifferent and difficult United States, Canada succeeded in negotiating a good agreement" (Hart et al., 1994: 387). Canadians have often doubted their government's ability to negotiate good agreements with the United States, not only because of problems of indifference and difficulty, but also because the United States is a large and powerful country and is presumed to have a more extensive talent pool upon which to draw. Former Prime Minister Lester Pearson, reflecting on his early diplomatic experience in Washington, became quite indignant on the subject, protesting that "the picture of weak and timid Canadian negotiators being pushed around and browbeaten by American representatives into settlements that were 'sell-outs' is a false and distorted one. It is often painted, however, by Canadians who think that a sure way to get applause and support at home is to exploit our anxieties and exaggerate our suspicions over US power and policies."[3]

---

[1] Allan Gotlieb (1991: 74-5). Gotlieb was not the only veteran of Canada-US relations who liked the image of the crowbar. During her term in office as US Trade Representative, Carla Hills took pride in pointing to a picture on her boardroom wall of President Bush presenting her with a crowbar as a symbol of the zeal with which she would pursue US interests in prying open foreign markets. US legislators, in a similar vein, often refer to section 301 as the crowbar of US trade policy, a tool available to the US government to force other countries to open their markets to US competitors. Gotlieb's image of the crowbar as a lever to force the United States into fulfilling its obligations to its neighbour seems more apt, particularly since close examination of Mrs. Hills' picture suggests that President Bush had handed her a wrecking bar rather than a crowbar. Many foreign observers of US trade policy would agree that as often as not, US officials tend to prefer the blunt approach of awrecking bar to the more delicate touch required with a crowbar.

[2] Donald W. Campbell Lecture in International Trade, Wilfrid Laurier University Chancellor's Symposium, Toronto, June 14, 1995.

[3] *Mike: The Memoirs of the Right Honourable Lester B. Pearson.* Volume I: 1897-1948. Toronto: University of Toronto Press (1972: 72-3).

Pearson's observation accurately reflects both the reality of bilateral negotiations and the inaccuracy of public perceptions about them. Canadian negotiators have proven more adept at negotiating with their US counterparts than at communicating the results to the public. Negotiating styles and approaches, however, have changed as Canadian officials have adapted to the constantly shifting requirements of dealing with their US counter-parts. This paper explores what is involved in negotiating with *an often indifferent and difficult United States*, and traces some of the techniques and attitudes Canadian governments have developed over the years in their determination to live distinct from but in harmony with the United States.

Three key challenges confront Canadians in their efforts to negotiate agreements and re-solve conflicts with their giant neighbour to the south: one is that the United States is temperamentally ill-suited to negotiate international commercial agreements; the second is that the United States is constitutionally ill-equipped to negotiate such agreements; the third is that Canada has an attitude to its neighbour that makes negotiations with the United States particularly difficult. In the Canada-US free-trade negotiations, one of the most public and controversial bilateral negotiations in Canada-US history, these factors were particularly challenging because the stakes – political and economic – were exceptionally high. Although not often thought of in such terms, the Canada-United States Free Trade Agreement (FTA) was conceived in large part as a mechanism for managing trade and economic relations between the two countries. As such it reflected a changing appreciation of the nature of that relationship and of the tools required to manage it. Of course, it was also many other things. It was equally an effort to make trade and investment between the two countries freer and thus expand opportunities for entrepreneurs on both sides of the border. That aspect of the FTA has been sufficiently explored elsewhere. This essay concentrates on the background to the decision to seek an improved way to manage bilateral relations, and on its impact as a management tool.

II   THE CHALLENGE OF LIVING NEXT DOOR TO A SUPERPOWER

The impact of history and geography has perhaps made the management of Canada-US relations more challenging than the relations of any other country with the United States. Canada and the United States, together with Mexico, share a continent and boast a common frontier more than five thousand miles in length. Unlike Mexico, however, the ties of language and common ancestry have always made Canada-US relations unique.[4] That uniqueness dates back more than two hundred years. The United Empire Loyalists, the dominant element in Canada's governing stock during the formative years of its history, arrived from the United States with an attitude. They had rejected the American Revolution. They were the first anti-Americans. They had made a conscious decision to remain loyal to the crown and to reject the ideology of the American Revolution. Over

---

[4] This is a uniqueness that is more readily apparent on the Canadian than on the US side of the border. Most studies of Canada-US relations are written by Canadians. Few Americans find the issues sufficiently interesting to devote a whole book to them. John Holmes (1989: 18) noted acerbically that "there is a small band of scholars and concerned citizens in the United States who might be called Canadianists, probably smaller than the number of Albanianists."

the next hundred years these Canadians proved time and again that they did not want to be Americans; they rejected American expansionism in whatever form it was presented. When the various colonies came together in 1867 to form a country, they did so on the basis of an Act of the British Parliament. Unlike the revolutionaries to the south a century earlier who had proclaimed their creed to be life, liberty, and the pursuit of happiness, Canadians declared their goal to be peace, order, and good government. Thus from the outset, Canada and the United States exhibited a sibling rivalry like no other. The United States was founded in revolutionary fervour, based on the values and ideas of the Enlightenment. The subsequent US conquest of a continent over the course of the nineteenth century and its military and economic success in the twentieth century helped to reinforce a peculiar, religiously based concept of manifest destiny, i.e., the secular version of the Christian duty to spread the gospel, with the gospel having become the *American way*. This good news was spread with a self-confidence that can only be exhibited by a people who know they are right and have God on their side. Not surprisingly, others did not always accept this gospel with equanimity. The American people, while professing a deep commitment to tolerance, proved in fact to be the most intolerant of people. Subconsciously, they exhibited attachment to a set of values and habits of mind that made it very hard to see other points of view, and to accept that there might be alternative, even better ways of doing things. In short, American culture developed a strong and abiding insensitivity to the views and preferences of others.

American self-confidence and expressions of manifest destiny tend to grate, particularly on the people next door. Canadians are not Americans. They are not governed from Washington. They do not get their views from *The New York Times*. They do not consider Hollywood to be the realization of the Canadian dream. Like their Loyalist ancestors, many Canadians glory in the fact that they are not Americans. They revel in it and often enough, in so doing, they exhibit their own cultural insensitivity.[5]

Americans may share some Canadian misgivings about American values. Some resent being governed from Washington; some have nothing but contempt for Hollywood; most do not get their views from *The New York Times*. But that is not the same thing as Canadians questioning so-called mainstream American values. Home-grown critics form part of the decision-making, value-generating whole that is America. They are on the inside.

Canadians are on the outside. They have their own values. They have their own clichés and caricatures. Their demons are in Ottawa, at the CBC, and at the *Globe and Mail*. Canadians have their own cauldron of hopes and anxieties. They have their own disagreements and make their own determinations of what is important, what they want to see, hear, and read, who they want to deal with, and more. They are determined to

---

[5] David Orchard's *The Fight for Canada: Four Centuries of Resistance to American Expansionism* (1993), which might more accurately have been subtitled Four Centuries of Canadian Paranoia, provides interesting insight into the pathology of modern anti-Americanism. J.L. Granatstein (1996) provides a sensitive and sensible appreciation of the issues by someone who started out as a "devout anti-American" but came to the conclusion that most modern anti-Americanism is "just plain silly."

maintain room for their own hopes and glories as well as their own inanities and banalities. As John Holmes (1989: 21) observed, "we chew the same gum, but our political lives are distinct."

Canadians are not alone in their desire to be distinct. Japanese, Malaysians, Norwegians, Italians, and Brazilians also want their own space. But none of these people live next door to the United States. With the exception of the Mexicans, no one else lives as close. No one else visits back and forth as easily and is as deeply saturated by the American presence as are Canadians. Nor have any other people had as long an experience of dealing with the juggernaut of the twentieth century. At the same time, Canadians are the closest thing to Americans, making Canadians insist even harder that they are not and leading Americans to wonder why. That is why Canada-US relations, viewed from the Canadian end of the telescope, tend to be as sensitive and intense as they are. From the other end of the telescope, awareness of Canada and things Canadian does not amount to much. Canada is the source of cold weather on the evening news and, unless you are professionally engaged, not much else. For many Americans, what happens in Canada is about as important as what happens in Wyoming or New Hampshire. Usually not that important in the global scheme of things! That attitude has its own way of grating. Notes Canadian novelist and Montréal *enfant terrible*, Mordecai Richler (1979: 38), "The sour truth is just about everybody outside of Canada finds us boring. Immensely boring."

Finally, to US missionary fervour and confidence must be added the difficult problem of dealing with a country with the single most concentrated share of global economic, military, and political power. Superpowers tend to behave differently and to have expectations that may be somewhat more pressing than those of others. The end of the cold war as the basis for organizing much official thought in the US and elsewhere, coupled with the perceived decline of the United States as a great power, has added a further note of uncertainty to the management of relations with the United States.

III   THE CHALLENGE OF THE US CONSTITUTION

As if life would not be difficult enough living next door to the United States, Canadian governments have discovered through bitter experience, as have other governments, that the United States is not constitutionally equipped to deal with the rest of the world on a basis that most countries would consider normal. The United States does not have one government or a single center of power, but many governments and many actors with authority to exercise power. Putting aside the problems of a federal state within which fifty states exercise the authority assigned to them by the Constitution, the much touted system of checks and balances and of divided or separate power can make the US government a very trying negotiating partner. In the words of Canada's diplomatic sage, John Holmes (1989: 26), "Canadians recognize that Americans have a beautiful Constitution, but we wish they would realize how difficult it is to be an ally of a country that can not make binding commitments."

The US system of government is not just a matter of an executive, a legislature, and a judiciary, all with interests to promote and powers to protect, but it is also a system that divides power so finely that it allows the noisiest and most idiosyncratic individuals to rise to positions of power and influence. Former House Speaker Tip O'Neill was not describing a universal truth when he said that all politics is local, but it is an American truth. In normal countries local politics is important, but there are also institutional provisions which make it possible for national or broader interests to prevail. The Helms-Burton law, aimed at discouraging non-Americans from trading with and investing in Cuba, provides only the most recent exhibit of the ease with which parochial, narrow interests can prevail in the United States. Negotiations in the spring of 1997 to conclude a Pacific Salmon Treaty provides a further illustration of the American truth that the more concentrated and local an interest, the less likely their American authorities will be prepared to make compromises and reach a reasonable settlement. Some may call this the cost of democracy; others would describe it as a perversion of democracy.

The impact of the doctrine of the separation of powers is particularly acute in the area of trade because the US Constitution assigns responsibility for regulating international trade to Congress, while it places the President in charge of the conduct of foreign relations. Thus the President may negotiate treaties, but the Congress is responsible for trade agreements, a subtle distinction not always appreciated by non-Americans. Treaties require two-thirds approval by the Senate before they become law; trade agreements must be implemented into US law by both Houses of Congress. Since 1934, the negotiation of trade agreements has been periodically delegated to the President under a series of arrangements which involve close congressional supervision and, through implementing legislation, ultimate approval by Congress.

The exercise of the president's negotiating authority can be so circumscribed as to virtually tie the hands of US negotiators. In addition to complex consultative and formal reporting requirements, the process of gaining congressional approval means satisfying the narrow interests of a sufficient number of members of Congress to pass the necessary legislation. In a country where party discipline is weak and responsible government is unknown, this is no easy task. In such circumstances, broad national interests play virtually no part. As Allan Gotlieb (1991: 43), Canada's ambassador to the United States for most of the 1980's, trenchantly observes: "in Washington, ... a foreign power is just another special interest, and not a very special one at that." Gotlieb (1991: 76) goes on to suggest that "the foreign government must recognize that it is at a serious disadvantage compared to other special interests for the simple reason that foreign interests have no senators, no congressmen, and no staffers to represent them at the bargaining table. They have no votes and no political action committees."

All they have is the State Department, and that is almost worse than having nothing at all because it creates a false sense of security. On issues that matter today, such as trade and investment, the State Department has little or no influence. Notes Gotlieb (1991: 91): "Notwithstanding the enormous importance of trade in current international relations –

unfair trade acts are a new form of international aggression – the State Department has at best a modest role in both the negotiating and policy processes." The important players are the United States Trade Representative (USTR), Commerce, and Treasury, all of whom respond to domestic interests and pay careful heed to the machinations of Congress.

Equally critical are the courts and various regulatory bodies and quasi-judicial administrative tribunals, all of which apply laws passed by a Congress driven by special interests. The US Constitution provides individuals with the right to use the courts, or *due process*, to an extent that goes well beyond what is required to defend civil society – again with serious implications for US trade relations with the rest of the world. It is not difficult to point to recent examples: the Loewen case in New Orleans (private pursuit of antitrust of a Canadian-based firm modernizing the delivery of funeral services); the pursuit of liability suits on products that fully conform to US and international standards; and the US embargo of Mexican tuna and Thai shrimp to protect dolphin and sea turtles respectively. In each instance, decisions in US domestic court cases ended up as unilateral extensions of US jurisdiction and regulatory fiat.

All this might be acceptable as the price of doing business with the largest, richest, and most lucrative trading partner in the world, if Americans were not so insistent that their approach to matters is not just the best way, but the only way. All other ways are suspect and must be rooted out and made to conform to American values, preferences, and practices. This is not just a matter of doing business with Americans in the United States, but also of doing business with Americans in one's own country. The United States is the only country in the world with a fully developed concept of the extraterritorial application of its laws. In effect, cultural insensitivity is an accepted, legal doctrine in the United States.

If truth be told, however, many American habits of mind, values, and preferences wear surprisingly well in relations between Americans and the rest of the world. The rest of the world is prepared to accept many of them, except when they come as official pronouncements out of Washington. They then become something else. They become hectoring in tone and difficult to swallow. In large measure, what happens in Washington is that these US cultural values lose balance; they become the aggressive act of a narrow interest, unprepared to place matters in perspective. Washington has become the home of the narrow-minded, as thousands of competing special interests try to prevail in law and policy. And foreign interests are the easiest to sacrifice or attack. That is the nub of the problem.

IV   THE ADVERSARIAL NATURE OF TRADE RELATIONS

The challenges presented to the rest of the world by the US temperament and Constitution are, of course, not unique to trade relations, but they are perhaps more acute because of the competitive or adversarial nature of trade, and the artificial intrusion of national frontiers into what are essentially transactions between private parties. What most people would find objectionable behaviour within a country is applauded when it involves an international transaction. At heart, most people are mercantilists, even when they know better. Most people instinctively believe that exports are good and imports are bad. Such economic nationalism may not be theoretically sound, but it is a creed to live by and, intuitively, most politicians live by it. David Henderson (1986: 11-2), once the chief economist at the OECD, believes economists are the least successful of academicians because virtually no one accepts the most basic tenets of their teachings, particularly when it comes to international trade. Most people continue to confuse comparative advantage with absolute advantage. They do not accept that countries export in order to import and that the benefits come from imports.

Similarly, most business people would like to be monopolists. They accept competition because governments and ease of entry will not let them become monopolists. But competition for many business executives represents a second-best approach; as a result, the purpose of competition becomes a matter of besting your competitor and, if possible, driving him out of business. Such an attitude is not considered acceptable within a domestic market; more to the point, in most societies there are laws against acting on it. But the prevalence of economic nationalism makes such behaviour legitimate on a cross-border basis. Indeed, government policy often makes it easier because much government policy is predicated on mercantilist thinking and is designed to serve producer interests rather than broader economic welfare and consumer interests. As a result, governments are often prepared to champion the interests of their own producers at the expense of foreign producers, even in matters that clearly suggest that broader societal interests are being sacrificed.

The US doctrine of the separation of powers accentuates this internationally anti-social behaviour. The assignment of the trade policy-making authority to Congress virtually ensures that US policy will be more attuned to narrow than broad interests and be more adversarial than is the case for most other countries. International trade rules and institutions seek to curb these natural tendencies, but their implementation always represent an uphill struggle. When there is conflict, politicians often portray them as a burden rather than as a help. Thus, even though the United States has long been a leader in the negotiation of international trade rules that seek to make national trade policies less discriminatory and more liberal, US politicians consistently characterize such rules as stacked against US interests and seek ways to neutralize their impact. In September 1996, then acting USTR Charlene Barshefsky told members of Congress that "the WTO dispute settlement mechanism is proving to be a very effective tool to open other nations' markets. ... [E]nforceability of the dispute settlement rules has made settlement of disputes a much more frequent, speedy and useful outcome." But she felt compelled to assure the members that "the WTO cannot force the United States to repeal or amend any provision of federal or state law or apply or enforce our laws in any particular manner."[6] Such ritualistic confirmations of a double standard colour US trade policy and frequently raise suspicions about US motives and goals in the negotiation of new rules.

From the US perspective, any negative fallout from international trade means that its trading partners must take steps to redress a US grievance. If US exporters fail to succeed in the Japanese market, the Japanese government is called upon to rectify the situation. If too much Canadian wheat or too many Canadian-made suits enter the US market, the Canadian government is enjoined to make amends. If low-cost exporters of textiles and clothing are too successful in the US market, it is their duty to restrain exports and stop disrupting the US market. If Canada takes steps to promote domestic consumption of Canadian cultural products, the Canadian government is called to account. A favourite mantra of US trade policy is "we have a problem, and you must do something about it." When other countries have a problem with US measures, US officials resort to discussion of the Constitution and the importance of congressional support for other policies. When other countries have a problem, they need to learn to live with it.

It is thus not difficult to appreciate why there is sometimes conflict between Canada and the United States and why such conflicts can be very adversarial. Most Canada-US trade disputes, of course, are not between Canada and the United States but between private parties in Canada and the United States. They may involve government programs or policies, as in a subsidy or countervailing duty case, or they may involve governments as champions of their citizens, as in antidumping cases. Bilateral trade disputes may require that the government take sides on an issue in which there are conflicting interests within Canada, for example, between producers and consumers. In all such cases, it is important not to confuse the vigorous defense of Canadian interests in a dispute and what Canada's broader public policy interests may be. Like a good lawyer, the government will defend a firm or province or policy, but a loss does not necessarily mean a loss for Canada. It may mean the establishment of better public policy. The long-running and difficult dispute about landing requirement for salmon and herring on the West Coast ultimately obliged Canada to change its requirements. From a broad public policy perspective, it is not at all clear that Canada's previous policy served anything other than a few narrow fish processing interests.

Conflict, of course, can be regarded as a healthy sign of a dynamic relationship. In a tough, competitive world, individuals, firms, industries, and countries will work hard to gain and maintain advantage. It is not unusual in such circumstances to see conflict. At any one time, it is not extraordinary to count dozens of issues being disputed between Canadians and Americans and between the government of Canada and that of the United States. The fact that there is a border between the two countries, for example, staffed by

---

[6] Statement of Ambassador Charlene Barshefsky, Acting United States Trade Representative, before the Subcommittee on Trade of the Committee on Ways and Means, US House of Representatives, September 11, 1996.

customs agents, is often enough to spark a conflict. Customs agents believe it is their job to defend domestic producers. What is surprising is not that there are conflicts, but that there are relatively few which are so controverted and difficult as to require formal resolution using available dispute resolution mechanisms. The question then becomes why these disputes contain so much rancour and why they project such an adversarial nature.

The question can only be asked by a Canadian. It is not an American question. Resolving conflict on the basis of an adversarial process is as American as apple pie. Nor do Americans wonder why there is rancour. If you believe in a case, you put it forcefully, and if the other side does not respond, you speak a little louder and you get your friends to help raise the volume. In the case of bilateral trade disputes, you ask your Representative or Senator to help make noise. The fact that Senator Max Baucus is shouting on behalf of US lumber producers should not be interpreted as meaning that the whole of the United States has made up its mind on the issue. The cacophony of noise generated inside the Washington beltway is just part of the way business is conducted in the world's greatest democracy. Diplomacy, particularly in the area of trade, is not something best left to professionals to sort out quietly. It is a matter of forceful advocacy.

Canadians have traditionally not liked this adversarial approach to bilateral issues. They prefer a more consensual approach. The parliamentary system of responsible government concentrates tremendous authority in the executive which is thus much better equipped to negotiate international trade agreements and to address problems in international trade relations. While over the years Canadian parliaments have assigned some powers to quasi-judicial tribunals under the general supervision of the courts, Canadian governments have tended to carefully circumscribe such delegated authority, even to the extent of providing the executive with continued power to intervene and overrule such tribunals. As a result, Canada has shown a strong preference for quiet rather than public diplomacy. Because Canada is a federal state, the role of the central government has increasingly needed to accommodate provincial concerns, particularly as international affairs have grown to encompass matters of provincial responsibility. But even here, Canadians have preferred a consensual form of decision-making. The federal-provincial log-rolling process and muddling through have been Canada's contribution to decision-making literature.

Given that issues are likely to be addressed in an adversarial manner between Canada and the United States, the challenge is to ensure that appropriate substantive rules and procedures are in place that will allow these issues to be resolved on the basis of law and due process rather than power and the rancour and entrenched interests of the moment. That has been the thrust of Canadian trade policy for the past sixty-plus years, still more so as the US decision-making process has become more and more fragmented and unpredictable.

V   SOME HISTORICAL PERSPECTIVES

Modern Canada-US trade relations date back to 1935 Only then did Canada and the United States finally succeed in negotiating a modern trade agreement. Canada was one of the first countries to take up the invitation of President Roosevelt to negotiate a new kind of reciprocal trade agreement under the revolutionary new delegated mandate provided by Congress in 1934. Canada followed up in concert with Britain in negotiating a more extensive agreement three years later by which time Canada had developed a team of experts with a solid base of experience in negotiating such agreements. Together with the colleagues responsible for political relations, they excelled at what became known as *quiet diplomacy*. They cultivated relationships with senior members of the US Administration, particularly in the then powerful State Department, which could be used to protect and advance Canadian interests. They were very good at their job and thus carved out a place for Canada in the US capital that far exceeded what could reasonably be expected of a small country just emerging from the shadow of the mother country. To be sure, there were frustrations and disappointments, but in a significant number of instances Canadian diplomats earned a role for Canada in international affairs that was more a tribute to their talents than to Canada's natural weight. They also managed frequently to resolve problems between the two countries in Canada's favour. Building on the warm personal relationship between President Franklin Roosevelt and Prime Minister Mackenzie King, they carved out a *special relationship* between the two countries that lasted through the 1960's. One of the hallmarks of that special relationship was a willingness on the part of US administrations to exempt Canada from measures aimed at other trading partners. Historian Robert Bothwell (1992: 10) cautions, however, that we should not exaggerate the efficacy of the special relationship. When US interests were clear, such as in efforts to shift on to western Canadian farmers the burden of US concessional wheat sales to third markets, there was nothing special about the relationship.

One of the early fruits of Canadian-American cooperation was the successful conclusion of the General Agreement on Tariffs and Trade (GATT) in Geneva in 1947. From a Canadian perspective it had the particular virtue of providing a set of rules and procedures for gradually liberalizing trade and resolving trade conflicts on a multilateral basis. Canada could pursue close relations with both of its major trading partners and not have to choose between them, as its had been forced to do in the triangular negotiations of 1937-38. In effect, the GATT became Canada's trade agreement with the United States.

The virtues of rules-based relations and the liberalizing bias of the GATT regime were, for most of the postwar period, offset to some extent by powerful interests in Canada that saw greater benefit in maintaining protection than in adjusting to competition. Thus, throughout the period, Canadian governments kept to a delicate compromise between the mercantilist interests of domestic groups, particularly manufacturers, and the broader interest of the nation in rules-based multilateralism. There was, therefore, not always a congruence of interests between Canada and the United States. Canada maintained protection that harmed US export interests while the US took measures that harmed Canadian interests. Canadians found US protectionism particularly galling in the face of the overwhelming economic superiority enjoyed by the United States.

While Canada professed a deep attachment to rules-based multilateralism, Canadian officials were not always convinced that the rules were enough. They were not prepared to take on US interests purely on the basis of the rules, preferring where possible to negotiate accommodations that reflected the neighbourliness worked out in the 1930's and 1940's. Both sides were loath to rely on third-party arbitration, fearful that such arbitration could lead to a loss of control by both officials and ministers. Despite a long string of irritants between the two countries, Canada did not formally invoke GATT dispute settlement procedures against the United States until 1973 when it joined in a complaint regarding the US Domestic International Sales Corporation tax deferral scheme. Until that time, close consultation and resort to pragmatic solutions were the preferred approach.

This quiet diplomacy worked better when Liberals and Democrats were in power than when Republicans were in office in Washington or Conservatives in Ottawa. The Eisenhower years saw more setbacks than triumphs as Republicans in both Congress and the Administration were more inclined to listen to US business interests than take account of broader geopolitical considerations, and tiffs between the Kennedy and Diefenbaker governments became legendary. With the return to power of the Liberals in 1963, however, neighbourliness was fully back in fashion, at least until Lester Pearson offended President Johnson over the Vietnam war. Even then, US officials worked hard to maintain good relations. The resolution of problems in the automotive industry by means of the GATT-inconsistent Autopact in 1965 typified what could be achieved as a result of the special relationship.

The auto agreement added further to the continental direction of Canadian economic development. By this time, opinion in Canada was beginning to question the wisdom of such close ties to the American economy. As if to prove the critics' case, President Nixon and his Treasury Secretary John Connally brought the special relationship to a crashing halt in 1971. Faced by a mounting drain of dollars caused by the Vietnam war and US overseas investment, as well as US responsibility as the reserve currency under the fixed-exchange regime of the International Monetary Fund, Nixon took dramatic action that effectively altered the postwar consensus on monetary cooperation. The various measures, including a ten percent import surcharge, hit Canada hard. Canadian officials trooped to Washington to explain that Canada should be exempted from the measures only to learn that they were considered a major part of the problem. There would be no exemptions and Canada would have to make its own adjustments. In case the point had been missed, President Nixon told the House of Commons the following year that he respected "Canada's right to chart its own course" – the United States would follow its own course and respect Canada's right to do the same. There would be no more special relationship.

Canada's ability to use quiet diplomacy to advance its trade interests had in part reflected the fact that during the first three decades after the end of the Second World War, trade was much less important to the United States than to Canada. With few exceptions, American firms manufactured goods and produced services for American consumers, and American consumers relied almost exclusively on American goods and services. Competition in the United States meant competition among American firms. Abroad, American firms might compete with European, Canadian, and other firms, but more often on the basis of goods produced by American branch plants than on the basis of exports. Until the 1970's, the value of neither American exports nor American imports ever exceeded five percent of GDP. The United States might formally have been the most open economy in the world during this period, but in terms of actual levels of trade, it was one of the most closed. Consequently, the number of special interests affected by Canadian and other imports was quite small, in part explaining why the State Department was allowed to subordinate so much of its trade policy to broader geopolitical considerations. The payments crisis that led to the Nixon measures of August 1971 was fueled in large part by the outflow of US investment as well as the cost of the Vietnam war, rather than by the inflow of imports or the paucity of US exports.

Trade played a much more important role in the Canadian economy, particularly trade with the United States. During the first decade and a half after the war, growth in the Canadian economy was spurred more by domestic than foreign demand, but by the end of the 1950's, when most European currencies had returned to full convertibility and reconstruction in Europe and Asia had been achieved, Canada was participating in a trade-led boom. For Canada, however, that boom was largely a matter of trade with the United States. Trade between Canada and Britain never recovered from the devastation of war, depression, and Britain's long attachment to a closed Sterling area. By the time Sterling was returned to convertibility in 1957, Canadians had developed a clear preference for American over British goods, and Britain had learned to rely more and more on European and other Commonwealth suppliers. In the following two decades, that pattern of close interdependence would accelerate further, fueled by the effect of growing two-way investment flows.

The intensification of trade and investment naturally added to the potential for tensions. Canadians might not be considered *foreign* by most Americans, but to those who had to compete with Canadians either at home or in Canada, Canadians did not always measure up to American standards and, without representation in Congress, were fair game for either protectionist measures at home or some extraterritorial arm-twisting in Canada. Managing these tensions proved more a Canadian than an American challenge. Even during the heyday of the special relationship, Canadians had learned that any irritant in the relationship was usually their fault and required them to take appropriate action to fix the problem. By the early 1970's, Canadian vulnerability to US actions had become acute, particularly as the long US economic lead over its trading partners began to erode and US firms learned that they would have to compete with foreign suppliers not only abroad, but also at home. Many were convinced that foreigners could only beat them on the basis of some unfair advantage, and Congress agreed by strengthening the US unfair trade laws.

The Trudeau government's response to the vulnerability created by Canada's close economic ties to the United States was the *Third Option*. Originally conceived by Secretary of State for External Affairs Mitchell Sharp (1994: 186) in response to the 1971 Nixon measures, it became an article of faith for some ministers and officials for the next dozen years, although in many instances it involved more rhetoric than action. Sharp came to have his own regrets, remembering that "the Third Option came to be invoked enthusiastically by the government and by others to support policies that were far more nationalistic than my paper had proposed, a consequence that I deplored."

Strengthening the Canadian economy was unexceptionable. More controversial, but widely accepted, were various policy measures aimed at *Canadianizing* the economy, i.e., reducing Canadian reliance on US investment capital and ensuring that new, particularly US, investments would be of "net benefit to Canada." Not as controversial but wholly ineffective was the effort to diversify Canadian trade relations. Trade is a private sector activity and the capacity of a democratic government in a market-based economy to influence the direction and content of trade is limited, particularly when the direction it seeks runs contrary to economic and geographic forces and private sector preferences. The 1976 "contractual link" with the EC and the "broadening and deepening" agreement with Japan represented political commitments, but were never backed up by policy measures with any clout. Sharp agrees that the policy contemplated "was never really seriously attempted and, in retrospect, was probably far too difficult an undertaking for any federal government of Canada, given the crucial role of the provinces with respect both to resources and industry" (Sharp, 1994: 186). Little Canadian trade and investment was in fact diversified.

As a technique for managing trade relations with the United States, the Third Option was less than helpful. But then, as Robert Bothwell (1992: 11) observes, "Trudeau was never very much at home with Americans, and never entirely came to grips with the significance of the United States in Canadian life." Because trade with the United States continued to expand, issues and irritants in the relationship also grew. While US officials could appreciate Canadian anxieties about over-dependence on the US market, they did not appreciate some of the policy measures chosen, whether in the realm of investment (the Foreign Investment Review Agency), energy (the National Energy Program), or culture (various measures to increase Canadian content in publishing and broadcasting). All were considered confiscatory and discriminatory. The net result was a deterioration in Canada-US relations. The Trudeau years not only saw an end to the *special* relationship of the 1950's and 1960's, but also witnessed the growing perception in Washington that Canada was becoming a *problem* country. There was no way that Canada could now count on the benefit of the doubt. Its friends were few and without influence.

Changes in the way Washington operated further undermined the traditional basis for managing trade and investment relations between the two countries. Exemptionalism not only did not work because Canada was no longer seen as an important and special partner, but because the centers of power had changed. In the period from the 1930's through the 1950's, Congress had ceded its trade negotiating authority to the President, who in turn had relied on the State Department to execute this delegated authority. In pursuing its mandate, the State Department often subordinated narrow commercial policy considerations to broader geopolitical interests. Canada counted on its willingness to view matters broadly rather than narrowly to defend its interests and thus concentrated its resources on diplomatic channels in the State Department. The latter was able to take a broad, national interest approach because, unlike most executive agencies such as the Commerce Department or the Department of the Interior, it did not have a natural domestic constituency. Other than a small, generally supportive foreign policy elite in New York and Washington, the State Department did not have to satisfy any special interests and could thus successfully appeal to broad geopolitical ones.

Most members of Congress were not happy with this state of affairs. While unprepared to return to the situation that had led to the excesses of the Smoot-Hawley Tariff Act of 1930, Congress did not want to be seen to be responding to the narrow interests of particular industrial and agricultural sectors. It extricated itself from this role by passing legislation which mandated separate agencies to provide embattled industries with relief from foreign competition when certain conditions were met, such as foreign dumping or subsidization or levels of imports capable of causing injury or harm to domestic industries. Over the years, it tinkered with these laws to make them more responsive to domestic interests and to make their application less and less subject to administrative discretion (Destler, 1995).

Congress also established a Special Trade Representative (later the US Trade Representative) to be the principal executor of US trade policy. The State Department lost its lead role and was reduced to just another agency participating in the policy formulation process, weaker than most because it lacked any domestic constituency of its own.

Finally, Congress began to reassert its role in the trade and economic policy-making process much more aggressively in the 1970's, at the same time as the traditional power-brokering system in Congress disintegrated. In the aftermath of the Watergate scandal and the rapid decline in the *Imperial Presidency* established by Franklin Roosevelt, power in Washington became even more decentralized. Canadian ministers and officials could no longer count on the State Department and the White House as centers of power that could be courted to help defend Canadian interests, nor could they rely on a few major figures on the Hill capable of applying the brakes when special interests got out of hand and sought measures clearly inimical to Canadian interests. As Allan Gotlieb (1991: 30) observed, by the 1980's the Speaker of the House could deliver his own vote and little more.

Thus while the 1971 Nixon measures may have symbolized the end of the special relationship, the handwriting had long been on the wall. Even if Canada had remained the most constant of US allies, prepared to give the US the benefit of the doubt in return for which Canada could count on its friends to defend its interests, its friends could no longer deliver what Canada needed. During its heyday, Canada did not expect to win all its battles in Washington, but it had won enough of them in the more than thirty-five years since the two countries had entered into a reciprocal trade agreement to make the special relationship into a central canon for the conduct of bilateral relations. By the end of the 1970's it was clear there would be no return. Other means would have to be developed to ensure that Canada could defend its interests in the US capital.

By the early 1980's, Canada's economic dependence on the United States had reached new heights, while rules and institutions to underpin that degree of dependence had not kept pace. A growing array of irritants led to heightened anxiety among Canadian business leaders about the management of the relationship. Efforts to launch a new round of multilateral negotiations at a ministerial meeting of GATT in 1982 proved premature, leaving Canada in what was perceived to be an increasingly intolerable situation: heavily dependent on a single market but without sufficiently free and secure access to make investment on the basis of a North American economy feasible.

VI   THE DECISION TO NEGOTIATE THE FTA

Against the background of a deepening but troubled relationship, what were the policy motives and objectives that led to the decision to negotiate a free-trade agreement? Free trade had proven one of the most divisive issues in the history of Canadian politics. At least two elections had been fought on the issue, in 1891 and 1911, and the supporters of free trade had lost both. Little wonder, therefore, that the origins of the decision to negotiate with the United States in the mid-1980's lay more in professional than in partisan considerations. It was not part of the agenda of new prime minister, Brian Mulroney, elected in 1984, nor had it played an important role in the agenda of the Conservative Party. Mulroney had categorically dismissed free trade during his successful leadership bid in 1983. It had been advocated by a number of prominent members of the party, including Finance Minister Michael Wilson and Justice Minister John Crosbie, but Crosbie had failed in his leadership bid and Wilson had other priorities. What mattered politically was that a number of other key Conservative goals lent themselves to a decision to pursue a Canada-US free-trade agreement: one was a commitment to place Canada-US relations on a less adversarial tone, and the second was a desire to reduce the role of government and allow markets to play a larger role in Canadian economic life. Finally, Mulroney and his ministers were prepared to accept the advice of officials and of other influential voices that free trade and better relations with the United States were not unrelated.

The immediate catalyst to the decision to pursue free trade with the United States was the combined impact of the conviction of business leaders that they needed a better way to defuse and resolve trade and investment disputes with the United States and the determination of senior civil servants to find a better way to manage Canada-US relations. The FTA responded as much to a management crisis as to an economic imperative in Canada-US relations. Civil servants responsible for both the broad spectrum of Canada-US relations and the narrower commercial policy concerns of Canadian exporters to the United States were looking for a better set of rules which would level the playing field between the two sides. The most important element in the equation was not that trade would be free – although that obviously had some important ramifications – but that it would be governed on an agreed basis, i.e., that the agreement would provide a set of rules that would be equally binding on the US and the Canadian governments and contain procedures to ensure that these rules would actually be implemented.

The FTA was meant to serve the twin objectives of enhancing and securing Canada's access to the US market, with both objectives enshrined within a binding agreement. The price for meeting these objectives would, naturally, be to enhance and secure US access to the Canadian market. Much has been written about the costs and benefits of enhanced and more open access to each other's markets for goods, services, capital, and technology. We need not rehearse the arguments here except to reiterate that this aspect of the agreement had the effect predicted: a major restructuring of the Canadian economy along North-South lines leading to greater efficiency and prosperity and much higher levels of two-way trade and investment (Schwanen, 1997)[7]. Whether one considers these results good or not depends on one's values. Some of these changes can be attributed directly to the FTA, others were a matter of more indirect effects, including attitudinal changes, technological developments, the consequent negotiation of the NAFTA, and the major expansion of the multilateral rules from the GATT to the WTO.

The debate in Canada on the merits of the FTA was in many ways a debate on the merits of deepening integration. It indicated that the compromises which governments now had to forge differed significantly from those that had animated the trade negotiations of the 1950's through 1970's. Then the debate had been largely between import-competing (read manufacturing) and export-oriented (read agriculture and resource) producers. Echoes of old imperial sentiments and appeals to new economic nationalism added spice but were essentially secondary considerations. By the 1980's, however, Canadian producers were largely of one view. Even import-competing sectors accepted that there had to be significant restructuring if Canadians were going to compete in the global economy and that such restructuring could best take place within a framework of rules that allowed them to compete in a larger market, even at the expense of more competition at home. The new opposition came from a coalition of populist groups worried about a range of issues – Canadian culture, health care, environmental protection, gender equality, and other largely non-economic concerns – believed to be threatened by a more

---

[7] Daniel Schwanen (1997) of the C.D. Howe Institute has provided the best continuous analysis of the trade impact of the FTA and NAFTA. In his third report (C.D. Howe Commentary no. 89, 1997), he concludes that "the pattern of trade between the two countries has shifted roughly in the direction of pre-FTA expectations, and the competitive position of Canadian and US producers in each other's markets has improved relative to those in third countries in many sectors that were liberalized under free trade."

open economy as well as by closer economic ties to the United States. The debate pitted a corporate internationalist vision against a populist nationalist one.

From the perspective of those charged with managing Canada-US relations, however, the intensity and far-ranging nature of the debate seemed at times to border on the bizarre. The claims and counter claims on both sides of the divide attained an extravagance that insiders had difficulty appreciating. What made it particularly puzzling was that there seemed to be little appreciation on the part of opponents that without a better set of rules and procedures, Canada's ability to promote and protect its interests in Washington would continue to deteriorate leading to precisely the kinds of outcomes opponents most feared. A well conceived and implemented trade agreement would do more to protect Canadian sovereignty and freedom of action than the continued drift toward a continentalism without rules, i.e., a continentalism in which the United States called all the shots. The nationalist alternative of a sturdy Canada going its own way and cocking its snout at the United States was hardly more reassuring.

Of course, to some opponents, the better alternative to the FTA was a revitalized multilateral system of rules. Proponents of the FTA, however, never opposed a better functioning GATT. Indeed, many of the professionals who contributed to the FTA and NAFTA negotiations also worked on the concurrent Uruguay Round of GATT negotiations, and saw all three negotiations as individual parts of a single whole. The FTA would simply achieve more quickly and more thoroughly what was equally desirable at the multilateral level. There was also some skepticism about the ability of the Uruguay Round to deliver, given both the delays in launching negotiations and the difficulty of bringing them to a successful conclusion. Many skeptics, while not perhaps prepared to concur with Lester Thurow's catchy judgment that GATT was dead, did not believe that the final result of the Uruguay Round would be as wide-ranging and professionally satisfying as it turned out to be. At a minimum, therefore, pursuing a bilateral agreement with the United States was an act of prudence.

The unitary nature of Canada's approach is demonstrated by the extent to which the FTA was firmly lodged within the structure and values of the multilateral GATT system. The provisions dealing with trade in goods follow closely the contours of earlier free-trade area agreements negotiated under the auspices of GATT article XXIV. The agreement also addressed issues that went well beyond a conventional FTA, including some that would normally be found in customs-union or common-market agreements. Characterized as *new* trade issues, they were in reality the kinds of issues that need to be addressed as economic integration deepens and as the potential for cross-border commercial conflicts intensifies. Even for these, however, there was a scrupulous effort to try to negotiate rules that would fit into a GATT-plus mold and that were congruent with what would flow from multilateral negotiations just getting under way.

Finally, the agreement included some innovative provisions aimed at reducing conflict and resolving disputes. In addition to a more robust version of the general GATT approach to dispute settlement, in some ways anticipating reforms adopted during the

Uruguay Round of multilateral negotiations, it included a special dispute resolution regime related to antidumping and countervailing duty procedures. The two sets of provisions responded to the original concerns of Canadian business that had given rise to the negotiations, but with the important difference that they were firmly ensconced within a fully articulated set of rights and obligations related to trade and investment.

VII   THE IMPACT OF THE FTA

Has the FTA worked? Has it helped the management of Canada-US relations? Yes, to the extent that Canadian governments have been prepared to use its rules and procedures. The existence of an international agreement does not mean there will not be conflict, only that there is a better basis for resolving conflict. The fact that there is a criminal code does not end crime, nor does the existence of courts stop civil litigation. Both the criminal code and the courts provide a more orderly, predictable, and just way of addressing conflict. They make it possible to bring a conflict to an end and resolve an issue. The same considerations hold true for international rules and procedures. A profound misreading of the FTA and the NAFTA led to many popular Canadian complaints about the rash of Canada-US trade disputes in the late 1980's and early 1990's. The existence of rules and procedures does not end disputes, and in fact, may increase the number of issues that need to be resolved on the basis of rules using formal procedures.

The agreement did at first seem to multiply disputes, as players on both sides of the border tested the will of the two governments to live by the new rules. Procedures under chapter 19 dealing with antidumping and countervailing duty cases proved particularly popular and have continued to engage parties in all three countries under the NAFTA. Under the FTA, a total of 35 cases were litigated, with a variety of results, some favouring Canadian parties, some American parties, but as William Davey (1996: 288-9) concludes in his study of all the FTA cases: "The dispute settlement mechanisms of the [FTA] have worked reasonably well, particularly the binational panel review process. The basic goal of trade dispute settlement ... is to enforce the agreed-upon rules. By and large, these dispute settlement mechanisms have done that."

Chapter 19, which was much less than Canada had originally sought, proved a pleasant surprise in reducing the cross-border temperature in trade remedy disputes, forcing administrators on both sides of the border to mind their P's and Q's, and reducing the capacity of US legislators to pressure tribunals to favour the home team. The more general dispute settlement provisions of chapter 18 of the FTA (20 of the NAFTA) have been used less frequently but as usefully. A variety of difficult issues, including salmon and herring landing requirements on Canada's west coast, the application of automotive rules of origin, and the continued right of Canada to maintain high tariffs to protect supply managed agricultural goods, have all been resolved with the help of high-quality panels and the procedures of the FTA or NAFTA. Additionally, the much improved multilateral procedures under the World Trade Organization (WTO) are now available to help resolve conflicts, as in the issue involving Canadian restrictions on imports of split-run periodicals. In all of these cases, the application of clear rules within a set of binding procedures that ensure the equality of standing of both parties has greatly facilitated the management of relations between the two countries. Canada has not won all the cases, in large part because Canada's policies have been inconsistent with Canada's obligations. The purpose of dispute settlement is not to guarantee that Canada always wins but to ensure that issues are resolved on the basis of agreed rules and procedures rather than power politics.

Some issues, however, have not lent themselves to resolution either through bilateral or multilateral procedures, in large part because the rules are not clear, such as Canadian willingness to restrain exports of wheat in 1995. In 1997, US requests for similar restraints have to date been met by refusal, in the knowledge that the US does not have a legal basis for its request, whereas Canada does have a legal basis for its refusal. Unilateral US action could be successfully challenged by Canada under either NAFTA or the WTO. Similarly, Canada has so far been adamant that as long as its exports of men's fine suits meet the NAFTA rules, it will not restrain their export, despite strong political pressure by the US industry on Congress and the Administration to limit their imports. Finally, the Helms-Burton law, while clearly an abuse by the United States of the security provisions of both the FTA/NAFTA and the WTO, raises troubling issues that go beyond currently agreed rules. Using dispute settlement to resolve this issue could place inordinate strain on the system without leading to clear results.

The exception that would seem to prove the rule is the continuing saga of softwood lumber. Originally written out of the FTA, trade in softwood lumber has continued to bedevil Canada-US relations for more than a decade and a half. Canada's current agreement to restrain exports of softwood lumber appears to have been based on a political judgment that while Canada had right on its side, the cost of proving this point, both economically and politically, outweighed the benefits of restraining the imports and thus ensuring peace in the industry for five years and keeping the scarcity rents in Canada. Reasonable people can differ about the wisdom of this political judgment and its long-term impact on the integrity of a rules-based approach to managing relations. With this single exception, the new era of more certain rules and procedures has proven its worth. Integral to this result, however, has been Canada's willingness to practice a new kind of diplomacy.

VIII THE FTA AND THE NEW DIPLOMACY

One of the lasting impacts of the FTA negotiations was acceptance by Canada of the need to practice a diplomacy more in tune with the reality of how Washington works. Canada's experience with the US Congress and US trade laws and procedures in the 1970's and early 1980's convinced the government that it needed an agreement that would give Canadians standing in these proceedings and help to reduce disparities in power between the two countries.

Canada's experience in negotiating agreements with the United States in the 1980's and in pursuing and defending Canadian rights under those agreements in the 1990's convinced the government Canadians needed not a larger but a different presence in the US capital and across the country.

Until the 1970's, Canadian representation in the United States consisted of an embassy in Washington and more than a dozen consulates general across the country. The embassy concentrated on the traditional diplomatic functions of representation and intelligence gathering, focusing on the State Department, but also building relationships with other executive agencies, including the Defense Department, Commerce, USTR, Agriculture, Treasury, Transportation, Justice, and others. The consulates general were primarily engaged in the promotion of Canadian trade opportunities and fostered private sector contacts.

In the 1990's, Canada still maintains a large and splendidly located embassy as well as some dozen consulates general. What these offices do, however, has changed radically. The traditional representational, intelligence gathering, and promotional activities, while still important, have been whittled down in order to make room for a range of new priorities. The embassy has become the nerve center of a vast information gathering and influence enhancing operation. In addition to its staff of traditional foreign-service officials and locally engaged specialists, the embassy now routinely uses the services of lawyers, lobbyists, and publicists to get its message out and reach the myriad of power brokers and decision-makers scattered around Washington. A congressional liaison team ensures that no law maker will be missed in an effort to ensure that Canadian interests are known and taken into account. Around the country, the consulates general spend as much energy on policy issues with both private and public contacts as they do on more traditional trade promotion activities. Taking to heart the lessons learned in the 1980's, they help to ensure that any US interest that coincides with a Canadian interest gets its message across in Washington.

Not everyone is happy about the turn Canadian diplomacy has taken in the US capital. Mitchell Sharp (1994: 184), veteran of the era of quiet diplomacy as both an official and a minister, bemoans that under the FTA, "Canadians will have to be as outspoken, aggressive, and litigious as those on the other side of the border." Sharp confuses cause and effect. The FTA provides a framework of rules and procedures within which Canada can aggressively defend its interests. The need to do so was dictated by changes in the relationship and in the way Washington operates. Anthony Westell (1989) agrees that Canada had little choice in raising the stakes in Washington, but cautions that media involvement will inevitably exaggerate the adversarial nature of disputes. Conflict sells; harmony is boring. Thus public diplomacy may make conflicts appear more rancorous than in fact they are.

Despite this disadvantage, the results speak for themselves. The Canadian embassy has become one of the most sophisticated lobbying efforts in the US capital, earning kudos from those in the know as the most effective foreign representation in Washington. It has adapted well to the demands of the fragmented, interest-driven Washington of the 1990's. From a Canadian perspective, the United States might still often be indifferent and difficult, as the 1997 salmon negotiations demonstrated once again, but its decision-makers certainly are better informed and the consequences of ignoring Canadian interests better known. This enhanced Canadian presence in the United States does not necessarily translate into one Canadian victory after another. It does mean, however, that Canada wins more than it loses. In Washington, that is an enviable record for any foreign government. It is a record that is in large measure the result of the agreements negotiated in the 1980's and the intelligent deployment of Canadian resources in Washington and across the country.

IX   CONCLUSION

Managing its commercial relations with the United States has always been a challenge for Canada. The explosive mix of Americans' unbridled pursuit of manifest destiny and Canadians' overdeveloped sense of paranoia makes it difficult for a government to maintain the confidence of the electorate. On occasion, Canadian officials have sought to exploit natural US neighbourliness and develop a *special relationship*, only to learn time and again the truth of Lord Palmerston's dictum that nations have interests rather than friends. In the United States, as Allan Gotlieb (1991: 56-7) observed, that dictum more often means that legislators, in the highly fragmented system of US decision-making, have special interests rather than enduring friends. A foreign government, no matter how friendly and neighbourly, can only rarely rise to the status of a special interest. To reduce the natural disadvantages that a small, trade-dependent country has in dealing with its superpower neighbour and ensure that legitimate Canadian interests are not too quickly sacrificed on the altar of political expediency, Canada needs the clout that comes from formal agreements with binding procedures. As Derek Burney, Gotlieb's successor in Washington, and one of the principal architects of the FTA, concluded: "Canada's pursuit of trade agreements, of rules and of dispute settlement mechanisms is not a matter of high-mindedness. It is a matter of survival. It is a reality that is brought home to us on a daily basis. As a small country living next door to a global power, we need these rules to reduce the disparity in power and thus allow us to reap the benefits of our proximity."[8] The FTA provided such an agreement. It raised the legal status enjoyed by Canadian interests to unprecedented heights and proved a critical step toward the further negotiation of even better rules and procedures in the NAFTA and WTO. Together with stronger representation, these rules are proving to be effective tools in the arsenal of measures Canada needs to live in harmony with but distinct from the United States.

---

[8] Donald W. Campbell Lecture in International Trade, Wilfrid Laurier University Chancellor's Symposium, Toronto, June 14, 1995.

References

Bothwell, R. (1992). Has Canada made a difference? The case of Canada and the United States. In J. English & N. Hillmer (eds.), *Making a Difference? Canada's Foreign Policy in a Changing World Order*. Toronto: Lester.

Davey, W. (1996). *Pine and Swine*. Ottawa: Center for Trade Policy and Law.

Destler, I.M. (1995). *American Trade Politics*. Washington: Institute for International Economics (third edition).

Gotlieb, A. (1991). *"I'll be with you in a minute, Mr. Ambassador": The Education of a Canadian Diplomat in Washington*. Toronto: University of Toronto Press.

Granatstein, J.L. (1996). *Yankee Go Home: Canadians and Anti-Americanism*. Toronto: HarperCollins.

Hart, M., Dymond, B. & Robertson, C. (1994). *Decision at Midnight: Inside the Canada-US Free Trade Negotiations*. Vancouver: UBC Press.

Henderson, D. (1986). *Innocence and Design: The Influence of Economic Ideas on Policy*. Oxford: Basil Blackwell.

Holmes, J. (1989). Crisis in Canadian-American relations: a Canadian perspective. In L. Lamont & J.D. Edmonds (eds.), *Friends So Different: Essays on Canada and the United States in the 1980's*. Ottawa: University of Ottawa Press.

Orchard, D. (1993). *The Fight for Canada: Four Centuries of Resistance to American Expansionism*. Toronto: Lester Publishing.

Richler, M. (1979). Canadian identity. In E.J. Feldman & N. Nevitte (eds.), *The Future of North America: Canada, the United States, and Québec Nationalism*. Montréal: Institute for Research on Public Policy.

Schwanen, D. (1997, March). *Trading Up: The Impact of Increased Continental Integration on Trade, Investment, and Jobs in Canada*. Montréal/Calgary: C.D. Howe Institute (C.D. Howe Commentary no. 89).

Sharp, M. (1994). *Which Reminds Me... A Memoir*. Toronto: University of Toronto Press.

Westell, A. (1989). A farewell to quiet diplomacy. In L. Lamont & J.D. Edmonds (eds.), *Friends So Different: Essays on Canada and the United States in the 1980's*. Ottawa: University of Ottawa Press.

ON TRACK FOR TAFTA?
DEVELOPING CANADA-EU TRADE RELATIONS IN THE 1990's

by Donald G. MITCHELL

I   INTRODUCTION

Fish and fur; disputes over these two commodities have dominated the Canada-EU trading agenda throughout the last two years. As a result, the future of Canada's trade with its largest trading partner after the United States[1] is often seen in terms of obstacles instead of opportunities. While there are obstacles that do present a challenge to closer economic integration between the two areas, there are also enormous opportunities which a rapidly expanding European Union offers for Canada, and vice versa. While booming Asian markets and *promises* of an APEC (Asia-Pacific Economic Cooperation) free trade agreement have captured the attention of business and trading strategists worldwide, the development of regional cooperation and democracy in Asia has not maintained the same frenetic pace. This discrepancy in the world's most rapidly developing region threatens to spark trading wars or even something hotter. It also threatens to slow the momentum of WTO-sponsored trade liberalization.

In such a scenario, the introduction of a TAFTA (Transatlantic Free Trade Agreement) could provide the initiative and framework to launch a whole new wave of global trade liberalization. The world's two most integrated trading blocs, NAFTA and the EU, are arguably best-suited to initiate such change. The success of a transatlantic agreement in this role, however, depends upon its ability to shed the image of a *rich men's club* and introduce *substantial* reform that would have positive repercussions not just for the two trading blocs involved but for other parts of the world. The Canadian seizure of a Spanish vessel off the Grand Banks of Newfoundland just beyond the 200 mile-limit established by international law set off a furious political struggle between Canada and the European Union. A dispute with the Spanish had become by extension a dispute with the EU. Just as Canada was on the verge of beginning negotiations on the Canada-EU Action Plan – intended as the launching pad for greater economic integration and political cooperation – the fishing issue paralyzed negotiations.

Similarly, the possibility of an EU ban on fur caught with leg-hold traps threatened to sour good relations. Recently, however, the conclusion of a framework agreement on international humane trap standards in Brussels removed the threat of this ban. In

---

[1] After the United States, the European Union is the largest market for Canadian exports (7 percent of total exports) and is the source of 9 percent of Canadian imports. The United Kingdom, Germany, France, Belgium, Italy, and the Netherlands occupy third, fourth, seventh, eighth, ninth, and tenth positions, respectively, in the ranking of the top 100 Canadian export markets. DFAIT (Department of International Affairs and Trade), 1995.

December of 1996, the Canada-EU Action Plan was signed by EU Commissioner for
External Economic Relations Sir Leon Brittan and Canadian Prime Minister Jean
Chrétien. These two achievements suggest that it is no longer sufficient to merely
study the problems at hand; there is a need to look to the opportunities that lie ahead.
Other disputes may emerge – and this article will address potential future problem
areas with particular regard to the enlargement of the EU – but there are also
enormous opportunities which transatlantic trade liberalization would offer to both
blocs.

A transatlantic free trade agreement (TAFTA) would, by the time it were negotiated,
give Canada access to a single currency zone of more than 420 million people.[2] It
would also link Canada to a trading partner that is in the unique position of expanding
not just demographically but territorially and is likely to include close to half a billion
people and twenty-five plus countries by the time the process of expansion is
completed. Before launching into a discussion of the idea of a TAFTA, however, a
number of other issues must be discussed: the current state of Canada-EU trade, the
enlargement of the European Union, and future trade trends.

II   OVERVIEW OF THE CURRENT STATE OF CANADA-EU TRADE

The European Union is Canada's largest trading partner after the United States, with
total trade in 1995 worth an estimated US$29.8 billion. That same year, the European
Union provided ten percent of all Canada's imports and was the destination for seven
percent of its exports. Since 1976, the growth rate for Canadian exports to the EU has
averaged 6.4 percent (Statistics Canada, 1996). In the past decade, Canadian exports to
the EU have grown in value by seventy-two percent (Statistics Canada, 1996). Yet the
most remarkable area of growth in economic activity between the two has been foreign
direct investment (FDI). In 1995, twenty-seven percent of FDI in Canada came from
EU countries. In the same year, over 20 percent of Canadian investment abroad
(CDIA) was channeled into the EU. A decade previously, the figures stood at 17
percent and 12.4 percent respectively. In relative terms that represents an 59 percent
increase in value of both CDIA in the EU and European Union FDI in Canada.

Measured in absolute terms, the change is even greater. European Union FDI in
Canada increased between 1985 and 1995 from US$14.8 billion to US$33.5 billion, an
increase of 126 percent. In the same time period, CDIA in the EU rose from US$6.7
billion to US$25.1 billion, a 275 percent increase. By comparison, over the same
period, CDIA in the United States dropped from 54 to 53 percent of total CDIA and

---

[2] This estimate is on the basis of the advent of EMU (European and Monetary Union) and the
introduction of a single currency, the *euro* in 1999. By 2005-08, when negotiations for a TAFTA
might begin, the EU is widely expected to have expanded to include Poland (38.8 million people), the
Czech Republic (10.4 million), Hungary (10.3 million), Cyprus (740 000), and possibly more Eastern
and Southern European countries. That would bring the Union's current population of 370 million to
over 420 million people.

the United States' FDI in Canada dropped from 76 to 65 percent of total FDI in Canada. These translate as relative decreases of two and thirteen percent, respectively.

2.1   Britain and Germany

Britain remains Canada's largest European trading partner, accounting for Cdn$5.47 billion in imports to Canada (2.4 percent of the Canadian total; almost a quarter of all imports from Europe) and Cdn$3.75 billion in exports from Canada (1.5 percent of the total; twenty-five percent of the European total). The UK is Canada's second largest source of FDI after the US and was the second largest destination for CDIA, surpassing Japan on both accounts. It is also the second largest market for business services. Great Britain acts as a gateway into Europe for many Canadian businesses which find common language and customs to be a business advantage. Many of the largest Canadian companies –names like Bombardier, Nortel, and Seagram's – have major investments in the UK. Similarly, over six hundred Canadian companies are owned or controlled by UK firms (Government of Canada, 1996). London also is Europe's preeminent (and one of the world's largest) financial centers. In the short-term, Britain's relationship with Canada is unlikely to change substantially. Longer term, however, in the context of Canada's relationship with the EU – in particular Germany – the primacy of Great Britain as Canada's principal European partner will be seriously challenged.

Since 1989-90, the strategic importance of Germany for Canada's European trade strategy has grown enormously. Through reunification, the Federal Republic grew to encompass 360,000 square kilometers and 81 million people, second only to Russia as Europe's most populous nation. Moreover, Germany provides the dynamic trade and investment link between Western and Eastern Europe. With companies like Volkswagen – who invested enormous amounts in the rebirth of Czech automotive manufacturer Skoda – leading the way, Germany's economic *Ostpolitik* is the catalyst for much of the economic growth in Central and Eastern Europe. Finally, the establishment of the EMI (European Monetary Institute) and as of 1999, the ECB (European Central Bank) in Frankfurt is likely to make it a rival if not a successor to London as Europe's preeminent financial center. That distinction will remain a point of contention for years to come; what is clear, however, is that Germany will be Canada's key European partner in the 21st century.

In Canadian *investment* terms, Germany is a distant second to the UK. In 1995, German FDI in Canada stood at US$4.97 billion (versus the UK's US$16.5 billion) and CDIA in Germany reached US$2.36 billion (versus US$13.8 billion invested in the UK). While Germany may lag behind the UK in terms of investment, its trade with Canada is growing at a far greater rate than that of the UK. In 1995, German exports to Canada reached US$4.8 billion and imports from Canada reached US$3.15 billion. The figures for Britain are US$5.5 and 3.9 billion respectively. A decade ago, the value of Canadian trade with the UK was close to double that of Germany. Today, it is roughly seventeen percent greater.[3] The trend is clear and may even mean that Germany will surpass Britain as Canada's primary European partner *before* the end of the century.

Canada's third largest EU trading partner is France. The importance of France has increased as a result of an enormous boom in investment, tourism, and the service industry. Between 1985 and 1995, CDIA in France grew from Cdn$190 million to Cdn$1.9 billion and French investment in Canada from Cdn$1.5 to Cdn$5.3 billion. Tourists from France spent close to half a billion dollars in Canada in 1995 while services account for a third of total trade with an estimated value of Cdn$1.6 billion. In addition to the purely economic nature of this relationship, a cultural affinity with Eastern Canada has helped to foster closer ties between the two countries. For a real insight into the European Single Market, however, one needs to take a closer look at Belgium.

2.2   Belgium – The Single Market Test Case

Figures for Canada-Belgium trade are somewhat misleading if taken at face value. On one level, the figures overstate the volume of trade and on another, they leave out important commercial considerations. The barrier-free nature of the Single Market and its location as a northern European, coastal country mean that a significant volume of Canadian imports are registered as entering Belgium even though their final destination is elsewhere in Europe. To a degree unmatched elsewhere in Europe, Canadian companies have a strong local presence in Belgium. Bombardier, the aircraft/subway car manufacturer is the single largest employer in the Belgian town of Bruges. McCain, the Canadian frozen food conglomerate, has beaten the Belgians at their own game; it is the nation's largest producer of French fries in a country that invented the food!

The establishment of local subsidiaries has meant a drastic reduction in transportation costs to the export market and also provides these Canadian companies with tariff-free access across the EU market. Furthermore, the standardization of legal and technical norms across the EU has meant that companies can operate much more easily across the Union. A Canadian firm that has established a subsidiary or joint-venture within say, Belgium, is free to do business as far away as Greece or Finland with few technical restraints. The challenges and opportunities for foreign-owned subsidiaries operating in the EU were discussed by Buckley et al. (1995: 77-86). The authors examined the experience of ten Canadian firms that entered the European market. The companies were operating in sectors as diverse as lumber and satellite equipment yet shared comparable strategies and faced similar obstacles. While the degree of

---

[3] In 1985 Canadian exports to the UK were valued at Cdn$211 million and to Germany, at Cdn$104 million. By 1991, exports to the UK and Germany had risen to Cdn$2.53 billion and Cdn$1.995 billion, respectively. Aside from the enormous increase in both figures, the most interesting thing is how much Germany gained on Britain as Canada's prime European target for exports; the latter's lead dropping from roughly 100 percent to 20 percent to the current 17 percent.

commitment varied according to the financial means of the company, all the companies that had achieved success had done so by actively engaging themselves within the Single Market.

In the case of the lumber company, it was a case of creating a number of joint-ventures with local companies. Other wealthier firms, such as Bombardier mentioned earlier, have wholly-owned foreign subsidiaries in operation. Aside from the material gains to be had from a presence in Europe, those companies with a strong presence on the continent benefit from a better and more up-to-date understanding of the EU's complex legislative changes and opportunities. For many of these companies, it is a concern that "polarization of economies into major trading blocs is raising barriers to business between the leading world markets and that a direct investment presence in key consumer markets is necessary to achieve profitable growth" (Buckley et al., 1995: 83). This will be key in 1998 when the monetary union becomes a reality on May 1st. All participating currencies will be locked together on December 31st. The majority of EU countries will no doubt qualify. Three, Britain, Sweden and Denmark, will decline to participate, for the time being anyway, despite their technical readiness. Greece will certainly stay out because it cannot yet apply the required standards of economic and monetary rigour.

2.3   Central and Eastern Europe

What then about opportunities for Canadian business in Europe beyond the EU, more specifically, in the rapidly growing markets of Central and Eastern Europe? The Canadian private sector is working closely with DFAIT and CIDA (Canadian International Development Agency) to provide entrepreneurial expertise for the development of local business and investment opportunities for Canadians in the region. Much of CDIA and trade in Central and Eastern Europe has been focused upon construction, telecommunications, and other infrastructural projects. The success of these joint projects is evident from recent trade statistics.

Table 1:   *Canadian Trade with the Visegrad Triangle Countries 1992-95*

	1992	1994	1995	% Growth '92-'94	% Growth '94-'95*
Czech Republic	**	96.67	138.77	**	43
Hungary	73.24	75.75	84.73	3.5	12
Poland	114.25	156.66	235.36	37	50

*   millions of dollars
**   independent figures for the Czech Republic are not available before 1994.

Amidst the general optimism about the emerging markets of Central and Eastern Europe, however, there is some cause for concern. An otherwise smooth last round of EU enlargement was ruffled by the problem of trade disputes between the EU, on the one hand, and Canada and third-party countries on the other.[4] The entry of Sweden, Finland and Austria into the Union meant the extension of higher EU tariffs to these countries. As the EU undergoes future enlargements, Canada is likely to face future tariff increases to Central European markets which will, in all likelihood, mean reduced access to these markets. While Canadian trade with the Central and Eastern European countries (CEEC's) has not yet reached particularly large levels, it is growing extremely rapidly as the table above suggests.

When Austria, Finland and Sweden joined the EU, a dispute arose over higher tariffs on Canadian exports of seafood, aluminum, wood products, and snowmobiles to these countries. If one considers that these are the primary Canadian exports to Scandinavia and Austria, we can also confidently predict likely problem areas that Canada might face in the next round of enlargement. These will be: electrical equipment, machinery, construction materials (and contracts), and wood products, which constitute the largest share of trade between Canada and the CEEC's. Problems of trade diversion may also develop. While the rapidly expanding markets of Central and Eastern Europe are currently open to all external partners and Canada shares Most Favoured Nation (MFN) status with the Czech Republic and Poland (and GPT – General Preferential Treatment – agreements with those two plus Hungary), these advantages are likely to be erased by the future admission of these three countries into the EU. The extension of EU tariff barriers to Poland, the Czech Republic, and Hungary is likely to severely weaken Canadian competitiveness in these markets. As the EU grows to absorb not only these three but, in stages, seven other Eastern European countries which have signed Association Agreements with the Union, the problem threatens to recur at each stage.

In the last round of EU enlargement, it took eleven months for the Canadian government to negotiate a satisfactory compensation package for the higher EU import duties introduced on large number of products to Austria, Finland, and Sweden. Negotiations for previous enlargement rounds have taken up to five years and even today, there remain outstanding tariff compensation issues between Canada and the EU. How should Canada tackle these trade disputes?

The aim of the Canada-EU action plan is to resolve current trade/political sticking points and lay the groundwork for a free trade agreement. This, however, is both a long-term as well as an optimistic goal. In the meantime, Canada can try and coax the EU into a more cooperative stance by further developing its own existing regional trade agreements. Canada is a key member of NAFTA and is expanding trade with Latin America, most notably Chile, with whom Canada recently signed a free trade agreement.

---

[4] This group is largely made up of WEOG countries (Canada, Australia, New Zealand, Japan) and the US; in other words, western industrialized countries not included in the Lomé Convention group of developing nations who enjoy tariff-free trade with the EU in almost all sectors.

The expansion of NAFTA would make Canada an increasingly attractive point of entry for European firms that want to gain access to the North-South American markets and force the EU to take steps to increase its appeal to its prosperous transatlantic partners. Yet at the same time, this runs contrary to Canada's wish to diversify its trading base – in other words, to reduce its dependence upon the US. Rather, in the case of Europe, Canada is trying to reinvigorate Canada-EU trade, with an eye to the coming attraction of an expanding, single-currency market with 370 million-plus people. A third strategy would be for Canada to publicly push for a lowering of EU tariffs rather than simply accept an extension of EU tariff levels with each successive wave of enlargement.[5] For this, there are two imperatives. Firstly, Canada cannot expect to do this alone. Rather, it must take advantage of its membership in the WTO and foster support for tariff reduction among WEOG countries who face the same obstacle in trading with Europe. Secondly, Canada must start this process of lobbying *before* each successive wave of EU enlargement begins. Rather than waiting till this loss of markets occurs and then applying for compensation to the EU afterwards, Canada must work to prevent this market restriction *beforehand*. Sympathetic to Canada's complaints, Dr. Lorenz Schomerus, State Secretary in the German Ministry of Finance, argues that European regional integration should not run counter to multilateral trade liberalization (Senate of Canada Report, 1996: 26).

III   TOWARDS A EUROPEAN TRADING BLOC?

A recent European Commission report, *Reinforcing Political Union and Preparing for Enlargement,* calls for the EU to act more cohesively in the area of trade policy and representation in international organizations. Because of the disparate interests of its member states, "the Union's negotiating position is weakened in many cases (…) the Treaty [on European Union] should include provisions explicitly designed to enable the Union to speak with one voice and defend all the relevant interests more effectively" (European Commission Opinion, 1996: 26). The EU is trying to invigorate its economic and trade policy so as not to be outmatched by the booming economies of Asia-Pacific and Latin America and a resurgent United States. This is already evident in the number of cases of dispute settlement at the WTO in which the EU, rather than individual EU member states, has participated. A real European trade bloc, however, is unlikely to exist as long as the *Deutsche Mark* is competing with the *franc*, pound and *lira*. Only when the *euro* gathers strength, are we likely to see the emergence of a real European trading bloc.

Constant speculation about the fate of the *euro* experiment and EMU in general was silenced by the public launch in Dublin in December 1996 of the design for the *euro* paper notes. The event put to rest any doubts that even the most hardened skeptics had as to whether EMU would "fly". On January 1st, 1999, the new currency will be

---

[5] While standard EU tariff levels are quite low on many items (3.6 percent), there are a number of key sectors in which high tariffs make it very difficult for Canadian companies to compete in these European markets. For example, EU tariffs on telecommunications equipment – one of the world's fastest-growing and most lucrative sectors – were recently raised from 4.5 to 7.5 percent.

launched; now, it is simply a question of where. Will it be introduced in just six core countries: France, Germany, Austria, and the Benelux, or will it be extended to include Italy, Ireland, and the three Scandinavian member states as well? Some argue that an initial *mini-currency* union would not work for two reasons. Firstly, they claim, it would be difficult to differentiate between core and non-core countries when the decisions are based upon often very minor differences in economic performance. Secondly, to not admit a country that is very close to meeting the requirements for EMU membership – particularly if such a country has undertaken severe austerity measures as a means of doing so – risks provoking a popular backlash against EMU in that country. The most obvious example of this is Italy where a real effort is being made to bring the *lira* into line for 1999.

Instead, critics of the mini-currency approach argue in favour of a *maxi-currency* union that would include up to ten or eleven member states. This would, in theory, prevent the creation of a sufficiently large bloc of member states who might oppose the selection of core EMU members. Of course, this begs the question whether EMU is more an economic means to a political end or an economic end unto itself. While some argue that EMU is primarily a political goal, its potential economic advantages would be enormous: a genuine single currency market incorporating at least 200 million people at the outset which would attract investors previously turned off by the number of different currencies and their inherent exchange rate headaches.

IV   FROM A G-7 TO A G-3?

The whole notion of a shift from a G-7 including Canada to a G-3 (the EU, the US and Japan) excluding Canada hinges largely on the success of EMU and the *euro* experiments. Even if it were adopted by ten EU member states in 1999, the *euro* would not become a reserve currency in the short term. Until the *euro* is perceived as a reliable currency, no one will want to exchange their reserve *Deutsche Marks* or dollars for it. Yet at the same time, it will not be perceived as a stable currency until businesses and banks put faith in it. This will leave the nascent currency in a difficult but not impossible position. The creation of a single currency and a European Central Bank (ECB) does not preclude EU member states acting individually on financial matters. There will be fifteen finance ministers of the ECB, one from each member state. Britain and possibly Italy will be left out of the EMU initially but that does not mean that they will cease to have a presence in international economic and monetary affairs.

The combination of the limited initial impact of the *euro* on reserve currency holdings combined with the fact that from its inception, EMU is not likely to incorporate all 15 member states mean that the shift from a G-7 to a G-3 configuration is unlikely to occur soon. Nevertheless, the emergence of a cohesive European bloc in international economic and monetary affairs at a later stage is inevitable, which would leave Canada as the awkward smaller partner at the G-7 table.

In spite of the potential offered by EMU, there has been a noticeable decline in the relative importance of the EU as a destination for Canadian exports. This is partially explainable by two distinct regional trends. Despite Canada's desire to move its trade strategy away from a dependence on the United States, the nation's share of trade with its southern neighbour has grown in relative terms at the expense of the transatlantic relationship. Much of the reason for this growth lies with the passage of the NAFTA which dramatically opened up trade and investment flows between Canada and the US. The second reason for this relative drop is because of a growth in Canadian trade with Latin America, China, Japan, and Southeast Asia. While trade among the APEC countries is booming and there is talk of creating an APEC free trade zone, discussions are moving at "a glacial pace" (The Economist, 1996, December 7: 15).

The slowing of European economic growth over the last two decades has meant a drop in the EU's share of Canadian trade. Nevertheless, as the statistics cited earlier show, Canada-EU trade continues to show robust growth. The sheer size of the European market ensures its value as a target for Canadian business. In spite of sluggish growth rates – the forecast average for EU growth in 1997 is 2.3 percent – the EU market is so lucrative and integrated that its GDP grows by US$200 to 220 billion annually, the equivalent of discovering a market the size of Taiwan's each year.

As Peter Cook (1996, October 2: 3), the *Globe & Mail*'s Brussels-based correspondent argues, "the value of the European market is that it corresponds exactly to Canada in terms of income levels and economic needs and is somewhere where we have a great deal of success selling high value goods" and, he continues, "with a single currency, that will be enhanced." The implications of a single currency for the world's largest trading bloc are enormous. The US dollar remains the world's global currency. Although this will not change overnight, the emergence of the *euro* threatens to eventually topple the dollar in *some* parts of the world as the reserve currency of choice. As the EU grows – with EMU to eventually incorporate all member states – and develop closer ties and freer economic trade with the New Independent States and Mediterranean rim countries, the whole idea of the *euro* as a reserve currency gains greater credibility.

Imagine the European Union thirty years from now. Its large elderly population – Europe's Achilles heel and the single largest reason demographers depict a doomsday scenario for Europe – will have largely died off. It will be a bloc of twenty-five plus countries with a single currency spread across most of its constituent countries and a young, well-educated population of close to 450 million.

Contrast this with Southeast Asia where in many areas, the inability of democratic development to keep pace with economic growth and a failure to organize closer economic cooperation threaten long-term prosperity in the region. Admittedly, the enormous diversity of the Southeast Asian nations – a fact which many westerners fail to recognize – makes APEC's challenge for the 21st century a daunting one. Nevertheless, without a solid framework for regional dialogue, rising economic competition threatens to ignite political disputes. Such a scenario is not, I will stress, a short-term trend. It is clear that the momentum lies with the Asian emerging markets both now and in the coming decades. Longer-term, however, it remains to be seen how well these economies will sustain their growth.[6]

V   THE BACKGROUND TO TAFTA

If a larger, leaner EU offers major opportunities in the coming century to Canada, what does an EU-NAFTA free trade agreement represent? Ideally, TAFTA would create a free trade zone representing close to fifty percent of the volume of world trade. It could also act as an enormous catalyst for global trade liberalization. By uniting the world's two single largest trading blocs, it could establish a precedent for future cooperation.

Here too, this begs the question of whether such an agreement is primarily economic or political in intent. Ultimately, the whole notion of TAFTA serves as an economic means to a political end. By this I mean that the economic gains of such a free trade agreement would be neither enormous nor sudden.[7] While these gains would be by no means insignificant, the political value of such an agreement outweighs the economic advantages.

What are the practical gains to be made? Firstly, exposing industry to transatlantic competition (and this is particularly true of European industry) would force it to become far more efficient and, by extension, more competitive. If European industry were able to open up to transatlantic competition and weather the major phase of restructuring that would be inevitable for it to survive such competition, it would find itself with tariff-free access to the entire NAFTA market including the rapidly growing Mexican and possibly even the Chilean economy.[8]

---

[6] This is the thrust of an article by Gerald Segal (1996) in which he argues that in future: i) the peaking of Asia's demographic bulge, ii) a decline in traditional family networks/rise in welfare costs, iii) flagging APEC activism, and iv) declining growth rates will all bring about a slowing in the Asian economic boom. This, Segal argues, combined with the onset of a single European currency, reform of the welfare state, and the "dying out" of the older generation will mean a radical rejuvenation of the European continent. While this is not likely to happen as nearly as Segal implies, some of his arguments do hold some validity and help to define Europe's value to Canadian trade in the 21st century.

[7] This opinion is expressed by a number of contemporary commentators on transatlantic trade, including Robert Wolfe of the Queen's University Public Policy Center. Thomas J. Duesterberg (1995), formerly assistant secretary of commerce for international economic policy in the US government, argues that any such trade agreement must be seen in terms of what Zbigniew Brezinski calls the "geopolitical situation." Duesterberg (1995: 77) concludes: "Non-economic factors in favour of an EU-NAFTA free trade and investment agreement may be more compelling, in fact, than the economic considerations."

[8] While Mexico is a fully integrated member of NAFTA, Chile signed a free trade agreement with Canada in December, 1996 and enjoys low-tariff trade with Mexico through the MERCOSUR trading arrangement but does not yet have a free trade agreement with the United States.

Trade blocs such as the EU and NAFTA are increasingly inward-oriented. Although this is inevitable to a certain extent, when the proportion of regional trade as a percentage of total trade exceeds seventy percent, as is the case with the EU, the bloc risks reaching an unhealthy balance.[9] An EU-NAFTA free trade agreement would give the EU a means of increasing its market share of extra-European trade, which has fallen significantly since the Single European Act in 1986.

A transatlantic agreement would give NAFTA countries access to the emerging markets of Central and Eastern Europe, the Mediterranean rim (Turkey, Cyprus, Algeria, Tunisia) and the New Independent States (NIS) on the same terms as currently enjoyed by EU member states based on the Association Agreements which these countries have signed with the EU. While the economies of Russia and its NIS neighbours continue to perform sluggishly, experiencing low or even negative economic growth, they hold huge potential one or two decades from now. For all its faults, the Soviet Union did an excellent job of educating its citizens. Many of the countries of the former Soviet Union also have enormous natural gas, oil, and other mineral reserves. While the region is still sorely lacking in capital for investment, a well-educated labour force combined with enormous energy resources provide it with the key elements for future growth.[10]

Despite the potential benefits, there are many obstacles to the development of a TAFTA, most of which stem from an absence of political will. The most frequent criticism of the NAFTA proposal in the run-up to its signing in 1988 was that Canada and the US would be unable to compete with Mexico where labour costs were dramatically lower. The laws of comparative advantage prevented this from becoming a problem. Nevertheless, the belief that freer trade will mean job losses remains and politicians on both sides of the Atlantic are reluctant to push for further trade liberalization if it threatens their popularity in any way.

With the deadlines for EMU and EU enlargement looming, the Union is unlikely to devote much time to developing a TAFTA in the next decade. This stems not so much from lack of will – the NAFTA market is eyed hungrily by those in Brussels – but from lack of time. The EU is simply too preoccupied with ongoing projects at the moment to devote the necessary attention to developing such an agreement.

If political will is the single greatest obstacle to the development of a TAFTA, what chance does such an agreement stand? As a sweeping free trade agreement covering all aspects of trade, none. As a smaller-scale initiative aimed at freeing up trade in a few, clearly-defined sectors and goals, it stands a much greater chance of succeeding. Moreover, the political rewards of such an effort could be reaped before an agreement is even signed. The onset of meaningful discussion of trade liberalization, let alone negotiations, would breathe new life into a static transatlantic agenda.

---

[9] Cfr. Duesterberg (1995: 77).
[10] The most vigorous advocates of this view are Richard Layard & John Parker (1996).

VI   THE PRACTICAL FRAMEWORK

Firstly, we must define what an EU-NAFTA free trade agreement would logically consist of. There are three main areas to be targeted for liberalization: trade, investment, and industrial standards. What sectors should be tackled first? It is perhaps easiest to answer this question negatively, i.e., by identifying what should *not* be tackled first, namely, agriculture and textiles. The difficulty with which textiles were incorporated into the GATT negotiations and the controversy surrounding agricultural subsidies in North America and even more so in Europe make these an inauspicious area to deal with first. Even though the potential gains are enormous, tackling agriculture would be so complex that it would be more likely slow the momentum for liberalization in other sectors than achieve real progress.

A better area in which to start would be foreign investment. As the figures quoted towards the beginning of this article suggest, transatlantic investment is already so prevalent that the removal of restrictions in this sector would, in all likelihood, prove to be a *relatively* non-complex place to begin. A successful start to TAFTA negotiations in this sector would provide it with the impetus necessary to tackle more complex and controversial sectors. Yet even changes to current investment rules would not be without controversy as measures such as local-hiring quotas for foreign subsidiaries would come under scrutiny.

Telecommunications, computing, and other high-technology industries have been the focus of much attention recently. One of the principal aims of the recent WTO conference in Singapore was to launch trade liberalization in this booming sector. Yet initiating real change will be difficult in an industry in which every country wants to champion the cause of its own national firms so as to ensure a competitive share in what is widely-viewed as the high-growth industry of the next century.

The impending conclusion of the Mutual Recognition Agreement (MRA) between Canada and the EU on product standardization will eliminate many of the technical headaches associated with trade liberalization. The agreement could also pave the way for transatlantic harmonization of other regulatory legislation. Ultimately, these agreements would provide an incentive (i.e.: common standards) for EU countries to orient more of their trade towards the NAFTA markets, and vice versa.

Some have argued that TAFTA represents a threat to global trade liberalization.[11] Critics argue that such an agreement risks creating a "rich men's club," tacitly endorsing the idea that trade liberalization is best reserved exclusively for the western industrialized world. Certainly, the main economic motivation behind such an

---

[11] Bergsten (1995: 105-20), a former adviser to the APEC, argues that "as the urgency of competitive liberalization has accelerated, the regional approach has increasingly come to the fore [in which] regional groupings are demonstrably willing to proceed more boldly." While Bergsten acknowledges that the "fears of some that regionalism would derail globalism have been overcome to date," he sees a veiled threat in a TAFTA.

agreement lies with the fact that the European markets share a similar standard of living and are consequently an ideal market for Canadian products. In this sense, TAFTA is a consciously western-oriented idea. On the other hand, the EU and NAFTA also represent the two most sophisticated and integrated trading blocs in the world and are arguably in the best position to forge ahead with global trade liberalization.

It is crucial that the WTO be seen as an integral part of the development of a TAFTA. In other words, a TAFTA must not be perceived as a final act but rather a step on the road to WTO-sponsored *global* trade liberalization.[12] If that could be achieved, then a TAFTA would be much more likely to gain the popular support needed to be able to shed its "rich men's club" image and gain serious, widespread consideration. The single most important step in this direction over the last three years has been the conclusion of the Canada-EU Action Plan signed in December in Ottawa by Prime Minister Jean Chrétien and EU Commissioner Sir Leon Brittan.

The plan is the most wide-ranging agreement of cooperation achieved since dialogue began with the 1976 Transatlantic Framework Declaration engineered by former Canadian Prime Minister Pierre Trudeau. Encompassing economic, political, and trade relations as well as technical cooperation, the Action Plan aims to eliminate the potential for disagreements such as the recent fishing dispute and lay the foundation for closer, lasting ties. More specifically, the Action Plan calls for a joint study into the removal of remaining trade barriers and incorporates agreement on labour rights and *extraterritoriality*, the issue at the heart of the Grand Banks fishing dispute (European Commission, 1996). The Action Plan should also ensure a speedy conclusion to the MRA which, as the *Cassis de Dijon* case did for the EU in the mid-1980's, would eliminate testing of Canadian products entering the EU and vice versa.[13]

Delays in the conclusion of the Canada-EU Action Plan threatened to derail the project entirely. Had this occurred, at a time when the United States had already reached a wide-ranging agreement with the EU, Canada would have risked losing much of its influence in the transatlantic forum. The MRA, however, is a sign of the reverse.

---

[12] Former US Secretary-of-State Warren Christopher was quoted as saying "any free trade agreement must advance our key objective of global trade liberalization; it must be compatible with an effective WTO and not disadvantage developing nations." Taken from Wolfe (1996: 365).

[13] The landmark legal case, named for the liqueur that a French importer was attempting to export to Germany, eliminated the need for national testing of products being traded within the EU.

VII   CONCLUSIONS

When, if ever, will a TAFTA occur? In the next decade? Unlikely. Neither the EU, which is too preoccupied with EMU and eastern enlargement nor North America, absorbed by closer economic integration with Asia and South America is ready to initiate serious discussion on the matter. This does not mean, however, that a transatlantic agreement is just a pipe dream. A TAFTA would offer significant opportunities to its members. Rather, the problem lies with the fact that the potential economic benefits of such an agreement would neither be immediate nor immediately apparent. Consequently, discussion of a TAFTA tends to get de-prioritized in favour of issues perceived to be more pressing.

The second problem a TAFTA faces has to do with the current economic climate. In a boom cycle such as much of the world is enjoying now, there is little incentive to alter any of the existing political structures. The 1996 US presidential elections are a good example of this. Bill Clinton was re-elected not so much because of his personal popularity but because the majority of the electorate believed that government continuity was the best way to ensure sustained economic growth. In short, *if it ain't broke, don't fix it*. For similar reasons, the idea of a TAFTA is currently not a popular one.

In the words of a former US government official, "what is lacking now, perhaps, is the crisis atmosphere that [...] engenders heroic wisdom and leadership" (Duesterberg, 1996: 80). It may indeed be the case that in less prosperous times, when *political* solutions are sought for economic woes, a transatlantic free trade agreement will come to be more clearly recognized for the potential it holds. In the absence of such an agreement, Canadian business must take advantage of the many opportunities that the European Single Market offers and increase its presence within the EU. Only by fostering trade ties between the two continents *now* can the foundations be built for a transatlantic free trade agreement in the future.

References

Bergsten, C.F. (1995). The ascent of regionalism, *Foreign Affairs* 75 (3): 105-20.

Buckley, P.J., Pass, C.L. & Prescott, K. (1995). The Single European Market initiative: a perspective from Canadian companies, *British Journal of Canadian Studies* 10 (1): 77-86.

Cook, P. (1996). Canada's stake in a new Europe, *Globe & Mail, Report on Business*, October 2: 3.

Duesterberg, T.J. (1995). Prospects for an EU-NAFTA Free Trade Agreement, *Washington Quarterly* 18: 71-82.

European Commission Opinion (1996). *Reinforcing Political Union and Preparing for Enlargement.* Brussels.

Government of Canada (1996). *Overview of Canada-United Kingdom Bilateral Relations.* Ottawa: Department of Foreign Affairs and International Trade.

Layard, R. & Parker, J. (1996). *The Coming Russian Boom.* New York: Free Press.

Segal, G. (1996). East Asia: don't look now, but Europeans are catching up, *International Herald Tribune*, October 9: 8.

Senate of Canada Report (1996). *European Integration: The Implications for Canada.* Ottawa.

The Economist (1996). *Spoiling World Trade.* December 7: 15.

Wolfe, R. (1996). Vers l'ALETA? Le libre-échange transatlantique et la politique étrangère canadienne, *Etudes Internationales* XXXVII (2): 353-80.

BEYOND INFRASTRUCTURE
EUROPE, THE UNITED STATES, AND CANADA
ON THE INFORMATION HIGHWAY

WHERE BUSINESS AND CULTURE COLLIDE

by Leen d'HAENENS

The Information Highway looks set to become the most pervasive mass medium of all time – a revolution born of and on a par with that ushered in by microcomputers. Beyond the essential technical infrastructure, we must not forget that the vitality of the Information Highway will be directly dependent on the content on offer. This is after all more than a mere matter of "big bucks and cables:" its basic principle must be the international diversity of angles of approach and languages, to the benefit of all users. The emphasis in supply must lie on openness, rather than concentration, and on diversity rather than one single angle of approach. Nor should the Information Highway become hostage to the narrow and often protectionist views G7 countries harbor on the subject. This contribution assesses some of the European, American and Canadian responses to two specific challenges, i.e., infrastructure development (the hardware) on the one hand, and cultural policy (software, content) on the other hand. The United States, Canada, and Europe all have the capability to build their own export-based telecommunications infrastructure. The question of the future role of the government in the expansion of the Information Highway is more problematic: issues include striking the right balance between competition and regulation, Canadian content and European content, the protection of privacy, information, copyright and intellectual property, and ways for Canada, Europe, the United States, and also Japan to be in tune with one another. This article does not offer any ready solution to all these questions, but attempts to provide some understanding of the different policy options.

I   BACKGROUND

A government's policy with regard to the mass media can be expressed in different degrees of state intervention: freedom of opinion and state control are the two poles between which all policy options are to be found. Traditionally the only choice has been one of three options: free speech; a partially regulated framework, and "the voice of the government" as was seen in the early days of television. In Western democracies policies regarding the print media are based on the "freedom paradigm." Conversely, the regulatory paradigm still dominates policy as far as the audiovisual media are concerned.

The Information Highway, which is rapidly becoming known as "cyberspace", can be considered a revolution in its own right, on a par with the microcomputer revolution which spawned it. It can potentially reach audiences on a scale unprecedented by any other medium. Such large-scale intercultural communication would have far-reaching social and cultural implications, and not everybody stands to gain from it, which promises some forceful opposition along the usual protectionist lines. Still, the Information Highway could become the carrier of choice for existing products and services: news, sporting events, films, drama, video games, videoconferencing, databases, etc. On the other hand, it is a medium suitable for interactive programs and services based on direct participation of the end-user. Almost all non-interactive content that will be delivered to the consumer via the Information Highway already exists and is currently carried by other media. In other words, the Information Highway would offer the consumer more user comfort (thanks to the integrated supply) at a lower price.

First in the United States and (to a lesser extent) in Europe and Japan, vertical and horizontal alliances are being formed between sectors that used to be clearly separate (each with its own regulatory framework), such as broadcast media, telecommunications and a variety of computer-based business activities. These are the characteristics of an information society in which multimedia, scale amplification and mega-mergers of all kinds are the order of the day (Bouwman, 1994: 2). One direct, global consequence of this blurring of boundaries between formerly distinct media is highly problematic for policy makers: effective mechanisms embracing new information technologies as a whole seem extremely difficult to find. Because of this lack of integrated tools, policy makers are failing to tackle the problem on a macro level, tending instead to look at it as a set of discrete aspects and trying to find meta-level tools they hope will be effective on specific issues such as privacy and the protection of information, universal access, interoperability, standardization, etc. Apart from this central issue – blurred boundaries between formerly well-defined media and the corresponding policy frameworks – we will see that national, supranational, or regional policies all vary according to the geopolitical, cultural-linguistic and, last but not least, business climates and realities in which they are developed and implemented. Trying to understand the differences and similarities in policy options in the regions under scrutiny, we found that some constant features (including mistakes) of past audio-visual media policy shed a great deal of light on those policy options currently being adopted by governments with regard to information and telecommunications.

II   AIM AND OBJECTIVES

First of all, this article intends to compare some major differences and similarities in the approaches adopted by governments and industrial partners throughout Europe, the United States and, to a lesser extent, Japan, in order to implement the information society – with the Information Highway seen as one of its driving forces. A look at the relevant literature (not only learned journals and books, but also government reports and official documentation of supranational organizations such as the European Union) shows that the overall goals are the same, although the methods adopted by the various governments may vary: (1) creating the best possible infrastructure and (2) enhancing the opportunities thus created, improving the overall quality of life and work of all citizens (if at all possible) through a global, significant improvement of information and communication technologies (ICTs). Key issues throughout these regions are societal and political aspects such as the impact on the job situation in the short, medium and long term, intellectual property rights, cross-ownership of media and anti-trust regulation, privacy, censorship, security of electronic information, and universal access. Such issues are crucial. To do them justice we would need to go way beyond the limited scope of this paper.

Furthermore, the article looks into the Canadian perspective on the Information Highway, since options taken in Canada can offer interesting perspectives concerning the potential path to be followed within the European Union. Apart from the necessary technical infrastructure (networks, terminals, databases), one cannot ignore the fact that the Information Highway's vitality will be directly dependent on the content on offer: we hardly need to point out that in the past many promising technological achievements went the way of the dodo because they failed to fire the imagination of the buying public. One may therefore contend that the Information Highway's success will be greatly dependent on the cultural sector as a prime content provider. So, beyond financial and technological issues there is a need for basic principles governing content supply, such as the following, to which the Canadian government subscribes without reserve:

- Content should reflect the international diversity of perspectives and languages for the benefit of a majority of users. The emphasis in the supply must be on openness instead of concentration; on diversity rather than one single perspective.
- What is on offer on the Information Highway should not be dictated by the G7 countries' narrow and often protectionist self-interest. According to the Canadian vision, what is interesting about the Information Highway has more to do with communication than information: this is the basic difference with the American stance, which emphasizes infrastructure and raw data sharing. Canadian government documents indicate that cyberspace should not be a mere hub regulating the flow of data crisscrossing the globe, but that it should be promoted as the meeting point for those various dynamic communities that make up Marshall McLuhan's global village – a space where creative minds cross-fertilize each other...

III   US, EUROPE AND JAPAN: DIFFERENCES AND SIMILARITIES

Before going any further, we need to briefly assess current trends in US, Europe and Japan, some of which are diverging while others are similar. In addition, we shall look into the changing role of the government and the difficult task of finding the right balance between freedom and regulation with regard to the establishment of standards for new information and telecommunications technologies. Since "the goal is to come to unambiguous, uncontested standards" (Libicki, 1995: 73), given the fact that the economic advantages of compatible standards are threefold – "they may lower supplier costs, increase consumers' willingness-to-pay, or alter the competitive dynamics among suppliers" (Lehr, 1995: 125) – we will take a look at the standardization process in the United States and Europe as well as, to a lesser extent, Japan.

Table 1 (Longhorn, 1995: 8) illustrates the differences in these three major economies, taking into account the following four criteria: information content, network structures, applications and software, and the "people" element.

Table 1:   *Information society differences between the US, Japan and Europe*

	In the US & Japan	**In Europe**
Information Content	Content is national in character. Single-language market predominates in most mass communication arenas. Large, integrated media companies exist with huge investment power for new technologies. Content sellers are mostly selling to a large single market.	National & multicultural in character. Multilingual market. Smaller national media producers can combine forces to approach the size and financial strength of single American media producers. Sales of information products are to national and European-wide markets.
Network structures	Manufacturers and users have access to basically a single set of standards, which have evolved in place over many years. Nevertheless there are interoperability problems. Most technologies are "home-grown," and developed as a result of direct national R&D programs. Wide distribution of basic infrastructure exists such as telephone, cable TV, inexpensive high-speed networks. This is less true in Japan.	Great success in mobile telephony (GSM). Multiple standards exist at many levels; many foreign suppliers and purchasers are more familiar with the US standards. Often competing technologies exist, developed as a result of national R&D initiatives; innovation is widespread. Distribution of basic service is complicated by national differences in both coverage and regulatory issues. Modern telephone basic infrastructures.

Applications & Software	In the US, a large, aggressive software product industry rules in critical basic software areas. In Japan, the software product industry is weak.	Specialist developers; many excellent niche market applications, e.g., in areas such as virtual reality systems, compression technologies, etc.
The "People" Element	Users, especially in business and industry, are technology-orientated and are reaching a level of technology maturity which increases their awareness of information use possibilities. Information producers, whether entertainment media, educational material, or simply personal communications, are familiar and at ease with the various technologies and applications. Awareness of information technology and of the information society is becoming much more widespread.	The historically lower level of penetration of ITC applications in business and industry, in the home and in secondary and advanced education, is now being rapidly remedied. Relatively late arrival of many information services to Europe means users and producers have not reached the level of their counterparts in the US; yet Europe has some of the largest publishing groups in the world. Awareness activity is increasing considerably.

One of the similarities found in every region under scrutiny is the trend towards – quick (US) or gradual (EU) – deregulation, especially as a means to eliminate or reduce monopolies. National, state-owned telecoms corporations no longer determine what is on the global agenda. According to Noam (1994: 7) the dynamics of the telecommunications policy in both Europe and the United States (this is also the case for Japan) go towards deregulation. While in the United States deregulation has expanded functionally from one business sector to the other, deregulation has also spread geographically from the United States to the UK, Japan, and, more gradually, to almost all EU countries. One of the major reasons why it took the European Commission so much longer than the United States to – slowly but surely – encourage this deregulation movement (Commission of the European Communities (CEC), 1987), is the huge differences in geopolitical contexts: while the United States separated network regulation from network operation as early as 1934, with the *Communications Act*, and established the FCC as its regulatory body, many European countries were still in the process of creating their national telecommunications ministries.

Given this pro-deregulation context, at least two major tools remain available to the government:

- The government can act as a *provider of sources of capital* for infrastructure. This is a thorny issue since all governments are currently faced with very tight budgets. How to finance the necessary telecommunications infrastructure remains highly problematic. Partnerships with the private sector are and will likely remain the most popular solution. The 1997 EU ministers' Bonn conference was attended by ministers and corporate figures mostly from Europe, but also from the US, Japan and Canada. One thing everybody agreed on was that Europe is still trailing far behind the US and Japan. North-American companies and governments spend twice as much money on information technology as their European counterparts. The partners in Bonn are aiming to bridge this gap as soon as possible.
- The government as a *regulatory body*: e.g. FCC, NTIA in US and ETSI in Europe are involved in standard-making. Since it is necessarily based on consensus within cumbersome organizations – which can be time-consuming – and extremely vulnerable to new events – which may be unpredictable –, standard-making has proven an extremely long-winded endeavour.

Originally, in addition to standard-making, US government interventions at the content level mostly focused on censorship with regard to (1) pornographic or indecent data on the Internet (see Decency Act, 1995) and (2) violence (see Telecommunications Act, 1996). Interesting against this background is the fact that in the US both Acts were struck down in June 1997 by the Supreme Court, which deemed these incompatible with the First Amendment (see also The Economist, 1997: 13). The ruling states that Government should not interfere with Internet content, not even with a view to preventing children being exposed to pornography, violence, or indecent language. In other words, the Supreme Court upheld the arguments of Internet users, civil liberties advocates and the Internet industry, namely that user-empowerment technologies are far more effective and far less restrictive than content regulations. It cannot be mere chance that only four days after the ruling, on July 1, President Clinton introduced a far less controversial, and therefore safer, text establishing a framework for worldwide electronic commerce while favouring limited government intervention and aiming at a harmonization of commercial rules.

While doing all of those things, the European Commission also looks at European content issues and the protection of Europe's cultural dimension in connection with copyright and neighbouring rights (CEC, 1995). Thanks to the Bonn Declaration (July 1997) on the protection of data, electronic commerce, and penal liability related to Internet use, for the very first time a unanimous European position has been achieved.

As for the Canadian government, it adds to this list – whose last item is directly related to the employment issue in local cultural sectors – the sovereignty issue. In a separate section, this paper will expand on the Canadian perspective.

The **US** industrial sector can rely on the highly visible support of President Clinton and Vice President Gore when it comes to the extension of the American Information

Highway. In September 1993 the *National Information Infrastructure* (NII) initiative was launched by the Clinton administration: thanks to a partnership with the private sector the development of broadband information infrastructure will be financed. On March 21, 1994, on the occasion of a speech to the International Telecommunications Union (ITU) in Buenos Aires, Vice President Al Gore outlined the five principles according to which the United States National Information Infrastructure is to be built:

- "First, encourage private investment;
- Second, promote competition;
- Third, create a flexible regulatory framework that can keep pace with rapid technological and market changes;
- Fourth, provide open access to the network for all information providers; and
- Fifth, ensure universal service" (Gore in Neuman, 1994: 3).

There is nothing particularly new about four of these five conditions: business enterprise in the United States is based on classic free market models, and the one distinguishing factor here is the fact that they are being applied to cyberspace. Such principles as "as few regulations and market corrections as possible" and "innovation springs out of competition in the first place" are also applied to the telecommunications issue. Nevertheless, some restrictions apply: broadcasting, cable and other new media technologies are not like many other so-called free market industries and should therefore be subject to some form of regulation. The reasons for this are diverse, but paramount among them are the related issues of scarcity, public interest, and local monopoly[1]. With respect to the fifth condition, the Telecommunications Act (1996) officially sets out to promote competition and reduce regulation in higher quality services for American telecommunications consumers as well as encourage the rapid deployment of new telecommunications technologies and advanced, quality services, accessible to the largest possible user groups (including rural and high-cost areas, schools, health care service, libraries, etc.) at low rates.

As regards standard-making processes, the United States and Europe pursued (and to some extent they still do) very different goals with their respective regulatory policies. The contexts in which these policy measures took shape were also very different: in 1984 the United States could be described as a "fully harmonized fixed network"; the

---

[1] In this respect, Johnson (1995: 505) criticizes the lack of consistency in the United States' policy regimes vis-à-vis the communications providers, thus limiting competition and access to services: "Federal, state, and local governments each play different roles in regulating service providers. Regulation has focused on four different kinds of information or transmission media:
- The press are not regulated because of the First Amendment.
- Telephone companies or Local Exchange Carriers (LECs) are regulated by the States. Congress allowed telephone service to be operated by a monopoly in return for stringent government oversight of rates and regulation of access.
- Cable television companies are regulated by the Federal government, local communities, and sometimes at State level.
- Wireless communications providers are regulated by the Federal Communications Commission (FCC) through the frequency licensing process." (Italics are ours.)

FCC's[2] priority concern around that time became to maximize the use of radio equipment by increasing inter- and intra-system competition. The reasoning behind this shift was the fact that a rapid establishment of technologically advanced and spectrum-efficient equipment could best be achieved by imposing only those few, strictly defined standards that were absolutely necessary; these should be mandated by a federal body or authority. The FCC – which adopts a participatory style – now plays a rather passive role insofar as it performs no long-term technology and/or spectrum planning. The FCC has now been increasingly in favour of a more flexible spectrum allocation policy in order to foster inter- and intra-wireless system competition.

The **European Union** also considers that the Information Highway is going to be a crucial tool for the continuation of political and economic integration. As early as 1987 a Green Paper outlined Europe's priority concerns in a variety of fields such as distance learning, health care, other services for public welfare, advanced services and networks in less favoured regions. Co-ordination regarding the future development of telecommunications throughout the European Union was set to be carried out by means of common infrastructure projects on the one hand, and pre-competitive R&D on the other hand, through programs such as RACE, ESPRIT, STAR, etc. Network development is considered crucial: ISDN, digital mobile communications and the development of future broadband communications, as well as a more efficient, comprehensive, and long-term European spectrum management process. Since equal access for all market participants is seen as another priority, the creation of a compatible European Union-wide market for terminals and equipment as well as the establishment of open and interoperable standards are considered a requirement (DAVIC, DCC in the TEN Telecoms Program are EC funded projects working on standards for interconnectivity).

The *White Paper on Growth, Competitiveness and Employment* (1993) first emphasized the significance of the information society for Europe's future. A High Level Group of experts, chaired by Commissioner Martin Bangemann, submitted its report to the European Council in Corfu (June 1994). The report specified that financing information infrastructure was a task best left to the private sector. The role of government should be that of a catalyst only. In 1994, the Commission presented *Europe's Way to the Information Society. An Action Plan* (1994), which is the general framework within which initiatives centering on the information society are assembled for 1994 and 1995. The four main lines of action include: (1) liberalization of infrastructure; (2) encouragement of initiatives in the field of trans-European networks, services, applications and content; (3) a High Level Group of experts to be set up to look into social and cultural aspects characterizing the development of the information society; (4) launching information society awareness actions. In July 1996, the European

---

[2] Johnson (1995: 510-4) criticizes the current US standards process for information technology: it is outdated and non-responsive to users; rural America is not served as cost-effectively as it should be; new standards are needed to transmit from the analogue based infrastructure to the NII's broadband digital infrastructure; and the United States lacks a platform where discussions on the development of the NII can be addressed.

Commission published a communication (*The Information Society: From Corfu to Dublin. The New Emerging Priorities*) identifying four priorities of equal importance (see also Verhulst & Goldberg, 1998): (1) improving the business environment; (2) investing in the future and its knowledge-based society; (3) putting people at the center; (4) meeting the global challenge.

One can always dream... The **European market** remains sharply different from that of the United States: Europe has traditionally been a fragmented market, without the benefits of economies of scale[3]. Consequently, users had to buy expensive terminal equipment and until recently competition was almost non-existent for both fixed and mobile-communications services. This is why since 1984, EU regulatory policies have been geared towards two goals: (1) developing pan-European communications standards (leading to the establishment of ETSI[4]) and (2) the introduction of competition for the provision of services. Contrary to the United States and the United Kingdom, where a clearly different pro-competition attitude was adopted earlier (in favour of free market access and/or spectrum auctioning, among other things), most regulators in continental Europe favoured "limited" competition (Paetsch, 1993: 348).

One major drawback in Europe's information and telecommunications situation is certainly its so-called *software debacle*[5]: Europe does not produce nearly enough mainstream software applications. With SAP – the market leader in applications software for business computer networks – a happy exception, Europe buys nearly as much software as America, but produces only a fifth as much (The Economist, 1994: 71). In fact, things are even worse: including in its own markets, European companies account for less than a third of sales, including in their own markets, while Americans software producers control over 60% of the European market. "As a result, Europe's trade deficit in packaged software is running at $18 billion a year. And things are getting worse: American firms now account for 19 of the top 30 money-makers in Europe, up from nine just five years ago (...)" (The Economist, 1994: 71). Among Europe's major difficulties are certainly its scattered markets, its language diversity, its different legal systems, cultures and currencies, not to mention a long tradition of xenophobia...

---

[3] Some figures: the largest national market in Europe is Germany, with just 11 million PCs (compared to a domestic market of 57 million PCs in the United States). (The Economist, 1994: 71). Absence or presence of economies of scale is precisely what makes the difference between the impact of market segmentation in Europe and the United States. In Europe, market segmentation and lack of interoperable standards proved to be disadvantageous (higher prices for end-users), while in the United States, lack of mandatory standards and uncontrolled dissemination of non-standard equipment led to an advantageous situation.

[4] "In March 1990, 61.8% of the members were manufacturers, 12.7% public network operators, 12.7% administrations, 10% users and public service providers, and 2.8% research bodies. These figures testify to the fundamental change in the European standardization process, which for the first time, incorporates manufacturers and users." (Paetsch, 1993: 270-2)

[5] "America is the computer heartland, and the Information Highway cannot undo that fact. Europe has its scattered technology parks, but it has no Silicon Valley (...)". (The Economist, 1994: 71).

In short, Europe's problem is basically a content problem. There is a marked similarity with Europe's audio-visual media policy, which still focuses far too much on hardware development and distribution. There is a clear and incomprehensible disregard for the production of software (content). On balance, Europe's audio-visual media policy is rather inadequate, and this has a decidedly negative impact on European culture and the economic health of the European audio-visual sector. Consumers and program makers are being overlooked in favour of financial interest groups. The *Television without Frontiers* directive (1989) provides for the free flow of audio-visual products. However, this free flow is not backed by any financially balanced policy initiative. While the MEDIA I & II programs provide a unique counterweight to the glut of one-sided hardware development and distribution initiatives, remedying the current imbalance between production and distribution seems all but impossible... Nevertheless, there is hope, since the emphasis has been gradually shifting from "information technology" towards "information content." INFO2000 has funded 80 content projects, 29 of which have reached the implementation stage. Thirteen of these are cultural heritage projects, such as CHAMPOLLION, NAVEGAR, or *Great Composers* (Echo Facts for Users, 1998: 2). More and more funds are now being made available for on-going or planned European Commission R&D programs as part of the Fifth Framework Program, whose (in)direct purpose is getting Europe's cultural heritage on-line (ESPRIT, ACTS, TAP).

Other countries such as **Japan** view the Information Highway as a radical solution to the growing problems of urbanization and pollution. The *Nippon Telegraph & Telephone Corporation* has already announced that by the year 2015 all school, homes and offices will be wired up and interconnected through optical fiber lines. In order to prepare this large-scale project the Japanese Ministry of Post and Telecommunications initiated a three-year project (worth US$50 million) in the spring of 1994 in a bid to assess the feasibility of integrated telecommunications and broadcasting using fiber optics. Three hundred homes and offices are involved in the project: video-on-demand, high-definition television, videoconferencing, teleshopping and telemedicine are the applications to be evaluated. Finally the Japanese committee of telecoms experts in charge of the project considers the Information Highway as a potential means to disseminate Japanese culture world-wide. In this respect – the question of content and sovereignty – the Canadian experience may prove highly interesting...

IV   CANADA'S PERSPECTIVE ON THE INFORMATION HIGHWAY: INFUSING SOME SOUL INTO THE NETWORK

In an attempt to assess the efficiency of Canada's governmental policy on the matter, we will now assess the answers given by the Canadian government to two specific challenges: the technical evolution (the infrastructure, the hardware) on the one hand, and the cultural policy (the software, the content) on the other hand. With regard to infrastructure, thanks to active government support, Canada can rely on an extraordinarily high telecompetitivity index (Sirois & Forget, 1995). Since the invention of telephony (in 1876), Canada has always considered the development of communications networks (always in the hands or under control of Canadians) as a priority. Other examples are the Trans-Canadian telephone networks established in 1932, the Canadian Broadcasting Corporation (public broadcasting service), created in 1936, the transcontinental microwave networks built at the end of the nineteen-fifties, the launching of the first communication satellite in 1972, the move into wireless telephony at the end of the Eighties and the installation of optical fiber lines from coast to coast in recent years. And now Canadians are setting up *freenets* – the community initiatives that provide local citizens with Internet access at attractive rates. Networks for distance learning are operational in almost every province. *SchoolNet* – a joint initiative between governments (federal and provincial), actors in education (teachers, universities, community colleges and schools) and industry partners – is intended to establish an electronic link between all 16,000 Canadian schools. The *Canadian Network for the Advancement of Research, Industry and Education* (*CANARIE*), a relatively slow speed[6] national network that needs upgrading, provides the funding needed to optimize *CA*net*[7], the Canadian component of the Internet. At the same time in Labrador and Newfoundland, a lot of efforts are being made to promote a more effective and efficient use of advanced information technology by local small and medium-sized companies. In the fall of 1995 a home communication service was installed in Québec (*UBI*)[8], providing interactive services such as *telebanking*, *teleshopping*, interactive mail, *video-on-demand* and government services on the television screen (instead of a computer screen) by means of an advanced remote control (instead of a keyboard). These examples show that Canada is able to build an export-oriented infrastructure, that can be considered an efficient and competitive approach in view of further developments on the Information Highway.

More problematic is the question of the future role of the government with regard to the development of the Information Highway. Indeed, almost everywhere (things are no different in Canada) governments have been struggling to curtail huge deficits and since January 1, 1998, in almost all EU countries, telecommunications monopolies have been pared down or altogether eliminated. In other words, governments everywhere can no longer play the key role they used to revel in: they now must rely a lot more on the private sector[9].

---

[6] "Despite the strong telecommunications base, Internet bandwidth and development of the commercial Internet in Canada lagged significantly behind the United States in the early 1990s." (Cronin, 1996: 105) This go-slow approach – however costly for the business community – was a conscious choice on the part of Canadian policy makers: "In the minds of some policy planners, however, the economic benefits of open competition do not outweigh the claims of Canadian culture and national identity." (Cronin, 1996: 107)

[7] The majority of Canadians have access to the Internet thanks to CA*net. The largest user communities are concentrated in universities, community colleges, government, industrial groups, companies and also a growing number of primary schools (Shade, 1994).

[8] UBI stands for Universality, Bidirectionality, Interactivity. A consortium of seven companies spent Cdn$750 million to develop UBI. Phase I began in the autumn of 1995: i.e. 34,000 families in the Saguenay region will get the necessary equipment installed in their homes. The companies in the consortium are: Vidéotron (20% participation), Hydro-Québec (20%), Canada Post Corporation (19%), Loto-Québec (11%), Videoway Communications (10%), National Bank of Canada (10%) and The Hearst Corporation (10%) (Montreal Business Magazine, 1994).

[9] The low profile currently being kept by the government with regard to the development of a

The current pro-competition attitude vis-à-vis the telecommunications industry contrasts sharply with the traditionally protective reflexes concerning the production and distribution of all kinds of software products. The Canadian experience in this field is exceedingly interesting: its officially bilingual cultural market is undoubtedly one of the world's most open[10] – and therefore one of the most vulnerable – markets to US influence. That is why the Canadian government has long been active in the promotion of Canadian content through electronic mass media and the film industry (*Broadcasting Acts*, 1968 & 1991). Institutions such as the *National Film Board* and the *Canadian Broadcasting Corporation* were created as part of this policy. Complementary to this is the financial support provided by the government through *Telefilm Canada* and fiscal compensations for investment in films shot in Canada. Moreover, legislation exists which guarantees some Canadian content on the television screens. This policy remains viable primarily through the granting and/or extension of TV and radio broadcasting licenses. In practice the CRTC (*Canadian Radio-Telecommunications Commission*) requires that 60% of the programs transmitted on public service channels (*CBC/Radio-Canada*) be of Canadian origin (see CRTC, 1984; Taras, 1991). Private stations are allowed to reduce this percentage by 10% in *prime-time* (between 6 p.m. and midnight). Canadian content rules also apply in principle to pay- and thematic channels. Nevertheless, *Much Music* (Canada's answer to MTV) and the *Sports Network*, two Canadian-owned, special-interest channels available on cable, respectively broadcast a mere 10% and 18% of Canadian content (Raboy, 1990).

In accordance with its chosen cultural policy, it is the Canadian government's objective – as indicated by government documents dealing with this issue – not to accept any expression of cultural hegemony or cultural monopoly on the Information Highway. Until now, a whole variety of governmental measures – financial compensations in film production and quota in radio and television – have contributed to the protection of Canada's cultural identity. These policy options, together with active support of local creative production, proved quite effective. The arrival of the Information Highway, however, is considered a potential threat. An initial, probably impulsive response could then be to clutch at the protective measures taken in the audio-visual sector and amplify them. Precisely because of the open character of the Information Highway (*homepages* and *web sites* can be designed to suit everyone's needs and tastes), the question remains whether the options chosen by the Canadian government to protect Canadian culture (mostly in the field of radio and TV) will prove applicable and effective with regard to the most recent challenge: the Information Highway...

Moreover, Canada's weaknesses being mostly geography and demography, they are being given special attention by the government in its attempts to reverse the already

---

global policy option contrasts sharply with the heavy government participation in the establishment of earlier infrastructure. Examples are numerous: railroads, air traffic control, the French Minitel (a precursor of the Information Highway) all resulted from government initiatives and direct government support.

[10] Foreign (read mainly American) films make up about 96% of the total screen time; 70% of the works aired on radio are foreign and foreign titles represent 75% of all sound recording.

pervasive Americanization of Canadian cultural products. But what is there to be done about (1) the sheer size of its territory and the poor accessibility of remote communities in the Northern Territories, as well as (2) the low population density – less than 30 million inhabitants heavily concentrated on a narrow strip of land along the border with the United States (whose population totals some 250 million people)? Precisely because of this specific context, the Canadian government does not feel comfortable with policy regimes and options that are being invented elsewhere (read the United States), in utterly different geopolitical contexts. This is the reason why the Canadian government has undertaken to come up with policy options of its own, an approach that still favours openness and a pro-competition regime, but based on the two following tenets:

(1)   Canadian end-users must be given the possibility to express their own identity in order to be able to "recognize themselves," as it were, on the Information Highway.
(2)   Canadians must be actively involved in the development of the Information Highway: not only as consumers, but as active creators, providers of services and products, and carriers of content.

Sirois & Forget (1995: 5) spell it out as follows:

> The goal is not to keep American-generated content out of Canada but to ensure that the wonders of technology are effectively used to expand our horizons, making the full spectrum of human interest, outlooks and creativity accessible to all, with as little bias as possible, in an open environment – while at the same time creating wealth and prosperity for Canadians. There should be room for the expression of Canadian talent and the exercise of Canadian entrepreneurship not just in Canada but in the United States and elsewhere. The question is: paying due attention to economic realities and the relatively small size of Canada and its proximity to the United States, how can such an open environment be fostered?

In Canada, the body in charge of assessing the threats and promises of the Information Highway is the *Information Highway Advisory Council* (IHAC) (which disbanded in September 1997 after submitting its final report, *Preparing Canada for a Digital World*; during its four years of existence, it came up with a wealth of recommendations and advice on how to carry forward Canada's policy agenda for the Information Highway). It comprised 29 experts from industry (telephony, telecommunications, data traffic, cable distribution), the cultural sector, academia and consumers associations. This committee, whose objective it was to advise the government, was established in April 1994. In order to enlarge the knowledge base of the advisory council, it was augmented later on with another 26 Canadian experts. Priority is given to the use of the Canadian component of the Information Highway, with a view to supporting local cultural and other content-related products and services. The IHAC considers that the goal must be the development of an information network of the highest possible quality at the lowest possible rates, including access for all Canadians to services that have to do with employment, education, investments, leisure, health care and overall improvement of the

standards of living. IHAC's activities are based on the three following strategic principles:
(1)   creating jobs[11] by means of innovation and investments in Canada;
(2)   strengthening Canadian sovereignty and cultural identity;
(3)   ensuring universal access at an affordable price.

These principles are to be translated into policy options based on the five following working methods:

(1)   development of a network linked to and interoperable with other networks;
(2)   collaboration between government and private sector;
(3)   competition in the fields of possibilities, products and services;
(4)   privacy and network protection;
(5)   permanent education (lifelong learning) as a key principle for Canada's information superhighway.

The IHAC also paid attention to the government as a model user. The following paragraphs describe a number of highly relevant issues[12] in the opinion of the expert committee; the goal is to foster the development of the Information Highway and Canada's position on the matter. Correct answers need to be found to the following questions:

(1)   What about balance between competition and regulation?
(2)   What about Canadian content on the Information Highway?

4.1   Competition and Regulation: A Difficult Balance

The Canadian advisory council believes that competition, rather than regulation, can and should be the driving force behind the development of the Information Highway, together with new information and communications services. Nevertheless the advisory council unanimously recognizes the need for a national regulatory body. Again according to this advisory council, a new role for the regulator should be urgently thought of: should it be an enforcer or an arbitrator? Central suppliers of network infrastructure, i.e., telecommunications and cable television industries, were regulated since their very beginnings. Fast technological growth and the free trade context naturally led to deregulation and a greater dependency upon market principles. What

---

[11] It is believed that the cultural potential of the Information Highway will lead to the creation of more jobs. Only in Canada the cultural and arts sector is worth Cdn$24 billion, or 4% of GDP, representing 700,000 direct and indirect jobs. The development of the knowledge-based information network is expected to breed still unknown creative possibilities and result in a tenfold enhancement of economic activity. In order to clarify this complex matter, the OECD was asked to write a report on (1) the content of the Information Highway, (2) the productivity of services to be supplied and, last but not least, (3) job perspectives.

[12] Those issues are dealt with in great depth in the research reports of the Canadian Advisory Council (in Industry Canada, 1994a; Industry Canada 1994b; Information Highway Advisory Council, 1994).

about the future? The evolution towards an open, more competitive system, seen by the Canadian government as the answer to ever-increasing pressure from the private sector, took place gradually.

The *CRTC*'s decision, made in the autumn of 1994, in accordance with the recommendations of the advisory council, to increase[13] the competition level within the telecommunications market, and the call for *public hearings* from the government with regard to the issue of convergence between the telecommunications and broadcasting sectors are welcome responses to the recommendations of the advisory council. They clearly show that the Canadian government is taking the initiative in order to create the most favourable conditions for the establishment of new information and communication services, ensuring that the necessary infrastructure is in place.

4.2   Canadian Content

The advisory council believes that government policy must aim to enhance the Canadian identity while promoting the development of the Information Highway. The council thinks that any recommendation made with respect to the Information Highway should be based on the provisions of the 1968 and 1991 *Broadcasting Acts*, especially since the Canadian content issue is intimately related to employment matters. The advisory council therefore recommends that exports of Canadian television programs and film productions should be facilitated in the future. Harmonization among national and provincial support funds is therefore necessary. The council makes it clear that the principle of freedom of speech as enshrined in the Canadian Constitution must not be undermined on the Information Highway.

Similarly to what has been happening in the other regions under scrutiny, a Canadian *Working Group on Access and Social Impacts* is examining ways to reformulate Canadian legislation with regard to offensive content transmitted through new information technologies. Since one can already find plenty of pornographic, obscene and hateful material in cyberspace (including Internet newsgroups), and given the fact that such content is easier to disseminate in digital format and therefore difficult to control, the working group will provide the Canadian legislator with recommendations for amending parts of applicable legislation, so as to more efficiently control children's access to such content.

---

[13] As an answer to the Advisory Council, the government reviewed the requirements regarding Canadian ownership and control over communications networks. The Council's proposal was favourable to a 20% to 33.3% increase in foreign capital in broadcasting companies, the obvious goal being to attract more foreign capital. By this decision, ownership regulations in both broadcasting and telecommunications are harmonized.

V   CONCLUSION

Converging of technologies are blurring the boundaries between telecommunications, broadcasting, computing and data information services. Such services as we now know them will be things of the past. This article showed among other things that governments are faced with confusing and sometimes downright chaotic situations. It all boils down to fighting vertical and horizontal alliances of content and service providers and manufacturers. National and supranational governing bodies are scrambling – rather ineffectually – to regain some control over the essentially horizontal, cross-national connecting abilities of the Information Highway and other advanced telecommunications systems. It must be clear, however, that governments still have a role to play: above all they must strive to put to right the infrastructure situation, which is currently characterized by the emergence of mega-mergers among suppliers. Furthermore, governments must ensure that power, currently in the hands of a few, is better distributed among larger groups of actors. Otherwise the only force in operation will be the market, which means that too many people may be left behind once and for all.

We saw that there is at least one government that is determined to do something about it: the Canadian government is taking steps to prevent the Information Highway from becoming a vehicle for cultural homogenization or an outlet for monopolies. Canadian policy makers want to make sure that their opinions on content issues are heard on the international scene, which means that Canadians may become more actively involved in the global co-ordination of the Information Highway. A lot of other regions, including the European Union, have also been looking for an approach which is more strategic and user-friendly. And most of them agree that the United States is never more aggressive in international matters than when it sees in them a means to boost economy...

Regardless of future policy options, there is a clear need for a complete change of paradigm concerning the regulation of infrastructure use and the production and selection of content on the Information Highway. The unavoidable international dimension of this global competition game must be reflected in policy measures. Advancing globalization will also prove useful in the long run inasmuch as it should help eliminate many of the multiple variants of existing standards. Based upon a realistic assessment of the needs of the global marketplace, it must be clear that truly international standards become increasingly necessary. Moreover, different user groups could play a vital and constructive role in the establishment of truly useful standards. Therefore, not only major user groups (multinationals or public administrations) – which sit already at the various negotiating tables – but also professional or trade associations and individuals using microcomputers should have their say, since they "share common expectations about standardization". (Ferné, 1995: 457) A number of national governments and supranational bodies such as the European Union are determined not to let government regulations or isolation from the rest of the world become priority criteria in the development of the Information Highway: openness and interoperability remain crucial.

What really matters is to use technology to recognize and stimulate creative activities, so that anybody who wishes to produce and distribute new products and services (from electrical cars to electronic music) may do so, to make institutions more flexible, to eliminate market boundaries and expand horizons, and perhaps ultimately to help draw humankind together.

References

Baer, W.S. (1995). Government investment in telecommunications infrastructure. In Computer Science and Telecommunications Board & National Research Council (eds.), *The Changing Nature of Telecommunications/Information Infrastructure*. Washington, D.C.: National Academy Press.

Bouwman, H. (1994). De doos van Pandora. In H. Bouwman & S. Pröpper (eds.), *Multimedia tussen hope en hype*. Amsterdam: Otto Cramwinckel.

Canadian Radio-Television and Telecommunications Commission (1984). *Public Notice 1984-94 on Recognition for Canadian Programs*. August 15.

Commission of the European Communities (1987). *Towards a Dynamic European Economy – Green Paper on the Development of the Common Market for Telecommunications Services and Equipment*. COM(87) 290, June 30.

Commission of the European Communities (1995). *Green Paper on Copyright and Related Rights in the Information Society*. COM(95) 382, July 19.

Cronin, M.J. (1996). *Global Advantage on the Internet. From Corporate Connectivity to International Competitiveness*. New York: Van Nostrand Reinhold.

Ferné, G. (1995). Information technology standardization and users: international challenges move the process forward. In B. Kahin & J. Abbate (eds.), *Standards Policy for Information Infrastructure*. Cambridge, MA: MIT Press.

Echo Facts for Users (1998). *Trading Cultural Heritage Information Assets*. Brussels: Commission of the European Communities - DGXIII (Telecommunications, Information Market and Exploitation of Research).

Industry Canada (1994a). *The Canadian Information Highway. Building Canada's Information and Communications Infrastructure*. Ottawa: Spectrum, Information Technologies and Telecommunications Sector.

Industry Canada (1994b). *Privacy and the Canadian Information Highway. Building Canada's Information and Communications Infrastructure*. Ottawa: Communications Development and Planning Branch. Spectrum, Information Technologies and Telecommunications Sector.

Information Highway Advisory Council (1994). *Canada's Information Highway: Building Canada's Information and Communications Infrastructure. Providing New Dimensions for Learning, Creativity and Entrepreneurship. Progress Report*. Ottawa: Minister of Supply and Services Canada.

Johnson, J.L. (1995). Standards for the information infrastructure: barriers and obstacles. In B. Kahin & J. Abbate (eds.), *Standards Policy for Information Infrastructure*. Cambridge, MA: MIT Press.

Lehr, W. (1995). Compatibility standards and interoperability: Lessons from the Internet. In B. Kahin & J. Abbate (eds.), *Standards Policy for Information Infrastructure*. Cambridge, MA: MIT Press.

Libicki, M.C. (1995). Standards: the rough road to the common byte. In B. Kahin & J. Abbate (eds.), *Standards Policy for Information Infrastructure*. Cambridge, MA: MIT Press.

Longhorn, R. (1995). The information society. Comparisons in the trio of Europe, North America and Japan, *I&T Magazine* 16: 5-9.

Montréal Business Magazine (1994). *UBI: Québec Expertise at the Forefront*, October: 53-7.

Neuman, W.R. (ed.) (1994). *Toward a Global Information Infrastructure*. Washington, D.C.: United States Information Agency.

Noam, E.M. (1994). Is telecommunications deregulation an expansionary process? In E.M. Noam & G. Pogorel (eds.), *Asymmetric Deregulation. The Dynamics of Telecommunications Policy in Europe and the United States*. Norwood, NJ: Ablex Publishing Company.

Paetsch, M. (1993). *Mobile Communications in the United States and Europe: Regulation, Technology, and Markets*. Boston, London: Artech House.

Raboy, M. (1990). *Missed Opportunities: The Story of Canada's Broadcasting Policy*. Montréal: McGill-Queen's University Press.

Shade, L.R. (1994). Computer networking in Canada: From CA*net to CANARIE, *Canadian Journal of Communication* 19 (1): 53-69.

Sirois, C. & Forget, C. (1995). *The Medium and the Muse. Culture, Telecommunications and the Information Highway*. Montréal: The Institute for Research on Public Policy (IRPP).

Taras, D. (1991). The new undefended border. American television, Canadian audiences and the Canadian broadcasting system. In R. Kroes (ed.), *Within the United States Orbit: Small Cultures vis-à-vis the United States*. Amsterdam: VU University Press.

The Economist (1994). *Europe's software debacle*. November 12: 71-2.

The Economist (1997). *Hands off the Internet*. July 5: 13.

Verhulst, S. & Goldberg, D. (1998). European media policy: complexity and comprehensiveness. In L. d'Haenens & F. Saeys (eds.), *Media Dynamics & Regulatory Concerns in the Digital Age*. Berlin: Quintessenz Verlag.

ABOUT THE AUTHORS

Louis Balthazar is professor of Political Science at the Université Laval, Québec, Canada. E-mail: balthazar@mercure.net

Leen d'Haenens is associate professor at the Department of Communication, University of Nijmegen, The Netherlands. E-mail: l.dhaenens@maw.kun.nl

Herman Ganzevoort is professor at the Department of History, University of Calgary, Canada. E-mail: ganzevoh@cadvision.com

Raymond Hébert is associate professor of Political Studies at the Collège Universitaire de Saint-Boniface, University of Manitoba, Canada. E-mail: rhebert@surf.pangea.ca

Cornelius J. Jaenen is professor emeritus at the department of History, University of Ottawa, Canada.

John F. Conway is professor of Sociology at the University of Regina, Canada.

James S. Frideres is professor of Sociology and Head of the Department of Sociology of the University of Calgary, Canada.

Michael Hart is professor of International Affairs in the Norman Paterson School of International Affairs, Carleton University, Canada. He is also visiting professor at the Center for Trade and Commercial Diplomacy at the Monterey Institute of International Studies in California. E-mail: international_affairs@carleton.ca

Donald G. Mitchell is the founder of Canada's only Full Service Trading Group (CTG) whose founding partners in 1986 include the Federal Government of Canada, Samsung Corporation of Korea, SNC/Lavalin, and Donald Mitchell's company D.G.M. Consulting.

Cornelius H.W. Remie is associate professor at the Department of Anthropology, University of Nijmegen, The Netherlands. E-mail: chwremie@telebyte.nl

Lorna Roth is associate professor at the Department of Communication Studies, Concordia University, Montréal, Canada. E-mail: roth@microtech.net

Jennifer Vrielink graduated in 1994 at the Department of Communication Studies, University of Ghent, Belgium.

Le papier utilisé pour cette publication satisfait aux exigences minimales contenues
dans la norme American National Standard for Information Sciences –
Permanence of Paper for Printed Library Materials, ANSI Z39.48-1992.

Printed in November 1998 by

in Boucherville, Quebec